NG DIGITAL
SERVICES:
ANDARDS
IG IT REAL

d by

Lankes

McClure

Gross

merantz

facet publishing

© R. David Lankes, Charles R. McClure, Melissa Gross and Jeffrey Pomerantz 2003

Published by
Facet Publishing
7 Ridgmount Street
London WC1E 7AE

Facet Publishing (formerly Library Association Publishing) is wholly owned by CILIP: the Chartered Institute of Library and Information Professionals.

First published in the USA by Neal-Schuman Publishers, Inc., 2003.
This UK edition 2003.

British Library Cataloguing in Publication Data

A catalogue record for this book is available from the British Library.

ISBN 1-85604-462-9

Printed and bound in the United States of America.

Table of Contents

PART I
Identifying the Need for Digital Reference Services

PART II
Managing Key Digital Reference Issues

PART VI
Evaluating Digital Reference Service Quality

List of Tables

List of Figures

Foreword

What a difference a year makes! Just last year the term "digital reference" had little meaning for many librarians. Few would disagree that the profession has been transformed by technology that has in some ways made us compete with our own users, many of whom think they no longer need the services and expertise of librarians. Most of us would agree that we need guidance and strategies to insure our relevance to new generations of library users, and further, that we need to be where our users are, even if they are not inside our libraries. How far we've come in just a year.

Implementing Digital Reference Services: Setting Standards and Making It Real, edited by R. David Lankes, Charles R. McClure, Melissa Gross, and Jeffrey Pomerantz, represents the newest set of tools to help librarians plan for, implement, and assess how reference services are delivered in the digital age. This exceptional book represents the evolution of excellence in an emerging field. It fills a need by contributing to the literature and practice of digital reference while blending both scholarship and practical solutions, just as the participants in the Virtual Reference Desk conference are a marvelous cross section of practitioners and researchers.

Last year R. David Lankes and his colleagues, John W. Collins III and Abby S. Kasowitz, chronicled the changing practice of reference and helped information professionals plan for and implement digital reference service. This year's conference and this accompanying book help us understand the broad definition of digital reference, from robust reference by e-mail to real-time chat, to 24/7 services that offer virtual training, homework help, and co-browsing. We see tools emerging for the assessment of digital reference, and an understanding of what to measure, when, and how. Further, we are reminded that digital reference succeeds when delivered by well-trained staff who can tell the story through effective marketing and promotion.

Digital reference is maturing: it is now a standard feature of the library landscape. However, in order to truly mature, the profession needs to agree upon an agenda that will guarantee the healthy future development of this essential service. This common agenda will develop through collaboration and exchange, and through the recognition that what digital and desk reference services have in common is greater than any perceived differences.

The editors have even structured the book in a way that is analogous to the development process, including identification of the problem, implementation of a solution, and evaluation. It will be easy to recognize the patterns of this process and draw useful and practical conclusions for your own library, no matter where you may be on the digital reference continuum.

The Virtual Reference Desk project is truly cutting edge because it recognizes that the circle is connectivity, information, and interaction, and that the most successful digital reference service must contain all of these components in order to be complete. The Internet is a tool that has transformed the way librarians are able to work and interact with our users. Lankes, McClure, Gross, and Pomerantz have wrapped the future neatly into a package that all of us who care about libraries and our users can adapt to fit our needs.

RIVKAH SASS
Reference and Information Services Coordinator
Multnomah County Library
Portland, Oregon

Rivkah was honored as a notable alumna by her alma mater, the University of Washington, in 2001 and was featured in the special "movers and shakers" edition of Library Journal.

Preface

Implementing Digital Reference Services began life at the Third Annual Virtual Reference Desk (VRD) conference, "Setting Standards and Making It Real," held recently in Orlando, Florida. The VRD conference is currently the only conference in the world dedicated entirely to digital reference, in all its aspects. Subsequent to the conference, the chapters in the volume you are now holding were organized, revised, and updated to reflect current technology and practice. The VRD conference and the ideas in this book represent the cutting edge of work, practice, research, and thinking in the digital reference community. Created for librarians and researchers, both for those new to digital reference and for old hands (if there can be said to be "old hands" in such a new field), the experiences and research findings included here represent the latest theories and practices available for implementing successful digital reference services.

As is the case with many innovations, there are several clearly identifiable stages in the emergence of digital reference: identification of the need for digital reference services, design of a solution to provide such services, implementation of this solution, and finally program evaluation and feedback that informs future development efforts. Articles started appearing in the library literature as long ago as the mid-1980s about extending the hours of availability of reference services; libraries began to envision and pilot the use of the nascent technology of e-mail to provide this service. Since the mid-1980s, many e-mail- and later Web-based reference services have appeared on the scene, implementing various solutions in a variety of different environments. Only within the past two or three years have criteria and processes for evaluating digital reference services begun to emerge.

Because this model has been used explicitly in the creation of individual digital reference services—as well as implicitly in the evolution of digital reference service in general, the editors have organized this book using an analogy with the development process described above. The six sections follow this chronological process of identification, implementation, and evaluation, both as they apply to individual digital reference services and to digital reference service in general.

Part I: Identifying the Need for Digital Reference Service, presents two digital reference projects in unusual settings. These chapters discuss how specific problems were identified, and begin the discussion of the implementation of solutions specific to these settings.

Part II, Managing Key Digital Reference Issues, provides analyses of three major issues in digital reference: artificial intelligence, privacy, and copyright. Although the solutions presented here were conceived with the digital reference environment in mind, these solutions may also have relevance to a broader context.

The next two sections, Part III: Implementing Real-Time Reference Service and Part IV: Conceiving and Implementing Collaborative Reference Services, present novel approaches to solving existing problems in digital reference. Real-time or "live" reference has sprung into existence in only the past year or two, and is rapidly becoming popular among librarians and users. Just as physical libraries have been forming consortia for decades, so too are digital reference services discovering the advantages of collaboration.

Evaluation has always been a contentious issue in reference, raising a host of difficult questions: What are the implications of obtrusive versus unobtrusive testing? How should accuracy and correctness of an answer be gauged? What is an acceptable percentage of questions to which a reference service should be expected to provide "correct" answers? These are questions of long standing in the world of desk reference, and they are no less contentious in the digital world. What may be different in the digital world are the criteria by which reference services should be evaluated.

The fifth and sixth sections, Part V: Using Key Findings from Research in Digital Reference and Part VI: Evaluating Digital Reference Service Quality, present several ideas for both formative and summative evaluation of digital reference services. Quality and usability of services are the focus of this section, emphasizing the importance of these measures in determining the success of a service. The book concludes with a comparison of two different types of digital reference service, providing a "compare and contrast"-style view of this evolving field.

Implementing Digital Reference Services: Setting Standards and Making It Real serves two important functions: first, it presents the state of the art in digital reference work; second, and perhaps even more important, it contributes to the setting of an agenda for the future of the digital reference community. Extending the metaphor of the model of the development process, this book—and the VRD conference itself—is performing a needs assessment for the digital reference community: establishing where the field is now, discussing where it wants to go in the future, and then exploring ideas for how to bridge that gap. The editors hope that this book will provide ideas and practical suggestions for building those bridges, to organizations both new to digital reference and those experienced in providing such services.

The VRD conference was hosted by the Information Institute of Syracuse, Syracuse University's School of Information Studies, the Information Institute at Florida State University's (FSU) School of Information Studies, and SOLINET. The conference was sponsored by the U.S. Department of Education, the National Library of Education's ERIC Clearinghouse on Information and Technology at Syracuse University, the Library of Congress, ALA Reference and User Services Association (RUSA), OCLC, and Syracuse University's School of Information Studies. On behalf of all of these organizations, the editors wish to thank the reader for your interest in digital reference, and to encourage you to continue the dialogue!

JEFFREY POMERANTZ
Editor

Acknowledgments

The editors would like to thank everyone who contributed to the planning and success of the 2001 Virtual Reference Desk conference. These include:

The conference sponsors: the U.S. Department of Education, the National Library of Education's ERIC Clearinghouse on Information and Technology at Syracuse University, the Library of Congress, ALA Reference and User Services Association (RUSA), OCLC, and Syracuse University's School of Information Studies.

All those at the Information Institute of Syracuse who made the conference possible: Blythe Bennett, Virtual Reference Desk Coordinator; Abby Kasowitz-Scheer, Head of Instructional Programs at Syracuse University Library (formerly Virtual Reference Desk Project Coordinator); Bob Pawlewicz, Network Administrator; Marilyn Schick, Conference and Event Specialist; Joann Wasik, Virtual Reference Desk Research Consultant/Communications Officer.

All speakers, presenters, panel participants, and attendees for their valuable contribution to the conference and the ongoing dialogue.

And, last but certainly not least, all those who assisted in the preparation of this book: Yvonne Belanger, indexer Laurie Winship, and Neal-Schuman Development and Production Editor Michael Kelley and Director of Publishing Charles Harmon.

Introduction

I Want My Flying Car

INTRODUCTION

The TV commercial had it right. An actor stands by a busy highway and asks where are the flying cars we were promised in science fiction of the past. Many visions of the future—flying cars, video phones, jet packs, and the like—have yet to materialize. The promised revolution of technology seems like an empty dream—hype that died with the implosion of the dot-coms and the high-flying stock market of the late 1990s. Is digital reference also going to be a casualty of the Internet hype, and the more mundane reality?

In his opening comments at the Library of Congress's 1998 Institute "Reference Service in a Digital Age," Thomas Mann took issue with the concept that we do indeed live in a digital age (Lamolinara and Grunke, 1998). As he looked around, he saw a huge body of human memory encoded in physical media like paper, stone tablets, and papyrus. He looked at the healthy book publishing industry and the fiction of the paperless office and concluded that in fact, we do not live in a digital world at all.

My visits to libraries and discussions with educators and librarians around the U.S. attest to the very real physical issues that face reference today. Certainly library stacks are not going empty, physical facilities are not contracting. Also, when libraries do go online they are far from swamped by users lining up in cyberspace to ask questions. So why the big emphasis on *digital* reference? After all, isn't it just reference anyway?

Before I convince you to put down this book (and a printed book at that!) let us address the issues and arguments against doing digital reference one at a time. Also, let us look at these issues not only as they stand today, but how we see them evolving in the future.

ARGUMENT ONE: THIS IS NOT A DIGITAL AGE

This argument centers on the concept that we are limited in what we can do with reference in a virtual environment (namely the Internet). The argument has two faces. The first goes as follows: why should an organization accept questions online when the answers will require users to come to a physical space to get a physical information source (such as a book or video), or access to a physical computer? The other argument is more a question of where the users are. Why should an organization invest in digital reference when the users are at the desk and they outnumber the users that come through virtually, via e-mail, real-time software, or instant messaging?

I argue that we are in fact in a digital age. The fact is that we live in an amazing time, technologically. We can converse with people halfway around the world for pennies on cell phones (which increasingly use digital, rather than older analog technology) that allow us to go anywhere. We have computers that can bend reality in images and movies. Entire movies have been made within the sound stage of RAM and CPU. Our entire lives are dependent on digital technologies, at least in the developed world. The overwhelming majority of the books produced in the world are digital at one point or another—whether they were authored using a word processor, or sent to the press in some digital markup language like SGML. Paper has in many ways become simply another interface that eases distribution and commerce. Nowhere is this more evident than in the music world, where Internet services like Napster and Morpheus have shown that while people may buy a CD, it's the music that is important, not the transport. The 1s and 0s stored on music CDs, once "ripped" from their aluminum prison of pits and planes, become fluid information that can flow through the Internet, into computers and special devices without a care in the world as to what container they are in. I regularly walk around with over 1,000 songs on my hip.

At home and the office, I am no longer bound to a set of wires sticking out from walls: the network flows wirelessly through my work space. In fact, I can fly into major airports, cross over bridges, even take trains where I can surf the Web with no more effort than turning on my personal organizer. At least in the developed nations, we *are* in the digital age.

While it is true that a huge volume of recorded human knowledge exists in static, physical form, the percentage of that information to the total volume of human knowledge shrinks with every passing second. Just consider that experts have estimated that the amount of information in the world *doubles* every 18 months (Wurman, 1989). Therefore, if print information constituted half of our information today, it would be a quarter in 18 months, and by the end of the decade only about 1/72 of our information. Now I know that assumes that all of the items printed are available in some electronic form, and I understand that the newly digital information does not replace the print information, but it does put some things into perspective. I would argue that we have become rather proficient in organizing print information. We have good inventory and cataloging systems for physical items like books, videos, and journals. I would further argue that we have a very long way to go to match these organizational skills in the digital world. Today the largest aggregation of digital information available to humankind is the Internet. Do we feel it is well organized?

That is not to say that there isn't clear evidence that the Internet and digital resources aren't useful, or can't be used in many ways to replace physical

sources in digital reference transactions. Joe Janes and Charles McClure (1999:36) found that:

> Taking all of the data into account, it appears that for these questions and for these subjects [those used in the study], the use of freely available, Web-based resources are roughly equivalent to the use of other resources.

Now, to be sure the McClure and Janes study is by their own admission limited (primarily by experience and number of reference experts). However, it does imply that for a certain set of ready-reference questions, the Web already works just as well as paper resources. As publishers continue to make information and reference resources available only in digital format this will only be more so.

ARGUMENT TWO: EVEN IF WE LIVE IN A DIGITAL AGE, USERS CAN'T ACCESS IT

This argument is frequently expressed in terms of the "digital divide" or the "information have-nots," but boils down to a general statement along the lines that "not everyone has a computer." This, of course, is true, but increasingly less so. Less so in that access to computing and the Internet is increasing, and having a computer is becoming increasingly irrelevant. Let me address those points separately.

While there is a sizable portion of the population that does not have access to the Internet, we nonetheless live in a connected, high-tech world. Consider that at least 51 percent of all U.S. homes have a computer and 41.5 percent of all U.S. homes have Internet access.[1] In the United States two million new users connect to the Internet every month[2] with nearly half the population of the U.S. now online! Also consider that 90 percent of children between the ages of 5 and 17 (or 48 million) now use computers and 75 percent of 14-17 year olds and 65 percent of 10-13 year olds use the Internet. As the National Telecommunications and Information Administration states:

> With more than half of all Americans using computers and the Internet, we are truly a nation online. At work, schools, and libraries, as well as at home, the Internet is being used by a greater number of Americans.

The second point is that a computer is no longer necessary to access the Internet. Today cell phones, personal digital assistants, public kiosks, and special low-cost "Internet terminals" provide access to millions of non-computer users. News, weather, jokes, and instant messages flow from servers to the air waves and into the pockets of businessmen and teenagers alike. Commuters read e-mail on pagers, and a whole new generation of smart phones are about to allow anyone with a phone number to surf the Web in full color. We've even seen the first computer virus released that infects cell phones. People can now configure their car stereos, home security systems, and watches through a Web interface. Why not ask reference questions through these devices—anywhere the question hits the user (cab, subway, beach vacation)? In many ways, the United States is behind the curve in this arena. While the number of wireless phones is about to exceed the number of wired phones in the U.S., this has been the case in Europe for some years. In the Philippines, cell phone networks are fighting congestion not from voice calls, but from instant messaging done with cell phones.

This is not to say that the whole issue of digital divide and underserved populations is unimportant, or that the problem of connectivity is solved. Libraries and schools still make up a valuable safety net of Internet access for the "have-nots." However, that is not my point. My point is that a huge population of users is now online, and looking for information. They are technology-savvy and have increasingly diverse means for accessing an increasingly diverse body of information. Digital reference is a means for meeting these users where they need help the most.

ARGUMENT THREE: EVEN IF USERS ARE ONLINE, THEY'RE NOT COMING TO MY DIGITAL REFERENCE SERVICE

Here it is, the most compelling argument against digital reference: where are the users? This is the question that has even the most ardent supporters of digital reference frustrated. The story is common: a large outlay in resources (time, money, staff time) to set up a digital reference service, followed by six to twenty questions a week. If digital reference is in fact the future of reference then why aren't users flocking to it?

I really wish I had a simple answer to this argument, but I don't. Rather I have some conflicting evidence, and some educated guesses (I'm an editor, I'm

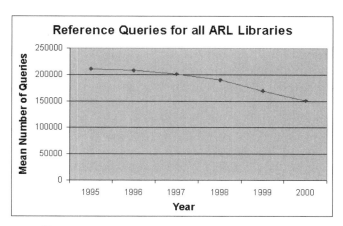

Fig. 1. ARL Reported Reference Queries

allowed). First, are we that surprised that digital reference statistics are low in light of falling reference statistics in general? A look at ARL reference statistics shows a steady downward trend in the overall number of transactions being reported (see Figure 1).

The fact is that even as traditional reference counts have fallen, I have never seen any published numbers that show digital reference queries have decreased. They may not be growing as fast as we would like, but are they declining like face-to-face reference?

Also, even these numbers are not consistent across libraries and digital reference organizations. Take a look at Cleveland Public Library (CPL). Their 24/7 service has reported usage at over 200 queries per day! In non-traditional services like the Internet Public Library and AskERIC (both located at library schools), reference numbers can easily exceed 300 questions per day. What do these services have in common? They are all services catering to the Internet population and have spent considerable effort to market their services. CPL did interviews on National Public Radio and CNN. AskERIC regularly exhibits at conferences and mails out posters. The Internet Public Library seeks out press coverage. These services are out there to be seen, targeted to their user base and not hidden twelve layers down on a Web site. Libraries long ago abandoned the idea of "build it and they will come" and turned to actively engaging a service population. Digital reference must avoid the same trap.

My last point on this argument will draw upon remarks made by Steve Coffman at the ACRL Annual 2001 Conference in Denver. His point was that current digital reference software is in its infancy. The eventual form of digital reference is not yet known. Will the future be framed Web browsers with a chat session snaking from top to bottom on the side? Will it be a set of Web forms or e-mail programs? Will it be video or voice over IP? The future is yet unknown. Perhaps users are put off by the existing interfaces. Who knows? There is no report of usability testing in digital reference.

In fact, there is little mention of the user at all in the digital reference literature. In one study Melissa Gross commented, "In the midst of this the voices of users and non-users are largely missing. The general attitude appears to be, 'if we build it they will come'" (Gross, 2001). If we don't ask the user what they want, if we don't include them in the design process, is it any wonder they vote with the feet (or lack thereof)?

SO WHAT DO WE KNOW?

Everett M. Rogers in his studies of adoption of technologies posits four stages of technology adoption: innovation, early adoption, adoption, and late adoption.[3] Innovation is seen as the cutting edge, where those organizations and individuals who are willing to deal with high levels of ambiguity and frustration (including false starts, or technologies that seem promising and then disappear) experiment and refine a technology often for the sole satisfaction of being first or new. The second stage is of early adopters, who see the early signs of success with a technology, and get involved at a point where the technology is nearing stability, but is still expensive and hard to find. Adoption is the stage where technology has been stabilized, costs minimized, or at least well understood, and the technology is widely deployed and understood. Late adopters are those that lag behind the majority in taking to a new technology either due to an installed technology base, or simply a strong resistance to change. It is arguable that digital reference has entered, and in fact come to the end of the early adopter phase.

That may come as a surprise to some. However, digital reference (also called e-mail reference) has been around for almost as long as e-mail itself. Certainly the earliest literature on it stretches back to the mid-1980s. Large-scale digital reference projects like the Internet Public Library and AskERIC have been around since the early 1990s. Early adoption

can be seen with the advent of the Virtual Reference Desk conference (on which this book is based), the first commercially available digital reference systems (LSSI, 24/7), and the first shedding of failed process models (where.com learned that it is at best difficult to charge end-users for reference services).

This is not to say that we are actually ready for wide-scale adoption of digital reference, or that large-scale adoption won't present challenges that will need to be solved. For example, in the predecessor to this book (Lankes, Kasowitz, Collins, 2000) I put forth two major challenges for digital reference: scalability (the ability for services to grow) and ambiguity (identifying the resources needed to meet users' needs before answering a question). While there is an increasing exploration of networked digital reference service (Lankes, Kasowitz, Collins, 2000) in existing or new consortia to solve the scalability question, there is still much to learn. Further, the issues of ambiguity remain nearly untouched, just now entering the research stage (EduRef, 2002). Also, issues such as training and quality standards are only now coming to light, both clearly issues concerning adoption as early adopters and innovators are often too focused on getting the technology to simply work to worry about transferability.

With all this said, however, the field of digital reference is increasingly ready for wide adoption. A market place for digital reference software is emerging with diverse players starting to compete on features and cost. Training and instruction is starting to be developed; a rich literature base of case studies (this book included) now exists to develop more generalizable and robust research-based concepts in digital reference.

MOVING FROM A FIELD OF A THOUSAND FLOWERS

At the end of the 2001 Virtual Reference Desk conference, Charles McClure called for a new approach to digital reference, and particularly digital reference research and development. He characterized the current work as a "field of a thousand flowers" approach. In this approach a thousand seeds are sown in a field hoping that some will grow. In other words, the current literature on digital reference represents many individual investigations with little synthesis, or common structure. He called for a new cooperative approach. In this approach a general research and development agenda in digital reference would be set by the community. Organizations would pool common resources to come up with solutions to common problems like quality definitions, technical standards, licensing of resources, the reference interview, and marketing among others. The results of these joint investigations will be made available to the whole community so that we can move forward faster, and with a more complete picture. There are good examples of that approach represented in this book on quality standards, consortia, and technical standards. Yet more needs to be done.

A CALL TO ACTION

Clifford Lynch called the digital reference community a movement. I have talked about an ongoing "reference revolution." These are apt descriptions of digital reference, but both imply action and involvement. If you are reading *Implementing Digital Reference Services*, you are interested in digital reference. You may be a librarian employed in a library that has a digital reference service, or investigating one. You may be a student trying to understand what digital reference is all about for a thesis, or future employment. Perhaps you are a business person investigating a new business opportunity, or means of improving customer support. Perhaps you are a government employee seeking insight for policy development or a new project. In any case, you have a choice. You can get involved now, join the dialogue and help shape digital reference's future, or you can wait and see what happens. Perhaps I am wrong, and this book will end up describing a flying car—an attractive idea that never sees full reality. Whatever the case may be, now is the time to get involved. Start a service, go to a conference, join a listserv, e-mail the authors of these chapters, whatever, but be an early adopter and innovator. It is more fun to invent the future than to dismiss it or wait for it to happen.

R. DAVID LANKES
Editor

REFERENCES

EduRef 2002. *Integrating Expertise into the NSDL: Putting a Human Face on the Digital Library* [Online]. Available: www.eduref.org/eduref/Default.htm [2002, June 11].

Gross, M. 2001. "What About the User?" Quality Study Bulletin 080102. Available from the Information Institute of Syracuse [Online]. Available: http://iis.syr.edu [2002, June 11].

Janes, Joseph, and Charles R. McClure. 1999. "The Web as a Reference Tool: Comparisons with Traditional Sources." *Public Libraries* 38, no. 1 (Jan./Feb.):30–39.

Lamolinara, G., and R. Grünke. 1998. *Reference Service in a Digital Age*, LC Information Bulletin, August 1998 [Online]. Available: www.loc.gov/loc/lcib/9808/ref.html [2002, June 11].

Lankes, R. D., A. Kasowitz, and J. Collins, eds. 2000. *Digital Reference: Models for the New Millennium.* New York: Neal-Schuman.

National Telecommunications and Information Administration. 2002. *A Nation Online: How Americans are Expanding Their Use of the Internet* [Online]. Available: www.ntia.doc.gov/ntiahome/dn/ [2002, June 14].

Wurman, R. S. 1989. *Information Anxiety.* New York: Doubleday.

FOOTNOTES

1. http://www.digitaldividenetwork.org/content/stories/index.cfm?key=168
2. http://www.ntia.doc.gov/ntiahome/dn/html EXECSUM.htm
3. He actually named four types of people: innovators, early adopters, adopters, and laggards.

PART I

Identifying the Need for Digital Reference Services

OVERVIEW

Digital reference services are becoming increasingly common in libraries of all types, as well as in organizations unaffiliated with any library, physical or digital. As more and more digital reference services grow and flourish, services already implemented can serve as models on which to base new services.

The chapters in this section present those models. These chapters provide a blueprint of the first steps in the design process: identifying specific problems and implementing solutions for those specific problems. These two case studies describe services offered in special library settings—a museum and a federal depository library—with special requirements. In exploring issues specific to these settings, these discussions shed light on digital reference services in more traditional settings by providing a glimpse into a unique set of needs and requirements.

Chapter 1.

Analyzing E-Mail Reference Service in a Museum Library: The Experience of Colonial Williamsburg's John D. Rockefeller, Jr. Library

Juleigh Muirhead Clark

OVERVIEW

As museums add their presence to the World Wide Web, e-mail questions come unbidden to the museum library. The John D. Rockefeller, Jr. Library, the research library of the Colonial Williamsburg Foundation that specializes in the history and culture of eighteenth-century Virginia, has taken a proactive approach and added a library Web site offering finding aids, the library catalog, and a reference question form. This has become a popular service and opened up the library collections to a wider range of users, thus making an impact on public services. Other museum libraries have been surveyed and the results described to illuminate current practice with the goal of formulating ideas for the future.

INTRODUCTION

Museum libraries differ from public and academic libraries in that they have specific subject specialties making them attractive to professional, academic, and personal researchers, but their first duty is to serve the research of the museum staff. Museum staff expect and receive extensive research assistance from library staff. During the past decade, museums have opened their doors to the Internet audience with subsequent consequences to museum libraries. These specialized libraries find themselves with new issues to confront as they continue to support the work of the museum. The John D. Rockefeller, Jr. Library, the corporate library for the Colonial Williamsburg Foundation—an established living history and decorative arts museum now celebrating its seventy-fifth year—has been receiving questions through e-mail for five years, and the staff continues to confront and solve the accompanying issues. In an effort to understand how other special libraries, especially museum libraries, are managing e-mail reference services, the author reviewed related literature and library Web sites, and sent a brief questionnaire to ten museum libraries. This research has provided some understanding of the current state of museum library e-mail reference service and some ideas for future development.

History of Mail / E-Mail Library Service at the Colonial Williamsburg Foundation

Colonial Williamsburg Foundation professional staff has a long tradition of answering questions about eighteenth-century Virginia history and culture by mail, and the library is part of this tradition. The reference collection includes files of answers/letters dating back to the 1930s that have been indexed by topic and are still much in use. For instance, a reference librarian answered a recently received question concerning the meaning of the designs on the coat-of-arms in the Governor's Palace with a thorough response originally written in 1961. The switch from sending answers by snail mail to sending them on e-mail started gradually, without anyone starting a formal e-mail reference service.

The first Web site for the Foundation went live in 1996, at a time when many Colonial Williamsburg Foundation employees didn't have Internet access and was geared to the outside world of potential

Table 1–1
Timeline of Internet Development at Colonial Williamsburg Foundation
and John D. Rockefeller, Jr. Library

February 1996	Colonial Williamsburg brings up its first Web site.
December 1996	The Colonial Williamsburg Foundation (CWF) Library and its branches close (to prepare to move to new library).
April 1997	The John D. Rockefeller, Jr. Library opens in the Bruton Heights Education Center with the addition of the Decorative Arts, Architecture, Archaeology, and Trades Collections.
October 1997	E-mail queries are received through a contacts page on the CWF Web site or forwarded from the Webmaster and the first e-mail reference statistics are kept.
November 1998	Rockefeller Library brings up a Web site with "mailto" reference desk (a blank e-mail form) on its first page.
November 1999	Rockefeller Library brings up a new edition of its Web page with a Web question form. (Library is linked from first page of CWF Web site.) This expanded access is publicized to scholarly groups via mail and e-mail.
February 2000	Library staff is overwhelmed with e-mail questions. The question form is edited to focus the users on eighteenth-century Virginia.
March–June 2000	The Reference Question form stops working due to changes on the CWF Web site.
June 2000	CWF redesigns its Web site, putting the Library three pages down in the hierarchy. A products catalog appears on the front page of the CWF Web site that confuses frequent users of the library catalog.
July 2000	The Library is moved up one level in the CWF hierarchy. Now from the front page, a drop down menu from "Education" links the user to the library pages.
March 2001	Ten finding aids to manuscript and genealogical collections were added.
April 2001	The CWF Web structure was re-designed. Library placed under heading "History," with illustration of children around a computer. When cursor is placed over that picture, text rollovers appear consecutively, one of which is "Visit our Libraries, Museums and Research."

visitors. The library didn't have an overt presence on the Web, although library staff were involved with the development of the Colonial Williamsburg Web site (www.history.org) and served on the Internet Advisory Group. When the public first began asking unsolicited research questions, the mail went to the Webmaster, who forwarded suitable questions to the Reference Department. Table 1–1 outlines the progress of the organization's Web site and the accompanying consequences to the library and can be used in conjunction with Figure 1–1 to interpret the statistics.

In November 1998, the library brought up its first Web page—a simple, straightforward site focused on a research audience, that offered introductory information about the library's collections, location, and staff, a finding aid to one of our photograph collections, links to favorite research sites such as other Virginia research libraries, and an e-mail link direct to the library, inviting direct communi-

cation with our librarians. E-mail questions began to rise, and, a year later, when the Web site was redesigned with more content and a query form added, the numbers of queries became overwhelming. This enthusiastic response was the catalyst needed to review library e-mail service.

ISSUES AND CONCERNS

Usage

A 1999 survey of ARL libraries states that although the librarians had feared an overwhelming number of e-mail questions when they started an e-mail reference service, their workload was manageable (Goetsch, Sowers, and Todd, 1999). Such was not the case at the John D. Rockefeller, Jr. Library as shown in Figure 1–1. After the 1999 upgrade to the library Web site, the library's e-mail reference requests increased over 500 percent in one month. Nevertheless, the library advertised this new, much

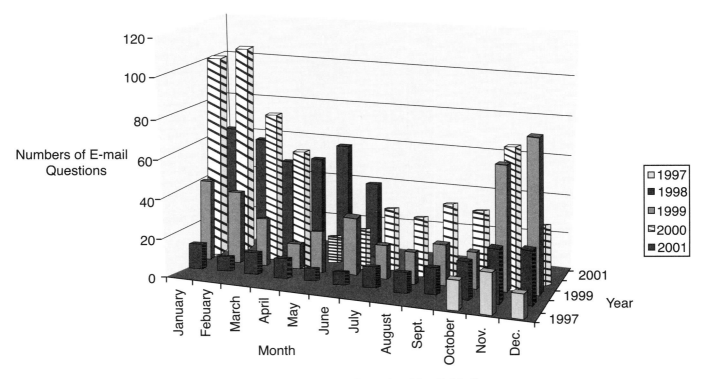

Fig. 1–1. Questions Received by E-Mail

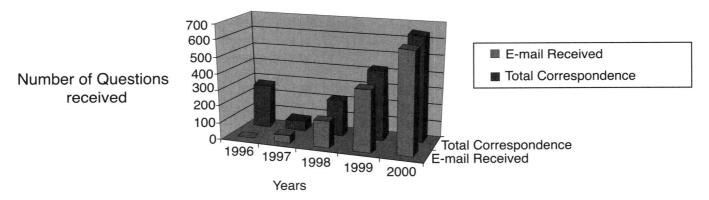

Fig. 1–2. The Progression of Written Queries with the Advent of E-Mail

expanded Web site through national and local professional and academic newsletters and listservs during December and saw the interest in the collections from the world at large continue to soar in the early months of 2000. A comparison of questions answered during the first quarter of 1999 to the first quarter of 2000 showed that e-mail requests increased by 166 percent. As you might imagine, this success both scared and elated the staff. We were pleased to have so much attention, but knew that we couldn't handle this popularity.

Central goals for the library's Web presence were

to alert serious researchers to our holdings and to invite them to communicate with us via e-mail. However, with Internet access, the library's user group has greatly expanded. The expected audience of scholars has been broadened by people using the service for personal reasons—to choose a colonial color to paint their house, to locate videos on silversmiths, or even to help out with science fair projects. Figure 1–2 shows that written inquiries have almost tripled in the past five years and that e-mail has outstripped traditional mail as a way to communicate.

With so much e-mail coming from the world at

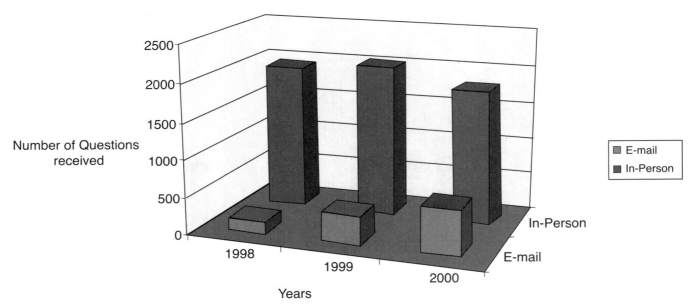

Fig. 1–3. Reference Questions Received Locally and Virtually

large, would the library reference staff still meet the needs of our primary users, Colonial Williamsburg staff? Only in the past year has Colonial Williamsburg Foundation staff begun to e-mail questions to the library, but these are less than ten percent of the inquirers.

E-mail reference is only part of the library's reference services, and it shouldn't overpower the service offered at the library for the staff. Since the library opened in 1997, Colonial Williamsburg staff consistently and insistently complained about library hours. In a user survey in 1998, Foundation staff vigorously lobbied for more library hours, but showed a distinct lack of enthusiasm when queried on electronic access. Therefore, more library hours would benefit the local community, while outreach via the Web would be a convenience (at least at first) for distance users. Could the library be fair to its primary users and still share library resources and expertise with the world? Figure 1–3 compares the number of reference questions received in the building with the number received virtually. Figures for the year 2000 may suggest that some of our local users have found us on e-mail, or may simply remark on other user patterns that have more to do with organizational rather than technical changes. Suffice it to say, that most of our questions are still received locally.

Placement and Wording on the Museum Web Site

Placement in the Colonial Williamsburg Foundation Web site makes an impact on the number of reference e-mail requests received. Researchers were a new audience for the Foundation Web site and placing the Rockefeller Library in the context of a tourist attraction Web site has been a challenge. At the times when the library was on the front page of the Web site, more requests were received. Not surprisingly, the path to the library on the Colonial Williamsburg Web site has varied during the past four years. While the library jockeys for a good position, library online catalog use and e-mail reference service similarly fluctuates. This is similar to hiding the reference desk and library catalog in a distant corner of the library where no one can find it—the number of questions at the desk would certainly go down.

Semantics also came into play when Colonial Williamsburg Products Division brought up its gift catalog on the Web in 2000, and it was featured on the front page of the Foundation Web site. Frequent users of the library's catalog were confused—they clicked on "catalog" and suddenly a choice of furniture, china, and bed linens confronted them. Not only was the gifts catalog on the opening page, but the library had dropped out of site from the first page and was in fact three levels down. A little nudge from some prominent researchers brought the library back up a level within a week. In the latest edition of the Foundation Web site (April 2001) the Library is one of the items advertised from the front page when the cursor hovers over "History."

Topic Suitability

It had never occurred to library staff that people would send Colonial Williamsburg questions unsuited to the library's research strengths. Internet patrons were sending questions outside Colonial Williamsburg's historical period and place—questions about the American Civil War, ancient Greece, the history of the Internet, and criticism for Romeo and Juliet. This phenomenon has been noted by Kristin Martin (2001) in her study of e-mail reference at the Southern Historical Collection at the University of North Carolina. She suggests that the Internet has opened the doors of archives to people who would never have found these collections previously, and who don't understand the scope of the archives they are querying. Receiving questions inappropriate to the collection is not unusual, and archivists and museum librarians can deal with this in two ways: referrals to appropriate libraries, and writing introductory pages on their Web sites that will target these new user groups.

The Rockefeller Library Web site has one e-mail question form for everyone, and while some patron information is requested in order to answer the question appropriately, no effort has been made to communicate with specific groups. We have merely edited the form to remind potential inquirers of our specialty—eighteenth-century Williamsburg. This has lessened the number of inappropriate questions received, but when such questions are received, staff responds politely with a description of Rockefeller Library collections and suggests people contact their local library. We also suggest specific Web sites for requests that are related to the scope of the collection, but not quite part of it. For instance, a question about Benjamin Franklin (not a Virginian) or the settling of Jamestown (not eighteenth-century) or glassmaking (not a craft that was known to be practiced in eighteenth-century Williamsburg) could be answered with recommendations to specific Web pages, books, or libraries. A sample taken from July 2000-June 2001 e-mail answers shows that librarians give specific information 75 percent of the time. More than half the time, these answers are accompanied by suggestions for further reading (books and

Web sites) or referrals to specific people or departments at Colonial Williamsburg Foundation. The other 25 percent are referrals without accompanying information.

MUSEUM AND LIBRARY LITERATURE

Very little is available about museum libraries and electronic reference service. Joan Stahl (1998), from the National Museum of American Art, wrote an informative article on the service offered by her library as early as 1993 on AOL. This service has evolved to
"Ask Joan of Art" (www.nmaa.si.edu) on the World Wide Web and receives an average of 700 questions per month (Taylor and Kalfatovic, 2000). That the museum is proud of her pioneering project is evident from the fact that it features the service on its front page. Stahl's reflections are extremely helpful for a museum planning an e-mail reference service.

In 1997, the Smithsonian Institution Libraries (Taylor and Kalfatovic, 2000) consolidated their e-mail service into one e-mail address, libmail@sil.si.edu, with staff to route the queries to the appropriate library. Receiving about 100 requests per month and directing them to staff at 21 libraries and divisions means that beyond administering the service, it has not affected the research library staff work load too much. The authors suggest that the placing of their link on the Smithsonian Web site could increase their statistics, and staffing would need to be similarly increased to handle it. As of September 2001, a library e-mail contact is linked on a second-tier page of the Smithsonian Libraries page, under "Branch Libraries" and on the front page of the National Museum of American History Library Web page.

Learning about e-mail reference in academic libraries is easy as most of the published literature comes from academic librarians. These articles can be helpful in a broad sense as they describe technical, formatting, and staffing decisions all e-mail reference services face. However, e-mail reference service seems to be a conscious decision made by academic reference departments and is focused on a relatively limited community. Furthermore, academic and public libraries may limit their services to the students enrolled in their institution or library cardholders from a town or region.

Museums bring up a Web site and open the lines of electronic communication with a Webmaster contact, and the library begins to get e-mail queries before they have consciously made the decision to offer the service. A museum is committed to lifelong learning and wants to turn the world into museum visitors and supporters. Everyone is a potential visitor or donor. In March 2001, Guiliano Gaia, National Museum of Science and Technology, Milan, Italy (www.museoscienza.org/), wrote convincingly of the efficacy of e-mail for museums to get their message out and to receive helpful feedback. He suggested that one contact person can direct the e-mail appropriately to the museum staff. Thus, the questions start, long before the library has designed a procedure or worked out staffing strategies. A look at the Science Museum of Milan's Web site in September 2001 shows that there is a general museum e-mail address, as well as several more specific contact people, one of whom is the librarian. To have added the librarian contact may imply that the Webmaster was forwarding enough e-mail to the librarian that he thought it useful to add the direct contact to the Web page.

SPECIAL AND MUSEUM LIBRARY WEB SITE CONTACT MODELS

In 1999, Rockefeller Library reference staff began reviewing the Web sites of nearby historical research libraries and museums. Some, like the Library of Virginia (State Library, www.lva.lib.va.us/) and the Virginia Historical Society (www.vahistorical.org/), did not accept e-mail questions at all and required a letter enclosing a $20 non-refundable deposit before any research was begun. Furthermore, they had a time limit for how much research the librarians would do. The Valentine Museum / Richmond History Center would do 30 minutes of research free and then charge $30 per hour after that. The Museum of the Confederacy (www.moc.org/Library/Index.html) in Richmond admitted to being swamped with questions, but hadn't come up with specific policies yet.

Two years later, the Library of Virginia accepts e-mail requests from Virginia residents with a one-week turnaround and no charge. The earlier policy (no e-mail and charges) is still enforced for out-of-state residents. The Virginia Historical Society now has a form for brief e-mail queries, and lengthier (one hour limit) questions require $20 with the "snail mail" question. The Museum of the Confederacy will

accept e-mail queries about their collections, but not research questions. These will be taken by mail with $10 enclosed for the first hour of research, $30 per hour after that.

THE SURVEY OF MUSEUM LIBRARIES

This researcher decided to look further at other museum libraries with a similar focus as ours—history or decorative arts—to help put Rockefeller Library's experience in perspective. The choices were based on museum method of exhibition, such as living history, or museums that Colonial Williamsburg curators and interpreters work with and visit for study trips, such as Plimoth Plantation and the Winterthur Museum. Staff size (neither of the library nor the museum) was not part of the selection process, as Colonial Williamsburg Foundation is larger in both space and staff than all the other museums. I reviewed the museums' Web sites, comparing similarity of purpose, before choosing only ten to contact. After choosing those that seemed most related, I examined the Web sites, especially looking for the amount of information about the libraries made public through the Internet and the ease of contacting the library staff. Table 1–2 shows the data revealed by examining the responding museums' Web sites.

Most museums have a link to a research section of their Web sites on the opening page of the museum's Web site—although some classify it under other more general headings such as Shelburne's "Education," Colonial Williamsburg's "History," or Old Salem's "MESDA." In some cases the e-mail contact was not located under "Library," but rather in the general "Contact Us" heading for museum staff, just as the Rockefeller Library had been listed in the first years of the Colonial Williamsburg Foundation's Web site. Forty percent of the museums listed only a Webmaster address for contact. In those cases, I made telephone calls to establish the best person to whom to direct my questions.

Five questions about current practice were sent to these ten museum libraries via e-mail. These concerned the length of time e-mail reference had been part of library services, the number of questions received through e-mail in 2000, the turnaround time for answering e-mail, what fees might be charged, and what other limits might be imposed. Finally, an area for general comments was included. Staff size was not part of the survey because of the complexity of the issue—it would require all the respondents

Table 1–2
Information from Museums' Web Sites about Library Research Assistance, August 2001

Museum	Direct contact to library on museum Web site?	Front page link for the library:	Online catalog on the Web?	Finding aids on the Web?	Research query policies on Web site?
Colonial Williamsburg Foundation (CWF) www.history.org	Yes	History	Yes	Yes	Yes
Fortress Louisbourg, Nova Scotia http://fortress.uccb.ns .ca/homeeng/	Yes	Drop down keyword menu : Library	Yes	Yes	Yes
Historic Deerfield, Massachusetts www.historic-deerfield.org/	Yes	Collections and Research	Yes	No	No
Mariner's Museum, Virginia www.mariner.org	Yes	Research Library and Archives	Yes	No	Yes
National Museum of American History, D.C. (NMAH) www.sil.si.edu/Branch Brochures/nmah-bro.htm	Yes-Smithsonian form	Collections, Scholarship, and Research	Yes Smithsonian	Yes	No
Old Sturbridge Village, Massachusetts www.osv.org	No, Webmaster	None	No	No	No
Old Salem / Museum of Early Southern Decorative Arts, North Carolina www.oldsalem.org	Yes	MESDA	No	Coming soon for Members	Yes
Plimoth Plantation, Massachusetts www.plimoth.org	No, Webmaster	Library (links to documents, not a department)	No	Answers to FAQs	No
Shelburne Museum, Vermont www.shelburne museum.org	No, museum information	Education	No	No	No
Winterthur Museum, Delaware www.winterthur.org	No, Webmaster	Library	Yes	No	No

Table 1–3.
E-Mail Services Beginnings

When did you first use e-mail?	
• Pre 1995	Louisbourg, Winterthur
• 1995-1997	Mariner's, NMAH, CWF
• 1998-1999	Deerfield, Sturbridge, Salem, Plimoth
• 2000	Shelburne

Table 1–4.
Number of E-Mail Questions Received in 2000

E-mail Q's Received in 2000	
• 0-50	Shelburne, Sturbridge
• 51-100	Louisbourg
• 101-200	Deerfield, NMAH, Plimoth
• 201-400	Mariner's, Salem, Winterthur
• 600+	CWF

to analyze their service beyond the simple annual statistics that most libraries report and policies that are already in practice. Nine libraries responded to the survey. Some follow-up was needed for clarification on answers and this was done by e-mail.

Findings

All the museums queried are using e-mail as part of their reference service. Table 1–3 shows that the earliest museum libraries to offer this service were Fortress Louisbourg and the Winterthur Museum who were answering e-mail reference questions by 1995. Most of the other respondents added this method of communication during the last half of the decade.

Table 1–4 shows the number of e-mail questions

Table 1–5.
Question/Answer Turnaround Time

Limits – Turnaround Time	
• 1-2 days	Louisbourg, Salem, Shelburne
• 3-5 days	Deerfield, NMAH, Sturbridge, Plimoth, Winterthur
• 4-6 weeks	Mariner's,
• 6-8 weeks	CWF

received in the year 2000 at the responding libraries. Interestingly, of the four libraries who receive the most questions, one doesn't have an e-mail contact on the Web site, but receives e-mail forwarded by the museum's Webmaster. Another librarian in this group mentioned that while they have a Web page contact, most of their e-mail requests were forwarded to them by the Webmaster.

Colonial Williamsburg Foundation received the highest number of questions, and, consequently the local bias has been how to limit the sheer number of questions, while still being accessible to those researchers that have questions not easily answered by local library collections. Thus, the respondents were asked specifically about limitations on the services.

Turnaround time has been a limit imposed by the staff of the John D. Rockefeller, Jr. Library, since the days of mail reference and has been carried over into e-mail, to give librarians plenty of time to complete the research without making an impact on the service offered to museum staff. When the library was inundated with research queries, we decided to extend the four to six week turnaround time to six to eight weeks. Inquirers are informed of this time frame at the top of the e-mail reference form.

Thus, library staff wanted to know if other libraries had similar turnaround times. However, as shown in Table 1–5 most of the libraries responding to this survey answer their reference questions within five days, and 45 percent within two. One of the respondents mentioned that if a question couldn't be answered within five days, the library notified the inquirer of the status of his request. One of the museum libraries that received the fewest questions (un-

**Table 1–6.
Maximum Time Allocated to Answer
a Reference Question**

Limits – Time on Task	
• Deerfield	• 20 minutes
• NMAH	• 1 hour
• Sturbridge	• 2 hours
• Mariners	• 6 hours

**Table 1–7.
Fees for Reference Service**

Limits - Fees		
$20-25 per hour:	Mariner's	Shelburne
$ 50 per hour:	Louisbourg	

Copying / Postage fees only:

CWF	Deerfield	NMAH
Sturbridge	Salem	Plimoth
Winterthur		

der 50) in 2000 has the goal of answering them in twenty-four hours but they limit the time spent on a question before research fees are charged. Impressively, one of the libraries that received between 201-400 questions answers questions in 48 hours and reports no limits or fees (except for database search fees).

The majority of those surveyed try to answer queries within one week. The longest turnaround time reported is four to six weeks, still shorter than the six to eight weeks at Rockefeller Library. In 2001, a sample of e-mail reference questions answered by Rockefeller staff showed that 70 percent were answered within two weeks, but because some questions are received at times when the librarians are involved in staff training or museum projects, occasionally it does take eight weeks for a query to be answered. If an inquirer states that s/he has a short deadline, the librarians try to reply quickly, either with an answer, if possible, or with an apology that needed information cannot be supplied within the requester's time limits. The service is free, but immediacy is sacrificed.

Research time limitations varied as well as shown in Table 1–6. A twenty-minute limit was imposed by one museum library; six hours by another. Three libraries reported that the time needed to answer the query was left to the librarian's judgment. Reasons for extensive work on a question included: 1) the research question is likely to be repeated, and 2) the information gathered to answer this question will be useful to the museum staff.

At the John D. Rockefeller, Jr. Library, one librarian answers 60 percent of the questions, and refers 40 percent to other librarians. During the past two years, the time on each question averages fifty-five minutes. No limits have been established, leaving the time expended up to the judgment of the librarian. Reference staff reviews the topic, its relevance to the collection and considers the patron's expressed limits when deciding how much time to spend, how much information to send and the best method for sending a reply. If it appears that the answer needed will be too extensive, part of the question may be answered, with suggestions for further research on the part of the inquirer—as when someone asked library staff to validate an anonymous article about what happened to ALL the signers of the Declaration of Independence.

Table 1–7 displays the fees mentioned by libraries. Three libraries charge research fees, with costs ranging from $25-$50 per hour. One librarian stated that while they didn't limit the time-on-task, they limited the free time. Another charges $25 per hour for questions answered within the usual turnaround time and $50 for rush answers. Sixty-six percent of the libraries do not charge for research, only for photocopying and mailing charges incurred. The information requested is often not in digital format, so U.S. mail still has a part of virtual reference desk service.

One librarian stated that if the information gathered would be helpful for her museum, then she wouldn't charge the inquirer who first raised the question. She mentioned as an example, a research request that was the catalyst for processing a collection of photographs of sawmills. In the course of the processing, the request was answered and the collection made available for further use.

Each library reflects its museum's mission and, therefore, has a built-in subject limitation so integral with everyday life that only one librarian mentioned it specifically; the others didn't mention it until a follow-up query. This reflected the Rockefeller Library's experience—librarians didn't tell people to ask only questions about eighteenth-century Williamsburg on the reference question form, as it was assumed that people had read the library's introductory screen before they ever made it to the contact stage. Museum librarians are so defined by their institutions that it surprises them to think that others don't understand what the museum is all about.

One follow-up about topic yielded two kinds of information—yes, topic was important to the librarian's answering the question and furthermore, that if the question was outside the scope of the collections, she would spend no more than 15 minutes on it. Another remarked that his library research practice stayed close to the museum's field of nineteenth-century Americana and wouldn't have the resources to answer questions on nineteenth-century European history.

Other considerations that affected the research decisions made by reference librarians mentioned were:

• Characteristics of the patron: Did the patron live in a remote locale where library resources might be severely limited? In this case, the museum librarian wrote "An older student or adult engaged in long-term research will generally get a bibliography of sources. An eight year old in Arizona, 40 miles from the nearest library of any size, will be more likely to receive a packet of materials."
• Type of question: Several librarians mentioned that e-mail requests are extremely vague, such as "Is Mary Jones related to the founder of the museum?" or "Do you have information about John Williams?" While these museum libraries have some genealogical information, they need to know more to adequately address these queries. In cases such as these, the librarians send e-mail with follow-up questions—and both reported that only occasionally do they receive an answer.

In almost every case, the museum libraries queried have set one or more limits, beyond that of sub-

ject, to serve with their virtual users. This knowledge has illumined our understanding of our situation while helping us focus on where we fall short and what we can do to improve it. Certainly, the enthusiastic response of the virtual public is a good thing that we can channel into more people knowing more about the eighteenth-century portion of American history. The number of questions we receive outstrips our colleagues, just as their ability to answer in a timely fashion outstrips ours.

FUTURE DIRECTIONS

Librarians must continue to study their usage and their users, keep up with technological options that can improve communication, and use this information to continually adapt and sharpen electronic service. Ideas gleaned from this study will be used to rework the Rockefeller Library's "Reference Desk" approach to soliciting questions and will hopefully communicate to each kind of virtual user how to communicate more precisely so that Rockefeller librarians can assist them successfully.

Furthermore, it is once again time to survey our primary users to ascertain how well we are serving them as a physical and a virtual collection, and how their access to e-mail may have changed. Day-to-day communication with library users gives librarians a flavor of their attitudes; however a formal survey provides statistics to support the anecdotal evidence.

Another arm of the Foundation's Research Department has begun a digitization project, to which the library has access. The first goal has been to digitize Colonial Williamsburg Foundation staff research reports on the historic properties. These documents were often consulted and quoted in their paper format in answering reference questions. Now, reference librarians are beginning to extract information from these documents, as they become digitized, into their e-mail answers. This speeds the accumulation and processing of information to answer the question and allows information to be sent electronically that heretofore would have been photocopied and mailed.

As previously mentioned, staffing was not part of this survey; however, the examination of virtual reference has resulted in some good news. This year, a new part-time professional position has been added to the Public Services Department to help improve service, and by 2003 the Web site will precisely describe the library's collections and services to each user group and the turnaround time on research questions will be shorter.

As museums establish a presence on the Internet, museum libraries can expect more questions through electronic communication and questions from non-traditional museum library users. A description of the museum library's collections and services should include information for various types of patrons—researchers and those looking for information for personal, nonacademic reasons.

Staffing issues—who does what and how much—need to be investigated so that managers can make more informed decisions on adding staff hours to the service or accepting limitations on that service—time or cost being the most usual limits. Most importantly, museum librarians need to stay close to their roots and offer services in whatever ways most benefit their primary users.

REFERENCES

Gaia, Guiliano. 2001.—"Towards a Virtual Community." Presented at Museums and the Web 2001 Conference, Seattle, Wash., March 2001 [Online]. Available: www.archimuse.com/mw2001/papers/gaia/gaia.html [2002, May 24].

Goetsch, Lori, Laura Sowers, and Cynthia Todd. 1999. *Electronic Reference Service: A Spec Kit*. Washington, D.C.: Association of Research Libraries.

Martin, Kristin. 2001. "Analysis of Remote Reference Correspondence at a Large Academic Manuscripts Collection." *American Archivist* 64, no. 1: 17-42.

Stahl, Joan. 1998. "Have a Question? Click Here": Electronic Reference at the National Museum of American Art.""*Art Documentation* 17, no. 1: 10-12.

Taylor, Gil, and Martin Kalfatovic. 2000. "E-mailing the Experts: Responding to Electronic Public Queries at the Smithsonian Libraries." Presented as a poster session at the American Library Association Annual Conference, Chicago, July 8, 2000 [Online]. Available: www.sil.si.edu/staff/ALA-2000/libmail/ [2002, May 24].

Chapter 2

Understanding Government Digital Reference: The DOSFAN Partnership at UIC

John A. Shuler and Lorri Mon

OVERVIEW

This chapter provides a case study of the DOSFAN digital reference service, in which federal depository librarians at the University of Illinois at Chicago answer e-mail questions for the U.S. Department of State Web site. The UIC DOSFAN service is discussed within both the context of government information policy for information management reform and performance review, and as a reflection of the growing e-mail burden of public digital reference demands on government. Future implications of digital reference services for e-government and the "more electronic" federal depository library system are also explored.

INTRODUCTION

The University of Illinois at Chicago (UIC) and the U.S. Department of State's Bureau of Public Affairs have long enjoyed a singular long-term collaboration in cooperative electronic public service. During the first years (late 1993 and early 1994) of William J. Clinton's administration, representatives from the university library's government documents department and State's Public Affairs Bureau agreed to deliver critical foreign policy information to the American public over the Internet. For the next seven years, both parties, along with the U.S. Government Printing Office (GPO), which became part of the project in 1997, evolved from simple text files of press briefings, news releases, major reports organized through a simple hierarchy of text files delivered by a gopher

server into a public high-speed electronic information network that used the full advantage of the World Wide Web's graphic and interactive features.

Within this time period, the DOSFAN (State Department Foreign Affairs Network) service experienced a steady increase in public electronic questions that led UIC and State to agree to the project's second stage of development. In 2001, earlier arrangements to answer the public's e-mail reference questions became more formalized when UIC and State agreed to a much more structured digital reference partnership in which UIC proposed, designed, and implemented a Web-based electronic reference service to handle questions sent to the State Department through its Web pages. This paper attempts to put this growth of e-mail information services in the context of several perspectives: first, by placing it within the broader policy framework of government management reform and performance review; second, by examining some of the lessons learned through the UIC experience; third, through the comparison of other federal information services that use e-mail; and fourth, by providing some general conclusions of what libraries and their organizations need to understand if they are to survive in this new world public information order.

The UIC/State Department partnership gained much of its spirit from Clinton's National Performance Review (NPR). In its final report (Office of the Vice President, National Performance Review, 1993), NPR set into motion a series of reforms designed to "reinvent government," strengthen and embed performance-based management measurements within agencies planning efforts, as well as instilling a stronger culture of customer satisfaction with federal services. The success of these reforms, the report argued further, depended on how well the government used the distributive technologies of the Internet and World Wide Web.

EARLY POLICY FORMATIONS AT THE FEDERAL LEVEL

At the beginning of the 1990s, several long-term policy and legal initiatives converged to form a new federal policy structure (High Performance Computing Act of 1991, P.L. 102–94) designed to support a rapidly growing national high-speed computer/telecommunications network: the National Education and Research Network (NREN). These initiatives included these policy aspects:

- Standardization of federal information technology acquisition, implementation and management (Information Technology Management Reform Act of 1996, P.L. 104–106), along with the creation of a viable core of Federal Chief Information Officers (procurement and information resource management).
- Promote the concept that the country's economic and political future depends on the rapid development of a national information infrastructure (Office of the Vice President, National Performance Review, 1993).
- Expand the traditional legal obligations to disclose and distribute information under the Freedom of Information Act to include electronic information (Electronic Freedom of Information Act Amendments of 1996, P.L. 104–231).
- Rationalize the government's records management through management plans and the Office of Management and Budget (Paperwork Reduction Act of 1980, P.L. 98–511, and the Government Performance and Results Act of 1993, P.L. 103–62).
- Transform the Government Printing Office and the National Technical Information Service tradition of print and distribution methods (Government Printing Office Electronic Information Enhancement Act of 1993, P.L. 103–40).
- Elimination of federal paper records and the legal acceptance of electronic signatures and records under administrative law by October

2003 (Government Paperwork Elimination Act, P.L. 105–277).

Each initiative, extolled as harbingers of enlightened federal information resource management, assumed that a direct consequence of their implementation would be a federal government both more responsive to the public and more efficient. The heart of this bureaucracy would beat through a steady stream of conversation with a citizenry actively engaged in a form of "direct electronic democracy," along with a more efficient management structure powered through information technology. In addition to these new efforts at reform, increased congressional oversight of existing laws put further pressure on government agencies to conform to performance-based standards widely embraced in the private sector. These efforts led the agencies to plunge into offering the public electronic access to information and services.

One of the side-effects of increased electronic access to information and services has been the ability of agencies to measure the quality of their services in very demonstrable ways. The Government Performance and Results Act, changes in the Paperwork Reduction Act, and the Information Technology Management Reform Act have forced agencies to respond to changes. Another emerging issue relates to the difficulty in defining what an electronic record might be. The policies encouraged, and in some cases required, that the government's procurement, implementation, and long-term management of information resources to reflect good economy, sound planning, and further "empower" citizens with new avenues of access to services and information. One of these avenues for citizen input grew to be the use of e-mail and electronic message exchanges with the public.

DEVELOPMENTAL HISTORY OF THE UIC/DOSFAN PARTNERSHIP

In the early 1990s, the State Department (DOS) did not have a coherent information resource management program. There were experiments with CD-ROM products, electronic bulletin boards offered through the Agriculture Department and GPO, as well as commercial electronic database providers. At the time, UIC enjoyed the advantage of having access to the very high-speed backbone of the Internet.

UIC's library had a long history of experimenting with electronic distribution schemes in the context of library applications and government publications. UIC library staff worked with State of Illinois Archives and State Library to distribute electronically simple land records from the nineteenth century, and began to experiment with early forms of the gopher to distribute text. UIC also enjoyed a history of innovative programs within its government documents department. By the spring of 1995, UIC Library systems staff created a graphical interface that took advantage of the Internet's first Web browser standard: Mosaic. About this same time, the White House began to push for every executive cabinet level office to have a Web page created by the end of October 1995. This extra work, and the growing complexity of managing a large number of files, prompted UIC and the State Department to agree to a more formal arrangement and a paid contract. E-mail accounts were also created so people could send questions to State's Public Affairs Bureau.

The next two years (1996–1998) witnessed an explosive growth in terms of size and scope of the project. By late 1996, following the presidential elections, the Web pages were redesigned and given a consistent look throughout in terms of graphics and naming functions. The gopher files that were not converted to HTML were declared electronic archives and removed from the current HTML files. By late 1996, UIC began discussions with GPO about formally recognizing the work with State under the depository library system, and began to wrestle with the issues of electronic archiving on a larger scale. These discussions led to the creation of the Electronic Research Collection (ERC); more involvement in answering the public's questions: technical and informational. As a step towards a more electronic depository system, ERC was declared the first Electronic Depository Library among other partnerships established by GPO.

In 1998, UIC librarians started a nascent digital reference service for DOSFAN e-mail questions, and in 1999 the UIC librarians launched DOSFAN Electronic Research Collection archive (http://dosfan.lib.uic.edu/ERC/) to provide permanent online access for DOS electronic archival collections covering 1993–1997. In 2000, the successful e-mail reference service was handling an average of 220 questions per month and in the first quarter of 2001, the UIC librarians were answering 100–150 questions per week. By June 2001, the UIC librarians further increased the speed and efficiency of the service by switching over to the QRC Web-based e-mail handling software created by Dr. Michael McClennen of the Internet Public Library (www.ipl.org). The DOSFAN digital reference service now stands ready for the next phase of expansion in which UIC librarians will be joined within the QRC system by staff of the Department of State's Bureau of Public Affairs and will work together in handling an estimated 1,500–2,800 e-mail questions per week using the Web-based e-mail software.

LESSONS LEARNED FROM THE DOSFAN EXPERIENCE AT UIC

E-mail received by the U.S. Department of State encompasses two major areas: foreign policy opinions and general questions. Foreign policy opinions receive an acknowledgment and are relayed to the DOS Bureau of Public Affairs, which apprises the Secretary regarding public opinion. General questions, depending on the e-mail address to which they are sent, receive an individual answer from either the Bureau of Public Affairs staff or the UIC federal depository librarians. Public Affairs staff receive approximately 1,500–2,800 e-mails per week, while the DOSFAN librarians receive approximately 100–200 questions per week. As UIC's role has been in a pilot program phase, the greater share of the e-mails has been handled by Public Affairs staff, but in future it is expected that UIC librarians will take on an expanded role in both answering and triaging questions.

DOSFAN questions initially are received to a Web-based "In-Box" for triaging. Triaging, which includes assigning a descriptive question title and determining whether the question should be assigned to either Public Affairs staff or UIC librarians for answering, is performed by senior DOSFAN reference administrators. Questions ready to be answered are moved into separate Web-based areas for UIC and Public Affairs, and can be claimed and answered by individual staff via Web browsers. The Web-based software makes it easier for administrators to keep track of questions needing to be answered and allows staff to work interactively on questions, posting internal suggestions for sources and research strategies.

E-mail messages received from the public include

foreign policy opinions as well as questions on a wide variety of topics, some of which fall within the scope of the State Department (such as questions about the Web site and State Department services) and others which are essentially misdirected research or reference questions (such as questions about other parts of the government, historical events in foreign countries, or older government documents). Because many members of the public no longer access State Department documents through the federal depository libraries, but instead go directly to the State Department Web site, the research and reference questions previously asked of federal depository librarians are now increasingly shifting to public e-mail messages sent to the agency's Web sites, bypassing the federal depository libraries completely.

In the course of operating the digital reference service, UIC librarians were found to be particularly well suited to handling the public's e-mail questions about research topics, government documents, and issues ranging outside the scope of the Department of State, while DOS Public Affairs staff excelled at handling questions requiring insider knowledge of the Department and of upcoming information releases. Frequently, "question exchanges" occurred between the two groups as the UIC librarians referred to DOS questions about upcoming reports while DOS staff referred to UIC questions on research topics, each group taking advantage of the strengths of the other.

Close working ties also developed between UIC librarians and the DOS Webmasters in various State bureaus and offices. The UIC librarians sometimes assumed a "watchdog" function as they traveled through DOS Web sites searching for patron answers by alerting DOS Webmasters to any technical problems they encountered along the way, thus solving problems in advance of public complaints. UIC librarians also noted common public requests and developed new Web resources to meet those needs, such as a biographical resource on U.S. Secretaries of State (http://dosfan.lib.uic.edu/ERC/secretaries/).

The top ten subject categories for public e-mail questions to the State Department were found to be: 1) Department of State (services, history); 2) Research (general topics and homework help); 3) Visas; 4) Passports; 5) Consular (travel); 6) Government (non-DOS); 7) Careers and Education; 8) Countries; 9) Contact Information; and 10) Immigration. In responding to questions, UIC DOSFAN

librarians commonly referred questioners to online sources in the State Department's Web sites and other federal government Web sites, as well as government print sources. When possible, UIC librarians also provided referrals to local federal depository or public library Web sites and contact information.

The UIC DOSFAN team made several key policy decisions for handling e-mail questions that have interesting implications for government digital reference services. One was that since a majority of "thank-you" messages expressed appreciation for fast answers, quick turnaround should be a priority, so in April 2001 an internal mandate for 24–hour turnaround 7 days a week was set for the UIC librarians. Another decision was for the digital reference service to be open to all questioners without any restriction on grounds such as geographic location or citizenship. This was an easy decision for a partnership with a federal agency that routinely deals with both American citizens and foreign nationals, but may not be as easy for other agencies lacking the same responsibilities for both foreign and domestic service as the U.S. Department of State.

Perhaps the most difficult UIC DOSFAN policy decision was in favor of attempting to provide digital reference services in multiple languages. Because the service frequently receives questions written entirely in other languages than the DOSFAN team's native English, the decision had to be made whether to tackle these foreign language questions. The UIC librarians had some language skills, but also had access to language dictionaries in the library and Web-based translation tools such as AltaVista's Babelfish (http://babelfish.altavista.com). In a decision that continues to be debated internally to this day, the UIC librarians decided to try to answer the foreign language questions, though for practical reasons of skill and ability this effort is limited to French, German, Italian, Portuguese, and Spanish. The UIC librarians were aware that the results were not perfect but viewed answering as better than not answering.

An important early lesson learned by the UIC librarians was the usefulness for both service providers and the public of creating and maintaining a publicly accessible "knowledgebase" of standard answers. UIC librarians built an electronic collection of "research pathfinders" and "standard answers" within the DOSFAN ERC Web site that could be easily copied and pasted from a Web browser into an e-mail message, providing a quick way to respond to commonly-asked questions (http://dosfan.lib.uic.edu/ ERC/ercdesk/). Among the most popularly visited of these by the public were online answers for visas and immigration, international adoption, immigration statistics, foreign aid statistics, diplomatic protocol, country information, birth certificates, dual citizenship, and travel advisories.

With the changeover to the Internet Public Library's QRC Web-based e-mail handling software in 2001, more than 70 "standard answers" written by UIC librarians were incorporated into the automated system, thus expanding the ability of a small number of staff to handle a large number of incoming questions. Detailed pre-written answers can now be included into responses at the click of a button, a development that highlights the dual role of the UIC librarians in not only answering questions but also in building and obtaining new tools and management systems to enhance the capabilities of the reference service.

As the DOS Public Affairs staff join the UIC librarians within the QRC Web-based system in late 2001, triage of the incoming questions may be the next area within which the UIC librarians will play a key role. The professional training of librarians in question negotiation and analyzing question content offer a significant benefit to agencies needing to quickly sift through hundreds or thousands of messages and determine where answers can be found. A particular problem for government agencies is that citizens often do not know where to send their questions, resulting in queries sent to the wrong federal agency or often even the wrong level of government, such as when a citizen seeking their state-level Secretary of State's office sends a question to the federal Department of State, in addition to homework help and research questions that would be better handled by local libraries. The experience of the UIC librarians in handling questions of all types across all levels of government has greatly benefited management efforts for questions sent to the Department of State's Web site.

DOSFAN IN CONTEXT: E-MAIL AND E-REFERENCE IN GOVERNMENT

Increasing numbers of citizens have home computers or access to the Internet through work and school, and there has been a proliferation of free e-mail services such as Yahoo! and Hotmail; indeed, it has been suggested that the U.S. Postal Service

Table 2–1
Estimated Public E-Mail to Selected Federal Agencies in 2001 (Mon, 2001)

Department of Agriculture Webmaster	10,000/yearly
Department of Energy Office of the Secretary	16,000/yearly
Environmental Protection Agency	30,000/yearly
Federal Communications Commission (FCC) Consumer Center (based on 6–month avg.)	68,000/yearly
General Services Administration Webmaster	5,000/yearly
Government Printing Office GPO Access	24,000/yearly
Internal Revenue Service Tax Law Inquiries	325,000/yearly
National Archives and Records Administration NNU Public Reference Inquire	150,000/yearly

should provide a free e-mail account for every citizen. The age of the "e-citizen" is here, bringing with it a deluge of e-mail to agencies at every level of government. The experience of the DOSFAN digital reference service with managing a rising tide of e-mail messages with a small staff is not unique, and has significant implications for the future.

For the percentage of the public that has become accustomed to using digital services and products, e-mail remains one of the preferred choices for communicating with the public bureaucracy. For instance, the U.S. House of Representatives received 48 million e-mail messages in 2000, with four million e-mails in the month of August 2000 alone (Congress Online Project, 2001). U.S. House and Senate offices together received an estimated 80 million e-mails in 2000 and 120 million e-mails in 2001 (Matthews, 2001). A look at e-mail statistics for federal agencies similarly shows a growing problem for government in meeting the public demand for e-mail services (see Table 2–1).

Although the statistics demonstrate strong public interest in communicating with government agencies by e-mail, there is no consistent commitment throughout the agencies to provide digital reference services or to regularize e-mail-answering policies and practices. For those agencies that do respond to the public by e-mail, there is great variance in how questions are handled and the speed at which each agency will respond. Agency policies on e-mail answering speed range from 24 hours or less, to two-five working days, to ten working days or more, and some agencies and offices still do not provide e-mail services but continue to rely on telephone, fax, letters, and office visits to answer the public's questions.

A major problem for the agencies is that e-mail is still a relatively new development and the necessities for engaging the public by e-mail, including sufficient staffing, budget, written e-mail policies, and training in digital reference skills, have not been made a priority within the government. Public demand is likely to force this issue as more and more citizens seek services online. However, the public often is not aware that in many agencies, thousands of e-mails are being handled by a mere handful of agency staff or sometimes as few as one or two government workers who also have other assigned duties. This reality has motivated exploration into alternative methods for government digital reference including partnership models such as the State Department's DOSFAN partnership with UIC, collaborative efforts such as the Library of Congress Collaborative Digital Reference Service (http://loc.gov/rr/digiref), and subcontracting experiments such as the U.S. Department of Education-funded AskERIC service operated by Syracuse University (www.askeric.org) or the Environmental Protection Agency's AskEPA contracts with companies such as GCI Information Services and ASRC Aerospace Corporation.

Partnership models similar to DOSFAN involve agencies working together with a partner that brings specific needed skills, such as digital reference expertise. Collaborative efforts such as Library of Congress CDRS involve many different institutions agreeing to share and exchange questions through a central coordinating agency. Subcontracting experiments employ specialists to operate services under the auspices of an agency.

The AskERIC service at Syracuse University's ERIC Clearinghouse, which answers questions on education-related topics for the Department of Education, has also branched outward into volunteer and consortial efforts by establishing the Virtual Reference Desk (VRD). Through VRD, question-answering services such as AskERIC and the Internet Public Library share and exchange questions through

a central coordinating agency, but in addition the Virtual Reference Desk (www.vrd.org) also recruits individual librarians as VRD volunteers. The AskERIC service is thus able to distribute out-of-scope AskERIC questions either to VRD volunteers or to other digital reference services within the VRD consortium, thereby focusing AskERIC's efforts on the remaining questions that fall within AskERIC's mandate and scope. Innovative efforts such as these are worth considering for government agencies faced with large volumes of e-mail to be answered and insufficient internal resources to accomplish the task.

CONCLUSION

What does the DOSFAN partnership reveal about how citizens and institutions responsible for the public's information (libraries, archives, and government information centers) will interact within the expanding universe of networked government information resources? Upon reflection, there is cause for both hope and concern.

On the side of hope are the depository librarians themselves. Their collective (and singular) professional skills as information experts who constantly evaluate information queries, and readily determine which level of government (federal, state, or local) might have the best information, remain a necessary resource within an environment where information is highly distributed and rapidly exchanged.

On the side of concern, however, is the fact that government information librarians, to judge from their professional literature, are at a crisis point. A century of practice binds them to a paradigm of information service that rests upon twin pillars rapidly eroding under the changes of technology and social organization. The first: a national distribution system (the Government Printing Office and its Superintendent of Documents) that delivers through the second: local service mechanisms (the more than 1300 individual libraries that are part of the system).

As long as the GPO controlled the means of production and distribution for the greater portion of printed federal documents (which it pretty much did from 1896 through 1965), the depository libraries served as informal information bureaus for the agencies—handing out tax forms for the IRS and providing information about taxes; helping with legislative histories and answering questions about the Congress and laws. However, the August 25, 2000, letter from the Superintendent of Documents to directors of the federal depository libraries has made it clear that fewer and fewer physical items will be printed and shipped to depository libraries (Buckley Jr., 2000). Take away the mechanics of national distribution and the purpose of local service buckles from the lack of material.

Reliance on the GPO as a centralized organization to provide both bibliographic records and documents has left the librarians without any other way of understanding government information. Much of the reaction and methods of dealing with the explosive use of electronic government information resources has largely been based on the traditions and practices of the print and paper world. In fact, government information librarians refer to electronic documents not handled through the GPO administrative apparatus as "fugitive" publications, casting a skeptical glance at those information resources not "sanctioned" by GPO's command and control. But the Web, along with the explosion of official government Web sites, has repatriated these "lost" titles, to much angst and worry among librarians and GPO about the permanence and legitimacy of the electronic material.

The Web turns all the information services back to the agencies; the agencies now are attempting to explain themselves to the public. E-government efforts such as GSA's FirstGov represent the government reclaiming services and information previously relegated to the depository library system, though without the interpretive guidance previously provided by federal depository librarians in helping citizens find their way to the correct bureau or office within the maze of government. In November 2000, Senator Ron Wyden partially addressed the issue of assistance to the e-citizen by advocating "an easy-to-use online complaint box" to be added to FirstGov.gov so that citizens would have a central place to lodge complaints (Matthews, 2000). FirstGov launched in September 2000 and by July 2001 was already reported to be "deluged by e-mail" with an estimated 70 percent of the intake consisting of questions needing to be triaged and sent to appropriate agencies for further assistance (Dean, 2001).

Clearly the movement of electronic government information to agency Web sites is being followed by a movement of citizen questions to the electronic venue. A recent reminder of the critical importance to the public of government digital reference service came in the wake of the September 11, 2001, terrorist attacks on Washington and New York. UIC librarians worked with the State Department's representatives to answer an unprecedented upswing in the public's messages, questions, and concerns about the attack. Even with the increased pressure and demands generated by this extraordinary event, the arrangement proved equal to the task and gives the authors further evidence that such partnerships can thrive in the worst as well as the best of times.

Given the new realities of electronic communication, it is essential for all libraries, especially the federal depository libraries, to rethink their role as information providers in the new electronic age. As the public goes online for more and more government information and services, it will become increasingly difficult to convince them that they should physically visit a federal depository library to ask government information questions. UIC's federal depository library in extending and redefining concepts of library service and constituency into the electronic world has rejuvenated its role in serving the public, creating both a dynamic digital reference service and a valued electronic depository archive. The U.S. Department of State's participation in the partnership experiment has likewise brought unique and unanticipated extra benefits to the agency in original online content, access to experimental software, and innovations in public service.

The new paradigm for federal depository libraries is a shift in focus from distributed collections to distributed services. Federal depository librarians must move beyond the artificial constraints of physical libraries and printed documents into the twenty-first century of electronic collections and digital reference services, as modeled by the UIC/DOSFAN partnership as well as the University of North Texas Libraries "Cybercemetery" partnership with the Government Printing Office, which provides permanent online access to documents from the defunct National Partnership for Reinventing Government, the Office of Technology Assessment, and other former federal commissions and offices (http://govinfo.library.unt.edu/default.html). We hope that the lessons learned from UIC/DOSFAN, the first federal electronic depository library, can help other federal depository libraries seeking to redefine themselves in this new era of electronic government information and services.

REFERENCES

Buckley Jr., Francis J. 2000. *SuDocs Letter to Directors: Changes in FDLP* [Online]. Available: www.access.gpo.gov/su_docs/fdlp/coll-dev/sdltr8–25–00.html [2000, August 25].

Congress Online Project. 2001. *E-Mail Overload in Congress: Managing a Communications Crisis*, George Washington University and the Congressional Management Foundation [Online]. Available: www.congressonlineproject.org/e-mail.html [2001, March 19].

Dean, Joshua. 2001. *FirstGov Web Portal Deluged With Citizen E-Mail*, GovExec.Com [Online]. Available: www.govexec.com/dailyfed/0701/070501j1.htm [2001, July 25].

Matthews, William. 2000. *Senator Seeks a "Send Your Gripe" Box at FirstGov*, Federal Computer Week [Online]. Available: www.fcw.com/fcw/articles/2000/1127/web-firstgv-11–27–00.asp [2000, November 27].

Matthews, William. 2001. *Congress E-Mail Volume Soars*, Federal Computer Week [Online]. Available: www.fcw.com/fcw/articles/2001/1217/web-e-mail-12–19–01.asp [2000, December 19].

Mon, Lorri. 2001. All statistics estimates in Table 2–1 are based on e-mail responses received from the agencies to personal inquiries during September 2001, as follows:

Department of Agriculture — USDA Webmaster, September 7, 2001: "E-mail received via the Internet by the Webmaster at USDA headquarters totals 10,000 per year."

Department of Energy — DOE HQ Webmaster, September 19, 2001: "The [DOE Secretary's] mailbox receives approximately 16,000 e-mails annually."

Environmental Protection Agency — EPA Headquarters Information Resources Center, operated by ASRC Aerospace, September 13, 2001: "Summer is a slow time for us, when we generally process (receive and answer) 2500 e-mails per month; last March (2001) we received 7,879 e-mails."

Federal Communications Commission — FCCINFO, September 17, 2001: "Customer service standards are at: www.fcc.gov/css.html." (Referred source indicates 17,118 e-mail inquiries received in the 3–month period of 4/1/01–6/30/01.)

General Services Administration — GSA Web Team, September 17, 2001: "GSA . . . receives 15–20 [e-mail messages through the Webmaster link] per day."

Government Printing Office — GPO Access, September 7, 2001: "You can search and retrieve information on statistics about GPO websites online via GPO Access at: www.access.gpo.gov/su_docs/aces/biennial/index.html." (Referred source indicates 23,457 e-mail messages for January-November 2001.)

Internal Revenue Service — Tax Law Inquiry section, September 20, 2001: "FY 2001 325,000 (approx)."

National Archives and Records Administration — NNU Public Reference Inquire, September 19, 2001: "We receive approximately 150,000 e-mails per fiscal year."

Office of the Vice President, National Performance Review, 1993. *From Red Tape to Results: Creating a Government That Works Better & Costs Less: Improving Customer Service*. Washington, D.C.: Government Printing Office.

PART II

Managing Key Digital Reference Issues

OVERVIEW

The chapters in this section investigate the issues of artificial intelligence, privacy, and copyright. Privacy and copyright have always been two of the stickier issues involved in the provision of reference services. The ease of duplicating electronic content and the difficulty of protecting personal information online has made these issues equally sticky for digital reference services. Artificial intelligence has for decades held great promise for automating the reference process, but this potential has to date far outstripped the reality; implementation in real-world settings has been rare.

These chapters explore these three issues from the perspective of the digital reference environment, but this consideration has clear application to other realms. In addressing these broad issues for this specific domain, the authors arrive at workable solutions that may then serve as models, not only for digital reference services, but for other domains as well.

Chapter 3

Exploring Virtual Reference: What It Is and What It May Be

Kwan-Yau Lam

OVERVIEW

One commonality found among prevalent virtual reference formats is that the computer serves only to store and deliver information. However, a computer is capable of doing much more, such as simulating human intelligence and problem solving. An expert system methodology is proposed to impart some artificial intelligence to virtual reference.

INTRODUCTION

The past few years have witnessed an extraordinary surge of interest in virtual reference among librarians. One important factor for such increasing interest is the rapid emergence of distance education programs offered by many colleges and universities (Coffman, 2001). Another key factor is of course the tremendous growth of the Internet and online information services of all kinds (Pack, 2000).

Undoubtedly, virtual reference is important and inevitable in this information age. Yet some critics may still ask whether it is just hype. This is an excellent question, and pondering this question would help us better understand the very nature of virtual reference. In fact, to provide effective virtual reference, librarians need to think deeply of other questions as well. For example: What exactly is virtual reference? What are the differences between virtual reference and traditional reference? Why is virtual reference indispensable in the eyes of many? What might be the future of virtual reference?

In an attempt to answer the above questions, the author reviewed extant literature and identified several different virtual reference formats. Virtual reference is considered in this paper as the type of reference that is provided through cyberspace, or more specifically, over the Internet. Prevalent formats of virtual reference include e-mail, AskA services, online pathfinders, chat, and real-time live Web reference. Similarities and differences among these formats, as well as their special attributes, strengths, and limitations, may shed light on the very nature and possible future of virtual reference.

One possible future direction is the development of a virtual reference system that possesses some degree of artificial intelligence. An expert system methodology that may be used to develop such a system is discussed in the second part of this paper.

PREVALENT FORMATS OF VIRTUAL REFERENCE

E-Mail

E-mail is the earliest and perhaps the most prevalent format of virtual reference. In many academic libraries, particularly health science and engineering libraries, e-mail reference can be dated back as early as the mid-1980s (Gray, 2000; Henson and Tomajko, 2000). With the proliferation of the Internet in the past decade and the availability of an e-mail account to almost everyone in society, e-mail reference service is no longer confined to large research and academic libraries. Many public libraries now have e-mail reference available to their patrons. One notable example is the Santa Monica Public Library in California, where librarians have been providing e-mail reference for more than ten years (O'Neill, 1999).

Obviously, e-mail reference has a number of advantages. First of all, it offers patrons the convenience of asking for information or reference assistance whenever and wherever they are, even in the wee hours of the night at some remote physical location where Internet is accessible. Lipow (1999) noted that more often than not, "people will go first to the most likely source that is convenient. *Convenience* is what governs the choice of where to go." It is therefore not surprising to find a lot of people who are more inclined to use e-mail reference than some other traditional reference services. For example, Bristow (1992) reported that many university faculty and graduate students at a mid-western state university had demonstrated overwhelmingly their preference for e-mail over telephone reference.

E-mail reference also has the advantage of providing more complete answers than what could possibly be given at a busy reference desk (Bristow and Buechley, 1995; Johnston and Grusin, 1995). When answering a question through e-mail, the reference librarian usually has more time to think about the question, the patron's information needs, and if necessary, consult with other librarians who have more related expertise or knowledge. Furthermore, since ASCII text is no longer the only format permissible in e-mail, librarians can include non-ASCII-text documents, such as image and sound files, in their replies to patrons (Tomer, 1994).

Like all other reference tools, e-mail is not perfect and it does have its limitations. Many librarians have expressed concerns over two major weaknesses of e-mail as a reference medium, namely, long response time (Coffman, 2001; Gray, 2000; Helfer, 2001) and difficulty to conduct reference interview (Abels, 1996; Garnsey and Powell, 2000). Although e-mail delivery is instantaneous, reply is not. It takes time for a librarian to respond to an e-mail reference question. The response time may vary from a couple of hours to as long as a week, depending on the volume of reference questions and the policy of the library. Long response time, coupled with the fact that an effective reference interview often takes several e-mail exchanges, may result in frustrations for both the patron and the librarian. Worse still, after a lengthy yet crucial and essential e-mail reference interview, the patron may find that the sought-for information is no longer needed by the time it is received.

One other drawback of e-mail reference is that all responses will become written records once they are sent out. Librarians generally have no problems verbally answering questions at a reference desk, but some may worry about putting their responses in black and white (Henson and Tomajko, 2000). Such worry is not totally unfounded for one can never tell what a patron may do with the written responses, including the possibility of suing the librarian or the library. As a matter of fact, the Santa Monica Public Library has a policy not to provide any medical, legal, or consumer product information over e-mail, although referrals to proper sources may be given (O'Neill, 1999; Santa Monica Public Library, 2000).

AskA Services

In this chapter, AskA services refer to Web sites that provide such services as AskA-librarian, AskAn-expert, and AskA-question, in which users' questions are referred to and individually answered by real people. Note that there are some Web sites such as AskJeeves.com that sound like AskA services but are in fact search engines and they are not considered here as AskA virtual reference.

There are many AskA services on the Web. Perhaps the one most well-known in academic circles is AskERIC, which was started in 1992 (AskERIC, 2001) and is one of the earliest AskA services on the Internet. Many public and academic libraries, as well as the Library of Congress, also offer AskA services. However, not all AskA services are provided by non-profit educational organizations and libraries. Some are run by dot-coms, such as AskAnExpert.com and exp.com.

Many AskA services provide online request forms for patrons to ask questions and to provide information that is usually obtained from an initial reference interview. For example, on the Internet Public Library's (2001) AskA-Question Form, patrons are asked to provide such information as how the sought-for information will be used, type of answer expected, and sources already consulted. This kind of information may help reduce irrelevancy and the number of subsequent communications (Henson and Tomajko, 2000), thereby to a certain extent alleviating the problem of a cumbersome reference interview process.

Although online request forms are popularly

used, they are not in themselves a communication medium between patrons and people who answer their questions. In fact, e-mail is the most prevalent communication medium for AskA services. Virtually all AskA services, particularly those run by libraries, require patrons to provide an e-mail address on their online request forms. In addition to e-mail, some AskA services use chat (e.g. exp.com), message tracking ID number (e.g. MadSci Network's AskA-Scientist, at www.madsci.org) and even phone (e.g. Library of Congress's AskA-Librarian, at www.loc.gov) as alternative or supplementary communication media. Despite these other means of communication, e-mail remains the most predominant and the most prevalent. To that extent, AskA services share the strengths and weaknesses of e-mail reference mentioned in the preceding section.

Online Pathfinders

Pathfinders are guides designed to help users find information on a particular topic. Libraries, particularly academic libraries, have traditionally been using pathfinders as reference tools for patrons. With more and more information available in electronic format and on the Web, online pathfinders are becoming increasingly popular not only in university libraries (Dahl, 2001), but also in public libraries. Examples of online pathfinders can be found at the Internet Public Library (ipl.org) and the Library of Congress (www.loc.gov) Web sites.

Like e-mail and AskA reference services, online pathfinders are available to patrons whenever and wherever they can access the Internet. However, online pathfinder users do not have to wait for hours or weeks for a librarian's e-mail reply, or to wait in an electronic queue for the next available librarian. This convenient, self-help nature of online pathfinders is definitely an important advantage.

The possibility of including Web links to electronic resources is another advantage of online pathfinders. Through these Web links, users may access not only textual materials, but also multimedia resources such as digitized images of historical documents and sound files.

A third advantage of online pathfinders is guided searching. Popular search engines available on the Web oftentimes return so many Web pages that a user has to go through a lot of irrelevant Web sites before finding what is needed. Worse still, one may even reach some dead end and find nothing useful

at all. Guided searching can help eliminate these problems of false starts and dead ends (Graves, 1998).

Though online pathfinders usually provide fruitful starts and useful information, their static nature is nonetheless one of their weaknesses. Most online pathfinders are static annotated lists of resources or Web links, and do not possess any interactivity with the users. Furthermore, Dahl (2001) noted that many online pathfinders analyzed in her study are more complex in structure than printed ones, and structural complexity can sometimes cause confusion to the user.

Another important weakness of online pathfinders is the lack of individualization. Though online pathfinders are generally customized, they are only customized to a specific target audience such as a group of students working on a particular classroom assignment. Specific information needs of a particular individual are not addressed and individual reference interview is not part of an online pathfinder.

Chat

Chat, sometimes referred to as instant messaging, is real-time communication between two or more computer users over the Internet. Every keystroke a chat user makes is instantly transmitted and appears on the monitors of all other users in the same chat session. Chat is a very popular means of communication over the Internet. However, as it now stands, chat communication is only text-based. Many libraries, such as Santa Monica Public Library (www.smpl.org) and Bowling Green State University Jerome Library (Broughton, 2001), have attempted to use Internet chat as a means to provide reference service.

Chat is the Internet counterpart of POTS (plain old telephone service). Since it is text-based, chat does not seem to be much more advantageous than POTS as a reference medium. Perhaps the main advantage of using chat reference is that, as Eichler and Halperin (2000) noted, it allows the patron to continue staying online while getting reference assistance. However, with the growing popularity of a second phone line, cellular phone, and high-speed DSL (digital subscriber line, though not available in all areas), this advantage may not be as significant nowadays as it was one or two years ago. Nonetheless, if one has an immediate reference question that must be directed to a particular library in another state or another country, chat may help save some money on one's phone bill.

As a reference medium, chat is far from perfect because it was originally designed for one-on-one personal "conversations" and it is simply not geared toward answering a high volume of reference questions (Coffman, 2001). Another limitation is the difficulty to multitask during a chat reference session. For example, a librarian cannot look for information while chatting online with the patron because he/she has to type in every word and letter. This would not only make chat reference much slower than POTS (Broughton, 2001) and other means of traditional reference, but would also require additional reference librarian staffing during busy hours (Eichler and Halperin, 2000).

Of course, the slowness problem can be further compounded by other factors such as a low-speed modem connection at the other end. Finally, the need to type in each and every word poses other problems as well. First of all, it could hamper potentially important communication between the librarian and a patron during a chat reference session. Schneider (2000) also noted that it would lead to physical and mental exhaustion very easily, especially when a librarian is under the covert pressure to give correct information immediately.

Real-Time Live Web Reference

Real-time reference live on the Web is the latest trend in virtual reference. Already some libraries are providing live Web reference services to their patrons. Examples are the Metropolitan Cooperative Library System's (MCLS) 24/7 reference service (24ref.org) and the CLEVNET Library Consortium's Know-It-Now service (www.cpl.org). MCLS is an association of 31 public libraries in the Los Angeles area, but participants in its 24/7 reference project also include many academic libraries such as University of Washington and University of Alberta libraries (Metropolitan Cooperative Library System, 2001). The CLEVNET Library Consortium has 29 member libraries in ten northern Ohio counties (Cleveland Public Library, 2000). Both 24/7 and Know-It-Now are available to patrons on the Web around the clock, except on certain holidays.

A significant round-the-clock, though not real-time live, Web reference project that should perhaps be noted here as a sidetrack is the Library of Congress's Collaborative Digital Reference Service

(CDRS). The mission of CDRS is to "provide professional reference service to researchers any time anywhere, through an international, digital network of libraries and related institutions" (Collaborative Digital Reference Service, 2001). At the time this chapter was written, CDRS was still in its pilot phase and there were around 100 participating libraries in the United States, Canada, Hong Kong, Australia, Germany, and the United Kingdom (Library of Congress, 2001). Though the final format and logistics are not yet certain, CDRS definitely deserves attention because it signifies the importance of collaboration among libraries from different time zones in providing 24/7 Web reference service anywhere in the world.

As exemplified by MCLS 24/7 and CLEVNET's Know-It-Now, real-time live Web reference is an extension of text-based chat reference. However, it has more features and capabilities than pure chat reference. The Virtual Reference Desk software developed by LSSI (Library Systems & Services, LLC) provides a prototype of what live Web reference is at present. In addition to text-based chatting between the librarian and the patron, Virtual Reference Desk allows electronic queuing of patrons, co-browsing, Web page sending, pre-defined or "canned" text messages, screen capturing, slide shows, demonstrations, chat transferring or conferencing, and complete transcript record of the entire session (Library Systems & Services, 2000). The software is also compatible with VoIP (Voice over IP), offered as an optional service, which enables the librarian and the patron to actually talk with each other over the same Internet connection for the live Web reference session.

The aforementioned capabilities of live Web reference surely make it a much more powerful and efficient reference tool than chat. On the other hand, because live Web reference is essentially chat-based, it shares all the limitations of chat reference discussed earlier. Moreover, quality live Web reference software never comes free, meaning considerable expenses for the library. For example, LSSI's Virtual Reference Desk requires an $8000 setup and training fee, and an additional $500 monthly maintenance fee (Broughton, 2001). If VoIP is opted for, additional expenses will be incurred. Note, however, that VoIP voice quality can vary considerably over the public Internet (TechEncyclopedia, 2001).

One final limitation of round-the-clock live Web reference, ironically, arises from one of its strengths—the possibility of collaboration and resource sharing among libraries from countries in different time zones. Potential problems may arise because different countries have different social and legal systems. For example, an Australian librarian who is not familiar with the U.S. educational system may have a hard time answering questions about GED (General Educational Development) from a patron seeking help on the Web at 2 a.m. in the U.S. An even thornier issue is copyright. Database licenses have already posed many problems for live Web reference and in certain cases have even forced reference librarians to snail-mail articles instead of sending them online in this country (Oder, 2001). The situation would certainly get more complicated when copyright laws of different countries are involved.

Differences and Commonalities

All of the virtual reference formats discussed above have different technological natures, and hence they differ in their capabilities and in how they are actually used. E-mail and AskA reference services may be grouped together technology-wise since e-mail is the most prevalent and primary communication medium for AskA services. Similarly, chat and real-time live Web services can be categorized together because of their underlying Internet chat technology, even though they have different capabilities and characteristics. Online pathfinders, however, stand on their own, for they rely neither on e-mail nor on chat technology.

There is an important difference between online pathfinders and the other four formats. As a reference tool, an online pathfinder is not human mediated while all the others are. The librarian only acts as a selector of information resources, but not as a human mediator between a patron and the pathfinder. Thus, to the extent that the word "virtual" implies simulation of something that is not actually present, online pathfinders are the most virtual of all the formats discussed in this paper.

Despite their differences, the five virtual reference formats have two commonalities. First, they all share the same goal of reaching out to patrons beyond the physical confines of a library at all times through cyberspace. The second commonality is the use of the computer as a powerful tool to provide reference services over the Internet. However, all five formats use the computer for nothing more than storing and delivering information. This distinction is an important one. Indisputably, the Internet is a valuable and efficient information delivery medium. But to use the computer as a mere information storage and delivery tool means that the computing power of the computer has not been fully utilized.

In what follows, an expert system methodology is proposed as an example of how the computer's computing power can be more fully utilized. The methodology can also be used to add a certain degree of artificial intelligence to virtual reference.

ARTIFICIALLY INTELLIGENT VIRTUAL REFERENCE?

Computer scientists, cognitive psychologists, and linguists have long been interested in artificial intelligence. With the ever increasing power and processing speed of computers, there are more and more computer applications that exhibit some kind of smartness, if not artificial intelligence as conceived by cognitive scientists. In virtual reference, there is a definite need for artificially intelligent software that can help patrons find information in accordance with their specific individual needs.

Studies have demonstrated that many students would rather change their research topics instead of asking librarians for assistance when they think the information they need cannot be easily found (O'Sullivan, 2000). For these students as well as those who prefer working on their own, an intelligent virtual reference system that can provide them with advice when looking for information may perhaps be more helpful than a reference librarian.

As mentioned earlier, online pathfinders do not require the actual presence of a librarian and are the most virtual of all prevalent virtual reference formats. They are therefore an excellent candidate for development into an intelligent virtual reference system. In this second part of the chapter, the possibility of developing an online pathfinder expert system is examined.

Expert System

Expert systems are one of four main branches of artificial intelligence. The other three branches are robotics, natural language processing, and voice recognition. In essence, an expert system is a computer program that "makes judgments or gives assistance in a complex area" (Neapolitan, 1992: 55), and it consists of two essential parts—an inference engine and a knowledge base. As its name implies, the inference engine makes inferences and is the reasoning part of an expert system. It decides what to do next based on data stored in the knowledge base and user's input. The knowledge base is where knowledge—that is, facts and data—in a specific area of expertise is represented and stored. Typically, knowledge is represented in the form of *IF [certain conditions are met], THEN [such and such action]* rules. Another method commonly used to represent knowledge is the use of frames, which allow coding of details and attributes of an object.

It is quite obvious that the traditional process of representing knowledge by if-then rules or frames is not an easy task. During the development of a frame-based reference expert system at the University of Houston Libraries, it was found that the construction of the knowledge base was time-consuming, complex, and required a detailed analysis of the actual reference process (Bailey, 1992). The same holds true for building a rule-based expert system (Glover, 1994).

Fortunately, not all expert systems have to be rule-based or frame-based. Some expert systems, known as normative expert systems, rely on statistical data rather than if-then rules or frames to make their decisions. A normative expert system is one in which "probability and utility theory are used" (Neapolitan, 1992: 56) when making the best possible judgments and inferences. The definition is definitely quite broad. Nonetheless, it is this broad conception that makes the idea of normative expert system applicable in many situations, for example, the development of computer adaptive tests (Frick, 1992). Normative expert systems are suggested here as a plausible methodology for developing an intelligent online reference pathfinder that is capable of self-learning and giving individual advice to patrons.

Online Pathfinder as Normative Expert System

Reference librarians often find actual usage data from past patrons very useful. These data contain much valuable information and they are an ideal type of data to be captured in a knowledge base. The problem is, however, how to do so. Let us now take an example and assume we want to transform an online pathfinder into a normative expert system. Our online pathfinder contains five fictitious annotated hypertext links (A, B, C, D, and E) to different information resources that are all related to a

Table 3–1
Frequency Distribution of Fictitious Concurrent Hypertext Link Visits

	A	B	C	D	E
A	10	300	250	10	5
B	300	10	350	5	10
C	250	350	10	10	5
D	10	5	10	10	350
E	5	10	5	350	10

particular topic. In this situation, the simplest way to develop a normative knowledge base is to construct a two-way frequency distribution table as shown above.

Table 3–1 shows the frequency distribution of concurrent visits by past patrons to five hypertext links. The diagonal indicates the number of patrons who have visited only one link. Of course, all numbers in Table 3–1 are fictitious. Note that the table is symmetrical about its diagonal. This is so because the order in which links are visited is not important in this example and is therefore not differentiated in the table.

Suppose a patron has just visited C, then A, and finally B. Not only will the numbers in the intersecting cells of C and A (first row/second column, third row/first column in Table 3–1) and of A and B (first row/second column, second row/first column) be increased by one accordingly, but so will be those corresponding to B and C (second row/third column, third row/second column) since the patron has indeed visited B and C concurrently. To avoid random browsing being counted as a hit, a link is considered visited only after a reasonable time has elapsed. Other criteria may be set as well. For example, back-and-forth jumping from one link to another can only be counted once. Link presentation order can be randomized to prevent any possible selection bias due to the position of a link in the pathfinder list.

The inference engine can now make use of Table 3–1 (that is, the knowledge base) to give advice to another patron. For example, suppose a patron has just visited link E but no other links. The inference engine looks up the table and finds out that 350 out of 380 past visitors to link E had also visited link D. It therefore infers that the probability of patrons visiting D after visiting E and vice versa is 92.1 percent. Based on this high probability, the inference engine recommends the patron to visit link D also.

Now suppose the patron does take the inference engine's advice and decides to visit D. After he/she has done so, the inference engine looks up Table 3–1 again. This time it finds out past visitors to D and E rarely visited A, B, or C. On the other hand, it also notices that although past A, B, and C visitors rarely visited D or E, they showed a high probability of concurrently visiting either of the other two links (95.7 percent, 96.3 percent, and 96.0 percent for A, B, and C visitors respectively). The inference engine may therefore advise the patron to visit A, B, or C and inform the patron that those links may contain some other information pertaining to a different aspect of the same topic.

The normative knowledge base in our example here is deliberately made simple for illustration purposes. Nonetheless, as demonstrated above, it contains much useful information about past usage patterns. The knowledge base can certainly have a more complex structure. Table 3–1 can be further broken down by some other variables. For example, patrons can be asked to input their satisfaction ratings of the links they have visited, and there can be two frequency distribution tables—one for patrons who have found the links useful, and another for those who are dissatisfied with the links. Note, however, that a frequency distribution table cannot be subdivided too elaborately, or else there will be too many cells but not enough data in each one to draw any meaningful conclusions.

Strengths

Methodologically, the greatest strength of a normative expert system lies in its elegant simplicity. Valuable information, such as past usage patterns in our example, is inherent in data stored in the knowledge base and is retrieved mathematically during run time. Normative information, or rather knowledge, is therefore more objective than knowledge represented by if-then rules or frames. In addition, there is no need for any painstaking, time-consuming but nevertheless subjective analyses of experts' knowledge.

Another very important methodological advantage is the ability of a normative knowledge base to self-learn and to make self-corrections. These two abilities are significant because they are manifestations of intelligence. Self-learning occurs when new usage patterns, previously unknown to the system, emerge as more and more data from actual patrons are stored in knowledge base. Accumulation of actual usage data may also result in refinements or self-corrections of usage patterns already known to the system.

Online pathfinders generally lack interactivity and individualization. These two weaknesses are addressed by the advising ability of normative expert system. As in our example, the system's advice is based on a patron's own path and/or satisfaction input. The idea of giving patrons individualized advice is not new. For example, Glover (1994) noted that rule-based expert systems can make hypertext links more usable by giving advice to patrons. However, unlike normative expert systems, a rule-based system is much more difficult to build and usually lacks self-learning ability.

As a virtual reference tool, an online pathfinder expert system is simple and easy to implement. The addition of a normative knowledge base and an inference engine does not change the fact that an online pathfinder is not human mediated. Since no live online presence of any librarian is required, it is the most convenient way to provide 24/7 virtual reference service. Also, unlike other virtual reference formats, there is no need for any special library policies limiting the use of an online pathfinder expert system to certain groups of patrons only.

Limitations

One major methodological limitation of normative knowledge base is that it requires a substantial amount of usage data in order to make any meaningful inferences. This problem is particularly crucial when the knowledge base is made up of many categories or subcategories. Of course, during the initial stage, a librarian may make reasonable data estimates that reflect some hypothetical relationships among the hypertext links, and then rely on the self-learning and self-correcting abilities of the expert system to make any necessary corrections subsequently as more actual usage data are available.

As aforementioned, the absence of human mediation is an advantage that makes an online pathfinder expert system a convenient and feasible 24/7 virtual reference tool. The same advantage, however, is also a weakness in the sense that it makes the system less flexible than any other human mediated reference format. As in our example, the hypertext links are fixed and pre-selected even though advice to patrons is not. Nonetheless, online pathfinder expert systems are particularly useful in situations where people keep coming and ask for information on the same topics. Such situations, of course, are not unfamiliar to librarians working in school or college libraries.

CONCLUSION

Though our example above is hypothetical, it has nonetheless demonstrated that both theoretically and logically, normative expert system is a promising and viable approach to virtual reference development. Normative expert systems definitely have a niche in virtual reference. There are many times when patrons ask for the same information over and over again. For example, academic librarians often find themselves helping students with class assignments on the same topics semester after semester. A 24/7, online pathfinder expert system would be particularly helpful in such situations. Moreover, since there is no lack of actual usage data in these situations, it can be safely assumed that any advice derived from the normative knowledge base is valid and reliable.

The methodological conception of a normative knowledge base may also be adapted to other reference formats. As an example, in addition to a searchable knowledge base of frequently asked questions, scripted messages and transcript records (Breeding, 2001; Coffman, 2001), a normative knowledge base can provide valuable statistical information to better empower a librarian during a live Web reference session.

Online pathfinder expert systems are not proposed here as a substitute for any traditional or virtual reference format. Rather, it is suggested with an intention to enrich the virtual reference environment for patrons. Virtual reference is no longer mere hype, but an inevitable fact of life given the abundance of authoritative and useful information existing in cyberspace. Many patrons have come to expect not only full-text documents, but also reference help, right now and right here over the Internet. Virtual reference is necessary to help these patrons, rather than alienating them from libraries. In fact, as inherent in the commonalities found among prevalent virtual reference formats, the essence of virtual reference is to reach out to patrons through cyberspace. Traditional reference formats, such as POTS and fax, are in general less efficient than the Internet in overcoming geographical barriers between libraries and patrons.

Future development of virtual reference in different formats is crucial in order to meet different information needs and to cater to different cognitive styles of patrons. The development of an online pathfinder expert system is one step in that direction. Most virtual reference development efforts so far have focused on adapting to and making use of hardware and software products available on the market. There is no doubt that these efforts are very important and productive. However, as illustrated on this chapter, it can be equally important and productive to develop our own innovative products based on sound theoretical principles.

REFERENCES

Abels, Eileen G. 1996. "The E-Mail Reference Interview." *RQ* 35, no. 3 (Spring): 345–358.

AskERIC. 2001. *About AskERIC*, Information Institute of Syracuse [Online]. Available: http://askeric.org/About/ [2002, May 24].

Bailey, Charles W., Jr. 1992. "The Intelligent Reference Information System Project: A Merger of CD-ROM LAN and Expert System Technologies." *Information Technology & Libraries* 11, no. 3 (September): 237–244.

Breeding, Marshall. 2001. "Providing Virtual Reference Service." *Information Today* 18, no. 4 (April): 42–43.

Bristow, Ann. 1992. "Academic Reference Service over Electronic Mail." *College & Research Libraries News*, no. 10 (November): 631–632.

Bristow, Ann, and Mary Buechley. 1995. "Academic Reference Service Over E-Mail: An Update." *College & Research Libraries News*, no. 7 (July/August): 459–462.

Broughton, Kelly M. 2001. "Our Experiment in Online, Real-Time Reference." *Computers in Libraries* 21, no. 4 (April): 26–31.

Cleveland Public Library. 2000. *Library Locations & Information: The CLEVNET Library Consortium*, Cleveland Public Library [Online]. Available: www.cpl.org/Locations.asp?FormMode=CLEVNET [2000, April 17].

Coffman, Steve. 2001. "Distance Education and Virtual Reference: Where Are We Headed?" *Computers in Libraries* 21, no. 4 (April): 20–25.

Collaborative Digital Reference Service. 2001. *What is CDRS?*, Library of Congress [Online]. Available: www.loc.gov/rr/digiref/about.html [2001, June 12].

Dahl, Candice. 2001. "Electronic Pathfinders in Academic Libraries: An Analysis of Their Content and Form."

College & Research Libraries 62, no. 3 (May): 227–237.

Eichler, Linda, and Michael Halperin. 2000. "LivePerson: Keeping Reference Alive and Clicking." *EContent* 23, no. 3 (June/July): 63–66.

Frick, Theodore W. 1992. "Computerized Adaptive Mastery Tests as Expert Systems." *Journal of Educational Computing Research* 8, no. 2: 187–213.

Garnsey, Beth A., and Ronald R. Powell. 2000. "Electronic Mail Reference Services in the Public Library." *Reference & User Services Quarterly* 39, no. 3 (Spring): 245–254.

Glover, Kyle S. 1994. "How Expert Systems Can Make Hypertext More Usable." *Technical Communication* 41, no. 4 (November): 628–634.

Graves, Judith K. 1998. "Research Pathfinders: Offline Access to Online Searching." *Multimedia Schools* 5, no. 3 (May/June): 26–29.

Gray, Suzanne M. 2000. "Virtual Reference Services: Directions and Agendas." *Reference & User Services Quarterly* 39, no. 4 (Summer): 365–375.

Helfer, Doris Small. 2001. "Virtual Reference in Libraries: Remote Patrons Heading Your Way?" *Searcher* 9, no. 2 (February): 67–70.

Henson, Bruce, and Kathy Gillespie Tomajko. 2000. "Electronic Reference Services: Opportunities and Challenges." *Journal of Educational Media & Library Sciences* 38, no. 2 (December): 113–121.

Internet Public Library. "IPL Ask A Question Form." Ann Arbor, MI: University of Michigan School of Information [Online]. Available: www.ipl.org/ref/QUE/RefFormQRC.html [2001, July 9].

Johnston, Pat, and Ann Grusin. 1995. "Personal Service in an Impersonal World: Throwing Life Preservers to Those Drowning in an Ocean of Information." *The Georgia Librarian* 32 (Summer/Fall/Winter): 45–49.

Library of Congress. 2001. *Collaborative Digital Reference Service Reaches 100 Participants*. Library of Congress [Online]. Available: www.loc.gov/today/pr/2001/01–089.html [2001, June 20].

Library Systems & Services. 2001. *Virtual Reference Desk: Here's How It Works*. Library Systems & Services [Online]. Available: www.virtualreference.net/virtual/02.html [2000, September 26].

Lipow, Anne G. 1999. "Serving the Remote User: Reference Service in the Digital Environment." Keynote address at the Ninth Australasian Information Online & On Disc Conference and Exhibition, "Strategies for the Next Millennium," Sydney, Australia, January 1999 [Online]. Available: www.csu.edu.au/special/online99/proceedings99/200.htm [2002, May 24].

Metropolitan Cooperative Library System. 2001. *24/7 Reference Communities*, Metropolitan Cooperative Library System [Online]. Available: http://247ref.org/communities.htm [2001, August 16].

Neapolitan, Richard E. 1992. A Survey of Uncertain and Approximate Inference. In *Fuzzy Logic for the Management of Uncertainty*, L.A. Zadeh & J. Kacprzyk, eds. New York: John Wiley & Sons.

Oder, Norman. 2001. "The Shape of E-Reference." *Library Journal* 126, no. 2 (February 1): 46–50.

O'Neill, Nancy. 1999. "E-Mail Reference Service in the Public Library: A Virtual Necessity." *Public Libraries* 38, no. 5 (September/October): 302–303, 305.

O'Sullivan, Michael K. 2000. "Pathfinders Go Online." *Library Journal* NetConnect Supplement (Summer): 40–42.

Pack, Thomas. 2000. "Human Search Engines: The Next Kill App?" *EContent* 23, no. 6 (December): 16–22.

Santa Monica Public Library. 2000. *Reference & Information Services*, Santa Monica Public Library [Online]. Available: www.smpl.org/library/services/divref.htm [2002, May 24].

Schneider, Karen G. 2000. "The Distributed Librarian: Live, Online, Real-Time Reference." *American Libraries* 31, no. 10 (November): 64.

TechEncyclopedia. 2001. *IP telephony*, CMP Media LLC [Online]. Available: www.techweb.com/encyclopedia/ [2002, May 24].

Tomer, L. Christinger. 1994. "MIME and Electronic Reference Services." *The Reference Librarian*, no. 41/42: 347–373.

Chapter 4

Rethinking Privacy for the Virtual Library

Scott D. Johnston

OVERVIEW

As more research is conducted outside of the physical library building, it follows that issues pertaining to library privacy are becoming more complex. In this shifting environment, the implications of privacy as it pertains to library services are taking on a new urgency. Over the past ten years interest in virtual reference service has been steadily increasing. What is missing from the discussion is an examination of virtual reference from a privacy perspective. Ethical and legal issues are having a significant impact on virtual reference service. This chapter is an examination of aspects of information privacy as they relate to virtual reference service.

INTRODUCTION

There has been a growing fascination with virtual reference service. While it has been much written about and discussed, the emphasis has mostly been on the mechanics of how it works and measuring the success of service (Coffman, 2001). The nature of library reference service is being rethought as more digital resources are becoming available to the general public. As more research is conducted outside of the physical library building, it follows that issues pertaining to library privacy are becoming more complex. In this shifting environment, the implications of privacy as it pertains to library services are taking on a new urgency. Over the past ten years interest in virtual reference service has been steadily increasing. What is missing from the discussion is an

examination of virtual reference from a privacy perspective. Ethical and legal issues are having a significant impact on virtual reference service. This chapter is an examination of aspects of information privacy as they relate to virtual reference service.

DEFINING PRIVACY

The concept of privacy is an important one in modern life, yet there is little agreement as to what it actually means. Much of the current understanding of privacy developed from a collection of legal judgments combined with philosophers' attempts to illuminate what a right to privacy can and should mean (DeCew, 1997). Privacy once dealt primarily with concerns of personal autonomy and the right to be left alone, but has now become part of the economic and technological fabric of contemporary society.

In both law and ethics, privacy is an umbrella term for a wide variety of agendas and interests. Roger Clarke provides a useful typology of privacy including areas such as individual behavior in public and the integrity of the individual's body (1996). Of greatest relevance in relation to virtual reference are:

- *Privacy of personal communications* addresses the right to communicate, using various media, without routine monitoring of their communications by others.
- *Privacy of personal data* addresses whether data about individuals is available to other individuals

and organizations, and whether the individual has control over the data and its use.

PRIVACY IN LIBRARIES

Library privacy is an issue that periodically captures the attention of the media and information professionals. These periods of interest most often correspond to some political or criminal sensation, whether it be the FBI's Library Awareness Program (Foerstel, 1991) or the investigation of the Unabomber's library visits (Chepesiuk, 1998). It is inevitable that privacy issues again have become a topic of discussion within the library community. Much of the current preoccupation with information privacy matters can be attributed to the mass popularity of the World Wide Web and the proliferation of e-commerce. Most recently, security issues related to terrorist activity in the United States have further raised concerns about personal privacy.

The significance of privacy in libraries is closely related to the social role of the public library in America. Public libraries have occupied an important role in American society for over a century. They have long promoted values that are fundamental to a democratic society by offering unrestricted access to essential tools for informed participation in the political process as well as articulating intellectual freedom (Rubin, 1998). In courts the public library has been recognized as a "quintessential locus" for access to "the discussion, debate and the dissemination of information and ideas" that is guaranteed by the First Amendment to the United States Constitution (Kreimer v. Bureau of Police).[1] Public libraries "came to be accepted as public responsibilities, civic goods benefiting the entire society and thus worthy of public support" (Molz and Dain, 1999:4).

In the traditional library setting privacy generally refers to the confidentiality of circulation records and other personal information related to patrons, such as the nature of the patron reference questions, and even the materials that are entrusted to libraries by individuals and intended for use by others. In its broadest terms, library privacy has been defined as "the ability to keep personal information from others, whether it be one's thoughts, feelings, beliefs, fears, plans, or fantasies, and the control over it and when this information can be shared with others" (Garoogian, 1991: 220).

Library culture has embraced and espoused the philosophy that: "It's nobody's business what you read or . . . what use you make of the library, whether it's materials or services or facilities" (Krug, 1988). History, however, serves as the best introduction to the pragmatic meaning and significance of privacy in libraries.

Privacy first emerged as an explosive library issue in the late 1960s when a series of conflicts between law enforcement agencies and librarians set the stage for the American Library Association's (ALA) development of its first library privacy policy. This movement toward library privacy was a response to nationwide investigations of radicals and counterculture organizations. United States treasury officials and FBI agents examined circulation records in several academic and public libraries. Outrage and confusion on the part of librarians and library advocates led to the creation of the ALA's "Policy on Confidentiality of Library Records" in 1970, which addressed the growing number of attempts by U.S. law enforcement agencies to examine patrons' library records as part of their investigations (Foerstel, 1991).

In the 1980s libraries once again became sites of government surveillance. In a program known as the "Library Awareness Program," the FBI systematically began monitoring the behavior of foreigners in public and research libraries (Foerstel, 1991). The program was harshly criticized as an unwarranted government intrusion upon personal privacy and a threat to the First Amendment rights of patrons' free access to information (Ault, 1990). Librarians across the country also condemned the program for its "chilling effect" on library patrons, fearing that those who are under surveillance cannot exercise their constitutional right to gather information there for their free use. Simply put, if people could not use the library because of fear, they would be denied free access.

The ALA and several other professional organizations attempted to work with Congress to establish a federal act protecting privacy in the library (Foerstel, 1991). But when the act was defeated, librarians began to work locally, lobbying their state legislatures to enact statutes to protect the confidentiality of library users (Bielefield and Cheeseman, 1994). Although the first state law was passed by Florida in 1978, it would take seventeen years before more expansive legislation was passed by forty-nine states and the District of Columbia that would provide some type of privacy protection to library patrons (Huff, 1999).

Library privacy protection acts were in keeping with the attitudes in the 1970s and 1980s when the primary privacy fears were related to excessive and unwarranted accumulation of personal information by the government.[2] Many of the existing privacy laws were intended to protect individuals from the kind of scrutiny that could result in combining data from a variety of sources maintained by government databases, such as health, education, welfare, taxation and licensing, and financial data (Flaherty, 1989). It was believed that if people could be monitored through their data, data surveillance would provide an economically efficient means of exercising control over the behavior of individuals and societies (Clarke, 1994).

Libraries inevitably gather personal information. Circulation systems have been described as social surveillance systems in which personal information on an individual can be called up at any time: "technology now enables one to query the computer concerning the past performance of any patron within a few seconds" (Garoogian, 1991: 218). The power of a circulation system pales beside many new online information systems. Libraries can now provide potential access not only to circulation records, but also to a veritable smorgasbord of online search systems, Internet usage data, and electronic reference records. The key difference is that unlike information collected through circulation records, much of this information is collected without librarian knowledge or control. Technology has led the library to unwittingly accumulate the same fragments of information from a plentitude of new sources. The new collector of these personal fragments is not the federal government and the new mode of collection does not come from library records or from covert investigations. It comes from within the very tools embraced by all for information gathering and entertainment. And it is the vessel for these companies—the networked computer—that is at the heart of the new public library.

PRIVACY AND THE INTERNET

The phenomenal growth of Internet use has led to a myriad of opportunities for data collection. There are many potential uses for personal data in an unregulated world of electronic commerce. Government resources and government regulated industries are no longer the major collectors and potential abusers of personal information (Berman and Mulligan, 1999).

When using the Internet, there is an assumption of anonymity, more so than in the physical world where an individual may be observed by others. But because the Internet generates an elaborate trail of data detailing every stop a person makes on the Web, this transactional data can provide a "profile" of an individual's online life (Berman and Mulligan, 1999).

At a time when more Americans from all backgrounds are using the Internet, the degree of online privacy is increasingly dependent on a confusing technical infrastructure. In the online realm, much of digital reality is constructed through the setting of technical standards (Lessig, 1999). The result is that users unknowingly surrender their privacy interests. Users are likely to know little or nothing about the circumstances under which personal information is captured, sold, or processed. Often this information is surrendered voluntarily not to government record keepers but to online commercial service providers. Personal data use in cyberspace increasingly is structured around an unenforceable process of consent that often leads individuals into making uninformed, involuntary gifts of personal information (Schwartz, 1999).

These are all issues that have the potential to impact virtual reference services as well.

PRIVACY AND THE VIRTUAL LIBRARY

Over the past decade, the role of libraries has come under scrutiny as familiar notions of individuality and community have been challenged. It has become a truism to discuss how technology has transformed the library. It is in fact more accurate to say that new information technologies have revolutionized information access, blurring the boundaries between actual library collections and the information stored beyond its walls. The growth of electronic information technologies has challenged the library's role and resulted in considerable instability and uncertainty among librarians as they are now forced to redefine and restructure library service, and in the process, the library itself (Rubin, 1998).

Most libraries in the United States are now connected to the Internet (Molz and Dain, 1999). The Internet contains an ever-expanding array of information and misinformation. Many librarians are at the front lines of technology training, educating new computer users in search techniques and helping them evaluate the relevance and validity of online information (Sutton, 1996).

The challenge for librarians in the digital library is "envisioning the shape of instruction, research consultations, computer support, document delivery, and general reference services through the network" (Gray, 2000: 365). As libraries struggle to define their role in face of these technological advances, numerous questions arise concerning the risks and benefits of Internet use, particularly in helping patrons use the medium wisely. Privacy concerns have long surrounded reference service. The individual disclosure of a person's reference questions is at least as great a breach as the release of circulation records. It has even been suggested that "the reference interview itself may very well infringe on a user's privacy" (Garoogian, 1991: 218).

The virtual reference phenomenon further complicates the matter. Virtual reference has emerged as a logical and efficient way of providing reference assistance and training to patrons. While there are many advantages to this service, one of the biggest drawbacks is that by giving patrons twenty-four hour-a-day digital service, there is no longer face-to-face interaction, which may make it problematic to maintain patron confidentiality. There is an assumption of anonymity by patrons when it comes to virtual reference, but, in fact, records may be kept of many things without a patron's knowledge. These records may not be easy to delete and once there can, of course, become a permanent part of a patron's record.

The utilization of e-mail in virtual reference deserves particular scrutiny. Because e-mail is often not secure, there are numerous opportunities for privacy violations. For example, even with the best of intentions, the information in e-mail messages can be used for reasons other than what they were intended for. It is not necessary to obtain an individual's consent before retrieving information in an e-mail. Finally, after an e-mail is responded to, it can be difficult to delete.

One of the ongoing debates surrounding virtual libraries concerns the relationship between automated query response and patron satisfaction. In virtual library environments, it remains to be seen how patrons would react to machine-generated responses over personalized responses (Gray, 2000). An efficient automated system has the potential to provide a wealth of information much more rapidly than a personalized system. But in order to provide a comprehensive system that successfully addresses patron needs, personal information will need to be gathered and kept on file. This could lead to patrons experiencing the same sort of unease with virtual library service that they feel with online shopping. In addition, the ability to systematically store user data would allow a more thorough analysis of the types of questions handled by a virtual reference service.

The next step for librarians and others involved in the design and practice of virtual reference is to thoroughly examine electronic privacy concerns. This entails evaluating technology in terms of confidentiality and security. It further demands an understanding of the social and technological aspects of virtual reference service. An example of this is the term, "code," which refers to the underlying infrastructure of cyberspace (Lessig, 1999). Code limits individual options on accessing online information without the voluntary and often unknowing surrender of personal details. The individual's ability to exercise any rights has been overwhelmed by the complexities of technology; understanding the meaning of "code" for one's privacy interests involves comprehending the presence and implications of the technical infrastructure such as "cookies" and the price of such innocuous actions as surrendering an e-mail address for entry to a Web site.

CONCLUSION: PRIVACY AND A NEW ROLE FOR LIBRARIANS

As a public institution that must embrace traditional democratic values and welcome new technology, the public library—and by extension virtual reference service—is particularly in need of a pragmatic understanding of privacy protection. It is the shifting nature of privacy that makes this topic so important and yet so problematic within a library setting.

The Internet is at once a public good and a public threat. This duality lies behind the tensions that exist in establishing a functional library privacy policy. Looming external forces no longer threaten privacy; it has become inexorably interconnected to the modern library. The very information and communication systems that now play an essential role in libraries are the very systems that threaten to undermine individual privacy. A workable library privacy policy must embrace the apparent contradiction between the public craving for information and the individual desire for privacy (Schmidt, 1989).

Privacy protection comprises legal, organizational, and technological features that together implement a complex balance among conflicting interests and reflect a value system (Clarke, 1999). The establishment of detailed, operational rules about privacy protection is a difficult exercise in a context of rapid technological change. Howard Besser argues that the evolution of the library calls for librarians to "not only become aware of this evolution, but that they actively intervene to help reshape the institution in ways that are consistent with the core mission of libraries" (1998:133). By accepting the existence of new privacy threats within the institution, it is possible to define an important new role for librarians. Building on such traditional responsibilities as evaluation of sources, monitoring of information systems, keeping abreast of new tools or changes in old ones, and addressing internal and external information flows, the librarian could become something akin to a privacy watchdog or auditor. By dealing with the vagaries and uncertainties of the technology within the library, librarians could help raise individual consciousness of privacy standards in the public library and in public life.[3] Such an undertaking would be in keeping with the values at the heart of the profession, and ultimately help unite ethical ideals with pragmatic policies.

ENDNOTES

1. Kreimer v. Bureau of Police, 958 F.2d 1242, 1255 (3d Cir. 1992). See also, e.g., Board of Education v. Pico, 457 U.S. at 886 (noting that "public library is 'a place dedicated to quiet, to knowledge, and to beauty'") (quoting Brown v. Louisiana, 383 U.S. 131, 142 (1966)); Minarcini v. Strongsville City School Dist., 541 F.2d 577, 582 (6th Cir. 1976) ("A library is a mighty resource in the free marketplace of ideas.").
2. A partial list includes: Privacy Act of 1974; Electronic Communications Privacy Act of 1986; Computer Matching and Privacy Protection Act of 1988.
3. One recent attempt to address this can be found in an ALA report, *The Task Force on Privacy and Confidentiality in the Electronic Environment*. This serves as a valuable augmentation to the ALA's idealist privacy policy statements by addressing numerous potential privacy violations that emerge from information technology in the library.

REFERENCES

American Library Association. 2000. *The American Library Association's Task Force on Privacy and Confidentiality in the Electronic Environment*, Final Report, 7 July 2000 [Online]. Available: www.lita.org/docs/privcon/report.html#recommend [2002, May 24].

Ault, Ulrika E. 1990. "Note, The FBI's Library Awareness Program: Is Big Brother Reading Over Your Shoulder?" *New York University Law Review* 65: 1532–1565.

Berman, Jerry, and Deirdre Mulligan. 1999. "Privacy in the Digital Age: Work in Progress." *Nova Law Review* 23, no. 2: 552–582.

Besser, Howard. 1998. The Shape of the 21st Century Library. In *Information Imagineering: Meeting at the Interface*, Milton Wolfe et al., eds. Chicago: American Library Association.

Bielefield, Arlene, and Lawrence Cheeseman. 1994. *Maintaining the Privacy of Library Records: A Handbook and Guide*. New York. Neal-Schuman.

Chepesiuk, R. 1998. Surviving the Unabomber Media Circus: An Interview with Sherri Wood. *American Libraries* 29: 27–28.

Clarke, Roger. 1994. "The Digital Persona and Its Application to Data Surveillance." *The Information Society* 10, no. 2: 77–92.

Clarke, Roger. 1996. *Privacy and Dataveillance, and Organisational Strategy*. Keynote Address to the Conference of the I.S. Audit & Control Association, Perth, Western Australia [Online]. Available: www.anu.edu.au/people/Roger.Clarke/DV/PStrat.html [2002, May 24].

Clarke, Roger. 1999. *The Legal Context of Privacy-Enhancing and Privacy-Sympathetic Technologies*. Presentation at AT&T Research Labs, Florham Park NJ [Online]. Available: www.anu.edu.au/people/Roger.Clarke/DV/Florham.html [2002, May 24].

Coffman, Steve. 2001. "We'll Take it From Here: Further Developments We'd Like to See in Virtual Reference Software." *Information Technology and Libraries* 20, no. 3: 149–153.

DeCew, Judith W. 1997. *In Pursuit of Privacy-Law, Ethics, and the Rise of Technology*. Ithaca, N.Y.: Cornell University Press.

Ferguson, Chris D., and Charles A. Bunge. 1997. "The Shape of Services to Come: Values-Based Reference Service for the Largely Digital Library." *College & Research Libraries* 58, no. 3: 252–265.

Flaherty David H. 1989. *Protecting Privacy in Surveillance Societies*. Chapel Hill, N.C.: University of North Carolina Press.

Foerstel, Herbert N. 1991. *Surveillance in the Stacks: The*

FBI's Library Awareness Program. New York: Greenwood Press.

Garoogian, Rhoda. 1991. "Library/Patron Confidentiality: An Ethical Challenge." *Library Trends* 40, no. 2: 216–233.

Gray, Suzanne M. 2000. "Virtual Reference Services: Directions and Agendas." *Reference & User Services Quarterly* 39, no. 4: 365–375.

Huff, James. 1999. "Patron Confidentiality, Millennium Style: Library Confidentiality Statutes." *American Libraries* 30, no. 6: 86.

Krug, Judith F. 1988. Statement of Judith F. Krug before the Joint hearing of the Subcommittee on Technology and Law on the Video and Library Privacy Protection Act of 1988.

Lessig, Lawrence. 1999. *Code and Other Laws of Cyberspace*. New York: Basic Books.

Molz, Redmond K., and Phyllis Dain. 1999. *Civic Space/ Cyberspace*. Cambridge: MIT Press.

Rubin, Richard E. 2000. *Foundations of Library and Information Science*. New York: Neal-Schuman.

Schmidt, C. J. 1989. Rights for Users of Information: Conflicts and Balances Among Privacy, Professional Ethics, Law, National Security. In *The Bowker Annual Library and Book Trade Almanac 1989–90*, F. Simora, ed. New York: Bowker.

Schwartz, Paul M. 1999. "Privacy and Democracy in Cyberspace." *Vanderbilt Law Review* 52: 1607–1702.

Sutton, Stuart A. 1996. "Future Service Models and the Convergence of Functions: The Reference Librarian as Technician, Author and Consultant." *The Reference Librarian* 54: 125–143.

Chapter 5

Examining the Impact of DMCA and UCITA on Online Reference Service

Min Chou and Oliver Zhou

OVERVIEW

The rise of shrink-wrap licensing agreements, the passage of the Digital Millennium Copyright Act (DMCA), and the emergence of the Uniform Computer Information Transactions Act (UCITA), have changed the legal landscape upon which libraries have relied to operate, such as fair use and first sale doctrines. In launching online reference services, libraries should strongly assert their fair use rights and first sale doctrine, and integrate themselves into the digital creation process, avoid scanning full-text copyrighted materials, and deliver them online to users. Libraries should create their own electronic publication databases of public domain works, of new, never before published materials, and of other copyrighted works after obtaining permissions from copyright holders. Another option is to negotiate more favorable licensing terms from publishers in order to offer more comprehensive online reference services to authenticated users.

INTRODUCTION

Online reference services have long been an ideal dream for librarians with a vision of "a library without walls." The rapid development of the Internet technologies in the last decade has made it possible for the realization of such a dream. Various online service providers have sprung up on the World Wide Web in recent years. Many Internet e-commerce companies and publishers have developed numerous computer programs enabling their customers to do various types of work online through their licensing agreements. For the purposes of promoting their business models, they have successfully pushed to develop a legal framework, which supports and protects their rights. The Digital Millennium Copyright Act (DMCA) and the Uniform Computer Information Transactions Act (UCITA) are the fruits of their successful campaign in this regard. More important, these new laws represent a new direction in the American copyright protection mechanism, and their impacts have reverberated in almost all walks of life, including with librarians. The first part of this chapter examines the recent legal trend in the United States including the UCITA and shrink-wrap licensing agreement. The second part discusses the relevant portion of the DMCA regarding online service liability and the most recent case law. The third part explores the fair use doctrine, the first sale doctrine, the implications of new statutory and case law, and the possible solutions for libraries in terms of providing online services. The fourth part provides practical suggestions for libraries in offering online services and possible defenses for copyright infringement concerns under the current legal framework.

NEW DIRECTION OF THE AMERICAN COPYRIGHT LAW

The Internet has undoubtedly become one of the most commonly used communication tools in the past decade. The availability of a vast amount of data on the Internet has brought enormous concerns about copyright piracy. On one hand, consumers demand high-speed, reliable services free of charge while copyright holders fear that the Internet has become a hotbed of global piracy, and their intellectual property rights have been degrading on a daily basis. The business operation model of many online service providers, such as Napster, has made them embark upon a collision course with many copyright or label holders and with American courts adhering to the traditional interpretation of copyright law.

The history of American copyright law demonstrated a remarkable record of balance between the rights conferred upon the authors of copyrighted works and the rights reserved to the public regarding their fair use (Aoki et al., 2000). However, the rapid development of the Internet technologies and the accompanying e-commerce practices has begun to subvert this delicate balance. Basically there are three major factors affecting this balance, i.e., the Uniform Computer Information Transactions Act, e-commerce for software and various other products via the Internet, and the gradual acceptance of shrink-wrap license agreements by American courts (Samuelson, 1999). "[Dramatic] changes in the publishing industry, combined with developments such as UCITA, threaten the historic balance struck in copyright law between the interests of authors and those of the public" (Aoki et al., 2000).

The purpose of the UCITA (1999) is to make uniform rules for computer information transactions, as the Uniform Commercial Code did much to the American commercial businesses. The drafter of the UCITA, the National Conference of Commissioners on Uniform State Laws (NCCUSL), is comprised of a good number of prominent judges, lawyers, and professors with the goal of promoting uniformity in the law among the different jurisdictions of the United States (McDonald, 2001). And the NCCUSL was trying to replicate the success of the Uniform Commercial Code. The underlying theme of the UCITA is to transform e-business from the contract-as-consent model to the contract-as-product model (Radin, 2000), given the fact that our society has moved from a tangible goods-based economy to a service-based economy (Shah, 2000).

Under this business model, what people get from buying a product under the UCITA is a license with restrictive terms set by the software and publishing industries alike in advance. Almost without exception, a consumer enters into a license with a software company without prior reviewing and under-

standing the incomprehensible contents of the license. A consumer's consent is confirmed so long as he or she engages in purchasing acts (UCITA, 1999). According to 112(a) of the UCITA, "a person manifests assent to a record or term if the person, acting with knowledge of, or after having an opportunity to review the record or term or a copy of it: (1) authenticates the record or term with intent to adopt or accept it; or (2) intentionally engages in conduct or makes statements with reason to know that the other party or its electronic agent may infer from the conduct or statement that the person assents to the record or term" (UCITA, 1999: 112(a)(1)-(2)). However, mass-market licenses such as shrink-wrap agreements are subject to the legal limitations of unconscionability, fundamental public policy, and express agreements between the parties (UCITA, 1999: 209(a), 105(b)).

The "shrink-wrap license" gets its name from the fact that retail software packages are covered in plastic or cellophane "shrink-wrap" (*ProCD v. Zeidenberg*, 1996). A shrink-wrap licensing agreement typically appears on the screen whenever a user is in the process of loading software after he or she bought from a store or via the Internet. Basically a user has to click a "Yes" in order to complete the installation. Do most people read and understand these shrink-wrap licensing agreements? The commonsense answer would be "No." The reality is that most of these shrink-wrap licensing agreements are incomprehensible to the majority of the general public, since they are usually very lengthy and contain further complicated technical and legal terms.

The rise of the shrink-wrap licensing agreement is the direct result of "private legislation" of copyright-type rights initiated by the software industry (O'Rourke, 1995), which believes that the American Copyright Law does not provide adequate protection for software. Traditionally, software is protected by copyright law. Article I, Section 8, Clause 8 of the Constitution provides that "The Congress shall have the power . . . to promote the Progress of Science and useful Arts, by securing for limited Times to Authors and Inventors the exclusive Right to their respective Writings and Discoveries . . . " This provision grants Congress the power of copyright legislation, which provides a copyright owner with exclusive right to reproduce, display, distribute and to perform copyrighted works (DMCA, 1998: 106).

"Establishment of a system of defined 'intellectual property rights' can help alleviate . . . [the public goods] difficulty . . . In granting a limited monopoly through copyright or patent, government attempts to compensate for distortions arising from non-exclusivity. According to this rationale, without the counterbalancing grants of monopoly power bestowed through copyright and patent, the inability of authors and inventors to appropriate economic returns from their labors would result in the under-production of new works and inventions" (U.S. Congress, OTA Report 185–186, 1992). "A public good is one from which everyone may benefit whether or not they contribute to its production" (O'Rourke, 1995: 485). It has "the property of nonexclusivity; once the good has been produced, it is impossible (or prohibitively costly) to exclude any individual from benefiting from, whether or not he or she pays" (U.S. Congress, OTA Report 185, 1992).

However, the software industry believes that copyright law does not provide adequate protection to computer software due to its nature. Software is more easily copied and distributed than hard copy works. For example, hard copy quality degrades with each copy, and photocopying is time-consuming, while software can make the copy as good as the original and can be disseminated to hundreds of thousands of subscribers (U.S. Congress, OTA Report 176, 1992). Therefore, software providers have tried to turn the software purchasers to copyright licensees. They use shrink-wrap agreements to achieve this goal. Purchasers of software usually are not aware of the license agreement until the time they start installing the software. They usually accompany mass-market software such as WordPerfect and Windows (O'Rourke, 1995). The terms of software licensing agreements are more restrictive than the rights that the Copyright Act would otherwise confer, since software providers have substantial interest in protecting their source codes and trade secrets to maximize the rate of investment return (O'Rourke, 1995).

American courts started to accept the validity of software licensing agreement in the 1990s. In *Pro-CD v. Zeidenberg* (1996: 1447), Judge Easterbrook, one of the most influential appellate judges in the U.S., ruled in 1996 that the shrink-wrap agreement was enforceable as a matter of state contract law. In that case, the plaintiff ProCD compiled information from more than 3,000 telephone directories into a computer database. It sold a version of the database with a trademark name "SelectPhone" on CD-ROM discs. Defendant Matthew Zeidenberg bought a consumer package of SelectPhone in 1994 from a retailer, and resold the SelectPhone database through his corporation on the Internet for anyone willing to pay its price. Plaintiff sued defendant, and the federal district court ruled the licenses ineffectual, since their terms did not appear on the outside of the packages. A purchaser did not agree to and could not be bound by terms that were secret at the time of purchase. Judge Easterbrook reversed it by arguing that "transactions in which the exchange of money precedes the communication of detailed terms are common" (*Pro-CD v. Zeidenberg*, 1996: 1451), such as an insurance policy, or an airline and concert ticket, etc. The software industry has its own particularity also, as much software is ordered over the Internet by purchasers who have never seen a box. Or software simply arrives by wire. Judge Easterbrook reasoned that UCC 2–204 allows contracts to be formed in other ways since it states "a contract of sale of goods may be made in any manner sufficient to show agreement, including conduct by both parties, which recognizes the existence of such a contract" (*Pro-CD v. Zeidenberg*, 1996: 1452). Here, the defendant accepted the contract with protest. Contracts do not create exclusive rights, and generally only affect their parties, while "a copyright is a right against the world" (*Pro-CD v. Zeidenberg*, 1996: 1454). Federal law preemption usually does not affect private contracts. He further believes that enforcement of shrink-wrap licenses may even make information more readily available by reducing the price. And they may have more benefits for consumers, as many licenses permit users to make extra copies, and to use the software on multiple computers, even to incorporate the software into the user's products. "A simple two-party contract is not 'equivalent to any of the exclusive rights within the general scope of copyright' and therefore may be enforced" (*Pro-CD v. Zeidenberg*, 1996: 1454).

After *Zeidenberg*, there are a number of cases continuing holding in favor of shrink-wrap agreement, such as *Hill v. Gateway 2000 Inc.* (1997), *M.A. Mortenson Co. v. Timberline Software Co.* (1999). However, there is another line of cases unwilling to enforce the shrink-wrap licenses under state contract law. In *Step-Saver Data Sys. Inc. v. Wyse Technology* (1991), the Third Circuit held that terms of shrink-wrap licenses were merely proposals for amending a contract of sale, but not a part of the contract of sale. These two lines of cases may continue to diverge rather than converge in the future, given the dramatic change of business landscape in the Internet e-commerce environment.

Under UCITA, shrink-wrap licenses are enforceable if three criteria are satisfied. First, the licensee must have reason to know that additional contract terms will be proposed after initial agreement. Second, a consumer must have a right to return the product at the licensor's cost. And third, the licensee must be compensated for reasonable costs of restoring the system if it is altered by the installation of license terms for review (UCITA, 1999: 209(b)). However, UCITA would be a state law if it was adopted. And case law has indicated that the terms of shrink-wrap licensing agreements will be preempted by the federal copyright law. In *Vault Corp. v. Quaid Software Ltd.* (1988), the Fifth Circuit held that a decompilation provision in a standard form license agreement was constitutionally preempted. If any terms of a shrink-wrap license or state laws are in conflict with that of the federal copyright law, they will be preempted by federal law. However, one commentator argued that Vault's holding has very limited precedential value (O'Rourke, 1995).

DMCA AND LIABILITY OF ONLINE SERVICE PROVIDERS

Librarians and information professionals already have a grand vision to create a digital library by developing databases of journal papers and other materials they subscribed. This vision, however, is somewhat in conflict with the new digital copyright law such as the World Intellectual Property Organization (WIPO) Copyright Treaty in 1996 and the DMCA. WIPO has established a legal principle, among others, that copyright owners should have an exclusive right to control the making of copies of their works in digital form and control the communication of their works to the public (Samuelson, 1999). This new statutory law and case law will have a major impact upon any libraries' effort to create electronic online services, since the digital environment is a completely different ball game than the traditional one.

Some digital library projects such as the digital library in the Library of Congress have already been successfully developed (Anonymous, 2000). This project does not encounter copyright infringement issues, since the materials are in the public domain. Nevertheless, many contents are copyrighted materials. Any Web sites or internal databases created by a library containing copyrighted materials may infringe the rights of copyright holders. If a university librarian scans a journal paper into a database and makes it available to faculty and students, even if the library subscribes to the journal, it may still constitute reproduction, which can make a perfect copy. Full-text scanning and online delivery to users are equivalent to publishing. Publication constitutes copyright infringement unless the library receives permission from the copyright owner, which could be the publisher or the author.

Libraries at present provide four types of online services: 1. Selective links on the library's homepage to external information resources; 2. Integration of Internet resources into the library's OPAC; 3. Online provider of course-related information; and 4. Online publisher of subject area information (Gregory, 1997). Online reference combines all services mentioned above to provide librarian assisted information services to patrons through the Internet. A library becomes an "online service provider" if it adopts one of these business models through electronic technologies. "Online service provider" generally refers to a content provider such as a Web page provider or an operator of a Bulletin Board Service (BBS) (Ravn, 1999). Generally speaking, the first two business models are legally acceptable with little copyright infringement concerns unless a link connects to circumvention devices or a library offers full-text scanning and online delivery. The next two categories will raise red flags from copyright owners if they allow users' access to e-reserves or copyrighted materials without limitations. While libraries can provide online reference services by using the information on public domain or from any databases they own with little copyright infringement concern, patrons usually want more information, or all information libraries possess, including copyrighted materials and electronic contents with licensing restrictions. Therefore, a full scale online reference service might still be fraught with potential legal pitfalls under the current copyright protection mechanism.

The potential legal liability for an online service provider is enormous, given the fact that to date, American courts still employ traditional legal theories such as vicarious infringement liability to hold online service providers liable. Vicarious liability theory originates from the agency principle and landlord-tenant relationship (*Shapiro, Bernstein & Co., v. H.L. Green Co.*, 1963; see also *Deutsch v. Arnold*, 1938). This doctrine can hold an online service provider liable if it has the right and ability to control the direct infringer and it further receives direct financial benefit from the infringing activities (Ravn, 1999). However, vicarious liability doctrine might incur massive lawsuits, since it is a liberal legal standard to be applied in copyright cases. Many online service providers have argued that the traditional legal notions of direct, contributory, and vicarious liability are not appropriate legal standards to be readily applied into the Internet environment. The uncertainty of judicial liability standards will make wide and indiscriminate Internet access more difficult and more costly (Hearing on H.R.2180, Dunn, 1997).

The academic community also has special concerns in this regard, since universities play a dual role of a service provider and a user. Academic institutions feel very vulnerable in facing the copyright infringement allegations, since many online activities are often conducted without supervision. They argue that the liberal legal standards of direct, contributory, and vicarious liability cannot be applied to them, since they really exercise no control over the availability of content on their online system (Hearing on H.R. 2180, Greenwood, 1997). In *U.S. v. LaMacchia* (1994), an MIT student managed a bulletin board using MIT's online service; MIT was sued for having provided the Internet service and therefore liable for the student's alleged copyright infringement, since the student facilitated the reproduction of copyrighted computer software. This case was finally dropped; it nevertheless revealed the potential liability for a nonprofit research institution and a university.

Congress responded to these concerns by introducing "the Online Copyright Infringement Liability Limitation Act," which further became a part of the "Digital Millennium Copyright Act" (DMCA) in 1998. DMCA amends the Copyright Act to include section 512(c)(1) "safe harbor" provisions for online service providers. Under this provision, an online service provider is not liable if it does not have actual knowledge, or is not aware of facts or circumstances of infringement activities not controlled by it, or does not receive a financial benefit directly attributable to

the infringing activities, so long as the service provider responds expeditiously to remove or disable access to the subject of the infringing activity (DMCA, 1998: 512(c)). This provision is generally regarded as a "safe harbor provision" for online service providers. Under the current copyright law, a copyright owner can hold an online service provider liable only if he or she can prove that the online service provider engages in direct, contributory, or vicarious infringement (Ravn, 1999). This "safe harbor provision" provides online service providers certain protection without incurring additional liability, notwithstanding there are some infringing materials on their Web sites. However, some argue that it may have unintended consequence of reducing authors' incentive to produce content for the Internet (Siegel, 1999). The recent Internet meltdown indicates that this is probably not a determining factor. The more important incentive is apparently the rate of investment return, as indicated by the online e-book publishing business, which is on the doorstep of a new Internet battlefield.

The "safe harbor" provisions require that a service provider must first comply with two prerequisite conditions that it first must have adopted and reasonably implemented a policy for the termination of services as it applies to those subscribers who repeatedly engage in infringing activity online, and that it then must accommodate and refrain from interfering with any "standard technical measures" (DMCA, 1998: 512) designed to protect or to identify copyrighted works. After service providers have satisfied these two prerequisites, they are entitled to limited liability of four types of situations, i.e., transitory communications, system caching, storage of information on systems or networks at direction of users; and information location tools (DMCA, 1998: 512). Transitory communications are passive conduits in nature. A passive conduit, once it satisfies five criteria, is exempted from monetary damages due to the "intermediate and transitory" (H.R. Rep. No. 105–551, Pt. 2 at 50, 1998) storage of infringing materials. First, the transmission of the alleged infringing material must be initiated by or at the direction of a person besides the service provider (DMCA, 1998: 512(a)(1)). Second, any unauthorized copying by the service provider must be solely the result of an "automatic technical process," in which the service provider does not select the material to be transmitted (DMCA, 1998: 512(a)(2)). Third, the service provider may not select the recipients of the material, except as an "automatic response to the request of another" (DMCA, 1998: 512(a)(3)). Fourth, none of the stored unauthorized copies may be made "ordinarily accessible" (DMCA, 1998: 512(a)(4)) to anyone other than the material's anticipated recipients. In addition, the unauthorized copies may not be stored by the service provider longer than necessary for the successful communication of the material. And finally, the service provider must transmit the material without modifying its content (DMCA, 1998: 512(a)(5)).

"System caching" (Halpern, 1999) is also qualified for liability exemption if it meets the following five criteria. First, the content of retained material must not be modified. Second, the provider must comply with rules about "refreshing" material—replacing retained copies of material with material from the original location—when specified in accordance with a generally accepted industry standard data communication protocol. Third, the provider must not interfere with technology that returns "hit" information to the person who posted the material, where such technology meets certain requirements. Fourth, the provider must limit users' access to the material in accordance with conditions on access (e.g., password protection) imposed by the person who posted the material. Fifth, any material that was posted without the copyright owner's authorization must be removed or blocked promptly once the service provider has been notified.

A service provider is also exempted from liability for having any information stored on its network at the direction of an Internet user. This section is intended to limit the liability of service providers from claims of direct, contributory, and vicarious infringement (H.R. Rep. No. 105–551, Pt. 2, at 52, 1998). Of course, service providers must satisfy three criteria to avail them the benefits. First, the service provider does not have the threshold knowledge regarding infringing material posted by the Internet user. Second, the service provider must not receive any financial reward from the infringing activity if it has the ability and right to control the activity. Thirdly, the service provider must expeditiously remove or disable access to infringing materials upon notice (DMCA, 1998: 512(c)(1)). However, the notice must contain six specific pieces of information for the purposes of complying with the substantive requirements of the Act. First, the notice must con-

tain the physical and electronic signature of the copyright owner or an authorized agent. Second, it must identify the copyrighted works that have allegedly been infringed upon. Third, it must identify the posted material that is claimed to be infringing, and include the information that is reasonably sufficient to help locate the material, and demand either removal or access to that material (DMCA, 1998: 512(c)(3)(A)(iii)). Fourth, the notifying party must enclose information that is reasonably sufficient to allow the service provider to contact them or their agent. Such information may include a physical mailing address, a phone number, etc. Fifth, the complaining party must have a good faith belief that the manner in which the service provider is using the material is not authorized by the copyright holder or its agent (DMCA, 1998: 512(c)(3)(A)(iv, v)). Finally, the complaining party must attest, under the penalty of perjury, that the information contained within the notification is accurate (DMCA, 1998: 512(c)(3)(A)(vi)).

"Information location tools" contain indexes or directories of the Internet materials and Web sites. A service provider can be exempted from liability if it only links or refers users to an Internet location by using the information location tool, even if such Internet Web sites may conduct infringing activity. However, this exemption will only be available after a service provider meets three criteria similar to the information stored in the network under the direction of the user. In other words, the service provider does not have actual knowledge, does not receive any financial benefits, and expeditiously discontinues the service (DMCA, 1998: 512(d)(1)(C)).

Because of strong concerns from the academic community, DMCA provides special provisions applicable to any public or nonprofit institutions of higher education that are acting in the capacity of service providers. With respect to those passive conduits or system catching, graduate students or faculty members are treated as separate legal entities from their universities, and their actual knowledge or awareness will not be attributed to the universities (DMCA, 1998: 512(e)(1)). These special provisions basically eliminate the legal doctrines of respondeat superior and vicarious liability for a university in the capacity as an online service provider.

However, a university must satisfy three criteria to avail it of the special provisions. First, any infringing activities conducted by a student, staff, or a faculty member must not involve the supply of network access to any instructional materials that were required or recommended in the past three years (DMCA, 1998: 512(e)(1)(A)). The sending of materials via e-mail is one type of supplying network access. "Required or recommended" are materials that have been formally and specifically identified in a list of course materials that is provided to all students enrolled in the course for credit, but do not include materials that a student or a faculty member informally or incidentally brings to classrooms for students throughout the semester (H.R. Rep. No. 105–796, at 75, 1998). Second, a university must not have received more than two notices of infringement regarding a specific student, staff, or faculty member in the past three years. However, these two notices of alleged infringement must not misrepresent material facts and be truthful. Assuming the two notices are bona fide, the university may only be held responsible for the infringing acts of that particular student, staff, or faculty member (DMCA, 1998: 512(e)(1)(B)). Third, a university must provide information materials to all of its system users to promote compliance and accurately describe the copyright law (DMCA, 1998: 512(e)(1)(C)). Faculty, administrators, and students must all receive information materials. However, the law only covers a university in its capacity as a service provider, and it actually does not interfere with common law principles of liability such as respondeat superior and contributory liability. It also does not alter any of the existing exclusive rights of a copyright holder nor does it intend to alter the fair use doctrine as applied to any research university and nonprofit institutions such as a library (H.R. Rep. No. 105–796, at 75, 1998).

The law further creates two causes of actions for fraud for the purposes of deterring the making of "knowingly false allegations" against service providers. If a service provider suffers damages as a result of such misrepresentations, it is legally entitled to claim for a host of potential damages, including costs and attorneys' fees, incurred by either the alleged infringer, or any copyright owner, or its agent (DMCA, 1998: 512(f)).

A&M Records, Inc. v. Napster, Inc. (2001) was one of the most closely watched landmark cases of the year 2000 in this regard. Defendant Napster operated a popular online file sharing service that allowed users to download and to share digital files comprising of copyrighted song recordings. Napster allowed users to share music files directly between their computers via the Internet, without having to transmit the music files through central computers operated by it. The plaintiff sued Napster for its liability of contributory and vicarious copyright infringement. The district court issued a preliminary injunction against Napster by holding that it engaged in the copying, transmitting, or distributing the copyrighted works without permission. Napster appealed. The 9th Circuit upheld a number of district court rulings that Napster did not engage in fair use of the plaintiff's copyrighted material, and that it contributed to infringement by actively encouraging and assisting its users in sharing and transmitting copyrighted material, and that it was vicariously liable since it realized direct financial benefits from its users' infringing activity while it had the ability to police and screen its system for infringing materials. This most recent case indicates that the contributory and vicarious liability theories are still the dominant legal principles in the Internet environment. American courts basically have embraced the new laws and blended them into their own traditional legal theories and procedures.

Given the fact that a library's online resources are either owned by the library, or licensed for use, or are links to other Internet sites, library online reference services have increasingly come to resemble Napster-like directory-guided sharing of materials among users. Under this kind of circumstance, library online reference services may face the risk of being "Napsterized" (Clark, 2001). Users' unlimited access to, and their ability to download and share with others, any e-reserved materials developed by libraries will make libraries' online service programs exactly like Napster's, especially if there is no operational method to authenticate the identity of each user. Under the current legal framework defined by Napster, libraries will have enormous difficulty providing full-scale online services by offering electronic resources such as unrestricted scanning and online delivery of copyrighted materials to unidentified patrons. The DMCA's "safe harbor" provisions are really not adequate to protect libraries from potential legal liabilities. And libraries will also find it hard to rely on the fair use doctrine alone for protection.

FAIR USE AND FIRST SALE DOCTRINES AND POSSIBLE SOLUTIONS FOR LIBRARIES

Under the fair use doctrine, a user can access copyrighted works in a reasonable manner without the consent of the copyright owner. This doctrine was first developed at *Folsom v. Marsh* in 1841. Section 107 of 1976 Copyright Act codified this doctrine by providing that the fair use of a copyrighted work such as reproduction in copies for purposes such as criticism, comment, news reporting, teaching, scholarship, or research, is not an infringement of copyright (DMCA, 1998: 107). It further provides a four-factor analysis, "(1) the purpose and character of the use, including whether the use is of a commercial nature; (2) the nature of the copyrighted work; (3) the amount and substantiality of the portion used in relation to the copyrighted work as a whole; and (4) the effect of the use upon the potential market for or value of the copyrighted work" (DMCA, 1998: 107). This statement can be summarized as "nature, purpose, amount and effect" four-factor analysis method.

First sale doctrine was first affirmed in 1908 in the *Bobbs-Merrill Co. v. Straus*. It provides that the owner of copyrighted works does not have the right to impose any limitation as to the price at which the book shall be sold at retail by a future purchaser with whom there is no privity of contract. This doctrine allows libraries or consumers to dispose of books as they see fit without further compensating the author. However, shrink-wrap licensing agreements, almost without exception, put limits on the reproduction and distribution of the electronic information products libraries or consumers purchased or leased. To some extent they are moving in the direction of "pay-per-use," which literally deprives libraries or consumers of their right of fair use. James G. Neal, Dean of University Libraries at the Johns Hopkins University, commented that "the first-sale doctrine must be viewed as media-neutral and technology-neutral" (Foster, 2000:A5). He believes that under the principle of the first sale doctrine, the reproduction of online materials will also be allowed, just like hard-copy material (Foster, 2000).

Fair use doctrine has been affirmed by recent statutory and case law. 17 U.S.C.1201 (f) (1998) provides, in pertinent part, that "a person who has lawfully obtained the right to use a copy of a computer program may circumvent a technological measure . . . for the sole purpose of identifying and analyzing those elements of the program with other programs, and that have not previously been readily available to the person engaging in the circumvention, to the extent any such acts of identification and analysis do not constitute infringement under this title." This statement is commonly regarded as recognition of a policy not to prohibit the reverse engineering where it is needed to be obtained for interoperability of computer programs (UCITA, 1999: cmt.3). This section is also the codification of prior case law, which has established that a consumer can copy the minimum amount necessary to understand the product, and that he or she has legitimate reasons to reverse engineer the software, and that disassembly must be the only reasonable way to understand the idea behind the software (Karas, 2001). The 9th Circuit Court affirms that reverse engineering does not violate fair use in *Sony Computer Entertainment, Inc. v. Connectix Corp.* (2000: 596). It even went further to reject the strict necessity test by holding that the frequency of copying is irrelevant (*Sony Computer Entertainment, Inc. v. Connectix Corp.*, 2000: 605) This case is also consistent with the prior case law authority such as *Sega Enters. v. Accolade, Inc.* (1992). The 9th Circuit Court believes that the novelty of software is restrained by its functional purpose, and that "computer programs are, in essence, utilitarian articles—articles that accomplish tasks" (*Sega Enters. v. Accolade, Inc.*, 1992: 1524). If the copyrighted work lacks essential creativity and novelty, then the copyright law affords thin protection (*Sega Enters. v. Accolade, Inc.*, 1992: 1524).

However, fair use doctrine and the first sale doctrine have recently been marginalized, as the DMCA has seriously undermined them, American courts have gradually accepted the enforceability of the shrink-wrap licensing agreements, and the UCITA has legally validated shrink-wrap agreements, notwithstanding the fact that the UCITA has not been adopted by the majority of states. This trend will certainly make licensors rely more upon shrink-wrap licensing agreements than ever before. Because of the unilateralist nature of the shrink-wrap licenses, licensors can insert almost whatever restrictive terms they want into the shrink-wrap licenses to restrain the rights of licensee's fair uses. Libraries are just like regular consumers, who are not able to know the terms of the license until they buy the product. And more often than not, librarians really cannot comprehend the lengthy legal and technical terms. In addition, information products have become licensed and leased from software developers or publishers. This practice will essentially destroy the first sale doctrine, since libraries no longer purchase and own the products. The combining practices of this type will inevitably put libraries in a very precarious position at a time when they start launching more comprehensive online services than the four categories mentioned before.

One possible solution for libraries to cope with this dire situation is to create their own databases to computerize the vast amount of data and information ranging from those items no longer protected by copyright law, to those items originally owned by libraries. Libraries can also electronically publish archival materials and unpublished items. Libraries, however, can only conduct this task in a piecemeal or an incremental manner instead of a grand scale, given the limited financial resources and technical expertise they possess. Libraries can also team up with other high-tech companies to launch a creation campaign if they have an ample budget. The University of Cincinnati Law School created two databases for the Web; one is corporate law and the other human rights (Gregory, 1997). The University of Kansas is in the process of developing a system for digitizing, compressing, storing, indexing, searching and retrieving video and audio information down to segmented content level (Clark, 2001).

However, given the fact that the majority of libraries (i.e., academic libraries) still subscribe to online services and databases provided by many publishers and software developers, the libraries will have difficulties providing full-scale online reference services to users other than their students and faculty. The reason is that almost all shrink-wrap licensing agreements will only allow registered students and faculty to access (including remote access) online databases. Under this circumstance, an academic library can only use these databases with publishers or software developers' permission to provide online reference services to registered students and faculty. The delivery of copyrighted information should be done cautiously, given the copyright and license restrictions. Reference librarians could scan and deliver a reasonable amount of information (say, approximately 10 percent in general or to be decided on a case-by-case basis) to users on the basis of fair use

and the first sale doctrines. Otherwise, publishers or software developers could suspend or cut the service right away if they spot any unusual large volume of usage. The strongest defense of a library's online service is the nature and purpose of the program, i.e., nonprofit and fair use for education and research. The defense of amount and effect will become less effective if a library's online service offers full-scale scanning and online delivery of copyrighted materials without securing advance permission from copyright owners. The safe harbor provision of the DMCA offers only limited protection to an academic library from copyright infringement action while unwary students and faculty members will still face harsh penalties if they receive two prior warnings. Thus this kind of online service is still far from the ideal dream of "a library without walls" for all patrons to utilize virtual library services.

Another possible way to solve this problem is to unite as many research libraries or public libraries as possible to increase their collective bargaining power for the purposes of negotiating more favorable licensing terms with licensors. Under the more favorable licensing terms, a library will have more room to provide online services to all of their patrons without fearing the copyright infringement actions from licensors while minimizing the costs associated with developing its own databases. This is one practical solution for libraries to provide sizable online service programs under the current DMCA legal framework. By and large, the real progress depends upon what kind of favorable terms libraries can extract from licensors. Therefore, large-scale online services from libraries remain far from certain if the fundamental rules of the game do not change. And licensors obviously still have the upper hand in this game.

CONCLUSION

The rise of shrink-wrap licenses, the passage of the DMCA, and the emergence of the UCITA have completely changed the legal landscape of copyright protection in the United States. They have brought many serious legal challenges to libraries that have traditionally played a role as a bridge to disseminate information to the general public under the shield of fair use doctrine and first sale doctrine. Under the restraints of many major legal hurdles, libraries will have difficult prospects of providing comprehensive online services to their patrons. Libraries have been put in an unprecedented precarious position at a time when they need to provide more effective and wide online reference services to their patrons. The DMCA not only fails to provide ironclad "safe harbor" provisions in terms of protecting libraries from legal liability as online service providers, but it also further seriously undermines the traditional fair use doctrine and the first sale doctrine. There is no simple solution to solve this complex legal phenomenon. Nevertheless, libraries shall first strongly assert fair use and first sale doctrine in the digital online service by relying upon their nonprofit motive and fair use for education and research in their business operation. Secondly, libraries shall continue to push the envelope by expanding their role as a Web provider and publisher in the digital environment, and to further integrate themselves into the creation process. And finally, libraries shall unite to increase their bargaining power to force publishers and software developers to make concessions to libraries for the purposes of providing more comprehensive online services comparable to their ideal dream of a library without walls.

REFERENCES

A&M Records, Inc. v. Napster, Inc., 239 F.3d 1004 (9th Cir. Feb. 12, 2001).

Anonymous. 2000. "Digital Libraries, Internal Databases, and Copyrights." *Information Outlook* 4, no.5 (May): 49–50.

Aoki, Keith et al. 2001. May 30, 2000. Letter from Intellectual Property Professors. (May 30) [Online]. Available: www.arl.org/info/letters/profs_ucita.html [2002, May 24].

Bobbs-Merrill Co. v. Straus, 210 U.S. 339 (Sup. Ct. 1908).

Clark, Jeff. 2001. "Libraries and the Fate of Digital Content." *Library Journal* 125, no. 11 (June 15): 44–47.

DMCA. 1998. 17 U.S.C., sec. 106, 107, 512, 1201.

Deutsch v. Arnold, 98 F.2d 686, 688 (2d Cir. 1938).

Folsom v. Marsh, 9 F. Cas. 342 (Cir. Court, Dist. Mass, 1841).

Foster, Andrea L. 2000. "Scholars and Libraries Want Permission to Copy Electronic Materials." *Chronicle of Higher Education* 47, no. 15 (December 15): A51.

Gregory, Vicki L. 1997. "Delivery of Information Via the World Wide Web: A Look at Copyright and Intellectual Property Issues." *ACRL 1997 National Conference Papers* [Online]. Available: www.ala.org/acrl/paperhtm/e40.html [2002, May 24].

H.R. Rep. No. 105–551, Pt. 2 at 50, 52 (1998).

H.R. Rep. No. 105–796, at 75 (1998).

Halpern, Steven E. 1999. "New Protections for Internet Service Providers: An Analysis of the Online Copyright Infringement Liability Limitation Act." *Seton Hall Legislative Journal* 23: 359–408.

Hearing on H.R.2180. 1997. The *On-Line Copyright Liability Limitation Act* Before the House Subcommittee on Courts and Intellectual Property, 105 [su'th'] Cong.1 (Sept. 16) (testimony of Ronald G. Dunn, President, Information Industry Association [Online]. Available: www.house.gov/judiciary/4007.htm [2002, May 24].

Hearing on H.R.2180. 1997. Before the House Subcommittee on *Courts and Intellectual Property*, 105 [su'th'] Cong. 2 (Sept. 16) (testimony of M.R.C. Greenwood on behalf of the Association of American Universities, the National Association of State Universities and Land-Grant Colleges, the American Council on Education, the National Association of Independent Colleges and Universities, the American Association of State Colleges and Universities, the American Association of Community Colleges, EDUCOM, and the University of Continuing Education Association) [Online]. Available: www.house.gov/judiciary/4014.htm [2002, May 24].

Hill v. Gateway 2000 Inc., 105 F.3d 1147 (7th Cir. 1997).

Karas, Stan. 2001. "Intellectual Property A. Copyright 2. Defenses A) Fair use: Sony Computer Entertainment, Inc. V. Connectix Corp." *Berkeley Technology Law Journal* 16: 33–52.

M.A. Mortenson Co. v. Timberline Software Co., 93 Wash. App. 819 (1999).

McDonald, Brian D. 2001. "Contract Enforceability: The Uniform Computer Information Transactions Act." *Berkeley Law Journal* 16: 461–484.

Nimmer, David. 1996. "Brains and Other Paraphernalia of the Digital Age." *Harvard Journal of Law and Technology* 10, no. 142: 1–46.

O'Rourke, Maureen A. 1995. "Drawing the Boundary Between Copyright and Contract: Copyright Preemption of Software License Terms." *Duke Law Journal* 45: 479–558.

ProCD v. Zeidenberg, 86 F.3d 1447, 1451, 1452, 1454 (7th Cir. 1996).

Radin, Margaret Jane. 2000. "Humans, Computers, and Binding Commitment." *Indiana Law Journal* 75 (Fall): 1125–1162.

Ravn, Michelle A. 1999. "Navigating Terra Incognita: Why the Digital Millennium Copyright Act Was Needed to Chart the Course of Online Service Provider Liability for Copyright Infringement." *Ohio State Law Journal* 60: 755–798.

Samuelson, Pamela. 1999. "Intellectual Property and the Digital Economy: Why the Anti-Circumvention Regulations Need to be Revised." *Berkeley Technology Law Journal* 14: 519–566.

Samuelson, Pamela. 1998. "Does Information Really Want to Be Licensed?" *Communications of the ACM* 41, no. 9 (September): 15–20.

Sega Enters. v. Accolade, Inc., 977 F.2d 1510, 1524 (9th Cir. 1992).

Shah, Pratik A. 2000. "Berkeley Technology Law Journal Annual Review of Law and Technology I. Intellectual Property; A. Copyright The Uniform Computer Information Transactions Act." *Berkeley Technology Law Journal* 15: 85–107.

Shapiro, Bernstein & Co. v. H.L. Green Co., 316 F.2d 304 (2d Cir. 1963).

Siegel, Michael L. 1999. "Online Information Provider Liability for Copyright Infringement: Potential Pitfalls and Solutions." *Virginia Journal of Law and Technology* 4, no. 7: 10–52.

Sony Computer Entertainment, Inc. v. Connectix Corp., 203 F.3d 596, 605 (9th Cir. 2000), cert. denied, 2000.

Step-Saver Data Sys. Inc. v. Wyse Technology, 939 F.2d 91 (3d Cir. 1991).

U.S. v. LaMacchia, 871 Fed. Supp. 535 (Dist. Mass, 1994).

U.S. Congress, Office of Technology Assessment (OTA). 1992. "Finding a Balance: Computer Software, Intellectual Property and the Challenge of Technological Change," *OTA-TCT-527,* 228p. Washington, DC: U.S. Government Printing Office. (September 2001) [Online]. Available: www.ota.nap.edu/pdf/1992/9215.PDF.

UCITA. 1999. [Online]. Available: www.law.upenn.edu/bll/ulc/ucita/ucita200.htm [2001, September].

Vault Corp. v. Quaid Software Ltd, 847 F.2d 255 (5th Cir.1988).

PART III

Implementing Real-Time Reference Service

OVERVIEW

Within the past two years or so "real-time," or "live" reference, has burst onto the digital reference scene. Whether supported by technology as simple as instant messaging applications or as complex as graphical co-browsing including Web form synchronization, real-time reference has become the next frontier for innovation in reference service.

The two chapters in this section describe the unique types of problems that real-time reference can address. These chapters are glimpses into decision-making processes that have led to successful implementation. Even more important, however, these chapters can provide guidelines for services considering implementing real-time reference—thus making the task of later adopters of the technology that much easier.

Chapter 6

Providing Chat Reference Service: A Survey of Current Practices

Matthew R. Marsteller and Paul Neuhaus

OVERVIEW

In the summer of 2001, the authors surveyed providers of library chat reference services. Chat reference service refers to online, interactive, remote transactions with patrons. In this broad definition, the chat function is essential but it does not exclude other software features utilized by librarians. The survey attempted to gather a variety of data that could serve as a baseline for further studies. The survey results will try to address such issues as variations among library types, satisfaction with chat vendors, hours for offering chat, costs associated with the service, and staffing issues.

INTRODUCTION

Carnegie Mellon University Libraries began its chat reference service on October 2, 2000, under the guidance of an ad hoc Chat Reference Task Force charged with implementing and monitoring the new service. As members of the task force, the authors also handled correspondence with outside contacts. We fielded numerous questions from other librarians whose institutions were contemplating starting a similar service. Realizing that a lack of survey literature existed for this new spin on reference services, we decided to institute a study. We wanted to discover what current practices were commonly in place and believed the survey results could be beneficial to libraries currently offering chat reference services or contemplating offering such services. The survey touched upon many topics and we hope the survey

may function as a baseline from which future trends can be determined.

METHODOLOGY

Development of the survey instrument required considerable effort. After composing an initial draft, the authors consulted a library staff member possessing an appreciable amount of social science statistical survey experience to bring additional clarity to the questions. A revised draft of the survey was piloted internally to selected colleagues familiar with Carnegie Mellon's chat service. The internal pilot proved to be only marginally successful. Feedback from chat providers outside of Carnegie Mellon would have proved useful. For example, a pilot study outside of Carnegie Mellon might have given us a better indication of how consortium members would answer the questions (one response per consortium versus one response per library). A follow-up with the respondents from consortia was conducted to clarify some results.

The original draft took the form of an e-mail message. Two things successfully gathered from the pilot were that the e-mail format would be too cumbersome for such a long survey and that certain questions would be confusing. We enlisted the help of our Computer Science Librarian to guide us in converting the survey to one that utilized HTML forms. Creating the first draft of the base HTML form proved to be a good project for one of our Information Assistants (a graduate student from the nearby University of Pittsburgh). Beyond the basic form creation, we developed two additional files that worked in conjunction with the form. The first file provided the survey participant with a copy of her/his submission; the second sent the results to the e-mail account of one author.

The authors utilized various means to solicit responses to the survey. They initially posted an invitation to participate in the survey on the livereference (livereference@yahoogroups.com) and DIG_REF (DIG_REF@listserv.syr.edu) listservs just prior to the ALA Annual Conference (June 12, 2001). Secondly, we distributed flyers advertising the survey to visitors investigating our ALA poster session (Neuhaus and Marsteller, 2001). We later posted the survey invitation to other pertinent listservs that we identified using the Library-Oriented Lists & Electronic Serials Web site (www.wrlc.org/liblists/). These tactics yielded just over 30 responses. Finally, we examined the lists of chat reference providers on Stephen Francoeur's "The Teaching Librarian" (http://pages.prodigy.net/tabo1/digref.htm) and Gerry McKiernan's "LiveRef(sm): A Registry of Real-Time Digital Reference Services" (www.public.iastate.edu/~CYBERSTACKS/LiveRef.htm) Web sites to identify individual libraries. We followed this by scouring each individual library Web site to determine if we could identify a contact person specifically for chat reference services. Each individual so identified was sent a direct plea to complete the survey. This additional effort doubled our number of responses. These solicitation efforts lasted approximately one month. Some responses came as late as mid-August.

We recognize that these methods do not represent an objective, scientific sampling methodology but we believed getting a large enough survey response to be of greater importance given the small population of libraries offering chat reference services. In his April 2001 survey, Francoeur identified 272 such libraries (Francoeur, 2001). As a consequence, any conclusions drawn from the data are confined to the survey respondents and cannot be extrapolated to the population at large.

The authors entered the data into a Microsoft Excel spreadsheet and developed a codebook for ease of data analysis. We utilized statistical features in Excel to produce the basic statistical results. Cross-tabulated statistical data was generated by importing the spreadsheet into Microsoft Access.

The authors also sought the advice of a research computing consultant who was proficient with statistical analysis software. This consultant analyzed the cross-tabulated statistics using SAS. Due to low frequency counts in the cross-tabulated results, the consultant used a test that is more rigorous than the chi square test. The test is known as Fisher's Exact Test. Since the tables were larger than two rows by two columns, an extension of Fisher's Exact Test, known as the Fisher Freeman Halton Test, was used. SAS software simply refers to both as Fisher's Exact Test. The results of this analysis are given in the cross-tabulated section below.

STATISTICAL RESULTS

The survey yielded 67 total responses of which 62 were deemed usable for the purposes of analysis. Most respondents answered all the questions. Any missing data is reflected in the results reported below. With a population of 272 libraries, our useable responses reflect an input of roughly 23 percent. All results will be rounded to the nearest whole percentage point. This chapter presents the most important findings from the survey. For readers interested in the complete results or a copy of the survey instrument, please contact the authors.

Basic Statistical Results

As one would expect with a relatively new service, the results of the survey show both interesting congruities and dissimilarities in institutional practices. The reader should interpret the results as a snapshot in time rather than a description of practices that will be equally applicable a few years from now. One of the first questions from the survey provides a good illustration. This question asked what chat service or vendor the institution utilized. Results are given in Table 6–1.

There are a number of comments that can be made regarding this distribution. The products represented in this sample probably will change considerably in the next few years. This survey took place a few months after LivePerson purchased Human Click. Following the sale, Human Click changed from free software with pretty basic technological features to a fee-based service (though still relatively inexpensive). It is doubtful that Human Click will retain such a significant portion of the market and may not even survive as a separate entity. At the same time, new vendors may enter the field. A good example of the latter is 24/7 Reference. This vendor

Table 6–1
Breakdown by Chat Service or Vendor Utilized

Chat Service or Vendor	Response	Percentage
Human Click	22	37
LSSI	11	18
Docutek VRL	3	5
LiveAssistance	3	5
LivePerson	3	5
AOL	2	3
ChatSpace	2	3
Egain	2	3
eShare NetAgent	2	3
WebMaster ConferenceRoom	2	3
Desktop Streaming	1	2
ICQ	1	2
Instant Service	1	2
LiveHelper	1	2
NetMeeting	1	2
"Home Grown"	3	5
Total	60	100

Table 6–2
Type of Library and Length of Time Offering Chat Service*

Type of Library	Response	Percentage
University	43	69
College	4	6
Community College	4	6
Public	8	13
Special	3	5
Total	62	100

How Long Has Your Institution Offered Chat Services?

	Response	Percentage
1 – 4 months	28	45
4 – 8 months	13	21
8 – 12 months	11	18
Over 1 year	10	16
Total	62	100

*percentages are rounded; some column totals may not agree with their parts

did not appear in the survey but has begun to make significant inroads into the market since then. The authors expect the number of companies in this business to diminish and for some companies to dominate the market within a few years. It also will be interesting to see how many "home grown" products survive as technology changes. "Home grown" solutions might provide a good alternative if commercial products become too expensive or might be the only alternative for some consortia that have to deal with multiple computing environments among their membership.

Some survey questions were asked to ascertain basic information about the institutions. The results themselves were of interest but also provided a means to compare chat reference across institutions. Table 6–2 provides a breakdown by type of library.

University libraries are easily the largest contingent among the survey respondents. Based on Francoeur's list of libraries offering chat reference, over one-half of academic libraries as a whole answered the survey. Unfortunately, the number of respondents from public libraries represents only a small percentage of such libraries. The small numbers for some of these categories made comparisons across library types problematic. Table 6–2 also

shows how long institutions have offered chat services. The results are not surprising. What will be interesting to observe is how soon the number of new entrants begins to decline.

Other general questions yielded additional information. Nineteen percent of institutions represented in the survey offered chat services as a member of a consortium. Given Francoeur's estimate of 210 libraries served by reference consortia, the authors believe they missed many consortia members—especially those participating in large public library consortia (Francoeur, 2001). The estimated user population varied greatly between institutions, ranging from 450 to 5,200,000 patrons. The mean was 184,887 patrons and the median was 11,600. The sizable disparity between the mean and the median reflects a few extremely large user populations served by consortia.

The survey asked a number of questions that dealt with library staffing issues (see Table 6–3). We thought these would be of great interest both to administrators thinking about adding a chat service and individuals who actually staff the service.

Approximately one-fourth of the respondents indicated their institution offered no training beyond training provided by the vendor. We hope this means

Table 6–3
Staffing Issues*

Average Hours of Training, Excluding Training by the Vendor	Response	Percentage
None	16	26
1 – 2 hours	23	37
3 – 4 hours	11	18
Over 4 hours	12	19
Total	62	100

Status of the Chat Operators
(Check all that apply)

	Response	Percentage
Reference Librarians	60	100
Other Librarians	17	28
Paraprofessionals	24	40
Students	5	8
Other	2	3
Total	60	100

For Each Chat Operator, the Number of Hours Devoted to Reference Services per Week:

	Response	Percentage
Stayed the same	44	72
Increased by 1 – 2 hours	7	11
Increased by 2 – 4 hours	8	13
Increased over 4 hours	2	3
Total	61	100

*percentages are rounded; some column totals may not agree with their parts

Table 6–4
Yearly Expenditures for Chat Services*

What Is Your Institution's Yearly Expense for the Chat Service, Excluding Salaries?	Response	Percentage
Under $2,500	42	69
$2,500 - $5,000	1	2
$5,000 - $7,500	1	2
$7,500 - $10,000	3	5
Over $10,000	4	7
Don't Know	10	16
Total	61	100

What Is Your Institution's Yearly Expense for Chat Operators' Salaries?

	Response	Percentage
Under $10,000	13	21
$10,000 - $20,000	0	0
$20,000 - $30,000	2	3
$30,000 - $40,000	5	8
$40,000 - $50,000	2	3
Over $50,000	7	11
Don't Know	32	52
Total	61	100

*percentages are rounded; some column totals may not agree with their parts

that the vendors provided very good training rather than administrators expecting their staffs to introduce a new service without any training. It is not surprising that the persons staffing chat reference reflect a variety of statuses in their institutions. We would expect this variety to mirror the staffing at reference desks though we did not try to ascertain through the survey whether or not this assumption is valid. One of the more surprising findings in the survey was the large percentage (72 percent) of respondents who indicated the number of reference hours per week stayed the same after the introduction of chat reference. At the same time, only three respondents indicated that their libraries hired additional personnel. Various explanations present themselves as possibilities. It may be that staff in some libraries handled chat questions at the reference desk while also serving other patrons; thus technically, the reference load

as measured by hours did not increase. The relatively small number of queries received each month by many institutions would support such an arrangement. Conversely, comments posted at various times to the DIG_REF listserv suggest that the majority of chat operators staff the service from their offices rather than from the reference desk. The authors also suspect that some respondents may have underreported the impact. The cross-tabulated section below (specifically Table 6–13) addresses this question further.

Another issue close to administrators' hearts is the cost associated with providing chat reference. Two questions dealt with the yearly expenses incurred by libraries. We asked for expenses (excluding salaries) and listed vendor charges, office space, and publicity as examples. Secondly, we requested an estimate for the yearly expenses devoted to chat

**Table 6–5
Rationale for Changing Vendors and Average
Number of Chat Questions per Month***

Rationale for Changing Vendors (Check all that apply)	Response	Percentage
Service with More Options	17	68
Less Expensive Service	0	0
Technical Problems with Current Service	3	12
Simpler Interface to Operate	2	8
Other	8	32
Total	25	100

Average Number of Chat Questions per Month		
Under 25	43	72
25 – 50	5	8
50 – 100	5	8
100 – 200	5	8
Over 200	2	3
Total	60	100

*percentages are rounded; some column totals may not agree with their parts

operators' salaries. Table 6–4 gives the results for these questions.

A couple of comments can be made regarding these responses. A preponderance of respondents (69 percent) reported yearly expenses under $2,500. With the change in status of Human Click and an interest in vendors that offer more sophisticated capabilities, the number of institutions utilizing a low cost option may decrease over time. On the other hand, because many libraries are consortia members, the cost for individual institutions may be relatively low even while employing the more expensive products. Secondly, the authors do not believe any conclusions can be drawn from the question regarding operators' salaries since over one-half (52 percent) of respondents were unable to venture an estimate.

This last question in particular was difficult since we did not know if respondents would have the requisite knowledge regarding salaries or know how to interpret the question. Does the question indicate only salaries (such as new hires) paid expressly for staffing chat? Or, should all elements of salaries be included such as a percentage of paid benefits and the costs associated with other tasks not being com-

pleted because someone is staffing the chat service? We believe the second interpretation is the proper one and it raises the estimated cost of providing chat reference services considerably above the first interpretation. Despite this uncertainty, we decided to ask the question to raise awareness of cost accounting in the profession as well as to gather some potentially interesting data.

We also wanted to know if any libraries planned to change services or vendors in the next year and the rationale underlying such a change. A significant number of respondents (42 percent) expected to change vendors. The rationale for those expecting to change is given in Table 6–5. Of the responses in the "other" category, three respondents expected to change as part of joining a consortium, one sought better customer support, one wanted better performance, one expected their free service to disappear, one predicted something better would come along, and one library was in the process of evaluating other services and expected to change.

Table 6–5 also shows the number of questions each institution answered in an average month. As this table clearly demonstrates, the majority of libraries answered a relatively small number of questions. One could argue that the numbers call into question the value of offering such a service. A look at the number of reference questions answered at Carnegie Mellon University provides some perspective. In the 2000/01 fiscal year, library staff answered 30,209 reference and directional questions. In the first year of offering chat reference (October 2000 – September 2001), library staff handled 596 queries (50 questions per month on average). Therefore, chat reference only accounts for about two percent of the total questions. Balanced against these numbers is the recognition that chat reference is a new service whose use can be expected to increase over time. This is especially true as electronic means of communication become increasingly pervasive and users become accustomed to remote access for reference services.

Two other questions on the survey asked respondents about the hours for offering chat reference. The majority of libraries focused their service hours between noon and 5 p.m. during the week. A fair number of services extended their hours into the morning and/or evening hours and offered service hours on weekends. The total number of service hours ranged from seven to one hundred sixty-eight with a mean of 50 and a median of 55. Looking ahead over the next year, equal numbers (47 percent)

Table 6–6
Chat Reference Compared to In-Person, Telephone, and E-Mail Reference *

	In-Person	Telephone	E-Mail
Much Better	(n=0)	(n=4)	(n=11)
	0 percent	7 percent	19 percent
Better	(n=1)	(n=20)	(n=22)
	2 percent	34 percent	37 percent
Same	(n=20)	(n=21)	(n=17)
	34 percent	36 percent	29 percent
Worse	(n=35)	(n=13)	(n=8)
	59 percent	22 percent	14 percent
Much Worse	(n=3)	(n=1)	(n=1)
	5 percent	2 percent	2 percent
Total	(n=59)	(n=59)	(n=59)
	100 percent	100 percent	100 percent

*percentages are rounded; some row and column totals may not agree with their parts

Table 6–7
Value of Chat Reference Services *

How Valuable Is the Chat Service for Providing Reference Services?	Response	Percentage
Excellent	8	13
Good	33	55
Fair	18	30
Poor	0	0
Very Poor	1	2
Total	60	100

Is the Chat Service Worth the Money that Your Institution Is Spending?		
Definitely	29	50
Probably	21	36
Maybe	6	10
Probably Not	2	3
Definitely Not	0	0
Total	58	100

*percentages are rounded; some column totals may not agree with their parts

expected the number of chat reference hours to remain constant or expected an increase; just five percent expected a decrease in service hours. It remains to be seen how cost effective it is for institutions to offer chat reference in the early morning hours.

The authors also wanted to gauge respondents' attitudes toward chat as a reference tool compared to in-person, telephone, and e-mail reference. Table 6–6 provides an assessment.

Overall, respondents rated chat as slightly superior to telephone and e-mail reference but inferior to in-person reference. These results are not a big surprise. A more nuanced investigation comparing the different reference media might make for an interesting study by itself.

The study concluded with two of the more telling questions in the survey (see Table 6–7).

Generally, the opinions are very favorable for both questions. Equally important may be that only one respondent rated the service as "very poor" and no one expressed the opinion that chat reference is "definitely not" worth the money. The following section of the chapter examines the value of chat reference in greater detail and also compares a number of other variables.

Cross-Tabulated Statistical Results

With such a large survey, opportunities abounded for a deeper view of the results. For this closer exami-

nation, the authors employed statistical tests to verify whether or not perceived relationships between categories actually were present. This section contains those tables that have been analyzed using Fisher's Exact Test. A "p value" resulting from the test is given. The p value indicates whether or not a relationship can be said to exist between the categories that are being compared. P values less than 0.05 indicate a relationship and those greater than 0.05 indicate no relationship exists.

The authors started by comparing the value of chat services to a number of other variables. One such comparison was a breakdown by the value of chat service compared to the vendor used to provide the service (see Table 6–8).

The p value for the Fisher's Exact Test was 0.0322 and because of this one can state that a relationship exists between value judgment and vendor used. However, one must consider the size of the table and the number of zero values in the cells of the table. Some statisticians might argue that even Fisher's Exact Test is inadequate for this particular table. Value judgment of the chat service was markedly less favorable for the most heavily used prod-

Table 6–8
Value of Chat Service as Compared to the Vendor Used*

Vendor	Excellent	Good	Fair	Poor	Very Poor
Human Click	(n=1)	(n=10)	(n=11)	(n=0)	(n=0)
(n=22) 38 percent	2 percent	17 percent	19 percent	0 percent	0 percent
LSSI (n=11)	(n=2)	(n=7)	(n=2)	(n=0)	(n=0)
19 percent	3 percent	12 percent	3 percent	0 percent	0 percent
LivePerson (n=2)	(n=0)	(n=1)	(n=1)	(n=0)	(n=0)
3 percent	0 percent	2 percent	2 percent	0 percent	0 percent
LiveAssistance (n=2)	(n=0)	(n=2)	(n=0)	(n=0)	(n=0)
3 percent	0 percent	3 percent	0 percent	0 percent	0 percent
Docutek VRL (n=3)	(n=0)	(n=3)	(n=0)	(n=0)	(n=0)
5 percent	0 percent	5 percent	0 percent	0 percent	0 percent
"Home Grown" (n=3)	(n=3)	(n=0)	(n=0)	(n=0)	(n=0)
5 percent	5 percent	0 percent	0 percent	0 percent	0 percent
AOL (n=2)	(n=0)	(n=1)	(n=0)	(n=0)	(n=1)
3 percent	0 percent	2 percent	0 percent	0 percent	2 percent
Egain (n=2)	(n=0)	(n=1)	(n=1)	(n=0)	(n=0)
3 percent	0 percent	2 percent	2 percent	0 percent	0 percent
eShare NetAgent	(n=1)	(n=1)	(n=0)	(n=0)	(n=0)
(n=2) 3 percent	2 percent	2 percent	0 percent	0 percent	0 percent
NetMeeting (n=1)	(n=1)	(n=0)	(n=0)	(n=0)	(n=0)
2 percent	2 percent	0 percent	0 percent	0 percent	0 percent
WebMaster Conference	(n=0)	(n=2)	(n=0)	(n=0)	(n=0)
Room (n=2) 3 percent	0 percent	3 percent	0 percent	0 percent	0 percent
Instant Service (n=1)	(n=0)	(n=0)	(n=1)	(n=0)	(n=0)
2 percent	0 percent	0 percent	2 percent	0 percent	0 percent
ChatSpace (n=1)	(n=0)	(n=1)	(n=0)	(n=0)	(n=0)
2 percent	0 percent	2 percent	0 percent	0 percent	0 percent
LiveHelper (n=1)	(n=0)	(n=1)	(n=0)	(n=0)	(n=0)
2 percent	0 percent	2 percent	0 percent	0 percent	0 percent
ChatSpace Community	(n=0)	(n=0)	(n=1)	(n=0)	(n=0) 0
Server (n=1) 2 percent	0 percent	0 percent	2 percent	0 percent	0 percent
ICQ (n=1)	(n=0)	(n=1)	(n=0)	(n=0)	(n=0)
2 percent	0 percent	2 percent	0 percent	0 percent	0 percent
Desktop Streaming	(n=0)	(n=1)	(n=0)	(n=0)	(n=0)
(n=1) 2 percent	0 percent	2 percent	0 percent	0 percent	0 percent
Total (n=58)	(n=8)	(n=32)	(n=17)	(n=0)	(n=1)
100 percent	14 percent	55 percent	29 percent	0 percent	2 percent

*percentages are rounded; some row and column totals may not agree with their parts

uct (Human Click) compared to the group as a whole. Users of Human Click gave a "Fair" value judgment for 11 of the 22 responses. Overall, the respondents gave a "Fair" value judgment or lower just 30 percent of the time. The exception would be those respondents that developed their own software (designated "Home Grown"), which we placed in its own category.

The comparison of the value of chat service versus the size of library staff is given in Table 6–9.

Table 6–9
Value Judgment of Chat Service Versus the Size of the Library Staff *

Size of the Library Staff	Excellent	Good	Fair	Poor	Very Poor
Under 25 FTE (n=17)	(n=0)	(n=7)	(n=10)	(n=0)	(n=0)
30 percent	0 percent	12 percent	18 percent	0 percent	0 percent
25 - 50 FTE (n=8)	(n=1)	(n=7)	(n=0)	(n=0)	(n=0)
14 percent	2 percent	12 percent	0 percent	0 percent	0 percent
50 - 100 FTE (n=10)	(n=2)	(n=5)	(n=2)	(n=0)	(n=1)
18 percent	4 percent	9 percent	4 percent	0 percent	2 percent
100 - 200 FTE (n=11)	(n=4)	(n=6)	(n=1)	(n=0)	(n=0)
19 percent	7 percent	11 percent	2 percent	0 percent	0 percent
Over 200 FTE (n=11)	(n=1)	(n=7)	(n=3)	(n=0)	(n=0)
19 percent	2 percent	12 percent	5 percent	0 percent	0 percent
Total (n=57)	(n=8)	(n=32)	(n=16)	(n=0)	(n=1)
100 percent	14 percent	56 percent	28 percent	0 percent	2 percent

*percentages are rounded; some row and column totals may not agree with their parts

Results indicate that respondents from libraries with large library staff place a higher value on the service than their smaller counterparts (under 25 FTE). The p value for Table 6–9 was 0.0128. Why would size matter? Perhaps the larger institutions had immediate needs that a chat reference service could support. A large university campus (or multi-campus setting) with numerous libraries might mean significant travel would be involved just to visit a particular campus library. Chat reference service would give the library staff of the larger institution a real-time exchange with their patrons without the patron having to travel. The same could be said for a public library system where a reference staff at the main library could provide reference to all branches.

Another cross-tabulation compared the value of the chat service to the length of time an institution had been offering the service. The results are given in Table 6–10.

Respondents having more than one year of experience with chat service software gave a value judgment of "Excellent" or "Good" to the chat service 90 percent of the time. Overall, 66 percent of respondents gave a value judgment of "Excellent" or

Table 6–10
Value Judgment of Chat Service Versus How Long the Institution Offered the Service

How Long Service Was Offered	Excellent	Good	Fair	Poor	Very Poor
1 - 4 Months (n=26)	(n=4)	(n=11)	(n=10)	(n=0)	(n=1)
43 percent	7 percent	18 percent	17 percent	0 percent	2 percent
4 - 8 Months (n=13)	(n=1)	(n=9)	(n=3)	(n=0)	(n=0)
22 percent	2 percent	15 percent	5 percent	0 percent	0 percent
8 - 12 Months (n=11)	(n=1)	(n=6)	(n=4)	(n=0)	(n=0)
18 percent	2 percent	10 percent	7 percent	0 percent	0 percent
Over 1 Year (n=10)	(n=2)	(n=7)	(n=1)	(n=0)	(n=0)
17 percent	3 percent	12 percent	2 percent	0 percent	0 percent
Total (n=60)	(n=8)	(n=33)	(n=18)	(n=0)	(n=1)
100 percent	13 percent	55 percent	30 percent	0 percent	2 percent

Table 6–11
How Long Chat Service Has Been Offered Versus Whether or Not It's Worthwhile*

How Long Service Was Offered	Definitely	Probably	Maybe	Probably Not	Definitely Not
1 - 4 Months (n=25)	(n=11)	(n=9)	(n=4)	(n=1)	(n=0)
43 percent	19 percent	16 percent	7 percent	2 percent	0 percent
4 - 8 Months (n=12)	(n=6)	(n=4)	(n=2)	(n=0)	(n=0)
21 percent	10 percent	7 percent	3 percent	0 percent	0 percent
8 - 12 Months (n=11)	(n=5)	(n=5)	(n=0)	(n=1)	(n=0)
19 percent	9 percent	9 percent	0 percent	2 percent	0 percent
Over 1 Year (n=10)	(n=7)	(n=3)	(n=0)	(n=0)	(n=0)
17 percent	12 percent	5 percent	0 percent	0 percent	0 percent
Total (n=58)	(n=29)	(n=21)	(n=6)	(n=2)	(n=0)
100 percent	50 percent	36 percent	10 percent	3 percent	0 percent

*percentages are rounded; some row and column totals may not agree with their parts

"Good." However, the p value was 0.7161, which indicates that no association exists between the value judgment of the chat service and how long the institution has offered the service. In this particular case, the difference was not significant. This is a good example of the need for statistical tests. The statistical tests showed that the difference noted by just looking at the table was small enough that it could have been due to chance.

There was no association between how long a chat service had been offered and whether or not it was worthwhile (see Table 6–11). The p value of Table 6–11 was 0.7771. This means that respondents with little operating experience thought the service was as worthwhile as those respondents with more experience. Some might think that we would see more skeptics among those with less experience with their service.

One would expect that written policies are more frequently found in larger libraries. Larger staffs have less of a chance to establish close working relationships among all reference workers. As a result, administrators may wish to ensure that existing policy is consistent across departments. Table 6–12 supports this belief with gradually larger numbers of respondents as the size of the library staff increases. The converse is also true—the larger the library staff, the less likely they will NOT have a policy. The p value for Table 6–12 was 0.0251. We also ran a trend test and SAS confirmed the trend.

In the basic statistical results section we reported that only 28 percent of respondents indicated that their reference hours increased by any amount. This suggests that many libraries covered chat at the physical reference desk. As we thought about the question a bit more, we wondered if larger libraries

Table 6–12
Existence of Written Policy Versus Size of Library Staff (in FTE)

Written Policy	Under 25	25 – 50	50 – 100	100 – 200	Over 200
Yes (n=24)	(n=2)	(n=3)	(n=5)	(n=6)	(n=7)
39 percent	3 percent	5 percent	8 percent	10 percent	11 percent
No (n=38)	(n=16)	(n=6)	(n=5)	(n=5)	(n=4)
61 percent	26 percent	10 percent	8 percent	8 percent	6 percent
Total (n=62)	(n=18)	(n=9)	(n=10)	(n=11)	(n=11)
100 percent	29 percent	15 percent	16 percent	18 percent	18 percent

Table 6–13
Size of Library Staff (in FTE) Versus Change in Reference Service Hours per Operator

Size of Library Staff	Stayed the Same	Increased 1 – 2 Hours	Increased 2 – 4 Hours	Increased Over 4 Hours
Under 25 (n=18)	(n=16)	(n=2)	(n=0)	(n=0)
31 percent	28 percent	3 percent	0 percent	0 percent
25 - 50 (n=9)	(n=7)	(n=0)	(n=2)	(n=0)
16 percent	12 percent	0 percent	3 percent	0 percent
50 - 100 (n=10)	(n=7)	(n=1)	(n=2)	(n=0)
17 percent	12 percent	2 percent	3 percent	0 percent
100 - 200 (n=10)	(n=6)	(n=0)	(n=2)	(n=2)
17 percent	10 percent	0 percent	3 percent	3 percent
Over 200 (n=11)	(n=6)	(n=3)	(n=2)	(n=0)
19 percent	10 percent	5 percent	3 percent	0 percent
Total (n=59)	(n=42)	(n=6)	(n=8)	(n=2)
100 percent	72 percent	10 percent	14 percent	3 percent

with multiple persons covering the physical reference desk accounted for the 72 percent of respondents able to add the additional reference medium without increasing staff. However, the p value for Table 6–13 wound up being 0.0772. This indicates that no relationship could be shown between the size of library staff and the change in reference service hours per operator.

This may mean that the situation is more reliant on the institution's particular reference setup. It may have more to do with whether a reference service is divided up into many subject areas or handled at one (or a relatively small number of) reference desk(s).

Another look at the data reveals the uncertainty in the vendor marketplace in the summer of 2001. There was a 50 – 50 split among those not planning to change vendors and those planning to change vendors for services that had been in operation longer than four months. Even nine of the twenty-eight institutions that had been operating four months or less planned to change (see Table 6–14). A p value of 0.5599 for the table indicates no relationship between the categories. It made no difference how long a chat service had been offered when it came to a choice about changing vendors. It is particularly interesting to note the willingness to change among services in operation a short time.

One would think that a higher frequency of technical problems would be a significant contributor to market movement, but Table 6–15 turns this assumption on its ear. The p value of 0.0938 for Table 6–15 indicates that no relationship exists between frequency of technical problems and whether or not a library is planning to change vendors. This odd result suggests a more complicated decision-making

Table 6–14
How Long Chat Service Was Offered Versus Plans for Changing Vendors*

How Long Service Was Offered	Changing Vendors	Not Changing Vendors
1 - 4 Months (n=28) 47 percent	(n=9) 15 percent	(n=19) 32 percent
4 - 8 Months (n=11) 18 percent	(n=6) 10 percent	(n=5) 8 percent
8 - 12 Months (n=11) 18 percent	(n=5) 8 percent	(n=6) 10 percent
Over 1 Year (n=10) 17 percent	(n=5) 8 percent	(n=5) 8 percent
Total (n=60) 100 percent	(n=25) 42 percent	(n=35) 58 percent

*percentages are rounded; some row and column totals may not agree with their parts

Table 6–15
Plans for Changing Vendors Versus Frequency of Technical Problems

	Technical Problems			
Changing Vendors?	Daily	1 – 2 Times per Week	1 – 2 Times per Month	Never
Yes (n=25) 42 percent	(n=1) 2 percent	(n=7) 12 percent	(n=9) 15 percent	(n=8) 13 percent
No (n=35) 58 percent	(n=5) 8 percent	(n=2) 3 percent	(n=15) 25 percent	(n=13) 22 percent
Total (n=60) 100 percent	(n=6) 10 percent	(n=9) 15 percent	(n=24) 40 percent	(n=21) 35 percent

process. The authors took a close look at all the data in this table and noted a couple of overriding factors. Those respondents that invested heavily in a software package up front, such as LSSI, were more reluctant to change vendors. On the other end of the spectrum, some of those with free software seemed content to stay where they were.

We wanted to verify that large library staffs were handling the higher chat reference service traffic (see Table 6–16). Just 29 percent of all chat services that responded received more than 25 queries per month. All but one of those services had at least 50 to 100 FTE on their library staff. Analysis showed the p value of the table to be 0.0091. A relationship did exist.

We tried to ascertain whether or not consortia handled more questions per month than the rest of our survey respondents (see Table 6–17). The p value

for the table of 0.6547 indicated that there was no relationship. We questioned the validity of these results. We were concerned that respondents from consortia did not answer the question "What is the average number of chat queries your library system receives each month?" in a consistent manner. We contacted the ten consortia participants who included their contact information in order to clarify their responses. Seven of ten replied and we found that three of the seven reported only statistics for their library and not for the entire consortium. In retrospect, in order to ensure an accurate comparison, respondents should only have given statistics for their individual library. It's important to note that statistical reporting for a consortium is far more complex than for libraries operating on their own.

The data concerning the types of libraries that

Table 6–16
Size of Library Staff Versus Questions per Month (QPM)*

Size of Library Staff	Under 25 QPM	25 – 50 QPM	50 – 100 QPM	100 – 200 QPM	Over 200 QPM
Under 25 FTE (n=18)	(n=18)	(n=0)	(n=0)	(n=0)	(n=0)
31 percent	31 percent	0 percent	0 percent	0 percent	0 percent
25 - 50 FTE (n=9)	(n=8)	(n=0)	(n=1)	(n=0)	(n=0)
16 percent	14 percent	0 percent	2 percent	0 percent	0 percent
50 - 100 FTE (n=10)	(n=5)	(n=2)	(n=1)	(n=1)	(n=1)
17 percent	9 percent	3 percent	2 percent	2 percent	2 percent
100 - 200 FTE (n=10)	(n=5)	(n=2)	(n=2)	(n=1)	(n=0)
17 percent	9 percent	3 percent	3 percent	2 percent	0 percent
Over 200 FTE (n=11)	(n=5)	(n=1)	(n=1)	(n=3)	(n=1)
19 percent	9 percent	2 percent	2 percent	5 percent	2 percent
Total (n=58)	(n=41)	(n=5)	(n=5)	(n=5)	(n=2)
100 percent	71 percent	9 percent	9 percent	9 percent	3 percent

*percentages are rounded; some row and column totals may not agree with their parts

Table 6–17
Participation in Consortia Versus Questions per Month

Consortia Participant?	Under 25 QPM	25 – 50 QPM	50 – 100 QPM	100 – 200 QPM	Over 200 QPM
Yes (n=11)	(n=8)	(n=0)	(n=1)	(n=1)	(n=1)
18 percent	13 percent	0 percent	2 percent	2 percent	2 percent
No (n=49)	(n=35)	(n=5)	(n=4)	(n=4)	(n=1)
82 percent	58 percent	8 percent	7 percent	7 percent	2 percent
Total (n=60)	(n=43)	(n=5)	(n=5)	(n=5)	(n=2)
100 percent	72 percent	8 percent	8 percent	8 percent	3 percent

participated in consortia were interesting. The response yielded a relationship between consortia participation and type of library. The p value of Table 6–18 was 0.0001757—a very strong relationship. The results reveal that public libraries and community colleges were more prone to participate in consortia. We wondered why so few university and college libraries were in consortia. It could be that licensing of digital tools appeared to be too much of a quagmire to overcome. Perhaps it's because institutions like colleges and universities feel that they are simply too different (or too complex) to provide reference for one another and maintain the quality desired for the service.

Table 6–19 is the very important listing by vendor of the frequency of technical problems. Keep in mind that this is only a snapshot in time (mid-June through mid-August of 2001). The authors have personally experienced software "upgrades" that eliminate technical problems and still others that bring a whole host of new problems to the fore. Although the p value for Table 6–19 is 0.0008113 and indicates a strong relationship, the table is quite large and many zero values exist.

CONCLUSION

One troubling aspect of the results was the overall use of the chat reference service. Sixty-nine percent of respondents indicated that they were fielding less than 25 questions per month. The average number of hours covered per week was 54 with a median of 40. This works out to an average of about one reference question every nine hours of service for a library that receives 25 questions per month. However, efforts at the time of the survey were still quite new and beginnings are always tough. Comforting news came when we contacted consortia members for clarification of their reports regarding questions per month. As of late 2001, some of these consortia were fielding more than a thousand questions per month. It's also important to note that a large por-

Table 6–18
Consortia Participation Versus Type of Library*

Consortia Participation	University	College	Community College	Public +	Special
Yes (n=12)	(n=3)	(n=0)	(n=2)	(n=6)	(n=1)
19 percent	5 percent	0 percent	3 percent	10 percent	2 percent
No (n=50)	(n=40)	(n=4)	(n=2)	(n=2)	(n=2)
81 percent	65 percent	6 percent	3 percent	3 percent	3 percent
Total (n=62)	(n=43)	(n=4)	(n=4)	(n=8)	(n=3)
100 percent	69 percent	6 percent	6 percent	13 percent	5 percent

+Includes response from "public library consortia"
*percentages are rounded; some row and column totals may not agree with their parts

Table 6–19
Vendor Versus Frequency of Technical Problems*

Vendor	Daily	1 – 2 Times per Week	1 – 2 Times per Month	Never
		Technical Problems		
Human Click (n=22) 37 percent	(n=1) 2 percent	(n=0) 0 percent	(n=10) 17 percent	(n=11) 18 percent
LSSI (n=11) 18 percent	(n=3) 5 percent	(n=2) 3 percent	(n=6) 10 percent	(n=0) 0 percent
LivePerson (n=3) 5 percent	(n=0) 0 percent	(n=1) 2 percent	(n=2) 3 percent	(n=0) 0 percent
LiveAssistance (n=3) 5 percent	(n=1) 2 percent	(n=1) 2 percent	(n=1) 2 percent	(n=0) 0 percent
Docutek VRL (n=3) 5 percent	(n=0) 0 percent	(n=0) 0 percent	(n=2) 3 percent	(n=1) 2 percent
Home Grown (n=3) 5 percent	(n=0) 0 percent	(n=1) 2 percent	(n=0) 0 percent	(n=2) 3 percent
Egain (n=2) 3 percent	(n=0) 0 percent	(n=2) 3 percent	(n=0) 0 percent	(n=0) 0 percent
AOL (n=2) 3 percent	(n=1) 2 percent	(n=0) 0 percent	(n=0) 0 percent	(n=1) 2 percent
eShare NetAgent (n=2) 3 percent	(n=0) 0 percent	(n=0) 0 percent	(n=1) 2 percent	(n=1) 2 percent
NetMeeting (n=1) 2 percent	(n=0) 0 percent	(n=0) 0 percent	(n=1) 2 percent	(n=0) 0 percent
WebMaster ConferenceRoom (n=2) 3 percent	(n=0) 0 percent	(n=0) 0 percent	(n=0) 0 percent	(n=2) 3 percent
Instant Service (n=1) 2 percent	(n=0) 0 percent	(n=1) 2 percent	(n=0) 0 percent	(n=0) 0 percent
ChatSpace (n=1) 2 percent	(n=0) 0 percent	(n=1) 2 percent	(n=0) 0 percent	(n=0) 0 percent
ChatSpace Community Server (n=1) 2 percent	(n=0) 0 percent	(n=0) 0 percent	(n=0) 0 percent	(n=1) 2 percent
LiveHelper (n=1) 2 percent	(n=0) 0 percent	(n=1) 2 percent	(n=0) 0 percent	(n=0) 0 percent
ICQ (n=1) 2 percent	(n=0) 0 percent	(n=0) 0 percent	(n=0) 0 percent	(n=1) 2 percent
Desktop Streaming (n=1) 2 percent	(n=0) 0 percent	(n=0) 0 percent	(n=0) 0 percent	(n=1) 2 percent
Total (n=60) 100 percent	(n=6) 10 percent	(n=10) 17 percent	(n=23) 38 percent	(n=21) 35 percent

*percentages are rounded; some row and column totals may not agree with their parts

tion of our respondents were from academia. These institutions routinely see about a 25 percent turn-over in their community annually. Continual market-ing (or perhaps we should say education) of the ser-vice will be necessary.

Some guidelines for new services can be culled from our analysis. Most services reported having only one operator at a time covering chat reference. With this in mind, we recommend that services start with that level until a need for additional operators is proven. An exception to this guideline might oc-cur when an extremely large population is being served and the marketing of the service is done in an aggressive fashion. Another exception would be the use of a fundamentally different product model such as Docutek VRL. This product begins with the assumption that at any given time, you will want multiple reference staff available for chat. Another consideration is the hours for providing chat. Ser-vices tended to focus on the hours from 10 a.m. un-til 6 p.m. Evening hours until 10 p.m. were also fairly common. New chat services should expect to provide some in-house training. Nearly 75 percent of respondents trained their staff for an hour or more beyond that supplied by the vendor. Surprisingly, only 5 percent of respondents hired additional staff to cover the new reference medium. This was a bit disturbing—are we spreading our resources too thin? Finally, new services will probably want to utilize a variety of staff to operate the service. In addition to reference librarians, many institutions employed paraprofessionals (40 percent) and other librarians (27 percent) as well.

Conducting a survey presents a number of

interesting challenges. Obtaining an adequate sample size and response rate are concerns with most surveys. The direct plea via e-mail certainly helped, but the small number of responses from places other than universities was disappointing. Consortia members may have been reluctant to respond due to some questions being difficult to answer from their perspective. Also, many of our attempts to send e-mail to libraries in other nations (from the IFLA list) "bounced back" to us as undeliverable. There is also the issue of randomness. We opted to query many libraries directly due to the small population size. Perhaps we would have been better served to use a tool like the *American Library Directory* and randomly chosen libraries to participate. If the response proved adequate, the results would have provided a scientifically valid sample.

In retrospect, the authors might have done some things differently to make this a more accurate and useful survey. We did not pilot the survey instrument outside the "ivory tower" of Carnegie Mellon, which is a standard practice for such studies (Busha and Harter, 1980). Such a pilot might have provided a better understanding regarding how respondents would answer the questions. For example, should a respondent who is part of a consortium answer the question on simultaneous users for the whole consortium or just for the individual library? There also are questions that we could have excluded such as asking five separate questions comparing chat to in-person, telephone, or e-mail reference—one would have been sufficient. Some topics we wish we had covered include exploring how well chat software functions as a teaching tool, the physical location of the chat operator while staffing the service, and marketing strategies.

Technology offers a challenge as well as an opportunity for conducting surveys. Using an HTML form for the survey allowed for the elimination of mailing costs. This could allow for less expensive surveys (for the researcher) than in the past. As standardized lists continue to include more and more e-mail contacts, we would encourage the shift to this technology for obtaining responses. We must, however, be conscientious about segments of the sample population that are still unable to utilize the technology.

There certainly are many areas that need further research. An important issue involves the cost effectiveness of chat reference services, which this survey only begins to explore. A majority of the libraries that responded to our survey were academic libraries that were not consortia members. Further investigation into consortial arrangements for chat reference and particularly the role of public libraries would be very interesting. The authors believe the present survey results provide a starting point from which further research efforts may proceed.

ACKNOWLEDGMENTS

The authors would like to thank the following personnel for their support and advice throughout our research. Missy Harvey, our Computer Science Librarian at Carnegie Mellon, guided us through the development of the files needed to utilize the HTML form. John Doncevic, our Information Assistant (now with the Carnegie Library of Pittsburgh), drafted the first version of the HTML form. Carole George, Information Analyst with the University Libraries at Carnegie Mellon, advised us on the order and wording of the questions. Danianne Mizzy, formerly with Carnegie Mellon and now with the University of Pittsburgh, generated a list of e-mail contacts from the library Web sites that we scoured. Finally, Charity Swift, a Direct Experience Summer Intern from Chatham College, helped to test the survey to ensure proper functioning.

REFERENCES

Busha, Charles H., and Stephen P. Harter. 1980. *Research Methods in Librarianship*. San Diego: Academic.

Francoeur, Stephen. 2001. "An Analytical Survey of Chat Reference Services." *Reference Services Review* 29, no. 3 (Fall): 189–203.

Neuhaus, Paul, and Matthew R. Marsteller. 2001. "The Chat Reference Experience at Carnegie Mellon University." Poster session at the 2001 American Library Association Annual Conference, San Francisco, CA. [Online]. Available: www.contrib.andrew.cmu.edu/~matthewm/ALA_2001_chat.html [2002, May 24].

Chapter 7

Testing the Road to Real-Time Digital Reference: Pilot Projects at the University of California, Los Angeles

Alice K. Kawakami

OVERVIEW

The challenges of developing and implementing a real-time digital reference project using collaborative Web browsing software are discussed. The University of California, Los Angeles tested modified Webline and E-Gain Web contact-center software for a year before being able to solve problems with authentication and access to the proprietary databases that are crucial to the research activities of the campus clientele. Overcoming obstacles was accomplished through a structured testing process and partnering with the Metropolitan Cooperative Library System. The lessons learned during the testing process were used to develop guidelines, scripted chats, and bookmarked sites for the resultant pilot projects. The academic environment offers unique challenges in that the primary mission is to provide instruction. The success of instruction via digital means is dependent upon the skills of both librarian and caller as well as upon technology. The evaluation of the pilot projects took into consideration user comments, librarian perceptions of the service, and statistical data.

INTRODUCTION

Beta-testing new technology and initiating a new service requires organizing staff, monitoring human, hardware and software performance, and applying what is learned from each pilot project to progress towards implementing an ongoing program. Issues of staffing, training, policies, publicity, and assess-

ment are critical to developing a viable method of delivering synchronous, real-time reference.

BACKGROUND

Seeking to provide further means to serve its clientele, the University of California, Los Angeles (UCLA) Library recognized the potential of a new technology to offer reference assistance to its users. In-person, telephone, and e-mail reference was already offered by campus libraries but as more and more resources were offered online, point-of-need online assistance was seen as a plausible means to extend service. The library asked Susan McGlamery, Coordinator for Reference Services for the Metropolitan Cooperative Library System (MCLS), to demonstrate Web-based contact-center software that had been modified for library use. Contact-center software was designed for "answering questions and providing live, interactive customer service on very high traffic e-commerce sites like L.L. Bean, Kinko's" (Coffman 2001). The main features include the ability for "agents to push Web pages to customers and escort customers through catalogs or databases, collaboratively fill out forms or search screens, and share slide shows and other content online" (Coffman, 2001). MCLS, an association of libraries in the greater Los Angeles area that shares resources to improve library service to the residents of all participating jurisdictions, had received a federal LSTA grant to help fund the 24/7 Reference project and was primarily working with Webline software. The UCLA library decided to test the potential of synchronous, real-time reference and began testing the Webline software in conjunction with MCLS in April 2000.

SCOPE OF PROJECT

A group of seven librarians representing the three largest (undergraduate library, Research Library, and Biomedical Library) of the library's dozen units were charged to test the software's ability to work with the library's electronic indexes, full-text journals, and other electronic resources. Each of the units submitted a proposal for a pilot project that included a time frame, list of participating personnel, and target population such as the General Education cluster classes, dormitory residents, medical staff, and computer lab users. It was envisioned that this software would extend service beyond the walls of the library and beyond the hours of in-person reference service.

TESTING

One librarian was appointed liaison between the testing group and the developers. The librarians were to experiment with the software and report comments on its performance. It was soon discovered that testing "when you have the time" doesn't produce results. Therefore weekly meetings were scheduled to insure that the librarians had a specific time to test. During 90-minute weekly sessions the testers alternately portrayed the caller and the librarian in reference transactions. This weekly session allowed the testers to discover as a group how the software functioned, and what chat messages and Web sites were used often.

Chat Protocol

It was discovered that the librarian's initial instinct was to type out long, grammatically perfect paragraphs to send to the caller. Meanwhile, the caller had no idea whether the librarian was ruminating about the question or disconnected. This prompted the creation of guidelines such as "send frequent, short messages to let the caller know that you are still there" and "tell the caller what you are going to do, do it, then ask the caller if he saw what you did." A guideline to send messages in the form of a question was established to ensure that the caller was still online. For example, instead of just saying "I will escort you to the library's catalog," the message

would be "I will escort you to the library's catalog. Ready?" This questioning technique proved useful when chat exchanges got out of sync. Occasionally the user or librarian would send a question or comment before the other's message had been transmitted. When this occurred the librarian would ask a question, and then wait for the user's response to that question before proceeding.

Additional Benefits

There were other benefits to testing during a regularly scheduled time. Having tested with colleagues on campus, the test was expanded to callers from outside the UCLA network. Selected librarians from local public libraries and other University of California libraries were asked to click in as callers during the weekly sessions to help test. As it became known that testing was regularly in progress on Wednesdays, between 2:00-3:30 p.m., other librarians who were interested in trying out the software clicked in as well. This allowed testing transmission times from remote locations.

Also, while testing there was either an e-mail or phone connection to the MCLS developers who were modifying the software. Problems and questions that arose during the session were relayed in a timely manner. A solid working relationship grew and the testing group's suggestions and comments were incorporated into the development of the software.

SOFTWARE ISSUES

Testing revealed that the Webline interface was cumbersome for both the librarian and the user. It required multiple windows and was not user-friendly as the user was faced with many icons that needed explanation. The unsophisticated users would have a great deal of difficulty with the software. There are "50 or more vendors developing software with varying degrees of sophistication in this area at present" (Coffman, 2001), but none offered the combination of chat and escorting ability that we wanted at the time. MCLS had been investigating other software as well, including a product produced by e-Gain that required fewer windows for librarian and user. When MCLS acquired and modified the e-Gain software we began testing it in January 2001.

For some time, a major obstacle was the inability to successfully use either the Webline or e-Gain software with the library's many proprietary databases. The databases of the California Digital Library (CDL) databases that are used heavily by the UCLA population were inaccessible. The reason for this problem was difficult to pinpoint since the source could be the UCLA network, CDL firewalls, or vendor configuration. The problem was solved by placing a server (technically a secure reverse proxy server) on campus within the library's network.

PILOT PROJECT I

Having tested with librarians, the next step was to try the software with real users in the Spring Quarter 2001. When the project first began we were unable to escort users through our proprietary databases but we could talk them through a search and take them to the opening page of the database. The unique feature of the software is the ability of the librarian to take a user to a Web site. Both librarian and caller see the same page, and any terms that are input into a search box or form. The librarian can instruct the user as to what terms to input or what links to click and see the result of the action. Conversely the user can see the librarian do the same. The icon linking to our "Online Librarian" service was placed on the home page of the College Library and offered service Monday-Friday from 3:00-5:00 p.m. The times were selected based on the high level of activity at the reference desk during those hours. Shortly after the College Library's project began, the Biomedical Library began offering service Tuesday and Thursday from 3:00-5:00 p.m. Note that both libraries were open the same hours two days a week.

What We Learned

During the 44 days of the pilot, we received only 15 questions. The Online Librarian icons were difficult to find, as they were two levels down from the main library home page that was the default page on each of the library's public workstations. The service got very little publicity. Although a number of ways to publicize the service were proposed, some administrators feared that the service would be inundated with an unmanageable number of callers.

Questions Received

A transcript of each transaction is automatically sent to the user's e-mail at the end of the session and a copy is stored on the server. Analysis of the tran-

scripts showed that most of the questions received required knowing how to search a database, not necessarily requiring subject expertise. Although there were questions on how to find articles on child abuse and hummingbirds, users also wanted to how to renew a book, and what time the libraries were open. Since this was the case, rather than having librarians at different libraries cover the same hours, a centralized service with one librarian covering all the "waiting rooms" (Web page entry points) would be the next pilot project. Questions that needed a subject specialist would be referred to the appropriate subject library.

User Response

Users were incredibly patient. Even when there were technical difficulties, users were "delighted," "loved the technology," "thought it was great," and "thought it was an interesting experiment." Because there were not a large number of callers, it was possible to follow up with each one. Callers were contacted via e-mail or telephone (this information is entered by the caller upon login) and asked what they thought of the service and what hours they thought would be most useful for them. Most callers were very pleased with this method of obtaining assistance. When asked when they would be most likely to use the service, students replied that they would like to see it offered in the evenings, 6:00-10:00 p.m.; on Sunday evenings; before classes 8:00-10:00 a.m.

Training Issues

Analysis of the transcripts indicated that there were certain procedures (e.g., sending a chat message before engaging the escort feature) that weren't being consistently followed. It became clear that there were gaps in training.

When testing began, the initial cadre of librarians made collective discoveries and informally developed policies, procedures, and scripts knowing the reasoning behind each one. As other librarians began participating in the pilot projects, they were trained by one of the original group, but the background behind the policies, procedures, and scripts was not passed on. A one-page "Quick Tips" sheet that was originally designed as a quick guide for digital librarians grew to three pages providing more detail and the "why you need to do this" that was previously lacking.

Also, the responsibility of those attending the weekly sessions was formalized to include disseminating the information to others in their unit. At least one representative from each unit was required to attend the session.

From the weekly discussion as well as by reviewing transcripts it was apparent that librarians were not familiar with the resources available on each of the libraries' Web pages. In response to this a workshop entitled "Digital Resources for Digital Reference" was organized in conjunction with RRISC (Reference, Research and Instruction Services Committee). This workshop consisted of librarians from various units (e.g., Music Library, Government Information, University Archives) highlighting the most useful resources from their Web pages. This well-received program indicated that whether or not they intended to cover digital reference, librarians in general wanted to learn about resources for reference.

PILOT PROJECT II

Using the information gained from the first pilot, a second pilot project was conducted during the Summer Quarter 2001. The service was offered Monday-Thursday, 6:00 p.m. – 9:00 p.m. This allowed us to test whether librarians could cover the service from home using DSL, cable modem, and 56K modem connections. For visibility and easier access, the icon was placed on the main home page of the library as well as on the Biomedical, College, and Music Library's pages. Bookmarks with the logo for the Online Librarian service were distributed to all reference desks. In addition, an ad publicizing the service was placed in the student newspaper.

Results

During the 41 days of the project we received a total of 54 calls. The calls were spread fairly equally among the three hours of service (6-7, 7-8, 8-9 p.m.). As suspected, the greatest number of users entered from the main library page, which is the default on all public workstations.

User Entry Points

- Thirty-eight from the main page
- Nine from the Biomedical Library page
- Five from the College Library page
- Two from the Music Library page

Days of the Week

- Twelve Monday
- Twenty-two Tuesday
- Nine Wednesday
- Eleven Thursday

Questions

Sample questions:
  "Do you have the first violin part to Sleeping Beauty on sheet music?"
  "What is the picture on the cover of 'Facts on File's Encyclopedia of Novels into Film'?"
  "What is the census code for Los Angeles?"
  "How do I find call numbers when doing a search?"
  "How do I access an e-book?"
  "Is the proxy server down? I'm trying to connect to any of the NCBI linked journals."
  "What time does Powell (Library) close?"
  "Can I have microfilms located at the UCSD library sent to me in Toronto, Canada?"

PILOT PROJECT III

The Fall Quarter Digital Reference project tested a combination of day and evening hours and a different staffing model.

Dates and Times

The Project ran for nine weeks, from October 8 through December 6, 2001, open Monday-Thursday from 2:00-4:00 p.m. and 6:00-8:00 p.m. The proposed days and times were chosen based on data from four sources:

- Data from the Spring Quarter project that indicated that there was little demand for this service on Fridays.
- Data for the month of August showing that the number of hits on the digital reference Web page was highest on Mondays and lessened as the week progressed. Data also showed highest hits 2:00-4:00 p.m.
- A report of the eight academic libraries participating in digital reference in the Alliance Library System of Illinois shows that traffic fell off sharply on the weekends. The report also stated that less than 50 percent of activity took place during typical business hours of 8 a.m.-5 p.m. (Sloan, 2001).

- Sampling of callers and students indicate they would like hours in the evenings.

Project Description

This project continued the centralized service piloted during the Summer Quarter. The four units participating were the Biomedical, College, Research, and SEL (Science and Engineering) libraries. The librarians covering the service answer calls coming in from any of the icons on UCLA library pages. Each unit may determine how long each day's shift will be. For example, there could be two two-hour shifts, four one-hour shifts, etc. Subsequent projects will test staggered hours based on data on when users click on the icon.

RECOMMENDED POLICIES

- Librarians cover the service either in the library or at home. If in the library, the librarian should be in the office or classroom, NOT at the Reference Desk. If a unit has an on-call librarian, this individual could cover digital reference during their shift. If at home, a cable modem or DSL is preferable, though a 56K modem will suffice. If there is not a PC or 56K modem available at home, the librarian may borrow a laptop to cover the shift.
- Schedules should be flexible; librarians covering in the evening should be able to come in later in the day. Or if working at home, work a split shift. Digital reference hours should be seen as part of each librarian's reference desk responsibilities. As Sloan (1998: 79) states, "Responsibility for electronic reference shouldn't be an add-on duty; it should be integrated into a reference librarian's assignments."
- Service in an academic library should be a hybrid combination of instruction and "giving answers." The technology does not lend itself to the same instruction methodology used at the academic reference desk. Librarians try to get the user as close to the answer as possible and inquire whether they feel comfortable in taking it alone from there.
- Electronic resources should be used to answer questions if possible (e.g. catalog, databases, Web resources). Refer users to print or other media as appropriate.
- Librarians should not hesitate in referring us-

ers to subject specialists if they cannot fully help the user. Direct the user to the appropriate library or subject specialist. Or offer to forward the question on to the appropriate person.

RECOMMENDED PROCEDURES

- Librarians should be periodically checking the software during their shift. The pilot project is a testing vehicle, and librarians should be assessing the functionality of the software.
- Keep messages brief and frequent. As Kelly Broughton discovered (Broughton, 2001), "users tended to send many short messages rather than one long paragraph." We need to communicate in the same way. Longer sentences can be broken up into parts and sent with ellipses indicating a continuing thought.
- Access databases as appropriate to the user's status. Be aware that certain databases are restricted to university users only. Do not escort non-affiliated users through these resources.
- Make sure that the caller's question is answered completely, worked on offline, or referred to a subject specialist. Follow up with caller if necessary.
- Create a listserv for librarians to report the day's activity including the type of question, librarian perceptions of the transaction.

ROLE OF THE PROGRAM DIRECTOR

- Liaison to testers, MCLS, and software developers.
- Provide updates to Assistant University Librarian for Public Services and Public Services Committee on the status of the project.
- Develop a digital reference planning guide that includes procedures and sample questions.
- Act as consultant to units.
- Oversee training, create training guides and exercises.
- Conduct weekly discussion with testers, and convene other meetings as necessary, e.g., with other UC libraries, developers, and administrators.
- Collect and analyze data for consistency of service and scheduling, including review of session transcripts. As Koyama (1998) states, "Within the context of the traditional reference interview,

librarians have operated rather independently. Today however in banking, travel and other service areas, it is commonplace to hear, 'this call may be monitored for quality and customer satisfaction.'"

- Communicate with callers for feedback.
- Communicate with other libraries providing digital reference.
- Present information at appropriate meetings and conferences.

ROLE AND EXPECTATIONS OF THE TESTER

- Test databases and features of the software.
- Make recommendations and find solutions to problems.
- Report technical problems to director and/or developers.
- Keep up-to-date on any software changes via communications from director.
- Provide timely digital reference service.
- Contribute to the weekly discussion.
- Disseminate information with unit heads and colleagues regularly to keep them informed.

CHALLENGES TO IMPLEMENTING DIGITAL REFERENCE

One of the challenges to implementing digital reference is addressing librarian fears. The fears are many and varied: fear of the phrase "24/7," fear that their clientele's questions can't be answered by non-subject specialists, fear they will have to answer questions outside of their own subject expertise, fear they will be expected to have all the answers, fear of learning new skills, fear that their accumulated knowledge and skills will be devalued in this new digital environment.

Rather than emphasizing the differences between digital reference and traditional reference—that digital reference requires increased multi-tasking skills, lacks visual and verbal cues—training should emphasize the similarities to traditional reference. The role of the reference interview, to elicit the nature of the question and make a referral to other libraries if appropriate, still applies in the digital environment. Training should stress that if you are a good reference librarian, you will probably be a good digital reference librarian. As Hathorn (1997) states, "some

argue that the rise of digitized information is an opportunity to elevate the role of the librarian."

NEXT STEPS

The goal is to make digital reference an integrated part of the reference services that the library provides. It is a delicate balance to publicize a service when the technology is not completely glitch-free; difficult to attract users when the hours of service are few; difficult to cover many hours when there are not a great number of trained librarians.

As more librarians become trained, the hours that the service is open can be increased. This increase is necessary for users to be able to depend on getting online assistance when they need it. A list of competencies that every digital librarian must demonstrate will be developed to ensure that all digital librarians are grounded in the fundamentals of the philosophy and skills necessary to provide good service.

The icon will be added to the home pages of the labs as many students do research in the computing labs rather than in the library. A plan will be developed to publicize the service by rolling out publicity on a timetable.

As at the in-person reference desk, service is given to all users, though only UCLA-affiliated users are escorted into proprietary databases. At the moment we "authenticate" users by checking to see if they use a UCLA e-mail address, enter a UCLA ID number, and ask them outright. Currently 80 percent of callers are UCLA-affiliated, but as the number of callers grows, it will be necessary to authenticate users by electronic means.

The long-term goal is to see how this delivery mode of reference fits in with other modes such as e-mail and phone reference. A multi-factor approach will be used to assess user response, librarian response, and technical issues.

REFERENCES

Broughton, Kelly. 2001. "Our Experiment in Online, Real-Time Reference." *Computers in Libraries* 21, no. 4 (April): 26 [Online]. Available: www.infotoday.com/cilmag/apr01/broughton.htm [2002, May 24].

Coffman, Steve. 2001. "Distance Education and Virtual Reference: Where Are We Headed?" *Computers in*

Libraries 21, no. 4 (April): 20 [Online]. Available: www.infotoday.com/cilmag/apr01/coffman.htm [2002, May 24].

Hathorn, Clay. 1997. "The Librarian Is Dead, Long Live The Librarian." *Pre-text Magazine* 1(October) [Online]. Available: www.pre-text.com/oct97/features/story4.htm [2002, May 24].

Koyama, Janice T. 1998. "http://digiref.scenarios.issues." Paper presented at Reference Service in a Digital Age, 30 June, Library of Congress [Online]. Available: http://lcweb.loc.gov/rr/digiref/koyama.html [2002, May 24].

Sloan, Bernie. 2001. "Ready for Reference: Academic Libraries Offer Live Web-Based Reference." Report on Evaluating System Use [Online]. Available: http://alexia.lis. uiuc.edu/~b-sloan/r4r.final.htm [2002, May 24].

Sloan, Bernie. 1998. "Electronic Reference Services: Some Suggested Guidelines." *Reference and User Services Quarterly* 38 (Summer): 77-81 [Online]. Available: www.lis.uiuc.edu/~b-sloan/guide.html [2002, May 24].

PART IV

Conceiving and Implementing Collaborative Reference Services

OVERVIEW

Physical libraries long ago discovered both the pros and the cons of forming consortia. Today, consortia are a nearly ubiquitous phenomenon of the library landscape. Consortia can be a way for libraries to reduce costs, share resources and expertise, and gain leverage with vendors. On the other hand, consortia can reduce local control of resources and budgets, bureaucratize decision-making, and take up staff resources and time. Is it any wonder that the library community has a love-hate relationship with consortia?

The advantages and disadvantages of collaboration in the digital reference sphere are still emerging. The chapters in this section are concerned with the issues involved in the planning, implementation, and management of collaborative reference services. These issues range from the media used to provide service, to the personalization of service, to technologies and standards for exchanging reference questions, to scaling these services up in their scope. The digital reference community may benefit from these lessons learned on the pros and cons of collaboration, so that all digital reference services can reap benefits from lessons from library consortia.

Chapter 8

Emerging Standards for Digital Reference: The Question Interchange Profile

R. David Lankes

OVERVIEW

This chapter outlines the concepts, terminology, and a proposal for a linking mechanism for digital reference services, called the Question Interchange Profile (QuIP). The logic behind QuIP, its proposed elements, and its implementation are presented. With such a mechanism digital reference services will be able to coordinate load and scope in a reference network. It is hoped that this documentation of the proposed standard will both generate discussion and promote tool development.

THE OPPORTUNITY

We live in a distributed world. Systems, people, and organizations must interact and create fugitive relationships. In an era of digital libraries and collaborative collection of documents and resources, the human/customer service aspect of distributed information networks must also be considered. Such networks of human expertise will have a profound effect on knowledge-based organizations such as libraries, schools, and corporations. Such a network redefines applications to services, and concentrates on interoperability over comprehensiveness.

Much of this opportunity has been discussed in other documents so will not be repeated here. Suffice to say that by turning questions and answers into digital objects with strong computation aspects, primary knowledge (that is what's in people's heads rather than in some static representation such as a book, video, or Web page) becomes accessible on a large scale. This primary knowledge revolution will have a dramatic effect on how we approach research and problem solving.

THE IMPORTANCE OF STANDARDS IN DIGITAL REFERENCE

One might not immediately see the need for technical standards in digital reference. After all, libraries and other organizations are actively engaged in providing service to Internet users, and through e-mail, chat, and the Web seem to be meeting demand. Why then add a level of complexity in conforming to a technical specification? The answer lies more in the future than the present.

Today many of the digital reference services operating function locally, that is, within a given library or organization. They take questions from users via infrastructure they control and answer these questions according to internal rules, policies, and norms. This model has been sufficient given the current reported levels of questions. However new consortia and cooperative digital reference services are emerging (see Kresh, 2000; Kasowitz, et al. 2000; Virtual Reference Desk, 2002a). These services seek to bring improved service and efficiency in digital reference by using a broad distributed network of answer sources gaining advantages of time (expanding hours of digital reference service by shifting questions over time zones) and geography (moving questions to expertise located in remote libraries and organizations).

These consortia seek to answer the question of scalability (Lankes, 2000) by creating a wide pool of reference expertise.

It is in this environment of distributed but connected digital reference that standards become not simply possible, but necessary. Either the digital reference network/consortia will have to standardize at the product level (all using a common digital reference platform) or on a means of inter-application communication. The library world has always worked with the latter model, as has the Internet itself. Open standards that allow diverse applications to talk to each other have meant that libraries have taken advantage of an open market of vendors and software. In cataloging, for example, MARC has allowed multiple OPAC vendors to compete on features and interface, while allowing the library field as a whole to gain economics of scale (such as interlibrary loan and copy cataloging). Why should digital reference be different? By developing a common set of communication/exchange standards the digital library field can realize the benefits of forming large diverse consortia without being forced into a single product, or compromising local assets (programming expertise, application knowledge, etc.).

STANDARDS IN DIGITAL REFERENCE: AN OVERVIEW

While this chapter will explore the Question Interchange Profile (QuIP) in detail, it is only part of the standards picture in digital reference. It is important to give a more holistic picture of emerging standards in digital reference to best place QuIP and make the reader aware of other important areas that are emerging, or will emerge as the field matures. While QuIP is "first out of the gate" it will not be the last.

In April 2001, a two-day workshop was held by NISO in Washington, D.C., to consider the question of standardization in the digital reference arena (NISO, 2001). This meeting pulled together stakeholders in the digital reference community and beyond to consider the question of where standards were needed to facilitate the growth of digital reference. In particular, an increasing installation of software that was unable to interoperate was noted. The workshop brought together much of the standards development to that point, and identified "ripe" areas to pursue.

While to this point only a question transfer protocol (see QuIP Background) has been pursued, a picture emerged of a possible standards layer in digital reference. This section of the chapter describes aspects of that possible layer to put question transfer in perspective. The author assumes that later standards work will pursue other aspects of this proposed standards layer. It should also be noted that this scenario represents the author's picture of digital reference standards, not one formulated by the workshop or NISO.

The digital reference space can be seen as an abstract "space" consisting of a number of digital reference services. The author will refer to this diverse space as a "digital reference cloud"; just as the Internet can be seen as an IP cloud, the scale and scope of the digital reference cloud are also indeterminate as are the potential connections between services (see Figure 8–1). Each of the services in the cloud may be part of different industries (government, commercial, non-profit, etc.). They may also represent a variety of types within a given sector, such as public, academic, and special libraries. Some of these services may be in well-established partnerships or consortia, while other services will form a partnership[1] for a single question.

In order to facilitate the interoperability of these heterogeneous services several predetermined functionalities, or standards, need to be in place. The first is a way to identify potential partnership organizations. This identification would exchange such information as question scale (the number of questions that can be handled) and question scope (the content of questions to be answered). Other information might include a means of getting and giving questions (through e-mail, the Web, or some other means) and/or restrictions placed on incoming or outgoing questions (a price for answering questions, a deadline for generating an answer, etc.). The information about an organization needed to identify a service and create a partnership would be a service profile.

Profiles are already in use in the CDRS (Kresh, 2000) where the National Library of Canada, OCLC, and the Library of Congress have done extensive work on profiles and profile-base routing. Here CDRS members create a profile that is used in a central routing system. Questions are entered with appropriate metadata (topic of the question using LC Classification codes, for example) and then question metadata is compared against profiles of CDRS

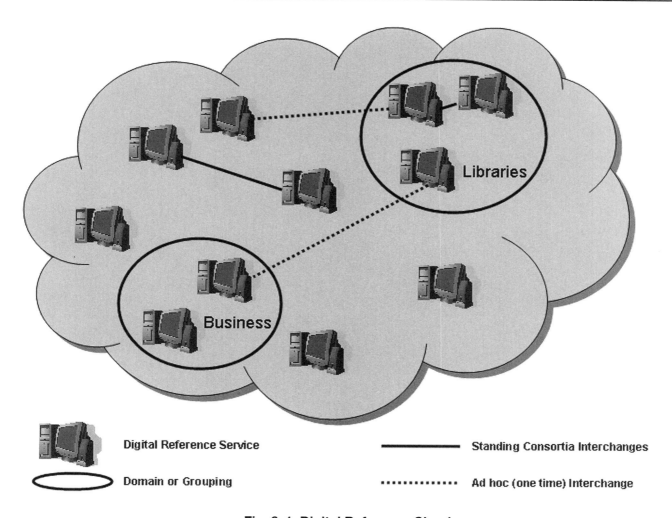

Digital Reference Service

Domain or Grouping

Standing Consortia Interchanges

Ad hoc (one time) Interchange

Fig. 8–1. Digital Reference Cloud

members and a service assignment is made. The next step in profiles would be to make a general digital reference profile that could be used in CDRS, as well as other digital reference systems, and/or for ad hoc partnership creation. One issue to be more fully addressed in profiles is that of resolution. Do you profile a service, an organization, a network, or an individual? Or, can a profile standard be created to handle all of these levels?

Another desirable standard in a networked reference environment relates to knowledge bases. Much of the current digital reference research and development involves the creation of knowledge bases, or a collection of previous questions with their corresponding answers. These knowledge bases vary from highly polished and selective (only the "best answers" get in) to comprehensive (all answers get in). While there is debate about the utility of such

systems (some feel such a knowledge base would be useful in answering frequently asked questions while others argue such systems have limited utility in intermediation, but a great deal of utility as a reference database outside the intermediation process) there is a general acceptance of knowledge bases as an important effort. Approaches to storing questions and answers in knowledge bases still remain diverse. There are questions of metadata associated with such information as well as of making these knowledge bases available for aggregation.

The issues in knowledge base creation and maintenance are manifold. Many of the complexities relate to the nebulous nature of knowledge. What do you do with changeable information (the name of the president of the United States, for example, or the height of Mount Everest), and the interpretative nature of answers (what is the answer to the question "what are the best books on raising children?"). These issues are matched in complexity with the issues of organization of information (should we use structured data such as the Dublin Core or MARC to organize this information, who will do the cataloging, what subject vocabularies shall we use, etc.). This is not to say that the creation of a usable knowledge base is impossible, it is done quite often, but rather that the aspects of knowledge bases that can be standardized (or the adoption of existing content standards for knowledge bases) is still a very open question.

The last identified area for standardization, and the focus of the remainder of this paper, is on question transfer protocols. That is, a means by which two or more services can exchange information (i.e., questions and/or answers). Currently such question hand-off is done ad hoc through existing tools like Web forms or e-mail. This makes moving such data laborious, often involving cutting and pasting to or from databases or e-mails. Creating a seamless means of interchange would greatly facilitate information sharing as well as a question economy.

QuIP BACKGROUND

The Question Interchange Profile (QuIP) was a concept first proposed in the Virtual Reference Desk's first White Paper (Lankes, 1998a) and research report on K-12 digital reference services (Lankes, 1998b). It was subsequently discussed in meetings sponsored by the Virtual Reference Desk (Virtual Reference Desk, 2002b) and AskA Consortium meetings. It was proposed as a means to distribute questions and answers among K-12 digital reference services (so-called AskA services). It has subsequently been extended as a generalized means of expressing discussion-like interchanges between one or more people or organizations.

At the heart of QuIP development has been the belief that reference interchanges can be both computational (that is able to be processed by software without human intervention) and extendable (into various domains for example) while retaining the value of human-to-human communication.

This chapter presents QuIP in the abstract. It is presented absent a specific protocol binding. It is envisioned that QuIP will be a two-part standard. The first part, presented here, is a metadata layer for the description of content being exchanged between two services. The second layer is that of a protocol that allows for more computational and complex exchange of data between two services. The QuIP metadata layer binds together profiles and content and provides human experts and/or digital reference services basic structures and description of what is being exchanged. This metadata could be exchanged in a variety of ways, from e-mailed XML files, to parsable text files, to Web page pointers. The protocol layer will define a set of services and functions allowing software to negotiate and control exchanges. The protocol layer may do little more than establish a connection between two services, pass data, and confirm that a question has been transferred. It may, however, evolve to handle more complex tasks such as recalling questions from a service, or determining the status of an in-process question. This protocol layer has only begun its development.

A final note: QuIP is a profile in that it sets definitions beyond a simple set of elements. Which elements are mandatory and repeatable, as well as predefined values for those elements may not work in all circumstances. Variations of these choices using the same base of elements would represent different profiles. Development was conducted in such a way as to minimize the need for multiple profiles, but it is not ruled out at this point.

QuIP FOUNDATIONS

The heart of QuIP is a thread. Digital reference exchanges are more than simply a question and an answer. These exchanges might go on over many interactions, with changing subjects and personnel. This concept of shifting, on-going dialogs is a thread. A simple thread can simply be a question, followed by an answer:

> User: How many senators are there in the Congress?
> Expert: One hundred, two from each state.

On the other hand, in the face of ambiguity, a thread may consist of several interactions:

> User: How many senators are there?
> Expert: In state government or in the federal government?
> User: The federal government.
> Expert: One hundred, two from each state.

Notice in this last example that questions (as in interrogative statements) can come from both users and experts. The difference, however, is that a user is asking a content-related question, while the expert is asking a clarifying question. These expert-based clarifying questions can be open-ended, or closed in nature. While much research has been done on the nature of an interchange between experts and users, we will simply conclude that questions can come from users or experts. Therefore a thread is NOT a series of questions and answers, but rather, more generically a series of events.

So a thread is a series of events. These events have several attributes. For example the event has content. That is, the question, or answer, or some other informative data. It also has a temporal indicator such as a date or time when it was sent, received, or acted upon. Each of these attributes also can have sub-elements. For example, the content of an event has the body of an answer, or question, but it also has a format that that text is expressed in, and a language that expresses it. For example, the content of the interchange may be an HTML file written in English such as:

```
<html>
<head><title>The Answer</title></head>
<h1>The answer is. . . . </h1>
<p>One hundred, two from each state.</p>
</body>
</html>
```

Since the author assumes that most of the processing and use of QuIP will be automated, this level of detail and metadata is seen as necessary. QuIP must be as specific and succinct as possible to allow for computational manipulation.

Other elements, attributes, and sub-elements will be fully explored in the next section. The purpose of this section is simply to lay the foundation concepts of QuIP. So while a thread may have one or more events, and events can have one or more temporal indicators, the idea of QuIP being hierarchical is important here.

Another important concept is that some elements of QuIP are mandatory, repeatable, and some attributes of these elements are pre-defined and extensible. Let's take those one at a time.

- Elements in QuIP are either mandatory, conditional, or optional: QuIP must have (in fact is)

a thread. A thread must have one or more events. It wouldn't make sense to have a thread with zero events. For this reason, the thread element and event sub-element are mandatory (threads have events, therefore events are sub-elements in that they are subordinate to a thread). However an event may or may not have restrictions (so restrictions are optional).

- Elements in QuIP are either repeatable or not: You can only have one thread . . . it is the fundamental unit in QuIP; however, a thread can have multiple events (in fact the simplest example of a thread would have two events: an originating question and an answer).

- Elements in QuIP can have pre-defined values: In some cases there is no limit to the values an element can contain (the body of an interchange for example is as varied as questions and answers being exchanged). In some cases, however, there is an established range of values an element can take. These ranges can be relatively small and controlled like the state of an event (it can have one of five values: new, assigned, answered, sent, closed). Ranges can also be expansive, but controlled like the language of an interchange, which can be any of the languages listed in RFC 1766.[2]

- Elements and attributes can be extensible: In order to make QuIP as accommodating of existing practice and software, key elements of QuIP are extensible. That is to say, QuIP has a placeholder, where other metadata standards and definitions can be used. For example, it is anticipated that digital reference services will use a variety of subject schema and thesauri. Rather than simply picking one, QuIP allows a service to specify a vocabulary to use, and the language of that vocabulary, and a place to look up that vocabulary. This means that a service can use any subjects they wish, so long as they indicate which one they are using, and how a computer can make sense of those terms.

Another foundation of QuIP is that it is process oriented. QuIP is designed to get data from one service to another. It is this action of exchange that drives QuIP, not the actual content of the exchange. This means that QuIP-formatted threads are not seen as fully formed document-like objects. While QuIP could be used as an internal file structure for digital

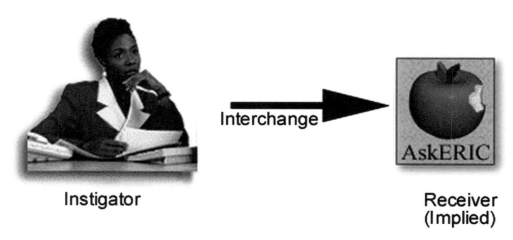

Instigator   Receiver
                                              (Implied)

Fig. 8–2. A Simple Thread Consisting of One Event Initiated by an Entity

reference services, it is assumed that most of the time services will parse apart QuIP data and transform it into some other format internal to a service (such as a relational database). This assumption also influences the predicative nature of QuIP—that is, the reason we need QuIP and structured definitions (rather than simply throwing e-mail from service to service) is that the format of the data is known in advance, and programs can be written to manipulate the data without human intervention. This goes back to the whole concept of metadata, and so the author will spend no more time on it.

Another fundamental tenet of QuIP is that it acts as a sort of metadata binder. It is a set of metadata that can point to at least two other first class objects (sets of standardized metadata controlled outside of QuIP). The first object QuIP points to is a profile. As described previously, a profile is a rich set of structured data that identifies and describes a digital reference service or individual. While QuIP will most likely contain a "fall-back" limited profile itself, the preferred method will be to use unique resource identifiers (URIs) to point to a full profile somewhere on the network, or elsewhere in the message being exchanged. This way, QuIP itself will not pass redundant data with each event as well as allowing ongoing parallel QuIP and profile development. The second object QuIP will point to is a content object. This object can be a binary file or textual data. For example QuIP may point to an audio file (MP3) used by one service or text from an e-mail exchange. Using this pointer approach QuIP does not constrain digital reference consortia in what they can

pass between its members, allowing consortia to create sophisticated ways to prevent the transference or duplication of large binary files (so one service in a consortia may simply pass a URI or URL to a large audio file rather than the whole thing).

Figure 8–3 shows how a more complex thread is made up of multiple instigators and multiple interchanges (the arrows). Note that the receiver in one case can become the instigator in another. Also note that while multiple instigators are involved, this is all one thread.

Two final concepts are key before entering a full element listing. One is the concept of identification and the other is the implicit dependency on repositories. In order to manipulate QuIP data computationally, unique identification of data is mandatory. Identification in QuIP is centered on QuIP Unique Identifiers (QUID). A QUID is composed of two elements. The first is a QuIP_Registry_ID. This ID is unique to a given digital reference service. So a service like AskERIC might be given a registry ID of 'ASKE.' The Local_ID is a number that is assigned by, and unique within, a digital reference service like 0000001. So a QUID in this case might be ASKE-0000001. This number will follow a thread no matter how many services may handle or hand off a thread. With a QUID, one can uniquely identify an interchange within a thread by a combination of a QUID and the sequence information associated with a given interchange (so the first interchange from the example thread might be ASKE-0000001.1 and the second interchange would be ASKE-0000001.2 and so on).

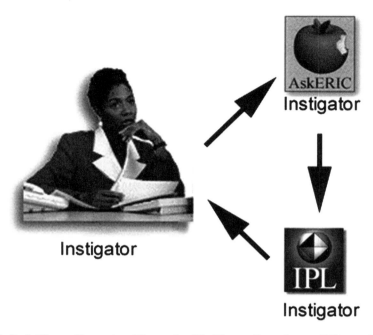

Fig. 8–3. A More Complex Thread with Three Events and Three Associated Profiles

QuIP ELEMENTS

The following is a list of elements with a definition, example (if applicable), restrictions (where a value or format is required), associated sub-elements, and the occurrence of the element. Occurrence designates whether an element is mandatory and/or repeatable. There are four possible values:

1. ZERO or ONE: The element is optional, but if present only one value is allowed.
2. ONE: The element is mandatory and only one value is allowed (non-repeatable).
3. ZERO or MORE: The element is optional and repeatable.
4. ONE or MORE: The element is mandatory and repeatable.

Obviously any sub-element's occurrence is dependent on its parent element.

PROGRESS WITH QuIP DEVELOPMENT

This chapter represents the third iteration of QuIP. The first came out of research in K-12 digital reference services and constituted an overarching metadata standard for K-12 AskA services. The intention was not merely to exchange questions, but also profiles and even internal process schemes. The second iteration was developed as a much streamlined metadata standard with an associated XML binding. This, the third iteration, is a result of a community development effort, including workshops held at Syracuse University and the Library of Congress.

Current efforts are mapping the current QuIP standard to real data, specifically question/answer pairs and other more elaborate threads from the AskERIC service's archive. This initial coding of questions will seek to identify gaps in elements and semantics. This coding will then be expanded to other services including archives at the Internet Public Library and the National Library of Canada. Once initial coding has been completed and any necessary adjustments have been made to the standard, software will be created to generate QuIP data, exchange QuIP content, and validate the exchange.

FUTURE DEVELOPMENTS

There are two future developments of note. The first is the development of a protocol layer for QuIP and the second is the announcement of NISO Standards Committee AZ. As mentioned previously, QuIP has two parts: a metadata schema and a protocol. The protocol will allow for computer-to-computer

Table 8–1
QuIP Elements

Element			Occurrence	Semantics
Thread			ONE	A series of interchanges based on a single information need of a user
	QUID		ONE	URI for the thread
		Service ID	ONE	URI for the service
		Local ID	ONE	Local designation for the thread
	Profile		ONE or MORE	First-class object with details on agent involved in manipulating thread
		PID	ONE	URI for a service profile
		P_Content	ONE	The profile being interchanged
	Event		ONE or MORE	A single interchange or state transition in a larger thread
		State	ONE	Type of manipulation of a thread
		Sequence	ONE	Ordinal place of this event in the larger thread
		Content	ZERO or MORE	First-class object with information being transmitted from one state to another
		Format	ZERO or ONE	MIME encoding of the content
		Language	ZERO or ONE	The language(s) of the intellectual content of the resource
		Body	ZERO or ONE	Binary information that is exchanged
		Subject	ZERO or MORE	Topical indicator of the content
		PID	ONE	Designation of which profile instigated this event
		Temporal_Indicator	ZERO or ONE	Indication of time and/or date in which state transition occurred
		Restriction	ZERO or MORE	Data used to control access to the event

transactions such as handing off questions, and other possible services like status querying. While initial discussions have looked at a series of functions for this layer, and possible architectural considerations (such as the use of SOAP), this work is only just beginning.

Much of this protocol work has emerged from the participation of the National Information Standards Organization (NISO). A proposal for creation of a QuIP standards process was put forth to NISO. This proposal resulted in the NetRef workshop. This workshop resulted in a series of possible standards efforts (profile, knowledgebase entries, etc.), but with a recommendation that work on a Question Transfer Protocol commence. A series of proposals and task statements have resulted, and in January NISO announced the creation of Standards Committee AZ to create a question interchange protocol. The model presented in this chapter, with a metadata layer and protocol layer, is represented in these task statements. It is assumed that QuIP development will fold into the NISO efforts.

CONCLUSION

The Question Interchange Profile is an emerging standard in building digital reference networks and linking disparate digital reference services. While there is much work still to be done in bringing the standard to completion, this work will progress quickly. Such a standard is essential if the digital reference arena is to grow. Already the AskA and library domain are calling for means of inter-operability.

There has been some resistance in the reference community to standards (Dig_Ref, 2002). While much of this resistance has centered on the more qualitative standards (Lankes et al., 2001) some have seen standards of any sort as an unnecessary complexity in the human-centered reference process. The author firmly believes that technical standards, in conjunction with quality standards, are essential for expanding digital reference and integrating it into the larger domains of libraries and customer service. Further, the author firmly believes that such standards processes should not be "left to technical services," but rather should include a large involvement from reference librarians and more broadly, the question answering community. Only with front-line knowledge can any standard hope to find wide and useful adoption. Further, only with well-established and understood technical standards can the digital reference community engage software producers and the technical community to help improve the practice of digital reference, and ultimately reference as a whole.

ENDNOTES

1. For this paper a partnership is defined simply as two digital reference services exchanging information for the purposes of answering a question.
2. See: http://rfc.asuka.net/rfc/rfc1766.html

REFERENCES

Dig_Ref. 2002. Listserv Archives [Online]. Available: http://groups.yahoo.com/group/dig_ref/ [2002, May 24] (in particular note the thread on "Standards for digital reference services?").

Kasowitz, A., B. Bennett, and R. D. Lankes. 2000. "Quality Standards for Digital Reference Consortia." *Reference and User Services Quarterly* 39, no. 4.

Kresh, D. 2000. *Offering High Quality Reference Service on the Web* [Online]. Available: www.dlib.org/dlib/june00/kresh/06kresh.html [2002, May 24].

Lankes, R. D., C. McClure, and M. Gross. 2001. Assessing Quality in Digital Reference Services. In *2001 Proceedings of the 64th Annual Meeting (Vol. 38)*. Silver Spring, Md.: The American Society for Information Science.

Lankes, R. D. 2000. The Foundations of Digital Reference. In *Digital Reference: Models for the New Millennium*, R. David Lankes, J. Collins, and A. S. Kasowitz, eds. New York: Neal-Schuman.

Lankes, R. D. 1998a. *The Virtual Reference Desk: Building a Network of Expertise for America's Schools*. White Paper for the Virtual Reference Desk. Syracuse, N.Y.: ERIC Clearinghouse on Information.

Lankes, R. D. 1998b. Building & Maintaining Internet Information Services: K-12 Digital Reference Services. ERIC Clearinghouse on Information & Technology; Syracuse, N.Y.

NISO. 2001. *NISO Workshop on Networked Reference Services* [Online]. Available: www.niso.org/news/events_workshops/netref.html [2002, May 24].

Virtual Reference Desk. 2002a. Part 5: Collaborative Reference Efforts. Part of the Electronic Proceedings of the 3rd Annual Virtual Reference Desk Conference [Online]. Available: www.vrd.org/conferences/VRD2001/proceedings/index.shtml#5 [2002, May 24].

Virtual Reference Desk. 2002b. The Virtual Reference Desk [Online]. Available: www.vrd.org [2002, May 24].

Chapter 9

Implementing KnowItNow24X7.net in 90 Days—or Bust!

Bob Carterette and Sari Feldman

OVERVIEW

Cleveland Public Library and the CLEVNET consortium created and launched a live Web reference service in less than 90 working days using project committees that provided input without slowing the project timeline. The methodology used to get the project off the ground, software and technical considerations, project strategy, and a description of finances is provided in this case study of a fast-tracked, 24X7 service.

INTRODUCTION

Cleveland Public Library (CPL) with its main library holdings of more than 10.5 million volumes, periodicals, photographs, microforms, and audio-visual materials has the most significant public research collection in northeast Ohio. The access to those collections and subject specialties is further increased through 28 branches city-wide and the 30 other libraries in the CLEVNET Consortium that share a catalog with Cleveland Public Library. That access grows exponentially through the communication tools of telephone, fax, e-mail, and the World Wide Web. But in fact most would put access through the Web first. The number of times people connect to CPL through remote access is 1.4 times the number of people who walk through the doors of all CPL main library and branches plus telephone reference questions answered. These facts and other dramatic changes in the library environment were strong determinants in our 2001 customer services initiatives.

While one picture of the customer was the individual visiting a library for professional reference expertise and library materials there was also interest in reaching the "individualistic or egalitarian user" (Wilson, 2000: 389), individuals who may use the Internet on their own but may also desire some support in navigating the Internet. Wilson concludes that reference service needs to provide "information about information" (2000: 389), to educate users "to access and evaluate the validity of information sources" (2000: 389), and to have reference staff function in clarifying user information needs. Taking the three key service elements to the future, CPL and the CLEVNET Consortium seized the opportunity to explore a digital or virtual reference service.

The CLEVNET consortium began in 1982 when the Cleveland Heights-University Heights Library asked to share in the benefits of Cleveland Public Library's automation system. Since that time CLEVNET under the leadership of CPL has grown to include 30 library systems in nine counties throughout Northern Ohio. CLEVNET now represents a robust resource sharing system serving 19 percent of Ohio's population. With combined holdings of over 2.6 million titles and over 10 million items, and access to a wealth of electronic databases, the CLEVNET system is one of the largest public library automation systems in the world. A users group established in 2000 led the way for increased input into initiatives of CPL on behalf of the consortium. After one CLEVNET library contracted for Web-based reference service with NOLA (previously the Northeastern Ohio Library Association) the CLEVNET users group began a drive to create its own. Never to be outdone, the goal was full service, 24 hours, and seven days a week, right from the launch.

GETTING OFF THE GROUND

A handful of overarching principles guided the planning and implementation process: (1) rapid development; (2) comprehensiveness of service; (3) organizational "buy in"; and (4) low administrative overhead. There was little in the way of literature, research, or experience from other public libraries providing live Web reference to help in the development of this project.

Rapid Development

Rapid development was served by first establishing a sparse model describing the service: it would be available 24X7; it would exploit the strengths of CPL's subject specialties; and it would build on quality standards as identified by Kasowitz and others. (Kasowitz, et al., 2000) A highly tentative, but aggressive timeline was then constructed with major milestones noted. Six workgroups were formed to work in parallel: (1) Agency Coordination, to select and coordinate the libraries staffing the service; (2) Service Guidelines and Standards, to establish broad guidelines for quality service; (3) Implementation, to manage the mechanics of vendor relations and purchasing, and to track progress against the timetable; (4) Training, to plan and organize training for the service providers; (5) Evaluation, to determine desirable measurements and monitor quality; and (6) an Executive workgroup, comprised of the facilitators of each of the other five workgroups and five administrators of CLEVNET libraries, to coordinate communication, provide overall administrative guidance, and to handle finance and marketing. The workgroups were instructed to determine and to do only what was needed to launch the service, without the burden of anticipating every possible problem or question.

Comprehensiveness of Service

To insure comprehensive coverage, the base model included plans to staff 24X7 service. It also included the guiding principles that the service would function as a consortium project, funded by all CLEVNET libraries for the benefit of all residents of their service areas, but the virtual reference desks would be staffed by selected institutions: all for one, one for all. KnowItNow would not only be available to remote users, but also serve as a backup service for branches and smaller libraries. Though not addressed in the initial model, comprehensiveness of service was an essential principle, with the intent that the librarian would be empowered to provide the best, quickest, most accurate, and authoritative answer, whether from the Internet, subscription databases, or the print collection.

Organizational Buy In

Involving staff from Cleveland Public Library's main library, and branches and outreach services with staff from other CLEVNET libraries, and aiming at a service comprehensive in scope and coverage resulted in immediate "buy in." Additionally, the Training workgroup arranged general orientations, formal training, and a week of testing by staff, involving providers and non-providers throughout the consortium, increasing interest and developing real excitement.

Low Administrative Overhead

With small, focused groups handling specific organizational and implementation issues, and the funding sourced in the CLEVNET budget, overhead was kept low. Most planning activities were handled through e-mail, with general information shared on a Web site established for the project.

The first planning meeting was on February 2, 2001. The service launched on June 11, 2001. By the end of August, 3,669 questions had been handled.

Service Schedule

The Executive Committee considered the work of all committees and determined the schedule handled using the following service pattern:

Monday through Saturday, 9:00 a.m. – 5:30 p.m.: Main library departments of General Reference, Business, Science and Technology, and Social Sciences, with CLEVNET backup for staffing problems. In addition the Cleveland Law Library (a CLEVNET member since 1985) would be a secondary provider Monday through Friday from 9:00 a.m. – 5:00 p.m. accepting referrals of legal questions from the four CPL departments. At 5:30 p.m. until 8:30 p.m., ten selected CLEVNET libraries provide the service. Two libraries share each weeknight including Friday. From 8:30 p.m. until 9 a.m. Monday through Friday, 5:30 p.m. Saturday until 1:00 p.m. Sunday, and 5:00 p.m. Sunday until 9:00 a.m. Monday, LSSI call center fields questions with professional librarians. Some adjustment occurs during summer hours.

TECHNICAL AND SOFTWARE CONSIDERATIONS

A demonstration presented by Steve Coffman of LSSI to the CLEVNET users group and CPL staff determined that the eGain/LSSI software was the first choice for this service. It offered a decentralized approach to providing service, the opportunity for co-browsing, comfortable chat protocols, and enough personalization for our library consortium. In addition the staff at LSSI are flexible, good communicators, and open to recommendations from the field.

The goal of making print information from the print collection easily available for inclusion in a Web-based system led to the location of software supporting scanning and delivery of the scanned document. Adobe Capture is used and also includes the ability to create an automated workflow. A page or pages are scanned, very much like making a photocopy, and the software "recognizes" layout and fonts, converts the document to PDF, and then can either save the finished product to the desktop or other directory, or immediately e-mail the document as an attachment. Currently about ten percent of patron queries are being answered with a page or two scanned from the print collection. Only portions of a given work are scanned with a result identical to photocopying, and can be used only for private study, scholarship, or research.

From the beginning it was assumed that unanticipated technical issues would emerge. To simplify troubleshooting we purchased all new equipment for the KnowItNow service. This insured that the workstations involved were using the same BIOS and operating system (Windows 2000); had the same computing resources (866 MHz, 128 MB RAM, 15GB hard drive); and the same software (Microsoft IE 5.5, Adobe Capture), configured the same way. Besides simplifying technical implementation, the new KnowItNow workstations, each equipped with a Hewlett Packard Scanjet 6250C, produced a feeling of *esprit de corps* among provider librarians. They were not only told they were taking on a pioneering project, they were also properly equipped

and connected with high-speed lines to the Internet.

No such control is possible over the user's equipment or Internet connection. The eGain/LSSI software uses a combination of Java, JavaScript, and server-side CGI to deliver services. Also, LSSI's servers mediate the communication between the librarian and the end user. This presents a complex system for troubleshooting technical problems experienced by users: Web browsers that freeze or crash, PCs that "freeze up," etc. Results of a survey of randomly selected transcripts indicate that failed calls may be as high as three to five percent of the total. Reasons for this may range from browser version or damaged installations to unreliable Internet connections or unidentified bugs on the vendor's end.

Staff and patron technical knowledge, skills, and expectations also complicate the picture. Bringing a kind of service that in many instances has been very personal out on to the public byways of the Internet, with unreliable connectivity, unruly Web pages, and mysterious plug-ins creates an environment in which no technical question can be easily answered, but an easy and direct answer is required.

Another area requiring additional technical development is sharing information from subscription databases. While the eGain/LSSI software includes a facility for doing so, it is currently far from seamless for the librarian.

LSSI has been very responsive to user suggestions. A forthcoming upgrade to the software incorporates features to streamline handling multiple calls; to share seamlessly pages from subscription databases; to manage unexpected Web page behavior cleanly; and to improve overall performance. CLEVNET is also upgrading its connectivity to the Internet to increase bandwidth. These refinements promise to resolve many of the technical issues that have appeared.

PROJECT STRATEGY

Libraries often attribute project success to careful planning and effective marketing. The planning for KnowItNow was precise but neither long range or strategic. Marketing brought extraordinary media attention, and probably some users were attracted through the brochures and newsletter. A news conference was held and over 150 news releases sent to local and professional media outlets. Approximately

5,000 brochures were distributed throughout the Greater Cleveland community. The CPL newsletter, "Speaking Volumes," featured a front-page story on KnowItNow and was mailed to over 10,000 residents with another 7,000 distributed from libraries, bookstores, etc. The major Cleveland newspaper ran a front-page story and an AP reporter pitched it to a number of publications including CNN and National Public Radio. Our own Web users were also a core patron group for KnowItNow. However, the success of KnowItNow is attributed to its quick integration into the fabric of the Cleveland Public Library culture and its immediate importance as a critical library service. These success factors are a result of the project's clear link to core values, the project participants' core competencies, leadership, confidence in the delivery system, consistent awareness of the customer's perspective, and the capacity to act.

Core Values

KnowItNow is a project of the CLEVNET consortium, which functions under the leadership of the Cleveland Public Library. This project speaks directly to many of the core institutional values of Cleveland Public Library (CPL). These basic values of access, information services, and cutting edge automation services are beliefs held by staff and the community. Commitment to access dates back to 1890 when CPL introduced open shelves. KnowItNow provides increased access for Web users and the opportunity for non-web users to enter a supportive environment while learning about the Web. Another core value of the system is the main library's role in public research and subject specialization. Despite the size of the city, CPL is among the largest public library research institutions in the country. KnowItNow was designed to take advantage of the expertise of librarians and the depth of the collections. By using high-speed scanners and Adobe Capture software, providers send PDF files of materials not restricted by copyright. Providers also promote the more than one million dollars worth of electronic database subscriptions of CLEVNET and teach the best of the Web. The third core value that directly impacted the success of KnowItNow is the effort to be at the cutting edge of automated services. Examples of this are seen in the creation of the CLEVNET consortium in 1982, the introduction of an online catalog in 1980, the dedication to providing access to networked information resources starting in 1989, the introduc-

tion of the Cleveland Public Electronic Library in 1993, and the introduction of the CPL Web site in 1995. Today the customer service enhancements introduced by e-business are important for the growth and development of the library's remote users.

Core Competencies

Core competencies were both present prior to the project and part of an on-going learning program. The basic talents and skills of question negotiation and reference work entered a changed environment that resulted in a higher level of accountability. Most staff were up to the challenge and in fact welcomed the change from "cyber-hostess," a self-deprecating term coined by librarians tired of teaching about chat rooms and e-mail, to a desire to be the best search engine on the Web. The investment in training presented by LSSI and peer training developed by the project training committee made being a provider of the KnowItNow service attractive to staff at Cleveland Public Library and CLEVNET libraries. It proved that it wasn't the length of training but the desire to be trained that made the difference. Staff viewed themselves as pioneers blazing a new cyber-trail and understood that additional training would be provided as needed.

There was some tension as the service went live to the public. Staff also expressed enthusiasm and an increased spirit of collaboration as they worked together to answer questions. Aspects of the live Web reference service have been more stressful. The staff members are encouraged to take the time to be complete in their answers and to use all available resources—however, the patron may be pushing for an immediate response. While there are no time guidelines, after about 15 minutes the staff member may feel the question is too complex to complete and ask for an e-mail address or phone number to follow up. The high expectations from patrons and the accessibility of KnowItNow transcripts increase the staff accountability.

Staff at the main library are doing other work while they wait for a bell announcing a question. During the day or busiest hours staff may be doing book selection, e-mail reference, interlibrary loan, or other computer tasks and the question load has been manageable. The smaller provider libraries covering the evening hours usually have their reference librarian "multitasking" and answering the questions of walk-in, telephone, and Web patrons. Again, the low volume, about two questions per evening per provider, has actually left the evening staff hungry for more.

Leadership

CPL leadership has changed during the past two and a half years. Despite this transition there was a clear vision that the purpose of new technologies was to provide enhanced customer service. Under the leadership of the current library director, Andrew Venable, Jr., the Automation Services Department has seen an increase of more than three full-time technicians and a full-time Web coordinator. There was support for redesigning the entire Web page and architecture that resulted in ease of access and continuous updating. The Greater Access Library card, which functions at CLEVNET libraries and at the Cuyahoga County Public Library, the first formal cooperative venture, was the brainchild of the director. Director Venable's leadership also resulted in the formation of the CLEVNET users group to prioritize projects and act as a clearinghouse for user needs.

Confidence

CPL and the CLEVNET Consortium members have confidence in the Automation Services Department and their ability to deliver projects in a timely and effective manner. the Automation Services Department has a diversified staff deployed for Web-based enhancements, training, technical assistance, and networking needs. The Automation staff is also focused on the customer service needs of the library and is able to collaborate with public service staff. The KnowItNow project model created joint committees with clear responsibilities and completion dates. This further contributed to the understanding and confidence in the delivery system.

Administrative and management responsibilities continue to be handled by a small committee of provider libraries from the CLEVNET Consortium and Automation Services.

Customer Perspective

The customer perspective was consistently at the forefront of this project. Many of the provider libraries had policy and practice that guided their own reference service. For this project everyone agreed that they could live without limitations or service rules. The customer needs would come first. The executive committee urged the provider libraries to be risk takers and to accept a kind of anarchy that would exist in such an original service. The agreed-upon goal was quality service and customer satisfaction and the standard restrictions of either walk-in or telephone reference would not be applied during the early stages of KnowItNow. It was the "just do it" mentality that made the project all the more exciting and gratifying to the provider libraries. The Web had already fostered new customer service enhancements such as CLEVNET's NetNotice. NetNotice subscribers receive weekly e-mails providing their up-to-date account and borrowing information and can renew materials with two clicks. Patrons can also subscribe to receive e-mail about programs on topics or at locations of their choice. The count of Web renewals is now rivaling circulation at CPL's busiest branch.

Capacity to Act

A live Web reference service was a high priority of CLEVNET and helped to spur the project into action. CLEVNET provides a capacity to act through the financial resources dedicated for automation services and through the collective energy and talents of the members. Designing KnowItNow as a 24X7 service required participation from Cleveland Public Library and ten other libraries with strong reference staff and collections. An Associated Press reporter, The Cleveland Plain Dealer, and even the American Library Association were surprised to discover that CLEVNET with Cleveland Public Library were first with live Web reference, 24 hours, and 7 days a week. However, based on the unique developments of CLEVNET and Automation Services, and the customer service philosophy that is critical to its project development, KnowItNow is probably just the next step in an evolutionary process.

FINANCES

While the Cleveland Public Library had a sincere desire to launch a live Web reference service without the collaboration and financial resources of the CLEVNET Consortium it would have been almost impossible to fast-track this project. As previously discussed in this chapter, the Consortium was represented by a group of people committed to an aggressive timetable. All costs are shared based among CLEVNET libraries through a cost recovery model based on the number of work stations, circulation statistics, and inventory statistics per library developed by Price Waterhouse in 1986. Cleveland Public Library's share is 33.68 percent.

The following is a summary of the costs associated with KnowItNow:

LSSI seats (5 seats per year)	$30,000
LSSI installation and training	8,000
LSSI service 8:30 p.m. to 9 a.m. (estimate)	14,400
HP Scan Jet 6350cxi scanners (15@ $479)	7,185
PC Workstations (15 @ $1,103)	16,545
Adobe Capture licenses (15 @ $606)	9,090
KnowItNow Web site development	7,000
Marketing and public relations (estimate)	5,000
Average annual staff costs (estimate)	40,000
Total	**$137,220**

While expenses for hardware, software, and LSSI training were fixed, costs for overnight service, marketing, and staffing are estimates. It is anticipated that the services will grow and become a standard in providing reference to the general pubic in our service area. However, at this time the average number of questions over a 24–hour period is 46. (This is based on the total number June 11–September 5 divided by the number of days.) At no time is staff solely dedicated to the KnowItNow service although they are expected to be poised and ready when the computer alerts them to a question. The cost for overnight service is based on 1,200 questions per year. We expect to exceed that before June 2002. Marketing and public relations consisted of a range of efforts from brochures, designed and printed in-house, to an extensive news release program including a news conference, outsourced to a local public relations firm.

HomeworkNow, a second wave of KnowItNow to direct students to the service, was launched with no additional staffing. However, as we develop a second marketing campaign directed to the school age user group and teachers we may see a significant increase in evening and overnight traffic. This could result in additional marketing, hardware, software, and staffing costs. HomeworkNow, introduced on September 4, has an initial question load that is easily absorbed by the current staff.

In October 2001 CPL piloted a program with MetroHealth Systems, our county hospital, to provide quality health information in the greater Cleveland area with the focus on interactive health content and live medical advice available via the World Wide Web. Nurses, already answering phone questions 24X7, were trained to use the software and began backing up librarians on health questions as the Cleveland Law Library backs up legal questions. The nurses proved to be excellent health information providers and love working with the public via the Web. We went public with this new service on February 4, 2002. This project should reach an entirely new client group for both the libraries and MetroHealth Systems.

Funding

A project modeled on the design of KnowItNow would be an excellent choice for outside funding. Foundations are often interested in new concepts and demonstration projects. Since one of the primary purposes of online Web reference is to increase the public's understanding of the Internet and to improve the quality of the Internet resources the public uses for information, a project of this scope is easily linked to current research on the "Digital Divide." In particular the "Final Report of the Digital Opportunity Initiative" (Markle Foundation, 2001) stresses that it is not access but education that divides Internet users. The availability of extensive data and transcripts provides both quantitative and qualitative evaluation tools that are essential to a successful proposal. A library can also set fixed project costs and specifically identify which operational costs can be absorbed in the existing budget.

Beyond grant seeking from community foundations, libraries should appeal to corporate foundations or for business marketing dollars. Few businesses have the Web traffic of a public library, yet many small companies, banks, and corporations are interested in e-commerce. A banner ad recognizing the support of one or more businesses is an attractive exchange for corporate dollars.

Foundations and corporations rarely want to make a long-term commitment to any project regardless of its value to the community or its potential. An appealing proposal should offer a financial plan that balances the initial costs of the project between the library and the business and ultimately demonstrates how the library will pay for the service through its operating budget.

A Web reference project also makes sense as a collaborative venture for groups of libraries. By sharing the costs and the activity no individual library

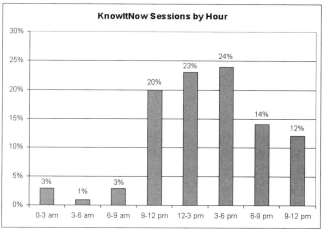

Fig. 9–1

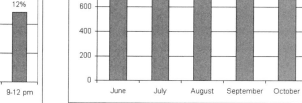

Fig. 9–2

feels an extensive financial burden or an additional strain on staff. These library partners can be near or remote and the same type of library or a mix of public, academic, and special. The Web reference service offers the greatest potential for creativity and new service models as demonstrated by our partnership with MetroHealth Systems.

CONCLUSION

The future of live Web-based reference service may be ultimately intertwined with the future of public library reference services. Unless library services can distinguish themselves from the other "search engines" available on the Internet the public will not ultimately choose the library sites over the commercial presence. Speed of service is one of the major considerations and staff, weighing the options of print vs. electronic databases vs. Internet sources, may not hold the attention of the autonomous "point and click" surfer. Promotion on the quality indicators of authoritative, instructive, non-commercial, reliable, and personal service may lure users to KnowItNow. Partnerships with specialized information providers such as the Cleveland Law Library and MetroHealth Systems for information referral services will also sharpen the image of KnowItNow.

As Figures 9–1 and 9–2 show, CLEVNET is off to a good start. From the inception on June 11, 2001, through the end of the year, business was steady and in sufficient quantity to justify the existence of the service. Furthermore, analysis by the time of day suggests one of the primary considerations is

convenience. Eighty-one percent of the KnowItNow sessions occurred during the libraries' regular business hours, indicating that extending hours is less important than extending reach—being available when and where service is needed.

CPL is a contributing member for the Assessing Quality in Digital Reference Study being conducted by Drs. Charles McClure and David Lankes. This project should provide some national benchmarks and best practices to evaluate existing and new services. Public libraries must seize this opportunity to say that not all services are created equal. Transcripts of interactions and other data easily captured by the software should enable libraries to fully assess the value and success of the service that may someday exceed both the in-person and telephone reference numbers. CPL and the CLEVNET consortium welcome the opportunity and are striving towards those standards of excellence.

REFERENCES

Kasowitz, Abby, Blythe Bennett, and R. David Lankes. 2000. "Quality Standards for Digital Reference Consortia." *Reference & User Services Quarterly* 39, no.4 (Summer): 355–363.

Markle Foundation. 2001. *Creating a Development Dynamic: Final Report of the Digital Opportunity Initiative* [Online]. Available: www.markle.org [2002, May 24].

Wilson, Myoung C. 2000. "Evolution or Entropy?: Changing Reference/Users Culture and the Future of Reference Librarians." *Reference & User Services Quarterly* 39, no.4 (Summer): 387–390.

APPENDIX I

Service Guidelines and Standards – KnowItNow Agreement

Classification of staff providing service:

In general, staff assigned to this service should possess the following: expertise, experience, and a strong interest in providing this type of reference assistance.

It is recommended that professional librarians with at least one year's relevant experience or library assistants with at least three years of relevant experience perform the reference function connected with this service. Library assistants must possess a bachelor's degree and should perform this work under the supervision of professional librarians.

Definition of services provided:

The service is designed to provide reference assistance to users requesting factual answers to brief questions or to users seeking general research guidance.

Definition of service area:

The service will be provided for the communities served by the CLEVNET consortium.

Standards to Maintain Quality of Service:

Transcripts generated by the "live" reference service will be made available to each CLEVNET library that has been assigned to provide this service. Participating libraries will be responsible for reviewing their own transcripts. In addition, Cleveland Public Library will conduct a periodic review of all transcripts. Representatives from participating institutions will meet at least twice a year to determine whether the service is meeting expectations.

Guidelines for Customer Service—Staff assigned to this service should:

Respond immediately to all inquiries.

Follow the principles of good business etiquette and "Netiquette."

Use clear language and correct grammar and spelling. Avoid the use of jargon or acronyms and abbreviations.

Clarify the question and identify the user characteristics in order to insure that responses are appropriate for the age and experience level of the user.

Use authoritative sources.

For additional guidance, staff should consult the "Guidelines for Behavioral Performance of Reference and Information Services Professionals," a publication of the Reference and User Services Association of the American Library Association. These guidelines are available on the Web at the following URL: www.ala.org/rusa/stnd_behavior. html.

Chapter 10

Moving from Virtual to Cooperative Reference Service Models

Lorraine Normore and Paula Rumbaugh

OVERVIEW

The recent move for libraries to provide reference service from their own Web sites has opened the door for a "virtual presence" for reference on the Internet. Going beyond providing virtual access to the local library or local library system, some projects, like the Library of Congress's Collaborative Digital Reference Service (CDRS), extend shared reference services across geographic and political boundaries. In these developments, we see a shift from "virtual" to "cooperative" reference. An analysis of the issues involved in cooperative reference brings to the fore a number of factors not present or less of a concern in the more locally controlled virtual reference. This paper will discuss these issues in the context of OCLC's activities relating to the definition and implementation of a cooperative reference service.

DEFINITIONS

The field of digital reference has expanded rapidly. Along with the growth in the number of practitioners has come a growth in the number of names given to similar services. Some of these definitions are related to physical characteristics of the service: We have a set of services that use the labels "virtual," "digital," "electronic," and "online" to represent the idea that this reference service is delivered when the question asker and question answerer are not in the same physical location. The terms "live," "real-time," and "chat" imply that the service is synchronous—that there will be some "conversation-like" interchanges between asker and answerer. The term "24/7" tells us that someone, somewhere could pick up the answerer's question at any time, that the service is not limited to the hours the local library itself is open.

Other definitions are related to the characteristics of the process of answering the question. The use of "librarian" or "expert" may suggest that librarians or people with specialized knowledge answer questions. This distinction has been important historically: both the AskA Consortium and many of the early dot-com "ask an expert" services were staffed by non-librarians. In some cases, the expertise was monitored by the service (e.g., the AskA Consortium), in others, expertise was self-declared. The use of "cooperative," "collaborative," or "networked" suggests that the answering process may be shared among a number of librarians and other experts in diverse locations. Questions can be routed from their originating institution to other institutions that have agreed to work together to answer questions from all participating institution's patrons.

In this chapter, we will use the term "virtual reference" to refer to more locally-based services and "cooperative reference" to refer to services that go beyond geopolitical boundaries, connecting local services and building a system for the common good of all the members. We will use "digital reference" to include both types of services.

OCLC AND DIGITAL REFERENCE

In many ways, virtual reference is not all that new. Reference librarians have long responded to questions posed from remote locations. According to Bunge: "The early years of the 20th century saw . . . the acceptance of reference questions via telephone and correspondence" (1980: 469). E-mail reference, which has become almost ubiquitous in libraries over the last two years, has been available far longer than that (Gray, 2000: 366). Recently, we have seen a number of projects that extend the boundaries of service beyond a single library or small group of libraries to transform virtual into cooperative reference.

As a result of a strategic planning effort, OCLC began to look at ways to extend the principles of cooperation on which it is founded from a focus on cataloging to library reference, where shared resources and workload could result in extended hours of service and could increase the library's subject reach while reducing duplication of effort. In the summer of 2000, OCLC approached the Library of Congress, which was already working with 16 libraries to establish a program that would "provide professional reference service to users anywhere, anytime, through an international, digital network of libraries" (CDRS, 2001). The Collaborative Digital Reference Service (CDRS) was conceived of as a global network of information professionals who can submit and answer questions directed by automated assignment software, based on profiles of availability, subject and language expertise, format strengths, geographic region, and service-level commitments. OCLC's purpose in seeking to participate in the program was to see if there was a special role we could play to help advance the program and to add value to the process. Since that time, the Library of Congress and OCLC have explored ways to deliver this service jointly.

In addition to working with the Library of Congress in this exploratory phase, OCLC undertook other efforts with two regional library networks, INCOLSA and METRO. In May 2000, the first phase of a pilot to test the concept of a local or regional virtual reference desk cooperative and to determine the components necessary to a useful service was begun. OCLC worked with INCOLSA and 15 Indiana libraries to implement and evaluate a very basic Web-based patron-to-librarian interface. In the fall of 2000, OCLC began talks with the New York City-based METRO Library Council about providing an "expertise" component, or module, for their online library directory. We saw this as an opportunity to explore in more depth the area of library profiles and the feasibility of gathering the many characteristics that describe a library into a single repository, for use by many interfaces, for many purposes, by many affinity groups and consortia.

Among our goals for the pilots was to establish a clear direction for OCLC's role in support of digital reference. We also hoped that we could determine how a stable, scalable, affordable service could be developed quickly. We wanted to include a usable, searchable database of profiles of library collections and librarians' expertise, and a usable, searchable, viable database of completed Q&A transactions. Finally, with the Library of Congress and its CDRS participating libraries, we hoped to identify best practices in this new world of cooperative reference. To understand the process and to provide perspective on the different needs of these pilot systems, the following analysis of digital reference components and of requirements underlying virtual and collaborative reference was undertaken.

ANALYZING DIGITAL REFERENCE

This chapter is structured around an analysis of three functional components underlying virtual and cooperative reference systems. The three functional components are: service delivery, reference resources, and profiling and routing. Service delivery refers to the technologies, management, and organizational issues that enable libraries to provide access to reference across the Web. Reference resources refers to the materials, both traditional and newly created, that are used to support the digital reference function. Profiling and routing refer to sets of data and associated technologies that maintain and use information about participating organizations or individuals and that support collaborative activities in a controlled and efficient way.

These components will be used as the framework for a discussion of issues to be considered in the evolution from virtual to cooperative reference service. Each has associated features that are affected by differences between virtual and cooperative reference. We shall also note OCLC's current activities within each venue.

Data Collection Methodology

Since 1999, there have been many changes in the technologies supporting digital reference and a phenomenal growth in libraries supplying such a service. To do the best job of reflecting this rapidly changing scene, this chapter has focused on data derived from ongoing discussions rather than employing traditional data gathering methods. Thus, much of the commentary was derived from public discussions at sessions on digital reference at ALA Conferences in 2000/2001, from OCLC focus group discussions at ALA Midwinter 2001 and with OCLC's Reference Services Advisory Committee, from listserv exchanges from mid-year 2000 to autumn 2001, in addition to the formal literature on digital reference.

Service Delivery

As noted earlier, traditional walk-up reference has been supplemented by both written and telephone reference service for a long time. Although e-mail reference was available before the recent wholesale move to the Web in the library community, the number of libraries that have e-mail links to their reference desks has shown an increase concomitant with that of library-based home pages. A recent innovation in Web-delivered reference is the development of chat software that allows both interactive discussion ("chat") and the "sharing/pushing" of browser pages, allowing librarian and patron to look at the same resource at the same time. This software, designed to add "high touch" in a digital environment, reflects the need for the traditional reference interview, even within the digital environment.

Experiences with the Delivery of Virtual Reference Services

Remote reference service has tracked technological trends for communication in the broader society, moving from mail to e-mail to Web-based services. In the 2000/2001 time frame, attention has focused on Web-based chat reference. An inspection of the archives of the listserv "livereference" shows the evolution of virtual reference from August 2000 to August 2001. The earliest systems described tended to be based on conferencing and chat tools like Microsoft's NetMeeting or AOL's Instant Messenger (IM) or "roll your own" systems created by technologically adept librarians for their patrons. In the course of the year, tools like Human Click, LiveChat, and LivePerson emerged. These systems were often derived directly from Customer Relationship Management (CRM) tools in use at online industrial customer help desk sites. The tie between reference and help desk systems was the surface similarity between the help desk task of asking and answering questions and keeping files of related information and the work of the reference librarian. As the difficulty and expense of using CRM software directly was experienced by smaller libraries (Livereference, 2001), systems designed to more directly support libraries grew up. These include products by LSSI, Inc. and 24/7 Reference and the extension of tools like the Internet Public Library's QRC or the Virtual Reference Desk's Incubator software.

OCLC, as a part of its strategy's charge to facilitate libraries' efforts to increase their visibility on the Web and to foster cooperation in new environments, was interested in understanding how to help libraries deliver virtual reference. The INCOLSA pilot was aimed at developing a bare-bones easy to use, affordable Web-mounted reference interface that met the needs of this Indiana Library Service Cooperative. Libraries would be able to communicate with their patrons and each other, while tracking the status and current work completed on patron requests. Through the pilot, we would gather valuable information about how librarians interacted with one another in their regional consortium, just what the Q&A process looks like, and what additional functionality is critical to the service. Our goal was to come away with a clear idea of the shape a regional service should take and to test the efficacy of such an interface to serve as a "front end" to the CDRS service. As of September 2001, six libraries have begun using the Web form service with their end users. Chat and page-pushing are under development.

Issues for the Delivery of Virtual Reference Services

Staffing virtual reference has been broadly discussed as an issue for many libraries. Reference desk management had already adapted to phone and e-mail reference. As chat-based reference was added as an access point for patrons, librarians became concerned that they would not be able to deal with the upsurge in traffic that could result if their services were as popular as free and fee-based Web "expert" services. If, in fact, libraries were able to become as accessible as AskJeeves, could they handle the increase in reference traffic? In the last year, reports made at sessions devoted to virtual reference at ALA and over the "livereference" listserv do suggest that volume is most often controlled by the amount of publicity given to the service and by the placement and number of links to the virtual reference desk on the library's Web pages.

The physical and organizational placement of the digital reference function has been widely discussed. Is it an additional service or simply another form of reference, to be included in the already existing workflow? Can this service be run remotely and, if so, what kinds of resources would the reference librarian have available? Although there have been reports from the field that digital reference has simply been added to existing reference desk duties, a "livereference" listserv discussion in September 2001 strongly suggested that digital reference, especially in a busy library, works best when it is established as a separate service point, often located physically separate from (although often near) the public reference desk.

Experiences and Issues for the Delivery of Cooperative Reference Services

From OCLC's perspective, the CDRS pilot was an excellent, already working, service that was successfully testing the concept of cooperative reference. That pilot afforded an opportunity to analyze the types of transactions such a service would facilitate and what metadata would best describe them, to learn about what information needs to be profiled to support automated question assignment on a large scale, and to discover and test the possibilities for storing completed reference transactions in a knowledge base, while examining the issues involved. There was a lot to learn!

In the evolution to cooperative reference, three new issues come into play: data interchange standards, jurisdictional concerns, and service level objectives. In a local library system, participants use common software and communication protocols. When reference questions must be moved from library system to library system, each of which may use a different package to deliver services, there is a need for standards to provide interoperability across systems. Data interchange protocols were part of an early white paper by David Lankes (1999). His Question Interchange Profile (QuIP) was among the earliest attempts to suggest standards for the virtual reference process. The NISO Workshop on Net-

worked Reference in April 2001 stressed the need for interchange standards to permit the exchange of questions and answers across different library systems and support technologies.

The second issue for delivery of cooperative reference is jurisdiction. In the United States, public libraries tend to be funded by local tax dollars and academic libraries by their institutions. Most libraries may be willing to answer occasional questions originating from patrons outside their funded mandate especially if the question concerns their local area or their own special collections. However, libraries need to decide how to balance the service needs of their sponsoring bodies with the needs of the larger community. In CDRS, jurisdictional concerns are incorporated as geographic proximity into the algorithm that finds a best match. As the number of participating libraries grows, it becomes more likely that there will be libraries in the same area that would be available to answer questions.

To deal with problems that arise because of increased traffic, cooperating institutions and consortia need to develop service level objectives. The Virtual Reference Desk's AskA Consortium developed a set of standards to support its reference referral service for K–12 education community (Kasowitz, Bennett, and Lankes, 2000). The CDRS also has embraced service level objectives. If only a small number of libraries agreed to provide the service that many others availed themselves of, inequalities would soon develop. Another possible scenario is that a disproportionate demand for the services of a small set of well-respected libraries (e.g., the New York Public Library) could occur. However, even smaller libraries have found their place in the global CDRS network. Cooper (2001) reported that her colleagues at the Boise Idaho Public Library, a CDRS member, were pleased to find themselves in a position to both ask and answer questions. The cooperative as a whole will need to develop and maintain a system of checks and balances that assures the participants of fair treatment.

Reference Resources

While reference resources are not of necessity different for traditional and digital reference delivery, the change to Web-delivered service has affected the ways in which reference resources are used and how they can be accessed. It has also raised questions about how and when access needs to be controlled.

Web delivery has extended the scope of reference resources that existed before the Web. Many libraries now produce Web-based versions of the subject guides that collections and reference staff have produced for a long time. Similarly, some libraries are creating online "question and answer" files, like the card and rolodex files traditionally kept to assist with either frequently-asked or hard-to-answer questions. Issues of ownership and copyright, of legal and privacy rights are increasingly present in the digital reference world. As we shall see, these problems are exacerbated when virtual turns into cooperative reference.

Reference Resource Issues for Virtual Reference

It has been noted on several occasions that virtual reference encourages the use of Web-based sources, especially if the service is delivered away from the reference desk (either in a separate area or by remotely located reference librarians). Because virtual reference is essentially electronic and most often Web-based, practice has shifted in the direction of using reference resources that are themselves most often Web-based or at least electronic. In some cases, libraries have also chosen to scan paper-based reference resources and sent the scanned image to users electronically. In this case and in the case of purchased or leased electronic resources, electronic rights management issues come to the fore (Butler, 2000). When access to fee-based electronic resources was confined to special workstations within the library walls, it was relatively safe to assume that the vast majority of users of the resource were patrons of that institution. As fee-based reference sources can be sent to patrons outside library walls, libraries may have to include some form of user or location identification or IP address authentication features in their Web-delivered services if they are to provide access controls that will meet the requirements of commercial information providers.

When new resources are created for Web-based services or in the course of digital reference transactions other kinds of ownership issues arise. Many libraries have invested both intellectual effort and significant amounts of time creating electronic subject guides. When these reference resources have been created by local libraries, the institution may have an interest in "branding" its product and in customizing the content to its own patrons' needs. OCLC's experiences with subject-oriented bibliographies (pathfinders) within CORC have suggested that intellectual property and branding were often important issues for its member libraries.

Other resources, like FAQ or "stumpers" files may be produced by the intellectual effort of reference and collections staff or may have been extracted from the reference process itself (patron-derived question-and-answer databases). These raise a host of other problems. What can be shown to patrons? What can be sent to remote patrons? What about copyrighted attachments that are sent in answer to a question? Can these be held in a knowledge base for possible reuse? How can currency and accuracy be maintained? These questions, of great concern to most librarians and publishers, are not easily resolved. There is a pressing need for policy to be established.

Reference Resource Issues for Cooperative Reference

Cooperative reference enables libraries to benefit from the lower creation and maintenance costs of reference resources created by local libraries. Whether these are pathfinders or question-and-answer databases, sharing the effort could bring to reference some of the synergy that catalogers have enjoyed for the last 30 years. Experts both from within and outside the library community are now available to all. Smaller libraries that have taken the "leap of faith" have found cooperative reference to be a big boost to the extent of their subject reach.

However, in a cooperative reference environment, the problems identified earlier still exist and intensify. Like virtual reference, participating libraries in a reference cooperative must be concerned about violations of their licensing agreements with fee-based reference resources. Questions and answers are themselves thought to be exempt from copyright. But reference service is often more bibliographic instruction than "answer" provision. If the reference approach is to provide a more directional service (rather than a direct provision of the answer), cooperating libraries must exercise caution. Helping users to high-quality resources appropriate to their need can be problematic when the resources of the requesting library is not the same as those of the answering library. Careful decisions must be made about what resources to supply directly to the patrons of distant libraries until sophisticated "appropriate copy" technology (Butler, 2000) for licensed works has become widely used in all types of libraries and until directories supporting rights management have been developed.

To meet the needs of libraries, systems need to protect the privacy rights of the patron and information provider. A shared database of question-and-answer pairs has long been seen as a valuable resource for CDRS. The CDRS board is establishing policy, in consultation with OCLC legal advisors. The retention on *any* server of information about a patron, about what question a patron may have asked, and of any transcripts resulting from chat sessions between a patron and a librarian is a concern. At this time, while CDRS maintains the full, unedited results of all transactions on its servers, these data are accessible only to CDRS administrative staff. License terms for a production service should guarantee protection of unedited transcripts following the close of a transaction. They should further stipulate that the data cannot be made available to any person or organization or system (although statistical information about the data may well be sharable).

Additional care is crucial if transactions in the reference system are captured for re-use (i.e., if patron questions and associated answers are included in an accessible database). If a database derived from patron interactions is to be created, institutions need to extract generalizable data while protecting patron privacy. In the CDRS pilot, it is understood that the completed transactions that appear in a sharable knowledge base have been edited to remove sensitive, personal information that could link the question to the patron generating the question. While the original participants are encouraged to complete as many fields as possible and to include information about sources already checked, editors may also need to add metadata (e.g., subject terms) to increase retrieval accuracy.

As with any database, a collection policy must be developed to ensure content quality. In the CDRS pilot, it is recognized that such a policy must be developed with the help of all the membership. Thus it is a policy that is likely to evolve and change over time. OCLC is currently working with its NetFirst staff—experienced library professionals who are also indexers and abstracters and Web site harvesters—to take on the role of knowledge base reviewers and editors. Together with volunteer editors from the participating institutions, they will develop guidelines for the review, editing, and collection of knowledge base data.

As discussed earlier, standardization becomes a major issue when data needs to be shared across participating libraries. In order to benefit from shared creation, these reference resources must have appropriate and consistent metadata attached. For service delivery, patrons' questions must be routed across a variety of interconnecting library systems. Lankes' (1999) QuIP included a proposal for question and answer metadata. At the NISO Workshop on Networked Reference (2001), there was consensus that standards for question-and-answer metadata were a necessary component for successful system operation. Component parts would include an identification of required metadata elements and their associated properties and related data to support record maintenance and reporting.

Profiling and Routing

In a world where everyone has the same basic knowledge, anyone can answer any questions. However, when things are less homogeneous, people looking for information will often choose to ask for help from someone who they believe has the information (or knows how to get it). When a group is small, people know each other's expertise. However, as the number of participants increases, it becomes difficult to identify and track expertise. As reference librarians reach outside their local area and, indeed, around the world, new practices need to be put in place.

These new practices involve the processes that we are labeling profiling and routing. Profiling refers to the process of creating descriptions of libraries, librarians, and other information resources (e.g., specialized collections, experts) that include names, contact information, expertise/collection strength, and availability. Routing refers to the process of using the information in profiles to identify available resource(s) and to move and track information requests as they move about in the system.

The extent to which profiling and routing are needed depends on the size and complexity of the digital reference service in question. In a system in which an individual library provides e-mail reference to its own patrons, an e-mail address could either be monitored within the library and questions sent to an appropriate staff member or separate links established for different reference areas. In a small consortium, manual searches in a shared member-profile database may be sufficient. As the scope of the digital reference system evolves into a multi-type global cooperative, automated assistance is required if a usable, efficient system is to result.

Profiling and Routing Experiences in Virtual Reference

Within small groups of participating libraries, profiles may be simplified and available as searchable files, rather than incorporated into a more complex routing system. In the current OCLC pilots, information about the identity and location of the institution, both specialized subject and collection strengths and availability are incorporated into the profiles characteristic of member institutions. Participating institutions complete their library's profile and are encouraged to keep it updated. As of the fall of 2001, the profile database for the METRO and CDRS pilots does not provide data elements at the individual librarian level, although this has long been a goal.

The METRO prototype was particularly interesting from a profiling perspective. In the fall of 2000, we began talks with the New York City METRO group about providing an "expertise" component, or module, for their online library directory. By combining the METRO library directory data structure with the CDRS collection strength data structure, we hoped to be able to present a much fuller, more rounded profile of any single library than is currently available in any known source.

OCLC's experiments with support for routing within a virtual reference context has focused on the INCOLSA pilot. The initial prototype allowed librarians to claim unassigned questions and work on questions assigned to them, to respond to the patron any number of times, to ask for clarification or refer the question to known libraries and reference centers, or to submit a complete question-answer pair for inclusion in a local knowledge base. At all times, librarians know the status of their work and of their outstanding questions. Librarians could establish a "buddy" list—a list of preferred libraries—that they could search by subject area to locate an appropriate library to which to route a question. A one-condition/one-location automated routing system that allows libraries to specify a backup location when they are closed is planned.

Profiling and Routing Experiences and Issues for Cooperative Reference

To successfully implement profiling and routing in a cooperative reference environment, several key features must be present and interoperable. These include directories that conform to metadata standards, sophisticated routing software, privacy protection (which has been discussed under Reference Resources), agreements on service level objectives, and quality standards.

To be effective, directories need to include institutions' and individuals' identities and contact information as well as expertise/subject strengths, including level and language. The directories also need to be able to incorporate information about availability and administrative details, including service restrictions. The third area identified as in need of standards development both in the QuIP (Lankes, 1999) work and at the NISO Workshop on Networked Reference (2001) is that of profile metadata. The Workshop report includes descriptive elements for the questioner and answerer that correspond to the question metadata to enable routing. Along with these elements should be contact information and business and administrative objectives. As always, a keen concern must be directed to privacy concerns.

Our experiences with cooperative reference routing have primarily been with the CDRS pilot system. In that system, after receiving a query or request for assistance that librarians are unable to address directly (for whatever reason), they will first search the knowledge base to see if the query has already been addressed in some way. If they need to go further, the request is submitted to the automated Request Manager for routing to an appropriate library. "Appropriateness" is based on subject depth, hours of availability, and geographic proximity, among other factors that include service level commitment and "load balancing." The assigned library can address the request, reject it, or ask for clarification. Answered questions are returned, including any necessary attachments, links, or reference citations. Requesting librarians retrieve the material and deliver it to their patron, completing the circle. Experience with the pilot has demonstrated that practical considerations require the previously mentioned contact, business, and administrative information be part of a usable profiling and routing system.

One of the objectives of the CDRS pilot has been to determine what profiling elements are needed to provide a good matching algorithm for the automated Request Manager. The current pilot profile requests more information than is currently used in the algorithm, though we expect to include additional elements as the service's membership grows. Jurisdictional issues, for example, can probably be handled via automated matching algorithms, by adding the "geographic areas served" profile elements to the Request Manager. While considerable testing has been done to evaluate the "best fit" algorithm now in place, we anticipate continuing evaluation and "tweaking" of the element weights as the service grows in membership. One of the major concerns in ensuring appropriate assignments by an automated request manager is up-to-date profiles. In the end, the match is only as good as the profiles provided by the libraries, so currency and accuracy are critical. To date, the CDRS service sends out frequent reminders on the lists to update profiles often. An obvious shortcoming of the profile as of this writing is its reliance on the primary use of LC higher level class structure as an indicator of subject expertise. There is a need for additional or alternative subject classes that better meet the needs of public libraries and special libraries (especially medical libraries). OCLC anticipates soon adding a cross-walk between the Dewey Decimal Classification structure and the LC classes to aid public and smaller public library profiling.

To ensure fairness, service level objectives need to be negotiated with the members of the cooperative and instantiated in the system to enforce adherence. CDRS libraries indicate on their profiles whether they will only ask questions, only answer them, or both and can specify the amount of service they would provide and the number of questions they would likely submit. The system provides load-balancing by tracking how recently a library answered a question. The assignment software takes into account recent activity and avoids assignments to libraries that have just been assigned a question. Such safeguards ensure that large libraries are not overwhelmed with work.

Libraries are currently concerned with identifying ways to assess digital reference quality. One can expect, and indeed we have encountered, questions and misgivings regarding cooperative reference that are reminiscent of the early days of cooperative cataloging. Questions such as "How can I be sure another librarian will treat a request with enough

care?" or "What will the assigned library think about my not being able to answer the questions?" are voiced. It is interesting to note that such questions do not seem to come from those actually involved with services like CDRS. While fear of lack of uniformity in standards or apprehension about "exposure" are not new in the reference area, Web-based cooperatives make libraries more visible. In time, some level of monitoring and quality control may develop within digital cooperatives. A study currently underway under the direction of Drs. Charles McClure of Florida State University and David Lankes of Syracuse University proposes to develop a "best practices" model for digital reference. The study will also develop and field test specific measurement instruments for measuring the quality of digital reference service, issuing a set of guidelines for such measurement.

OUR FUTURE DIRECTION: THE REFERENCE COOPERATIVE

Based on our analysis and informed by our experiences with the pilots and marketing research, OCLC and the Library of Congress are jointly developing and offering a reference cooperative, to be introduced in the Spring of 2002. The cooperative service is envisioned to be a powerful, inexpensive, and easy-to-use end-to-end solution for providing and managing reference services through the Internet. The service enables Internet users to ask questions and receive answers from their local library via the Web. To fully support service delivery needs, the system will support e-mail-based interaction, Web forms, and live chat.

Questions answered through the service are kept as candidate entries for a Q&A "knowledge base," which could be used as a shared resource across members of the cooperative. If desired, the knowledge base could also be accessed directly by the patron, addressing some questions before they reach the desks of busy reference librarians. To ensure user confidentiality, all content will be reviewed by participating libraries or NetFirst content creators and all identifying information removed before being including in the database. Designed especially to meet the needs of multi-type library programs, the service must track and manage reference traffic, with the capability of referring unanswered questions to other libraries in the library's cooperative or of forwarding the question to expert resources through the global, Web-based CDRS network. A database of institution and individual profiles facilitates the manual and automatic assignment of questions to an appropriate resource beyond the local library, when necessary.

Both the profile and the knowledge base(s) are cooperatively built databases that can be shared locally, regionally, and/or globally. Local/regional software and all databases reside on OCLC servers. CDRS Request Management software automates the routing assignment. Libraries are not required to download anything in order to be full participants. Those who wish to customize the question form or to customize the look of their home page and place their logo on it may do so. It is intended that the system will both adhere to and help lead the way to the establishment of standards and "best practices," working hand-in-hand with emerging standards being developed by the VRD, NISO, and the quality assessment study.

We don't believe we have all the answers to the issues that have surfaced for this new reference arena, nor do we assume that the service we are developing is the only possible solution. We do know that libraries cannot wait until we know with certainty that we have the "right" answers. We all must move ahead if we are to remain a viable and valuable resource for our users. We'll learn from our mistakes, gain experience and come back. We can't afford not to be in this new environment.

REFERENCES

Bunge, Charles A. 1980. "Reference Services." In *ALA World Encyclopedia of Library and Information Services*. Chicago: ALA.

Butler, Brett. 2000. "Designing a Virtual Reference Desk: Intellectual Property Considerations." In *Digital Reference Service in the New Millennium*, R.D. Lankes, J.W. Collins, and A.S. Kasowitz, eds. New York: Neal-Schuman.

Collaborative Digital Reference Service. 2001. "What Is CDRS? Mission Statement" [Online]. Available: www.loc.gov/rr/digiref/about.html [2002, May 24].

Cooper, Rosemary. 2001. Panel, "OCLC – Virtual Reference: Opportunities for Collaboration." ALA Annual Meeting, San Francisco, June 18, 2001.

Gray, Suzanne M. 2000. "Virtual Reference Services." *Reference & User Services Quarterly* 39, no. 4 (Summer): 365–375.

Kasowitz, Abby, Blythe Bennett, and R. David Lankes. 2000. "Quality Standards for Digital Reference Consortia." *Reference & User Services Quarterly* 39, no. 4 (Summer): 355–363.

Lankes, R. David. 1999. "QuIP: Question Interchange Protocol" [Online]. Available: www.vrd.org/Tech/QuIP/ [2002, May 24].

Livereference. 2001. [Online]. http://groups.yahoo.com/group/livereference [2002, May 24].

NISO. 2001. Workshop on Networked Digital Reference Services, Washington, April 25–26 [Online]. Available: www.niso.org/netref-report.html [2002, May 24].

Chapter 11

Collaborating with Our Users: Examples from the Excelsior College Virtual Library

Judith Smith

OVERVIEW

Virtual reference services for adult distance education learners require a personalized and proactive approach that can only be created through an understanding of this population's unique attributes. This chapter discusses the services of Excelsior College Virtual Library, a partnership between the Sheridan Libraries at Johns Hopkins University and Excelsior College.

INTRODUCTION

Adult learners who are also distance learners often have an especially challenging experience trying to locate, use, and evaluate information sources. This chapter describes how the Excelsior College Virtual Library (ECVL), a partnership between Johns Hopkins University and the nation's oldest and largest virtual college, Excelsior College, provides reference services for non-traditional adult learners across the globe. It discusses some specific needs of the adult learner, and the implications for digital reference services. It will explain how dealing with these distance adult learners in a virtual environment requires a shift to a more proactive and personalized model for reference services. Reference librarians who want to effectively serve these patrons in a digital environment must consider these learners' unique backgrounds and information needs and tailor services accordingly.

There are two challenges faced by ECVL that inform our approach to library services: 1) distance;

and 2) the type of student. The first part of the chapter will examine the issues involving distance and the type of student, and the second part of the chapter will describe the ECVL and illustrate how it addresses these issues in its implementation of digital reference services.

DEFINING A NON-TRADITIONAL, ADULT STUDENT

Imagine that you are under pressure to finish your degree so that you can maintain or improve your work position. To complicate matters further, envision trying to work on the degree while taking care of your two children and continuing at your job full-time. You are just learning how to use your computer, all of your classes are online, and you have a bibliography due for a research paper for the first time in 15 years. This is a generalization of the type of student to which this chapter refers. These students typically are returning to school after a long hiatus, or they may never have finished their first degree. They are balancing multiple responsibilities and trying to work on their studies in a drastically different information landscape than that which they encountered the last time they were in school. Adult students often choose to return to school for specific reasons, such as job improvement or the loss of spouse. While many adults are returning for life-enrichment purposes, numerous students are dealing with a great deal of pressure to finish their degree, which adds to a sense of urgency and insecurity.

Although this chapter interchanges the terms

"adult" students and "non-traditional students," this author is adopting the meaning of what Nouwens (1997) refers to as "mature" students. Students leaving their high school for college are essentially adults, but their characteristics differ greatly from mature students who have "a longer experience of living autonomously and independently" (Nouwens, 1997: 2). It is true that other students, such as traditional undergraduates or graduate students share certain characteristics with adult learners, such as the need to juggle multiple tasks in their lives. However, non-traditional students have a range of work and life experiences that differentiate them from the average student fresh out of high school, or the student who moves directly from undergraduate school to a graduate degree program. These adult students have many years of life and work experience behind them, which influence the way they approach their studies. Taylor explains that "a younger person is still anticipating most of the responsibilities in which an adult is fully engaged" (2000: 4).

It is tempting to try and neatly sum up these students' characteristics, but their characteristics are complex, and they do not always fit completely into one category. A student may have been out of school for many years, but may be completely confident in approaching her studies, and highly computer and information literate. Many have written about the characteristics of adult learners and the difficulty in trying to make universal characterizations about their common traits (Ezzo and Perez, 2000). And some have warned against pigeon-holing students into a particular category, rather than treating students as individuals (Givens, 2000). Nouwens (1997) delineates the core characteristics of adult distance education students that distinguish them from traditional students. These students: 1) have experiences that may help or thwart their current learning; 2) begin study with a clear motivation; 3) need support to deal with previous educational experiences; 4) prefer learning that is problem-centered; 5) may feel vulnerable; 6) have preferred learning styles; 7) protect their egos; 8) have other responsibilities; 9) have personal goals; and 10) work best under some pressure.

Similar to attempts to describe the typical adult student, efforts to clearly delineate a single theory of adult learning are challenging. In providing an overview of the core foundational theories of adult learning, andragogy, and self-directed learning

Merriam explains that we do not have "one theory or model of adult learning that explains all that we know about adult learners, the various contexts where learning takes place, and the process of learning itself . . . what we do have is a mosaic of theories, models, sets of principles, and explanations that, combined, compose the knowledge base of adult learning" (2001: 3).

Knowles describes several assumptions about adult learners: their need to know why they are learning something before embarking on it; the self-concept of being "responsible for their own lives"; the role of their life experience; a readiness to learn; an orientation to learning based on how the things they learn will help them "apply to real-life situations"; and motivation, primarily internal. He carefully notes that these assumptions differ from an ideology, which he defines as "a systematic body of beliefs that requires loyalty and conformity by its adherents" (1984: 55).

Although there are many generalizations about adult students, what follows are the characteristics that resonate most clearly in our reference work with Excelsior students, and the characteristics we base our digital reference services upon.

Need for Strong Level of Emotional Support

As described above, most adult learners may be smart, focused, and motivated, but they have multiple life responsibilities and (in many cases) have not been in school for many years. The combination of these circumstances often creates a learning situation in which students need a great deal of emotional support throughout their studies. In delineating how andragogical concepts can be applied to distance education students, Rossman (2000) touches upon the importance of setting the "psychological climate" of the learning space. This type of non-traditional student requires an extra level of support, although this may initially seem counterintuitive since they are adults, and not especially young students. Taylor (2000: 3) depicts these adults as "paradoxical learners . . . motivated to learn *yet* will sometimes focus on evaluations and grades . . . self-directed *yet* they may feel shortchanged when an educator explains that she intends to be less of a source of answers than a resource for learning" (2000: 3).

As mentioned earlier, many of these students are entering a vastly different information environment than what they experienced the last time they were in school. The amount of information and the variety of formats can be mind boggling to these students. While they may have some experience searching the Internet, they may not have had much success finding relevant information, or they are under the misconception that *everything* can be found on the Web (Cahoon, 1998). Their inexperience with electronic material can lead to a high level of "technostress" (Quinn, 2000), and they may be confused about the variety of information options. In addition to the influx of electronic information, the students may have had negative schooling experiences that they carry with them to their new education environment. They may not have been highly motivated or focused students in the past, and several years have passed since they have tried to study for anything. They often do not have confidence in their skills and abilities, and become overwhelmed at the prospect of writing a paper or studying for an exam. Due to their life experience, it seems logical that these learners would be confident, capable information seekers, but we see that this is not necessarily the situation.

Unique Backgrounds and Life Experience

Although adult learners often require a solid level of emotional support throughout their studies, we must not in any way let this negate in our minds the numerous strengths that they bring to their academic work. These students are far from being "blank slates" waiting to be filled. These students are teachers, nurses, accountants, and lawyers. They are dealing with, and have been through, a multitude of life experiences. The professional and life experiences of these learners must be appreciated and acknowledged in the digital services we provide.

These students have many responsibilities, but may be inexperienced in the new type of research they now must conduct. In most cases, students *already* conduct information seeking in their work environment, but do not see the parallel between the information seeking performed in routine work duties, and the information seeking that their academic pursuits require. Because they are not clear about the connection, students are not always aware of the information environment and how to take advantage of it. For example, when at work, students may feel perfectly comfortable seeking information and assistance from co-workers, yet they hesitate to use the librarian (or their professors or advisors) as information resources to be tapped.

Another issue stemming from their life and work experiences is the students' need to directly connect with what they are being taught. Adult learners tend to personalize their learning, and want to closely relate to their subject matter. This need to find immediate relevance to their academic material can sometimes be an obstacle, in that they may ignore the complexities of subject matter, or get stuck in their own experiences (Taylor, et al., 2000). For example, they may want to know how the material will be useful to them in their work. They don't want to waste their time with material that is not immediately "useful" to them. Although they are motivated and focused learners, this attitude sometimes interferes with their being open to exploring a range of information options. Fishidun (2001: 104) notes that "if middle-age and older women view the introduction of computers to their job as not important to the scheme of their lives, or if they believe that they are unable to learn computer skills, they may not be willing to follow through with learning" (2001: 104).

EXCELSIOR COLLEGE VIRTUAL LIBRARY (ECVL) DIGITAL REFERENCE SERVICES

When planning the digital reference services for the Excelsior College Virtual Library (ECVL), we closely kept in mind the student demographics: the Excelsior student is a non-traditional, adult student, with an average age of 40.5 years. We took adult learning theories as well as their adult learners' individuality into consideration (Givens, 2000) when creating digital reference services. Also at the forefront of our mind when developing digital reference services was the level of stress that this type of user has in the virtual environment, and how an "adult-to-adult approach based upon the recognition of mutual competence and respect" (Moslander, 2000: 111) is the most appropriate model for such services.

The Excelsior College Virtual Library (www.library.excelsior.edu) began in the spring of 2000 as a collaborative partnership between Johns Hopkins University's Sheridan Libraries and Excelsior College, a virtual college with offices in Albany, New York. The actual office of the virtual library is located in Baltimore, Maryland. Excelsior College, formerly known as Regents College, has been providing distance education to students across the globe for 30 years, and currently enrolls 18,000 students in the fields of nursing, liberal arts, business, and technology.

Excelsior is a leader in the educational community for its focus on outcomes-based assessment. The student body is primarily comprised of associates and bachelor's students, but the college does offer two master's programs: a nursing master's in informatics, and a master's of liberal studies. The Entrepreneurial Library Program at the Johns Hopkins University's Sheridan Libraries designs and implements auxiliary (external) enterprises that bring revenue and varied experience to Eisenhower Library. The Sheridan Libraries are known nationwide as leaders in their support of teaching and research needs with digital collections and services. The library system is also recognized for its development of innovative entrepreneurial programs.

The ECVL has no physical collection, but similar to any physical academic library, it supports the research and teaching needs of Excelsior College students, faculty, and staff with a wide range of library services that are specifically created for their academic programs. ECVL provides carefully selected electronic reference material, including general and specialized dictionaries, almanacs, and directories. It also offers licensed and free bibliographic databases and discipline-specific material, including online full-text books and electronic journals. The library presents all resources with evaluative annotations to help users choose the best resources for their information needs.

A core goal of the ECVL is to provide students, in as many ways as possible, the equivalent services that they would receive if they were physically situated on a college campus. The ECVL believes in and makes every effort to ensure that these students have support to help them in their current studies, and to develop them as lifelong learners. A crucial component of this is to offer full reference services to these students, despite distance and varying computer and information literacy skills. ECVL offers research and reference assistance through phone, e-mail, and fax, as well as instructional services to assist students in the use of specific library resources and to promote lifelong information literacy.

The rest of this chapter will focus on the e-mail and online chat components of ECVL's virtual reference service.

The ECVL model of digital reference services for adults includes three main aspects: creation of a climate of respect; development of a personalized service; and attempts to actively connect with students.

CREATION OF A CLIMATE OF RESPECT

As reference librarians, we are aware of how our interaction with students impacts the reference interview, as well as their perception of what the library and librarians can offer them. We strive to make our users feel comfortable by being accessible and nonjudgmental. In the "physical world" we can convey these messages with body language, eye contact, and the tone of our voice. However, messages by e-mail can be misconstrued and inadvertently convey a harsh tone, leading a student to be fearful of asking another question. They are also likely to be unaware of Netiquette, and may need to be, for example, gently told that writing in all caps can convey an unintentionally harsh tone.

With adult students, the potential awkwardness of communicating at a distance through e-mail is magnified. These students are people who may have a very good job, handle their children adeptly, juggle many responsibilities, but have no idea how to use a bibliographic database. This contrast of competencies creates insecurities, as these students are uncomfortable with the level of uncertainty they face with their academic work. Although all library services are geared towards creating a respectful environment for students, three main ways we engender a climate of respect is through our choice of language, our active listening skills with our users, and the prompt responses we provide.

Careful Choice of Language

In the ECVL, we try to be cognizant of how a student might feel "coming in" to our virtual environment and asking a question. One way we act upon this understanding is by our use of language. We are very careful with our language, realizing that e-mail is a different medium that masks non-verbal cues. To create a "safe" environment for students to ask questions, we carefully craft all of our reference responses to clearly convey that we welcome their question, that their question is important to us, and that they can reach us at any time by phone, e-mail, and fax. Our language is the first "face" we present to our patrons, and if our language comes across as unwelcoming in any way, we may be alienating the student from the library. We pay attention to details when we write to students, which we may not think of in ordinary correspondence to co-workers. For example, we never write a quick response without a salutation and closing. Although this might be a perfectly acceptable way of corresponding with friends and co-workers, a message lacking a simple hello can seem harsh to a student writing for information.

Listening to Our Students

Although it may seem like a truism to encourage better listening skills with our users, we find that it is an essential aspect of working with adult learners in the digital environment. We are careful to not only listen to their information needs, but to try to finely tune our listening skills so that we can hear beyond the student's query. We validate their feelings and reassure them that asking for assistance is the best thing that they can do. A common occurrence is for a student to e-mail us looking for a specific book or journal article to study for their examinations. They ask their initial question, but often comment that "it's the first test I've taken in eight years," indicating that they are looking for something more from us than just the information. In the ECVL we also get less subtle indications that students want the extra support.

We get students who are open and honest about their academic fears, who will note that they are "scared to death" of failing their exam or starting their research, and ask what should they do. The students will—due to the nature of their needs, their level of stress, and the perceived intimacy or anonymity of the e-mail—confide in ways that they probably would not reveal at a physical reference desk. It is not unusual for someone to confess how lost they feel or how they are paying for college or other circumstances of their life. We take the time to truly listen to what the student tells us beyond their initial need, and in doing so, we can serve as a better "information mentor" to these students.

Prompt Responses

We also are sure to respond to their e-mail messages promptly (within 24 hours on business days) so that they don't feel that they have sent an e-mail message to a black hole. We may not always be able to answer their question within 24 hours, but we can send an acknowledgement to let them know that their message has been received. Students may feel insulted to send a question, no matter how small, and have to wait for days for any response. We explain to students that their question has been received, and that

it is important to us, but that we are working on messages that arrived prior to their query. These quick responses help engender an atmosphere of trust in the library.

DEVELOPMENT OF A PERSONALIZED SERVICE

The creation of an appropriate and comfortable virtual learning environment for these adults is a pervasive component of ECVL's services. An extension of this philosophy is ECVL's model of creating as personalized a service as possible. While we do have reference policies to which we adhere, our policies are not rigid, and we try to be creative and flexible. Our conversations with users probe for unique circumstances and attempt to meet them.

Assisting Students Without Computers

A prime example of a way we are creative with our services is how we serve the Excelsior student who does not know how to use computers. Although Excelsior students are distance education students, they gain their credit in a number of ways: through portfolio assessment, through examinations, through classes at other institutions. Not every Excelsior student takes classes online and is computer literate. We accommodate these students by seeking out the circumstances that would allow them to get the information they need. One ECVL student needed several articles for her class. She had never used a computer and did not have an understanding of how they are used to conduct research. Based on our telephone conversation, it was clear that this situation required a more "hands-on" level of service. It was not feasible for her to conduct her searches at this point in her studies. We explained to her how she could go about researching for her material, that we would conduct some searches based on our conversation, and that we would e-mail her the full-text articles. She was an equal participant in the process, even if she was not at the computer herself. After brainstorming with her to determine how to get her the material, we realized that the best option would be to e-mail the articles to her sister-in-law. The student would be seeing her sister-in-law over the weekend, and she could print out the articles for her.

The above situation exemplifies how the ECVL has successfully avoided a rigid mindset about the best ways to provide service. The extended conversation with the student allowed us to find alternative means to getting her the material. There are other ways we assist non-computer users, such as sending e-mail newsletters to these students by regular mail.

Passing Along Additional Information to Students

Another way of creating a personalized service is by selectively passing along additional information to students related to their studies by e-mail. One benefit of working with students in cyberspace is that it seems possible to contact the students even after the initial reference transaction. Relationships are established in a more continuous way, so that we have time to ask students by e-mail: "Would you be interested in receiving references to material in the future?" There are many times we work at a non-virtual reference desk and come up with a solid approach to users' research questions *after* they have left the desk, and we have no way to contact them. Even if we do, by chance, know the professor's or student's name, it may not be appropriate to track them down and send them the material. This ultimately depends on the user, but since we do not have the opportunity to ask them ahead of time, we are unlikely to look them up and send additional information. Most of the students we have had the opportunity to ask are interested in this service. This service not only gives the users information they need, but it also keeps the library on the students' radar so that they continue to think of the library as a useful and relevant part of their studies.

We also have a built-in way of passing along additional information to students. In one Excelsior graduate class, students have to write a research paper and are required to pass their bibliography along to the ECVL by e-mail. This assignment allows us to give them ideas about additional resources and search techniques, and provides an opportunity for us to send any relevant resources we find in the future.

Instructing Students by E-Mail

The ECVL views instruction as an important component of digital reference services. This instruction not only serves to meet their immediate reference question, but also offers them encouragement to work together with a librarian in the future to find what they need and to become better researchers.

The ECVL encounters students with varying degrees of computer and information literacy. We accommodate all students and meet them at their computer skills and information-literacy level, with the goal of giving them the skills to become better information seekers for both their immediate and lifelong learning needs.

We regularly write out lengthy instructions for students via e-mail to assist them with specific sources and search strategies. We never just "give" them the answers, but we never solely give them directions. We find that it confuses students, and is ultimately detrimental, to give them citations without any context. Similar to on-site reference patrons, they need to be instructed on how we found the items so that they can conduct their own searches in the future.

Our philosophy is to give them some resources that we found to reassure them that there are resources that they can quickly access, and to also provide them with the tools for them to find additional information on their own. We give them search terms to try and other suggestions about ways to search (e.g., conducting a broad search and then narrowing down the search through examination of subject headings). We never tell them the virtual equivalent to "go look over there" without additional guidance. We always provide ways to search that we have tested and know will work, so that we do not lead students down a frustrating path. This type of frustration can damage the level of trust that we continuously work to build with our users. We don't have the opportunity to bump into them at the library and develop a level of trust through familiarity. Our answers must steer students in the direction of appropriate resources to ensure a strong relationship with the students by building their confidence in our abilities to assist them.

Efforts to Get Students Involved

As with any library, it is an ongoing challenge to get students to take advantage of library services. With adult learners, it is crucial to involve them in the process. Adult learners tend not to connect to the assignment unless they can see how it relates to what they need to know (Taylor et al., 2000). They are juggling many aspects of their life, time is scarce, and they often do not want to participate in activities in which they see no purpose. Described below are a few ways we try to get students "into" the library.

Continuously Ask for Feedback

One way we try to meet their needs is by providing opportunities to get their feedback. On most pages in the site we have a link with a star to the reference librarian, and an invitation to contact us by phone, e-mail, or fax. We try to make it as easy as possible for students to contact us.

Participation in Online Chat Sessions

Excelsior College has an online student study support network called the Electronic Peer Network (EPN) for undergraduates and graduates, which contains information about workshops to prepare students for exams, discussion groups, chat sessions, a book exchange, and test-taking strategies. Students can also look for a "study buddy." We hold two to three chats per month within the EPN to reach the students, and to maintain a close relationship with a core learning center of Excelsior. In these chats we discuss whatever library and information-related question they have, and we encourage them to write or call us with additional questions.

Our experience has been that students are often apologetic because they believe their question is overly simple, and they are occasionally defensive. As described above, they are successful in their "real" life, yet may be struggling trying to make sense of the new research they have to conduct. We want to make joining the library chats as welcoming as possible. When we had difficulty drawing students in to a general library chat, we changed the chat session to cover a specific topic. By having a set topic, students would not have to feel apprehensive about potentially being the only one in the chat with a question. While having a defined topic did attract more students, we continue to look for new ways to draw students into the chat rooms.

Newsletters via E-Mail

Another way we reach out to students is through periodic newsletters, distributed by e-mail and on the ECVL site. These newsletters contain highlights from the library, as well as a section with research and searching tips. For example, one newsletter encouraged students to examine the information available about databases' indexing when they are conducting searches. We provided an example for them to try using the core nursing database *CINAHL (Cumulative Index to Nursing and Allied Health Literature)*. The newsletters serve as a marketing tool, but also serve as an informal instructional vehicle for those students who have not yet contacted the library for individual assistance.

IMPLICATIONS FOR DIGITAL REFERENCE SERVICES WITH ADULTS

While we certainly have not come up with a complete set of answers, the ECVL is working to build as proactive a model as possible for virtual reference services and to use technology wisely. At the ECVL, we continue to search for the answers to many questions to improve our services: how can we reach this user population that we do not get to see? How can we involve additional users in the online chat sessions? What is the best way to instruct these students at a distance? While we do not have all the answers, we have no doubt about our mission, which is to mold our services to this user population. Based on the characteristics that we find with these adult students and our experience with them, we can draw some general implications about servicing this user population in a digital environment.

Need to Spend More Time Explaining

In working by e-mail, we need to go beyond sending someone in the appropriate direction of material. It is crucial to give the direction, but also to give examples and context. We may not get another opportunity to demonstrate that we can help them be better students. For example, if a user needs assistance locating material for a paper, a librarian could give the student a combination of information: resources you know they can find; search terms that will provide relevant resources; and an overall search strategy. To help them avoid frustration in their information-seeking process, it can also help to specifically explain to students that research is an iterative process, and not often a straight line.

Need to Acknowledge Their Experience

Adult students have a lifetime of experience in their work lives and personal lives. We need to be sure that we are not condescending or overly "jargony" in our written and verbal correspondence. We also need to ask for their input whenever possible so that we can incorporate their learning experiences into library services. When conducting a reference interview, ask users questions to find out more about their skills and their work experience. While we do not want to be intrusive, we do want to probe for information that will assist us in understanding their background and skills.

Need to Provide a Safe Place for Students to Ask Questions

Offering a secure place for students to reach out to the library may be the most important and overriding theme to providing services to these users, especially in a virtual environment where they may be more unsure of themselves than they would be at a physical reference desk. Lawrence (2000) explains in his discussion of literacy tutors that students can react to a problem according to "their basic temperament." Some students may be shy and timid, while others may become aggressive and arrogant, and "boastful." Lawrence writes that enhancing self-esteem in students requires communication skills of acceptance, genuineness, and empathy, as well as a respect for students' views. The same types of skills that apply to adult-literacy tutors apply to our digital reference world. We not only need to provide personalized services but we often need to be comfortable with the personal nature of some of our transactions. We also need to find the fine line between giving them the support they need while providing enough of a challenge.

Need to Provide Transferable Skills for Continuous Learning

Technologies are changing more rapidly than we are able to teach. Rather than giving students fixed skills that they can only apply to one database, or one computer software program, an effective approach would be to incorporate "experimentation and problem-solving" (Cahoon, 1998: 13) into our digital reference services. When instructing students on the use of a particular database, point out the attributes that they can find in most databases so that they will see how the information that they are learning has a wider relevance. For example, librarians can bring students' attention to descriptors in a database record and tell them how they can be used in most databases—or the librarian can explain how to take advantage of a database's thesaurus. It is important for us to stretch beyond the initial question to provide them with information about how what they are learning now is a skill that they can use with other resources.

FUTURE DIRECTIONS FOR EXCELSIOR'S VIRTUAL REFERENCE SERVICES

The Excelsior College Virtual Library (ECVL) is still in its infancy and is working on ways to learn more about its user population, their information needs, and their comfort level with technology. We strongly believe in using technology appropriately to meet the needs of our students and will continue to closely monitor developments in digital reference software. As Francoeur (2001) describes, there are many critical considerations in establishing a chat reference service, including administrative support, demands on staff, and knowledge of users' needs and the types of questions they would ask. Our interest is to continuously mold our virtual reference services to the adult learner population. Some short-term goals of the library include conducting a survey with students to better understand their use of the library, their expectations and interests, and their satisfaction with services. We also plan to conduct remote usability tests to determine if the design of the Web site allows the students to quickly and efficiently find the information that they need.

CONCLUSION

The number of adults participating in adult education is growing. In 1991 there were an estimated 58 million adults that participated in adult education activities, and by 1999 the number reached an estimated 90 million (Kim and Creighton, 1999). These learners are coming from all segments of society; as Cahoon mentions, "the explosive growth of the Internet is evidence of an extraordinary adult learning phenomenon that cuts across traditional demographic lines" (1998: 5).

The adult-learner population will be accessing virtual reference services in a wide range of libraries. Having a greater understanding of the needs of these adult learners can only strengthen our connection to this growing group of library users. This understanding helps students in their lifelong learning process, and also serves as a vehicle for increased use and appreciation for all types of libraries. Dority (2000) describes that one added value in helping these learners is that it serves as a marketing tool for the capabilities of libraries and librarians. We live in a time in which there is a common misperception that everything can be found quickly and efficiently on the Web. We have the opportunity with these students to demonstrate the value of libraries in their lives.

In creating user-centered library services for adult learners in a variety of settings, we have the ability to play a valuable role by providing solid emotional and intellectual support that may positively affect all aspects of their lives, whether it be their work or home life. They may become more confident, capable, and skilled workers, and may in turn assist members of their family with their information skills. By understanding and working with the strengths that adult students bring to their learning environments, we can go beyond meeting immediate information needs to participating in stronger communities, where confident lifelong learners use their skills for the communal good.

REFERENCES

Cahoon, Brad. 1998. "Teaching and Learning Internet Skills." *New Directions for Adult and Continuing Education*, no. 78 (Summer): 5–13.

Dority, Kim. 2000. "Online Learners and Public Libraries: Annoyance or Opportunity." *Colorado Libraries* 24, no. 4: 23–26.

Ezzo, Anita, and Julia Perez. 2000. "The Information Explosion: Continuing Implications for Reference Services to Adult Learners in Academia." *The Reference Librarian*, no. 69/70: 5–17.

Fishidun, Dolores. 2001. "Listening to Our Side: Computer Training Issues of Middle-Age and Older Women." *Women's Studies Quarterly* 29, no. 3/4: 103–125.

Francoeur, Stephen. 2001. "An Analytical Survey of Chat Reference Services." *Reference Services Review* 29, no. 3: 189–203.

Givens, Lisa. 2000. "Envisioning the Mature Re-Entry Student: Constructing New Identities in the Traditional University Setting." *The Reference Librarian*, no. 69/70: 79–93.

Kim, Kwang, and Sean Creighton. 1999. "Participation in Adult Education in the United States: 1998–1999." [Online]. National Center for Education Statistics. Available: http://nces.ed.gov/pubs2000/2000027.pdf [2002, May 24].

Knowles, Malcolm. 1984. "A Theory of Adult Learning: Andragogy." In *The Adult Learner: A Neglected Species*. Houston: Gulf Publishing Company.

Lawrence, Denis. 2000. *Building Self-Esteem with Adult Learners*. Thousand Oaks: Sage Publications.

Merriam, Sharon B. 2001. "Andragogy and Self-Directed Learning: Pillars of Adult Learning Theory." *New Directions for Adult and Continuing Education*, no. 89 (Spring): 3–13.

Moslander, Charlotte. 2000. "Helping Adult Undergraduates Make the Best Use of Emerging Technologies." *The Reference Librarian*, no. 69/70: 103–112.

Nouwens, Fons. 1997. *Designing Material for Adult Learners* [Online]. Rockhampton, Queensland, Australia: Central Queensland University. Available: http://cedir.uow.edu.au/programs/flexdel/resources/AdultLearners.html [2002, May 24].

Quinn, Brian. 2000. "Overcoming Technostress in Reference Services to Adult Learners." *The Reference Librarian*, no. 69/70: 49–62.

Rossman, Mark H. 2000. "Andragogy and Distance Education: Together in the New Millennium." *New Horizons in Adult Education* 14, no. 1 [Online]. Available: www.nova.edu/~aed/horizons/vol14n1.htm [2002, May 24].

Taylor, Kathleen, Morris Fiddler, and Catherine Marienau. 2000. *Developing Adult Learners: Strategies for Teachers and Trainers*. San Francisco: Jossey-Bass, Inc.

Chapter 12

Implementing Virtual Reference for OhioLINK: 79 Peas in a Pod

Kathleen M. Webb and Belinda Barr

OVERVIEW

Consortia-wide Web-based reference services are emerging all over the country. Many of these projects consist of relatively small groups of similar institutions. The OhioLINK consortium serves over 600,000 faculty, staff, and students from 79 institutions and 139 campuses. Members range from small, independent liberal arts colleges to large, public research institutions. A project has recently begun to implement Web-based reference service for Ohio-LINK. Phase one of this project is an innovative approach to broadening e-mail reference services. Phase two will be to provide a shared chat service. The challenges of defining and implementing these services for a large and diverse consortium are addressed.

INTRODUCTION

The OhioLINK consortium is already well known for the breadth of shared resources provided to its member libraries. With tightening budgets, and the number of resources growing more slowly, the consortium has started to concentrate on expanding the services offered to our end-users. Web-based reference services are becoming more important as our users are accessing our resources from places outside the library buildings. OhioLINK members have begun a two-phase project to implement shared, Web-based reference among all 79 member institutions. This chapter will describe the organization of the

project, planning for both phases, and the implementation of the phase one pilot.

BACKGROUND

The Ohio Library and Information Network, OhioLINK, is a consortium of virtually all of Ohio's college and university libraries and the State Library of Ohio. OhioLINK members include 17 universities, 23 community/technical colleges, 38 independent colleges and the State Library of Ohio. OhioLINK resources and services reach more than 600,000 faculty, staff, and students at 113 campuses throughout the state. Formed in 1990 by the Ohio Board of Regents, OhioLINK's mission is to address the issues of resource sharing and information access for Ohio's institutions of higher education. Twelve years later, OhioLINK provides access to a central catalog of library holdings: 98 research databases, document delivery, and over 4,000 electronic journal subscriptions.

In many ways OhioLINK operates differently from other consortia. While OhioLINK currently employs 16 central staff, decisions are made by committees composed of representatives from member libraries. A governing board of college and university provosts provides overall direction for the programs. The Library Advisory Council (LAC) reviews and approves the policies proposed by the four standing committees, approves major funding, and participates in strategic planning. LAC consists of library directors from all original OhioLINK members (see

Appendix One) and representatives from independent and community colleges. The four standing committees are Cooperative Information Resources Management Committee (CIRM), Database Management and Standards Committee (DMSC), Intercampus Services Committee (ICS), and the User Services Committee (USC).

PROJECT BEGINNING

There were a number of key events in late 2000 that led to the consideration of this Web-based reference project. First, the OhioLINK Governing Board and the LAC approved a vision document, which stated that OhioLINK needs to "create an overview plan describing how the look and functionality of OhioLINK services should evolve and how the community should best support these services, such as 24X7 reference services" (Sanville, 2000: 6).

Second, there was growing interest in the idea of chat reference service at several member institutions. Three members of USC were experimenting with chat reference services at their campuses and a number of USC members attended the Second Annual Virtual Reference Desk conference. Several conversations took place about OhioLINK's possible use of call center software to extend the reference services currently offered to our users.

Third, the OhioLINK Web Taskforce had submitted a detailed report on the status of the OhioLINK Web site. One of their recommendations (based on the results of a survey of member institutions) was to investigate methods of implementing an electronically enhanced, 24X7, cooperative, Web-based reference service. It was thought that given the breadth of shared resources among OhioLINK members, the high cost of call center software, and the central computing support provided by OhioLINK staff, a shared consortium-wide project was a logical choice.

In early 2001, at the direction of OhioLINK's Executive Director and with the support of the LAC, a USC subcommittee was formed and charged with implementing a Web-based reference service for OhioLINK, preferably within the next year. The subcommittee is comprised of representatives from large public institutions, medium-sized and small independent institutions, a medical college, a community college, and an OhioLINK staff member. There are varying degrees of chat reference experience among the members. With no appointed project manager for this initiative, all subcommittee members and their libraries are volunteering their time in order to design and implement this project.

PROJECT DEFINITION

The first step in defining the project was to determine what was meant by 24X7 reference service. The subcommittee decided that the options for delivering 24X7 Web reference included FAQs, telephone, e-mail service, and chat. This combination of electronic services means that a user from an OhioLINK institution, using an OhioLINK product from a remote library service point, would have some type of assistance available 24X7. The subcommittee felt that a combination of synchronous and asynchronous reference services would accommodate most users while enabling all member libraries to participate in the project from the beginning. As the User Services Committee had already worked with OhioLINK staff to develop a complete set of database documentation and help tips, we felt that the FAQ portion of the service was mostly in place already. That left the e-mail and chat portion to be addressed by this project.

The second step in the definition process was to establish a timeline (see Table 12–1). We decided that Phase I would be establishing an e-mail service and Phase II would be the chat service. There were two reasons to start with the e-mail issue: the new OhioLINK Web site was scheduled to debut in August 2001 and we wanted an e-mail procedure ready for use on the new site; and an e-mail service would allow all member libraries to participate from the beginning of the project.

PHASE I: E-MAIL SERVICE

As the planning for Phase I began, the conversations about e-mail reference centered on a way of distributing e-mail inquiries throughout the state using a process similar to the Internet Public Library reference service. For example, if a user clicked an e-mail link while using an OhioLINK database their inquiry would be sent to a central e-mail queue. Librarians from around the state could login to that site, see the questions waiting to be answered and claim one to answer. This would allow librarians to do two

Table 12–1	
2001 Timeline	

Task	Feb	Mar	Apr	May	June	July	Aug	Sept	Oct	Nov	Dec
Subcommittee formed	■										
Project defined, phases identified		■	■	■							
Establish procedures for Phase I (e-mail)				■	■	■					
Videoconference						■	■				
Prepare RFP for call center software							■				
Distribute RFP							■				
Implement Phase I											
RFP responses due								■			
Evaluate RFP responses								■	■		
Write proposed service guidelines and staffing models								■	■	■	
Select software, purchase, and install									■	■	
Hire programmer										■	
Create criteria for performance tests										■	
Customize software											■
Select Phase II (chat) pilot participants											■
Hold conference to present proposals to OhioLINK members											■

things: claim inquiries from local users and answer questions in their area of expertise.

We began investigating two topics: what e-mail and other virtual reference services were currently in place at OhioLINK member libraries and what collaborative e-mail software was in use by other library systems. A survey was conducted to determine which OhioLINK members were currently offering e-mail or other Web-based reference service. An analysis of the data showed that the majority of OhioLINK schools were offering some form of e-mail reference, either with Web forms and/or e-mail addresses.

Next we researched collaborative e-mail systems. A review of the proceedings from the 2nd Annual Digital Reference Conference helped to identify some systems worth investigating (Footz 2000; Reed, 2000). We also looked at some of the literature available on the Internet Public Library project (Irwin, 1998; Janes, et al., 1999). A list of questions was developed to help us evaluate these software systems.

We found that while the functionality of these systems was impressive, we were not sure a collaborative e-mail approach was the direction to follow. With all the large and many of the smaller OhioLINK institutions already offering e-mail reference, a shared e-mail project seemed to add a new layer of complexity to a service already in place. A decision was made not to use a collaborative e-mail system, but rather to develop a method for sending e-mail inquiries directly to the home institution. Each OhioLINK user is assigned a home location based on their IP address. Once a user clicked a help link it would be a simple matter to display their institution's contact information and e-mail address.

As part of our research into local library contact information, we casually polled our colleagues about their e-mail reference usage. Although most campuses reported low e-mail statistics, the few institutions with high usage statistics tended to have prominent links to their e-mail services, i.e., on the institution's home page. We hypothesized two reasons for low e-mail usage: e-mail service links are not visible when our users have their questions; and there were not enough links on our pages to the e-mail services. A recent article on e-mail reference services in ARL libraries discussed these issues and suggested offering several different paths to e-mail reference links in order to facilitate use (Stacy-Bates, 2000). Our task was to determine how to put links where our in-house users seemed to have the most

questions, i.e., how do I use this database, and to put links in a variety of places.

An evaluation of how research database vendors (Ovid SilverPlatter, FirstSearch, DIALOG, and Ebsco) offered links to local assistance from within databases showed that this option is not widely available. Ovid was the only vendor to offer subscribers an Ask-a-Librarian feature. In this system, users request assistance by filling out a Web form. Information from the form is submitted to an e-mail address designated by the subscribing library (Ovid, 2002). There is no option to include other types of local contact information.

Fortunately, OhioLINK locally mounts many databases that are searched with a universal interface called Dataware (DW) and maintains a database of electronic journals, the Electronic Journals Center (EJC). Since OhioLINK staff customizes these screens, it is a simple process to add functionality. Placing links to e-mail services, contact information, and other virtual service options on all pages within DW and EJC meant that the links could be positioned where we felt the questions were likely to arise.

For the Phase I pilot a decision was made to place links to contact and e-mail reference service options in three places: on the EJC pages; on pages within two highly used DW products (one multi-disciplinary database, *Periodical Abstracts*, and one more complex, subject-specific database that uses a

Fig. 12–1. The OhioLINK AskUs Button

thesaurus, *PsycInfo)*; and the *Contact Us* page in the newly re-designed OhioLINK Web site. After much discussion, the links within the EJC and DW products were labeled Ask Us. The placement and design of the buttons was a joint project between the WebRef subcommittee and OhioLINK staff working within OhioLINK Web publishing guidelines. The button appears on all pages within the two DW databases in the toolbar area (see Figure 12–1.) and on the menu bar of the EJC (see Figure 12–2). The Ask Us buttons appear in addition to the existing Help and About this Database options.

When a user clicks on Ask Us an institution specific page is dynamically delivered (see Figures 12–3 and 12–4). Stacy-Bates (2000) made several useful suggestions for the type of information to include on contact pages. Options for this information page may include an e-mail address, URL to a Web form, URL to a chat service, or simply a URL to a local help page. Currently the dynamic Ask Us pages include a message about the developing nature of the project. The information for these pages is stored in a database developed by OhioLINK staff. Each OhioLINK member institution has identified a person responsible for maintaining contact information for their institution.

Members may also include links to:

Phone number, e-mail address, and a link to Interactive Chat.

Once the mechanics of the new service was developed, the subcommittee needed to inform all OhioLINK institutions before the August 6, 2001, rollout day. Since this service had the potential to increase the number of e-mail questions and other reference transactions, we wanted the opportunity to inform and prepare the librarians who would be involved in providing the service. For instance, members needed to know the timeline for the Phase I pilot, how the service would be implemented, how to maintain local contact information, and what the screens would look like.

We decided to incorporate an informational session into a videoconference already scheduled at various member institutions across the state. OhioLINK e-mail lists were used to invite heads of reference to an afternoon session tailored to present Phase I pilot details including the how-to of maintaining the local contact database. On July 12, 2001, the videoconference was successfully broadcast from the OhioLINK offices to member institutions across the state. On August 6, 2001, the new features debuted in the targeted databases and the OhioLINK Web site.

PHASE I PILOT EVALUATION AND FULL IMPLEMENTATION

Given that we were unable to estimate the impact of these links on local institution's e-mail services, the Phase I pilot project started with only the two DW products and the EJC. This pilot will run through December 2001. Full implementation for Phase I will be to add the Ask Us links to the remaining OhioLINK mounted databases and to examine the use of the links.

Anecdotal evidence from the first six weeks of service leads us to believe that the Ask Us links within the databases and the institution-specific Contact Us page on the OhioLINK main Web site have generated more e-mail questions. Unfortunately the current e-mail process does not identify the referring page (i.e., we don't know if a person clicks on Ask Us from DW, EJC, an OhioLINK Web page, or a local Web page). Once the service has been in place

Fig. 12–2. Phase I Pilot AskUs Link in the Electronic Journals Center

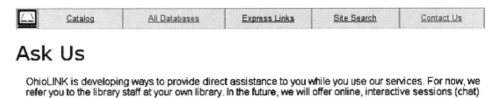

Ask Us

OhioLINK is developing ways to provide direct assistance to you while you use our services. For now, we refer you to the library staff at your own library. In the future, we will offer online, interactive sessions (chat) with librarians.

Options for assistance at Miami University/Main Campus

- Ask-a-question form: http://www.lib.muohio.edu/libinfo/ask_new.html
- Library information page: http://www.lib.muohio.edu/libinfo/

Or visit your library.

If you have a basic question about using this interface, you may wish to check these Quick Tips.

Fig. 12–3. Phase I Pilot DW and EJC Ask Us Page

Contact Us

If you have a question about or problem with an OhioLINK database, please contact your library.

Options for assistance at Miami University/Main Campus

- Ask-a-question form: http://www.lib.muohio.edu/libinfo/ask_new.html
- Library information page: http://www.lib.muohio.edu/libinfo/

Or visit your library.

If you are having trouble connecting to OhioLINK databases from your home or office off-campus, please check our Off-Campus FAQ.

For other questions, please check the general OhioLINK FAQ.

Fig. 12–4. Phase I Pilot OhioLINK Contact Us Page

for several months we will examine OhioLINK logs to determine which institutions had the highest number of hits. We will try to analyze the types of questions received to see if we can determine what proportion of questions were received from the Ask Us links within databases or from the Contact Us link on the OhioLINK Web pages.

PHASE II: PLANNING FOR CHAT

While Phase I offered challenges they were minor compared to the ones we faced and continue to face with Phase II. The biggest issue is that the consortium was again embarking on a new service. The first major service offered by member libraries was the patron-initiated, reciprocal borrowing feature of the OhioLINK central catalog. This service required many institutions to reallocate personnel to process the large numbers of lending and borrowing requests. This new method of interlibrary loan significantly affected the workflow of all OhioLINK members' circulation and/or interlibrary loan departments. Chat reference has the capacity to raise the same issues. While it has the endorsement of deans and directors, the reference staff that will implement this service may have not been consulted.

Another issue is that given the current pricing model used by many call center software vendors, OhioLINK could not centrally fund the software for all institutions. We knew that the money issue needed to be dealt with first since it would dictate any further planning on this project. An LSTA grant application was submitted, which included a request for funding for call center software, hardware to run the system, and a consultant to configure the system. The matching funds required would come from the OhioLINK budget. The grant was approved at the end of September 2001.

The next task was to prepare an RFP for the call center software. In June 2001, the committee began to investigate the call center software market and to develop a list of mandatory, highly desired, or desired features (see Appendix Two). As the list was developed, the committee was intrigued by the possibilities of multiple "queues" for a consortia environment (queuing means that calls can be put "on hold" and answered in the sequence received). The committee thought an ideal scenario would be an individual queue for each member institution and a shared queue for the consortium. An institution would have the option of routing calls from their community (based on IP address) to their local queue. This would allow the user to be in touch with someone most familiar with his or her local environment. We are looking for call center software that would route calls in this way:

- If the call was identified with a member institution (using an IP check) and someone from that institution was logged into the system, the call would go to the institution queue.
- If the call was identified with a member institution and a local person was not logged in, the call would be routed to the shared queue.
- If the call was not identified with an institution, the call would go into the shared queue.

As a result of the discussion, multiple queues became a mandatory feature of the RFP.

After further deliberations about staffing, equipment, and guidelines, the finalized RFP was submitted to vendors at the end of July 2001 with responses due by mid-September.

In the course of preparing the grants and the vendor RFP, we adjusted our timeline that will run through the end of 2001 and continue into 2002 (see Table 12–2).

As the timeline depicts, the pilot chat project will be evaluated from April-May. The primary evaluation methods will be an optional survey offered to users when they log out of the chat call and a survey of the library staff when they log out of the system. We are looking for an 80 percent satisfaction rate from users during the pilot. From library staff we are looking for enhancement requests, problems or peculiarities with the software, problems with the chat environment, and/or training issues.

Between May and July, we anticipate adjustments and enhancements will need to be made to the surveys, the software, and the training modules. After the adjustments are made, statewide training will begin in July 2002 and the Web-based reference project will be a reality for all OhioLINK members in fall 2002.

ONGOING CONSIDERATIONS

One issue we still need to consider is how to deal with inquiries from non-authenticated users. Since the Phase I pilot e-mail project is being limited to two licensed databases and users are required to authenticate before accessing the databases, it is a simple matter to assign each user to a home library. The next step of this project is to implement the Ask Us buttons in the other DW databases and OhioLINK's central catalog. Since the catalog is open to the world, many users will not be authenticated when they ask questions. A method is needed to route such questions.

The next issue is obtaining support from the reference librarians from across the state. We are still in the beginning stages of forming service guidelines, determining hours of operation, and developing staffing models. In order to gather input from all participants and to keep all OhioLINK member institutions informed, we held a conference in December 2001. This was an opportunity to bring together heads of reference and other librarians responsible for staffing reference points. There were four goals

Table 12–2
Revised Timeline for 2001 – 2002

Task	Oct - Dec 2001	Jan - Feb 2002	Mar - May 2002	June 2002	July 2002	Aug - Sept 2002	Oct - Nov 2002
Purchase and install hardware and software	■						
Hire programmer	■						
Customize software	■						
Design logo	■						
Create criteria for performance and functionality testing	■						
Create service policies and guidelines	■						
Conduct functionality and performance testing		■					
Train librarians participating in Phase II pilot		■					
Plan Phase II pilot service schedule		■					
Design service evaluation survey		■					
Conduct Phase II pilot			■				
Present project update to LAC for full approval			■				
Collect surveys from users			■				
Analyze user surveys				■			
Collect feedback from pilot project librarian participants				■			
Review and revise service policies and guidelines				■			
Recruit additional institutions for full implementation				■			
Determine staffing and scheduling requirements for full implementation				■			
Enhance systems as needed					■		
Conduct regional training for full implementation					■		
Full implementation						■	
Prepare and distribute promotional materials						■	
Review and revise user survey						■	
Collect and analyze user surveys							■

for this conference: to present various staffing models and hours for the shared service; to gather input about what model or models seem most manageable in our various environments; to present service guidelines and gather input; to discuss the changing face of reference and how institutions are dealing with these changes.

The conference was a success. Of the 189 people registered, 178 attended. Approximately 75.5 percent of the attendees were heads of reference or held primarily reference positions. Overall satisfaction of the conference was quite high: 81.7 percent rated it as excellent or good. Many discussions were held and several useful suggestions were brought to the attention of the WebRef subcommittee members.

Another issue involves handling libraries that do not wish to participate. While we hope to have 100 percent participation, we realize there may be members who have no interest in taking part. Previous OhioLINK projects potentially affecting all members have either required member-wide participation (e.g., the patron-initiated, reciprocal borrowing project where the software dictated full participation) or gave members the option (e.g., institutions decide which resources they will participate in purchasing with access to the resource limited by IP). Developing a policy for institutions that opt out of participation and service for Phase II will require answering hard questions: if an institution does not participate, what is the impact on their constituents and do their users get assistance via chat? If so, how does one financially thin institution extend itself to assist clients from other institutions?

RECOMMENDATIONS

While there are still many questions yet to answer, we can offer some recommendations to other consortia planning a chat service. First, the success of the service requires a commitment from all levels of library staff. Involve directors and reference librarians in the process from the very beginning. Second, the planning committee needs to have representatives from all types of libraries in the consortium. In addition, the planning committee should have people with varying degrees of responsibility. Include public service directors, heads of reference, and reference librarians. This broad representation from types of libraries and types of jobs will allow for a balance

between different institutions. Third, communication is vital to the success of this type of project. Also, the communication channels should be varied. There are some people who do not read e-mail and a paper announcement may work better for them. Others do better in a face-to-face environment and so regional meetings might work best for their style.

CONCLUSION

This project is unique in many ways. For instance, we know of only one vendor currently offering links to virtual reference assistance from within a database. The concept is exciting and we hope to be able to report an increased use of Web-based reference services and an increase in satisfaction from our users. The success of this point-of-need placement of service links could encourage other vendors to offer this option to their subscribers.

In addition, while there are consortial-wide chat reference projects underway, there is no group as large as OhioLINK. Although our large base of common resources makes a shared chat service easier in some ways, the diversity and size of our group provides other challenges. We still face the issue of staffing and acceptance of the service by every institution independent of their size.

In the end the goal for this Web-based reference project is to help our patrons better use the resources of their libraries. This service will provide new means of assistance, whether they come to us though our physical or virtual doors.

REFERENCES

Footz, Valerie. 2000. "Ask A Question! A Collaborative Virtual Reference Service." Presentation at the Virtual Reference Desk 2nd Annual Digital Reference Conference, "Facets of Digital Reference," Seattle, Wash., October [Online]. Available: www.vrd.org/conferences/VRD2000/proceedings/footz-intro.shtml [2002, May 24].

Irwin, Kenneth. 1998. "Professional Reference Service at the Internet Public Library with 'Freebie' Librarians." *Searcher* 6, no. 9 (October): 21–23.

Janes, Joseph, David Carter, Nettie Lagace, Michael McClennan, and Schelle Simcox. 1999. *The Internet Public Library Handbook*. New York: Neal-Schuman.

Ovid. 2002. *Ovid Documentation: Complete Features List* [Online]. Available: www.ovid.com/documentation/features/ [2002, May 24].

Reed, Donna. 2000. "Managing and Improving Digital Reference Service: Case Study." Presentation at the Virtual Reference Desk 2nd Annual Digital Reference Conference, "Facets of Digital Reference," Seattle, Wash., October [Online]. Available: www.vrd.org/conferences/VRD2000/proceedings/reed-intro.shtml [2002, May 24].

Sanville, Tom. 2000. *Connecting People Libraries and In-*

formation for Ohio's Future – 2000 and Beyond: Continuing the Task. The OhioLINK Program Vision, Priorities, and Strategic Activities. Columbus, Ohio: OhioLINK.

Stacy-Bates, Kristine. 2000. "Ready-Reference Resources and E-Mail Reference on Academic ARL Web Sites." *Reference & User Services Quarterly* 40, no. 1 (Fall): 61–73.

Appendix I
Original OhioLINK Member Institutions

- Bowling Green State University
- Case Western Reserve University
- Central State University
- Cleveland State University
- Kent State University
- Medical College of Ohio
- Miami University
- Northeast Ohio U College of Medicine
- Ohio State University
- Ohio University
- Shawnee State University
- State Library of Ohio
- University of Akron
- University of Cincinnati
- University of Dayton
- University of Toledo
- Wright State University
- Youngstown State University

Appendix II
RFP Features List

A. General Features

1)	Server software can be loaded and run at OhioLINK	Mandatory
2)	Supports common and current versions of major browsers (Netscape, Internet Explorer, Opera, etc.) and other user agents that conform to current specifications for HTML, CSS, and other relevant specifications	Mandatory
3)	Librarian can send to patron's browser an individual active Web page with a click of a link, image, or button	Mandatory
4)	Individual librarian settings (e.g., incoming call notices), as well as saved bookmarks and scripts (canned messages), are maintained at the server level and permanently saved	Mandatory
5)	Bookmarks and scripts (canned messages) are easily available to the librarians in session	Mandatory
6)	Includes database of statistics information	Mandatory
	a) Statistical information includes: patron home institution, time of day in hour increments, day of week, page or database from which patron connects (referrer page), hold time, length of transaction, librarian, queue, and librarian institution	Mandatory
	b) This database should be able to be queried by these fields, be able to combine any or all fields, and be able to export data in a delimited file	Mandatory
7)	Librarian and patrons are offered option to have transcripts of sessions e-mailed to them	Mandatory
8)	When the service is not available, the service displays customizable information	Mandatory
9)	Access to administrative functions (e.g., librarian IDs, customization settings/options for graphics, bookmarks, scripts, hold messages, instructions, patron login forms, surveys, as well as access to statistics and transcripts) is by password	Mandatory
10)	Server software runs on a Unix operating system	Highly Desired
11)	Twenty simultaneous librarians	Highly Desired
12)	Ability to modify and customize to allow access and searching of OhioLINK subscriptions databases (See Appendix II-B)	Highly Desired

13) Librarian can choose to send to patron's browser all visited active Web pages as they are retrieved by the librarian with a single click of a link, image, or button   Highly Desired

14) Librarian and patron can send to each other's browsers all visited active Web pages as they are retrieved   Highly Desired

15) Librarian and patron can see as a Web form is completed in either of their browsers   Highly Desired

16) Librarian can send patron static screen shots   Highly Desired

17) Multiple queues available   Highly Desired

18) Queues are associated with institutions or the consortium   Highly Desired

19) Ability to provide a common pool of callers and provide for the possibility that any OhioLINK institution can monitor individual queues anytime   Highly Desired

20) Ability to direct patron calls based on coordination with OhioLINK and its patron information   Highly Desired

21) Librarians can monitor multiple queues and answer multiple calls   Highly Desired

22) An automatic hold message displays to a patron as he/she enters a queue and includes some approximation of the wait time, e.g., how many already on hold   Highly Desired

23) The hold message is customizable so that other service options can be presented   Highly Desired

24) Customizable graphics, bookmarks, scripts, hold messages, instructions, and user login screens. Some customization options are for the consortium and apply to all librarians and queues. Some customization options are for the institutions and apply to all librarians and queues associated with a specific institution. In some situations, institutional settings may need to override consortium settings (e.g., graphics). In other situations institutional settings would be added to consortium settings (e.g., scripts)   Highly Desired

25) Each session is identified by a unique session number   Highly Desired

26) Bookmarks and scripts can be created and saved by the librarians   Highly Desired

27) Bookmarks and scripts can be created at the institutional level and can be made available to all librarians associated with an institution   Highly Desired

28) Bookmarks and scripts can be created at the consortium level and can be made available to all librarians   Highly Desired

29) Includes a database of session transcripts   Highly Desired

   a) Transcripts in databases are anonymous (patron identifying information (e.g., e-mail, name) are not included)   Highly Desired

   b) Transcripts can be accessed by date, librarian, institution, or subject category assigned by librarian   Highly Desired

   c) Institutions can opt to receive, via e-mail, transcripts of all sessions of users and/or all librarians affiliated with that institution   Highly Desired

30) Multiple service surveys can be created and be set, as needed, to automatically be offered to patrons or librarians at the end of each session   Highly Desired

31) Ability for the server administrator to broadcast a message to all librarians that would be immediately available to all online librarians and also available as librarians login to the system   Desired

32) Voice over IP option available   Desired

33) Video over IP option available   Desired

B. Librarian Interface

1) Librarian options to perform tasks in I.A.6 – I.A.10, if available, as well as access to scripts and bookmarks are located on the main screen and do not require cut and paste operations   Mandatory

2) Audio and on-screen (visual) notification of patron call. Librarian can decide whether one or more of these notifications are used   Mandatory

3) Librarian identification by password   Mandatory

4) Librarians are associated with a specific institution   Mandatory
5) Librarian can see information from patron login form   Mandatory
6) Librarian logout option   Mandatory
7) Librarian notification when patron logs out   Mandatory
8) Upon librarian logout, patron call is removed from the queue   Mandatory
9) Transfer of a session from one librarian to another within a queue   Mandatory
10) Librarian functions work for Windows and Mac   Highly Desired
11) Ability for librarian to add information that will not be available to the patron to the
    session transcript during or at the end of a session   Highly Desired
12) Upon librarian or patron logout from each session, librarian can assign a category
    from a list of pre-defined categories developed by OhioLINK   Highly Desired
13) Transfer of a session within from queue to queue   Highly Desired
14) If a librarian's browser crashes or computer fails, librarian can resume session   Highly Desired
15) Librarian sees the URL of the page from which the patron connects (referrer page)   Desired
16) Librarians can view the usernames and institutional affiliations of other librarians
    logged into the system while monitoring any queue   Desired

C. Patron Interface
1) Patron functions work for Windows, Mac, and LINUX users   Mandatory
2) Patron can view chat and Web pages on same browser screen   Mandatory
3) As patron initiates session, they are offered a customizable login screen   Mandatory
4) Patron logout option   Mandatory
5) Patron notification of librarian logout   Mandatory
6) Upon logout patron call is removed from the queue   Mandatory
7) No plug-ins or downloads required   Highly Desired
8) Upon logout patron retains a list of URLs used   Desired

D. Training, Support, Documentation
1) Vendor must provide technical support for the system   Mandatory
2) Vendor must provide training, both system installation/management training and user
    training.   Mandatory
3) Vendor must provide documentation   Mandatory

PART V

Using Key Findings from Research in Digital Reference

OVERVIEW

Scholars in the field of library and information science complain that there are too many "how we done it good" articles in the library literature, while library practitioners complain that the more theoretical work in the literature is divorced from the practical realities of librarianship.

The chapters in this section bridge that gap, proving that theoretical work can be firmly rooted in the realities of the creation and management of digital reference services. This section presents research studies on reference service in a government agency, the development of an automated question and answer service, and users' information-seeking behavior. These chapters all make valuable contributions to theories and models in the field of reference. In addition, these studies also make valuable contributions to the practice of reference librarianship in the digital age.

Chapter 13

Building a Generic Framework for Virtual Web Assistance: OPAL

David C. Bradbury and Georgina F. Payne

OVERVIEW

The Online Personal Academic Librarian (OPAL) project is an investigation into the possibility of developing a fully automated Web-based question and answer service for use by distance learning students. The initial scope of OPAL is to handle routine inquiries, freeing up library staff to handle more complex queries.

This chapter reports on progress since the start of the project in November 2000, and considers: 1) the results of a statistical analysis of Open University Library inquiry patterns and experiments conducted into user inquiry behavior; 2) the current state of the art across technologies and disciplines related to OPAL; 3) an outline of the OPAL prototype, the benefits of employing a genetic algorithm, and the generic framework behind the prototype; 4) a synopsis of the evaluation strategy designed to assess the success of OPAL with respect to its intended purpose; and finally, 5) recommendations are provided outlining possible future directions for the OPAL project.

INTRODUCTION

In November 2000 the U.K. Open University Library[1] (OU) embarked on OPAL[2] (Online Personal Academic Librarian), an 18-month research project to investigate the development of a fully automated 24-hour question-answer service for use by distance learning students.

The Open University is the U.K.'s biggest distance learning institution, with approximately 200,000 students who live across the U.K. and, increasingly, in mainland Europe and other parts of the world. The university offers more than 360 courses in Arts, Modern Languages, Social Sciences, Health and Social Welfare, Science, Mathematics and Computing, Technology, Business and Management, Education and Law. Degrees are awarded at both the undergraduate and postgraduate level. The Open University method of delivering courses is called "supported open learning"—students work essentially on their own at home, with high-quality course materials mailed to them. These materials typically include print materials, audiotapes, and videotapes, with some courses also being taught online. Every student has support from a named tutor (employed part-time by the University) and optional face-to-face group tutorial sessions.

With the assistance of three project partners—the Open University Knowledge Media Institute, Birkbeck College Library London, and the University of Leicester Library Distance Learning Unit—the Open University Library is conducting desk and field research into the development of an automated reference service for use by distance learners. While the OPAL project is based at the Open University, the vision behind OPAL is to create a generic framework for automated online virtual assistance that will be transferable to other libraries in the academic and public sectors. Birkbeck College and the University of Leicester will act as test-beds for the various iterations of the OPAL system. We are also liaising with colleagues in the public sector to ascertain whether or not the concept of an online virtual assistant could operate in the public library domain. In summation, the aims of the OPAL project are:

- to develop an automated question-answer system that can be used by students outside office hours and that is capable of handling repeat and routine inquiries 24 hours a day, 7 days a week.
- to develop a service capable of responding to user questions posed in natural language.
- to build an application that is efficient and acceptable to the user in that it helps to make the library site experience simpler and more rewarding.
- to ensure the system reduces the repeat and routine inquiry workload of library staff, freeing up library staff for more complex tasks and inquiries.
- to ensure the system can be seamlessly and beneficially integrated with existing and future Open University Library electronic services.
- to develop a generic system that is transferable to other libraries supporting distance students and lifelong learners, both in academic and public libraries.

This first section of this chapter outlines how the need for a service such as OPAL has arisen. This is then followed by discussion of research undertaken to date. In the Background Research section the results of a statistical analysis of Open University Library inquiry patterns and experiments conducted into user inquiry behavior are examined. This is followed in the Background Research section by an examination of the current state of the art across technologies and disciplines related to OPAL, in particular looking at existing question-answer systems. In the Building the OPAL Prototype section, the OPAL generic framework and prototype is outlined, while the Evaluation Strategy section is given over to the discussion of the criteria that will be used to assess the success of OPAL with respect to its intended purpose. Finally, in the Future Directions section recommendations are provided outlining possible future directions for the OPAL project.

WHY DO WE NEED OPAL?

Prior to the emergence of the Web and its associated technologies the Open University Library served aca-demic staff and research students who were based at the Open University's Milton Keynes headquarters, providing mainly print-based and on-site resources. With the arrival of the Web, the Open University Library was able to develop a new virtual library service, called Open Libr@ry[3], whereby information resources could be delivered electronically to the homes and workplaces of Open University distance learners based throughout the U.K. and across the world.

Yet delivering and providing access to information resources is only one aspect of the Open Libr@ry service. Students also need support and guidance from professional library staff. Accordingly, the Open University Library has developed the Learner Support Team—a team of library professionals dedicated to supporting the information needs of Open University students, answering user inquiries via e-mail and telephone. However, distance students' study patterns do not fit in with traditional office hours. Consequently, more than 50 percent of inquiries are asked outside office hours, and around 60 percent of these inquiries are of a routine and repeat nature. An analysis of inquiries received shows approximately 70 percent of answers to user inquiries can be found using existing information on the Open Libr@ry Web site. Students may also have to wait until Monday morning if they have posted a query on a Friday before receiving a response from the Learner Support Team. The new service paradigm needs to match the expectations of students' experience of the very best online services. The objective of the OPAL project is to improve service to students by investigating the feasibility and the development of a 24-hour, fully automated inquiry service capable of handling routine natural language questions and providing an immediate response to the user. This will also leave the Learner Support Team more time to deal with complex inquiries. The underlying aim is to create a satisfying automated question-answer service that Open Libr@ry users will wish to use time and time again. Repeat usage of such an automated service would be a key indicator of the quality of the service and the value placed upon it by Open University distance learners (Nielsen, 1999). It should be noted, the project does not aim to replace the inquiry service provided by the Learner Support Team; instead the project aims to supplement this service, enabling students to find useful information resources outside office hours.

BACKGROUND RESEARCH: EXAMINING INQUIRY PATTERNS AND USER INQUIRY BEHAVIOR

During the early months of the OPAL project, initial research focussed on understanding and analyzing inquiry patterns and the way in which users asked inquiries. This section of the chapter outlines these research findings, in particular looking at three areas. Firstly, the impact of inquiry context on the selection of a suitable enquiry response is examined. This is followed by discussion of field research conducted by the OPAL team to assess how student interaction with a question-answer system is affected by the agent—human agent or computer agent—that they believe to underpin the system's responses. Finally, general consideration is given to inquiry patterns and paths revealed by statistical analysis of the Open University's Learner Support e-mail archive, a collection of several thousand enquiries sent by students to the Learner Support Team.

The User's Context: Understanding the Essence of Reference Inquiries

To help determine the operational requirements for the OPAL system, a selection of U.K. information professionals from academic, public, and research libraries were invited to share their ideas and expertise at a focus group held on February 12, 2001. As it is planned for the OPAL concept to be extended for use in libraries beyond the Open University, input from a range of information professionals is of importance throughout the project to ensure the system meets the needs of a diverse user base. The focus group of 13 information professionals were invited to the Open University Library to discuss the patterns underpinning reference inquiries and to describe the functionality and capacity of an ideal automated reference inquiry system. In particular, the focus group emphasized the need for understanding the whole inquiry context, usually ascertained during face-to-face inquiries via the reference interview process. The inquiry context includes all the verbal and non-verbal clues that give the librarian the information they need in order to select the appropriate answer, such as the manner, language, and terminology in which an inquiry is expressed. This context also includes the user's previous library experience, their level of information and IT literacy, expectations concerning the level of service available,

cultural and professional background, the specific course being studied, and the urgency of the information need. In addition, many university inquiries follow a seasonal pattern, following the course and assignment schedules of students. All these contextual factors impact upon the answer selected by a real librarian, and where possible the OPAL system will need to be able to identify these differing user contexts by means of user profiling in order to deliver a more specific answer to the user. In the case of universities, much of the information required for user profiling is already held on centralized university student registration systems, or could be gathered via the development of a Personal Information Environment (PIE). The PIE concept has already been tested through the UK HeadLine (Hybrid Electronic Access and Delivery in the Library Networked Environment) project (Gambles, 2001). HeadLine was a U.K. Joint Information Services Committee (JISC) project to develop a PIE for hybrid library users by employing portal type technology such as that used by My Yahoo. As with My Yahoo, the PIE presents the user with an information environment that is tailored to their needs, also allowing user personalization. The Open University Library is now planning a My Open Libr@ry PIE style facility, within which the OPAL system could sit. Public libraries, with their particularly wide user base and remit, pose greater problems for user profiling, and represent a further area of research for the OPAL project.

Interfaces, Agents, and User Perception

In addition to understanding the iterative nature of the reference interview process and the importance of the inquiry context, another key part of the OPAL project is to get a clear picture of the system's users, and an understanding of the way they interact with Web-based applications. To this end a series of experiments were conducted at an Open University Psychology residential school held in July 2001. Some Open University courses include a residential school where students can discuss ideas, take part in group activities, and carry out practical work with other students and teaching staff. Due to the Open University's distance learning model, with the exception of the residential schools, it is often difficult to find a time and place where students gather together in a group. For the purpose of collecting data to help in modeling our users, the psychology residential school provided a suitable forum. The aim of the experiment conducted at the residential school by the OPAL team was threefold:

- To gather a clean data set for the analysis of question types and potential keywords.
- To see if there are any significant differences between the type of questions asked depending on the nature of the agent answering the question (see the details of the experimental design set out below).
- To see if there is any correlation between the type of question asked and the level of experience that the student has in using Internet applications.

In total 60 students took part. Participants were read a scenario explaining that a new Open Libr@ry question and answer service had been introduced, called OPAL. In the scenario they were told they were about to begin a new course assignment and had decided to see if the OPAL service could be of assistance. They were then invited to put a question to OPAL. The scenario was read to participants, as opposed to them being given a written version, so as to avoid giving cues that might bias their responses. Each student was allocated to one of three groups. Each group undertook a slightly differing experiment:

- In the first group participants were not given any information about the nature of the agent who would be answering their query, i.e., they were not informed whether they were dealing with a human agent or a computer agent.
- In the second group participants were told that an artificial agent, in other words a computer system, would be answering their query.
- In the third group participants were told that a human being would be answering their query.

Each student was then asked to put a question to the system, and to phrase it in three different ways. This was done to ensure that a wide variety of requests were obtained. Finally the participant filled out a short questionnaire detailing which Web-based applications they had used. Each inquiry was automatically archived into an access database.

Our hypothesis was that the nature of the agent participants believed they were interacting with would make a significant difference to the length of

Table 13–1

Relationship between the Agent Type Participants Believed to Underlie the System and the Mean Word Length of the Participants' Inquiries

Agent Type	Mean Length of Inquiry (In Words)
No information given as to the nature of the agent	4.35
Software agent	4.83
Human agent	4.9

the question they asked. Specifically, if the participants thought they were interacting with a human being they would ask questions in grammatical sentences (e.g., "What Psychology journals do you have in stock?"). Whereas if the participants thought they were interacting with an artificial agent they would ask questions in the form of a list of ungrammatical keywords (e.g., "psychology, journals")—in much the same way as a person would use a search engine.

In fact our results showed there was no significant difference between any of the three experimental groups in terms of the length of the query that was submitted. Table 13–1 above illustrates this by showing the mean length of query in terms of numbers of words.

Another possibility was that there was a correlation between the experience a person had in using Web applications and the nature of the question that was asked. For example, this correlation could be in terms of the length of the inquiry, the subject matter, or the manner in which the question was posed, i.e., keywords or natural language. Each participant was given one point for each of the various Web-related activities they had undertaken. Again, there was no correlation.

From these results it is clear that neither the nature of the agent with which they were communicating, nor the participant's level of experience, made any significant difference to the length of query they submitted to the system. This is largely counter intuitive, so what could cause the participants to behave in such a way? One possibility is the nature of the visual clues given by the online form itself. Despite the text box being much larger than those used in typical search engines, the interface still had the general appearance of a search engine and this could have been the determining factor in many cases.

These findings correspond with Restivo and Steinhauer's (2000) work on visual literacy theory, which argues that our reactions to user interface design are culturally determined by our visual gestalt.

Another aspect of natural language-based search engines is that many of them have an avatar as part of their look and feel, see for example AskJeeves.[4] This helps to humanize the system so that people feel asking a question in natural language is a natural thing to do. Again this need for an avatar could be part of our visual heritage and literacy, and is an area for further research.

Inquiry Patterns and Paths

From keyword analysis of the data gathered during the Open University residential school, it was found that the majority of participants formulated subject inquiries using subject specific keywords drawn from within the psychology knowledge domain, such as model, modeling, cognitive, cognition, memory, psychology, and neuropsychology. This is as opposed to resource and access specific keywords, such as journal, password, and database.

With respect to the participants' keyword usage, the dominance of subject-related rather than resource-specific keywords could be an indicator of the participants' subject and course-centered perspective. It could also indicate a general lack of awareness about the types of electronic library resources available via the Web, e.g., databases, e-books, and electronic journals. Clearly, if the student does not know a service or a resource type exists, they then lack the language and awareness to ask for that particular resource type. This indicates the need to undertake user modeling and to conduct research into user perceptions and expectations about online library services in order to understand how best to develop and convey online library services to the user.

Interestingly, the analysis of the inquiry data set gathered at the Open University psychology residential school yielded different results to an earlier analysis of e-mail inquiries submitted to the Open University Learner Support Team. Repeat and routine e-mails to the Learner Support Team showed a much higher concentration of requests for passwords or for access to particular databases and journals, totaling around 60 percent, and on the whole were less subject orientated. This may have resulted because the residential school experiment measured student inquiries that were connected to their initial information need, i.e., information for their course assignment. Whereas repeat and routine e-mails received by the Learner Support Team are often submitted by students who have already identified a suitable database for their course assignment, but have since encountered access difficulties.

Taking the inquiry data collected from Open University students at both the residential school and via e-mails sent to the Learner Support Team, it would appear that there are three main paths of questioning that student inquiries follow:

- Subject inquiries
- Resource and service inquiries
- Access inquiries (e.g., how to access a database or obtain a password)

These three inquiry paths form the core of the OPAL system as outlined in the Building the OPAL Prototype section, incorporating both the students' subject, topic, and assignment orientated perspective as well as the librarians' often more resource orientated perspective.

TECHNOLOGIES AND POSSIBLE SOLUTIONS

As well as understanding the role of the reference interview, the inquiry context, and the user's subject orientated perspective, the team has also been examining a number of already existing in-house solutions and third-party software products for the delivery of 24-hour automated reference.

Firstly, in considering in-house solutions there have already been several attempts in both the U.K. and the U.S. to build automated library systems capable of handling natural language inquiries. In 1997, the U.K. Newcastle University created NERD (Newcastle Electronic Reference Desk)[5] (Gleadhill, 1997), a database of common inquiry questions and answers searchable in natural language powered by Orbital Organik Knowledgeware.[6] Using NERD, students can ask a question of the automated system, and if an answer is not on the system, the student can choose to e-mail the question to a librarian. The librarian then answers the inquiry and chooses whether or not to add the new question-answer pair to the NERD database. The concept behind NERD was derived from Mark Ackerman's (1994; 1996) work at MIT on the Answer Garden. In the Answer Garden new questions, those not already included

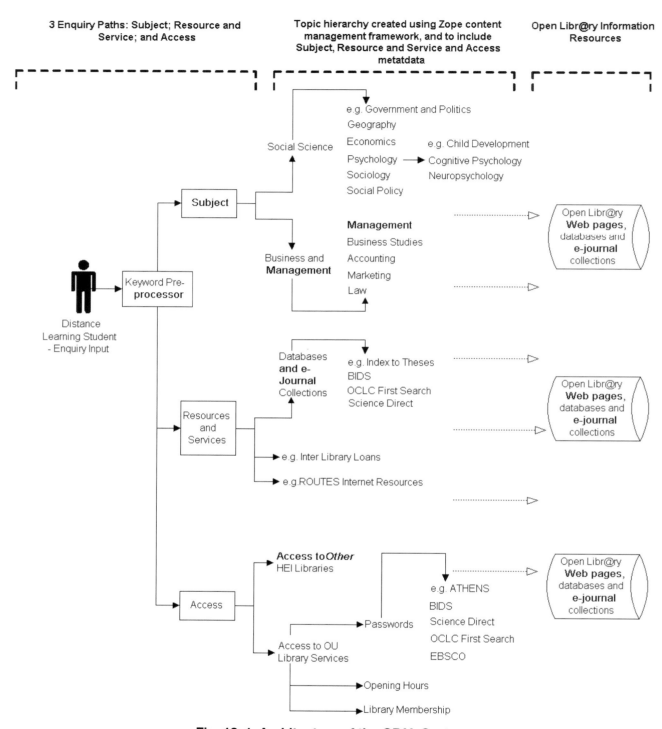

Fig. 13–1. Architecture of the OPAL System

in the knowledge base, were fielded to a group of experts who could then add their answer to an ever growing database of questions and answers, hence the "Answer Garden." While providing obvious benefits, the OPAL team also felt this question-answer model posed possible issues surrounding mainte-nance and quality control, with the potential for un-controlled answer proliferation and record overlap as the knowledge base grew. Nor did it take into ac-count the user's inquiry context or reflect closely enough the iterative, diagnostic nature of the refer-ence interview process between the librarian and student. Fully automated question answer services have also been developed in the U.S., the most successful of which include the Indiana University Knowledge Base[7] and the Massachusetts Institute of Technology's START Natural Language Question Answering System (SynTactic Analysis using Reversible Transformations)[8] (Katz, 1997). These systems do provide reliable answers to user questions and also have good quality control mechanisms in place, but could also represent high maintenance or complex development; for example, by utilizing already existing databases, such as the Internet Movie Database, the START system cuts down on the time required to maintain its repository of possible answers; however, START's natural language processing and artificial intelligence capacity is particularly complex and beyond the scope of the OPAL project. Conversely, the Indiana University Knowledge Base can process input in keywords and simple natural language as is within the scope of the OPAL project but takes an estimated 300 person hours per week to maintain.[9]

Recently there has also been an emergence in the use of Web-based virtual assistants for the delivery of customer service (Lees, 2001; Chartrand, 2001; Denison, 2001). These virtual assistants, also known as conversational bots and vReps, can receive and respond to questions submitted by the user in natural language. They are programmed to recognize and respond to questions within their predefined knowledge domain, and this knowledge domain is usually based upon topic hierarchies. Most often these virtual assistants take the form of a text box accompanied by an avatar, where the avatar is used to make the service seem more personable and human. There are several software developers now creating bespoke conversational bots for a number of big name companies. The OPAL team is also investigating and testing this style of conversational bot software, which could offer diagnostic possibilities if programmed correctly. These virtual assistants usually provide the user with a single answer response that can be as broad or specific as required, or they can also direct the user to an appropriate Web page. However, each response, and each possible pattern of interaction between the user and the bot must be predicted and anticipated in order for the bot to engage in this type of back and forth diagnostic dialogue, and could again represent potential quality control and maintenance issues.

It should be remembered that one aim of the OPAL project is to free up staff time to concentrate on more complex tasks while the OPAL system will handle routine inquiries on their behalf. It is important that any system developed does not absorb all free staff time with maintenance of the new OPAL service.

Finally, there are also a number of natural language search engines already in existence, most notably AskJeeves.[10] The AskJeeves model has been examined by the OPAL team. However, while AskJeeves acts as a general question and answer search engine across a broad subject domain, the team anticipates OPAL will be much more library specific, using keyword rule sets based on language derived from the library subject domain and from student library enquiries. The OPAL prototype, and the genetic algorithm used to develop these library specific keywords rule sets, are outlined in the Building the OPAL Prototype section.

Taken individually, none of these existing solutions was seen to provide a suitable model on which to base the OPAL prototype. In the case of the in-house solutions, those evaluated presented problems connected to high maintenance or high levels of complexity, and so presented an unsustainable, non-transferable solution. Problems associated with the commercial alternatives included maintenance, high cost, and dependency on the software provider for training and support. Consequently, the OPAL team has continued to pursue the development of its own prototype, incorporating selected concepts and ideas derived collectively from the commercial and in-house solutions.

BUILDING THE OPAL PROTOTYPE: A GENERIC AND TRANSFERABLE FRAMEWORK

In accordance with the project's objectives to provide both a transferable, generic model and a low-maintenance solution, a system has been devised that the team anticipates will fulfill these aims. Shortly, this prototype will be outlined in greater depth, but first several key points should be noted with respect to the first iteration of the OPAL prototype:

- Subject Domain: for the purpose of prototyping, OPAL has been developed focusing on two subject areas: *Social Science* and *Business and Management*.

- Answer Source: The OPAL prototype aims to *direct students to relevant information already contained on the Open Libr@ry Web pages*. At this stage in the development process the prototype does not yet interrogate databases, such as the library catalog, in order to provide answers. Currently effort is instead being concentrated on developing a system that can correctly identify the user's question and their associated need.
- Inquiry Categorization: The prototype has been developed with respect to the three possible inquiry paths outlined—*Service and Access, Subject,* and *Resource*—as already discussed in the Background Research section.
- Generic Framework: The prototype provides a simple generic framework that can be easily transferred to other university libraries, including the OPAL partner libraries at Leicester and Birkbeck.

Question Processing: OPAL Rule Sets and the Genetic Algorithm

In the first iteration of the OPAL prototype, the user submits their natural language question via a simple Web interface by inputting their question into a text box. Their input is first stemmed using a Python stemming program, and then OPAL sorts through the stemmed input, identifying keywords and phrases that match keywords and phrases contained in the OPAL rule set. In essence, the OPAL rule set is formed by keywords/phrases that are triggered by corresponding keywords/phrases in the user's natural language input. In the first iteration of the OPAL prototype, these rules have been developed manually and have been categorized into three main groups—*Service and Access, Subject,* and *Resource*—but future rules will be calculated via a genetic algorithm (GA). As more and more students enter their questions into OPAL and as these questions are archived, the genetic algorithm script will be used to analyze data in this archive, examining the way in which students ask questions. The genetic algorithm will compare the questions users ask against OPAL's actual responses, and also against the responses that OPAL should have given. Over time the genetic algorithm will gradually refine OPAL's in-built rule set, which at present has been constructed manually, eventually building a much more exact keyword rule set, which will in turn improve the system's success rate, en-

abling OPAL to become smarter over time and with increased usage. This genetic algorithm is now undergoing training using student inquiry samples. It is hoped long-term use of the genetic algorithm will provide the following benefits:

- Speed: There are too many possibilities and variables for rule sets to be created entirely "by hand."
- Adaptability: The adaptability of the genetic algorithm will reduce the need for human maintenance.
- Confidence and Accuracy: It is possible to see how the genetic algorithm reaches its conclusions. This makes the GA a preferred option to other adaptive algorithms where causality is not always so clear (for example neural networks).
- Generic Application and Transferability: Providing an institution has an archive of user questions, it is easy for them to configure a new set of rules to suit their own requirements, either manually or with some statistical or artificial intelligence method such as genetic algorithms.

In the present version of OPAL, if a rule is found that sufficiently matches the user's input, a Web page is built containing one or more links to those pages that are associated with the rule. This methodology is easy for other institutions to replicate, and again ensures OPAL is transferable and falls within a generic framework. Other institutions can simply create their own rule set, and link the required Web pages to each rule.

OPAL is a flexible concept, which could be applied to a range of academic and public libraries. The key to OPAL's success will partially reside in the quality of each institution's Web architecture, requiring a well-defined and consistent structure that provides good potential for interoperability. The more "fine grained" the architecture, the more responsive OPAL can be.

Why Zope, Python, and Perl?

The OPAL prototype has been developed in a combination of Zope,[11] Python,[12] and Perl.[13] Zope is an open source application designed to build dynamic interactive Web-based applications. It has been chosen as the platform for the OPAL prototype because it is a free open-source product and contains features that have helped to speed up the prototyping process. Zope would not necessarily be chosen as a tool for the final implementation of the final OPAL system (see the Evaluation Strategy section). Likewise, the current iteration of the OPAL prototype uses Python to embody the logic of the OPAL process. Python is the language in which Zope is written and is the default scripting language used to extend Zope's capabilities. For the purpose of the prototype, Python is a useful scripting tool, but as with the Zope system itself, Python would not necessarily be the language of choice for the purpose of a full-scale implementation of the OPAL system (see the Evaluation Strategy section). Lastly, the genetic algorithm, the tool used to improve and modify the OPAL rule sets, has been written in Perl. Originally this genetic algorithm was written in Python, but this script exhibited a slow processing time, and was re-written in Perl to provide a much faster processing time.

To develop this first prototype the OPAL team is working with our partners in the OU Knowledge Media Institute (KMi). KMi specializes in the development of near-term future technologies for sharing, accessing, and understanding knowledge, such as the use of organizational memory and the use of intelligent agent systems.

EVALUATION STRATEGY

The first phase of the OPAL project is scheduled for completion in July 2002, and the team is currently evaluating the prototype. If OPAL is to be taken forward into an implementation phase, the prototype should demonstrate that it could become an effective component of a digital library. Three aspects of the system will be evaluated:

- Response Accuracy: The accuracy of responses given by OPAL will be tested by submitting a set of archived student inquiries to the system, and examining the responses given. It should be noted that the set of test questions used to evaluate the accuracy of the system will be different to those used to train the genetic algorithm from which the initial OPAL rules sets have been developed. The team will also be looking to minimize the number of false positives. This is when an inquiry triggers a rule set and when an incorrect response is given. It will be far preferable for OPAL to provide a "don't know" response than a false positive, as this is

less damaging to the credibility of the system in the eyes of its users, than a completely incorrect response that could mislead the user.

- Comparison with Staffed Helpdesk: The second aspect of the evaluation will consist of a comparative study of the speed, cost, and accuracy of OPAL responses in comparison with the Learner Support staffed helpdesk.
- Usability and Acceptability: The third aspect of the evaluation will investigate the efficiency and ease of use of the interface, as well as looking at how acceptable and credible such an automated system is with students, and if they would use the system if it were available.

FUTURE DIRECTIONS AND RECOMMENDATIONS

Research to date has shown that OPAL represents a promising avenue for research with the potential to become a significant piece of software. Consequently, following completion of the evaluation in July 2002, it is hoped the project will move into an implementation stage. From the research already conducted it is now possible to make the following recommendations with respect to this second phase:

- Migration from Zope to Java: Zope was chosen as the platform for prototype development due to the opportunities for rapid development that it afforded. However the Zope development community is small at present and there are other available technologies more suited to the implementation of OPAL in the second phase of the project. In particular Java has emerged as the de facto standard language for Web-based application development, offering opportunities for distributed processing and interoperability with legacy systems. For this reason, a migration of the OPAL system to Java has been recommended.
- Development of a Diagnostic System: At present, OPAL simply starts afresh when it is asked each question. However there is the possibility of developing a more "interview" style interaction, enabling the answer given by OPAL to be a function of previous questions asked in a particular session. This could be seen as being analogous to the reference interview process between librarian and library user that occurs

during face-to-face inquiry interactions.

- Interoperability with Database Resources: Currently OPAL only points the user to existing Web pages. Its power would be greatly increased by enabling it to interrogate the library's already existing databases in order to find more detailed information, for example, what journal articles are held on a particular topic. This would enable the user to ask very detailed subject-specific questions. This would provide functionality similar to that now becoming available through information portal style technology, such as that under development both commercially and also by the MALIBU[14] (MAnaging the hybrid LIbrary for the Benefit of Users) research team (Cave et al., 2001; Pinfield et al., 1998). MALIBU is a project led by King's College London in partnership with Southampton University and Oxford University that uses a community of intelligent agents to search databases on behalf of the user. The project aims to develop a single search interface, currently known as GIGA (Global Information Gathering Agent), by which students can simultaneously search multiple online databases, the Internet, digitized archives, and Z39.50 compliant catalogues. In order to provide answers to more specialized student inquiries the OPAL team will be considering the possibility of developing such a community of intelligent mobile software agents capable of traversing Open Libr@ry's network of databases in order to answer more specialized questions. Further discussion about the possible use of intelligent agents within the context of library reference work can be found in work by Laura Zick (1999; 2000) and Susan Feldman (2000).
- Integration with a Personal Information Environment, such as MyOpen Libr@ry: Often much detailed information about a user and their preferences can be gleaned from existing systems. The Open University is currently developing a MyOpen Libr@ry personal information environment that will link to information about a student's course and subject of study held on existing Open University registration and authentication systems. Such systems can provide extremely helpful information about the user's context that often acts as an indica-

tor of the type of response required. Further research needs to be undertaken to determine how OPAL could be integrated within a system such as MyOpen Libr@ry.

- Extension of Subject Coverage: the current prototype only covers Social Science and Management and Business. It is now planned to extend the range of subjects covered by the prototype to all faculties within the university, and to provide a framework for assimilating subjects into the OPAL framework.
- Development of Prototype at Partner Institutions: in order to test the transferability of the OPAL prototype and the generic framework, and in collaboration with staff at the Open University, sibling prototypes will be developed at the OPAL partner institutions, Birkbeck College and the University of Leicester.
- Personal Digital Assistant and Post-PC Devices: The OPAL project team must also look ahead to the possibility of the post-PC age. The last few years have seen a steady emergence in the use of devices other than PCs to access the Internet. Some analysts have talked about the "death" of the traditional PC and the rise of household objects with access to the Web. Whilst OPAL does not yet cater for these, the design should allow extension to be able to handle such devices in the future.

These recommendations present future directions for the OPAL project. The climate under which the prototype is being developed is currently under rapid change, with new technologies and resources emerging both within and without of the library sector. Students' inquiries will move with this changing climate, and any system developed must be easily adaptable and easy to maintain to keep pace with this change. It is hoped that use of the OPAL genetic algorithm should enable the system to adapt to this changing climate with a minimum of human maintenance being required. Nevertheless, it will only be through testing the various iterations of the OPAL prototype with Open University distance learners that we will truly be able to determine the types of questions that are asked, the way in which students choose to ask those questions, and whether or not the system can provide satisfactory answers.

ENDNOTES

1. Open University Library: http://oulib1.open.ac.uk/
2. OPAL: http://oulib1.open.ac.uk/wh/research/opal/
3. Open Libr@ry: http://oulib1.open.ac.uk/open library/index.htm
4. AskJeeves: www.ask.co.uk/
5. NERD: www.ncl.ac.uk/library/
6. Orbital Organik Knowledgeware: www. orbitalsw. com/
7. Indiana University Knowledge Base: http://kb. indiana.edu/
8. START Natural Language Question Answering System: www.ai.mit.edu/projects/infolab/
9. Indiana University Knowledge Base: http://kb. indiana.edu/data/acte.html
10. AskJeeves: www.ask.co.uk
11. Zope: www.zope.org
12. Python: www.python.org
13. Perl: www.perl.com
14. MALIBU: www.kcl.ac.uk/humanities/cch/malibu/

REFERENCES

Ackerman, M. S. 1994. "Augmenting the Organizational Memory: A Field Study of Answer Garden." Proceedings of the ACM Conference on Computer Supported Cooperative Work (CSCW 94), Chapel Hill, N.C., October [Online]. Available: www.ics.uci.edu/ ~ackerman/pub/94b12/cscw94.html [2002, May 24].

Ackerman, M. S. 1996. "Answer Garden 2: Merging Organizational Memory with Collaborative Help." Proceedings of the ACM Conference on Computer Supported Cooperative Work (CSCW 96), Boston, Mass., November [Online]. Available: www.ics. uci.edu/~ackerman/pub/96b22/cscw96.ag2.html [2002, May 24].

Cave, Michael, Valeda F. Dent, Jessie Hey, Ann Lees, and Astrid Wissenburg. 2001. "Travelling at the Speed of Discovery: The MALIBU Project's Most Valuable Lessons." *Ariadne*, no. 26 [Online]. Available: www.ariadne.ac.uk/issue26/malibu/ [2002, May 24].

Chartrand, S. 2001. "Software to provide 'personal' attention to online customers with service untouched by a human." *The New York Times*, Monday, August 20, 2001.

Denison, D. C. 2001. "Bots for Business." *Boston Globe*, 13 May 2001, p. C1.

Feldman, S. 2000. "The Answer Machine." *Searcher* 8, no.1 [Online]. Available: www.infotoday.com/ searcher/jan00/feldman.htm [2002, May 24].

Gambles, A. 2001. "The HeadLine Personal Information Environment—Evaluation Phase One." *D-Lib Magazine* 7, no.3 [Online]. Available: www.dlib.org/ dlib/march01/gambles/03gambles.html [2002, May 24].

Gleadhill, D. 1997. "Electronic Enquiry Desk. Does NERD Have the Answer?" *Library Technology* 2, no. 2: 35-36.

Katz, B. 1997. "From Sentence Processing to Information Access on the World Wide Web." AAAI Spring Symposium on Natural Language Processing for the World Wide Web, Stanford University, Stanford, Calif. [Online]. Available: www.ai.mit.edu/people/ boris/webaccess/ [2002, May 24].

Lees, J. 2001. "The Gift of the Gab: Virtual Assistants." *InternetWorks* 48 (August): 12.

Nielsen, J. 1999. *Designing Web Usability: The Practice of Simplicity*. Indianapolis: New Riders Publishing.

Pinfield, S. et al. 1998. "Realising the Hybrid Library." *D-LIB Magazine* 4, no. 9 (October). Available: www.dlib.org/dlib/october98/10pinfield.html [2002, May 24].

Restivo, S., and A. Steinhauer. 2000. "Toward a Socio-Visual Theory of Information and Information Technology." Proceedings IEEE International Symposium on Technology and Society, La Sapienza University of Rome, Rome: 169-175.

Zick, L. 1999. "Artificial Intelligence and Libraries: A Primer for Librarians." School of Library and Information Science, Indiana University [Online]. Available: www.dochzi.com/l600/ [2002, May 24].

Zick, L. 2000. "The Work of Information Mediators: A Comparison of Librarians and Intelligent Software Agents." *First Monday* 5, no.5 (May) [Online]. Available: http://firstmonday.org/issues/issue5_5/zick/ index.html [2002, May 24].

Chapter 14

Creating a System for Shared Information and Referral: The Importance of Ontology

Jeffrey Pomerantz and Joanne Silverstein

OVERVIEW

This chapter reports findings regarding the use of taxonomies and ontologies in building an information and referral system utilizing pre-existing information sources found within an organization. These findings are based on a case study that sought to standardize the process of sharing organizational knowledge. It is concluded that information and referral activities can be streamlined, improved, and standardized by building taxonomies and ontologies based on existing information sources. These ontologies may be used to create shared software tools, and are especially effective when they are created in concert with partner organizations.

INTRODUCTION

All organizations, from small mom-and-pop stores to the largest organization, receive questions about themselves or their services. Stores are asked about their hours of operation and their available stock, corporations are asked about their products, human services organizations are asked about the services they provide. For reference services this situation is compounded, as the primary service provided is that of answering questions. Many organizations utilize software applications to manage and even answer questions. Like much software development, however, these software applications are designed and built without any firm theoretical basis.

This chapter describes a process for designing an information and referral system based on an ontol-ogy reflecting existing information sources found within an organization. It describes a case study that sought to standardize the process of sharing organizational knowledge across the distributed locations of a call center. This call center serves the function within the organization of a reference service, answering questions about the organization and the programs and projects run by the organization, for employees of the organization as well as for the general public. The remainder of this chapter is organized in the following order: Case Study Description, Definitions, Methods (Data Gathering and Analysis), Findings and Implications, Discussion, Future Research, and Conclusion.

CASE STUDY DESCRIPTION

The research described here was conducted in what will be referred to as the Organization. The Organization is a governmental agency that serves the national public through multiple programs and offices. Supporting the over 5,000 employees in those offices is a network of information and referral services, which will be collectively referred to as the Call Center. The Call Center serves the function within the Organization of a reference service, answering questions about the organization and the programs and projects run by the organization, for employees of the organization as well as for the general public.

Employees of the Call Center, like employees of any reference service, use a variety of information sources on many different types of media. Like many reference services too, some of these information sources are out of date, and some contain information that is inconsistent with information contained in other sources. As a result, the Organization loses time as Call Center employees struggle to find accurate and reliable information. Call Center employees are faced with a confusing array of information sources, and report that they often refer calls to the wrong offices, offer inconsistent information, and lose callers in transfers from office to office.

Call Center management decided to explore the state of their referral function and asked the research team to conduct research into information flow in the Call Center. This study was driven by the research question, "How can the process of sharing information and referral knowledge be optimized in a large, diversified organization?" The findings from this research formed the basis for development of specifications for an information and referral software application, referred to here as the Organizational Referral System (ORS).

DEFINITIONS

Information and referral services (commonly called "I&R" by practitioners) provide a central point of access to information about government, private, and community-based resources and social services. I&R services exist in many states and countries and provide a human-intermediated link between people in need and available resources in a myriad of human service arenas. Similar to telephone directory assistance, I&R services provide contact information for organizations that provide social services—but I&R services provide not just a telephone number, but a referral to the most appropriate organization to meet an individual's particular need. Similar to a library reference desk, I&R services provide information that attempts to meet an individual's specific and situational need. However, I&R services do not provide services themselves, but rather provide referrals to other organizations that do provide specific services.

In evaluations of library reference transactions, often only questions that are answered fully and correctly are considered to be successful (Hernon and McClure, 1986). According to these evaluation criteria, a referral is a failed reference transaction. For an I&R service, unlike for a library reference service, a referral is the only successful transaction.

Taxonomy

According to the Oxford English Dictionary, a *taxonomy* is "a classification of anything." This rather broad definition does not differentiate a taxonomy from a classification scheme, which Kwasnik (1999) describes as a representation of knowledge in a domain. Kwasnik continues, stating that a classification scheme, like a theory, connects concepts "in a useful structure" (1999: 24). What makes this structure useful is its "richness" in describing the domain in question and its utility for the task for which it was created.

Anyone can create a classification; indeed, everyone creates informal classification schemes (for example, a classification of books by room in a house—cookbooks in the kitchen, "work-related" books in the study, fiction in the den, etc.). On the other hand, a taxonomy reflects expert knowledge about a domain. The Linnaean taxonomy of all living things (named after Carolus Linnaeus, 1707-1778), for example, reflects biological knowledge accumulated over the course of centuries by many scientists and natural philosophers. Linnaean taxonomy is an "is-a" hierarchy: every class is divided into "child" subclasses that inherit all of the properties of their parent class. For example, the classes Mammalia and Aves are both children of the phylum Chordata; while animals in the "sibling" classes Mammalia and Aves differ in many of their characteristics, they all possess a vertebral column, a characteristic that can be inferred from their being subclasses of phylum Chordata. Indeed, according to Kwasnik (1999: 25), "a true hierarchy has only one type of relationship between its super- and subclasses": the is-a relationship.

Ontology

Ontologies are closely related to taxonomies, though they are not equivalent. An *ontology* is a "domain-specific vocabulary of entities, classes, properties, predicates, and functions, and [is] a set of relationships that necessarily hold among those vocabulary items" (Fikes and Farquhar, 1999: 73). Like any classification scheme or taxonomy, an ontology is composed of entities grouped into classes, which are related in some way. An ontology may be developed based on a pre-existing taxonomy, or "from scratch," independent of any taxonomy. Ontologies are different than taxonomies in two ways. First, ontologies include functions or rules that classes of entities may perform. For example, the class Mammalia would include the function *bears live young*. Second, ontologies are shared, reflecting consensual knowledge. Ontologies are not private to some individual, but accepted by a group (Studer et al., 1998).

Guarino (1997), Vickery (1997), and Uschold and Grüninger (1996) refer to this shared quality of ontologies as "reusability." There is some disagreement in the literature over the appropriate degree of an ontology's reusability. Mahesh (1996) claims that ontologies should be built for specific tasks, and thus should not be made to be reusable. Guarino (1997) opposes this view and claims that ontologies may be built for specific tasks, but should be made to be reusable. Findings from the current research suggest that an ontology built for a specific task may also be built to be reusable by ensuring that the categories of the ontology are sufficiently abstract that they will be generalizable to any individual or group involved in that specific task. In the case of the current research, the ontology was built to be reusable by creating classes like Project and Program, subclasses of which were created according to the structure of the organization, but which could be replaced with different subclasses for a different organization.

METHODS

Data were gathered from producers, owners, and users of referral information within the Organization, who participated in focus groups. These focus groups enabled the researchers to collect data about how respondents expected and wished ORS to affect organizational policies and job functions, and enabled the respondents to articulate lengthy or hard-to-describe concerns on these subjects.

Forty-eight respondents participated in the focus groups. Six focus groups of eight participants each were conducted, with respondents drawn from most offices across the Organization, and from all organizational levels. Focus groups were organized so that all members of a given group had approximately the same level of computer skills. (The focus group questions are available upon request from the authors.)

Focus groups were conducted using electronic meeting software. The software application allowed anonymous, text-based responses of any length to the researchers' questions. Focus group questions were projected onto individual respondents' screens, and onto a large room-sized screen. Thus, as respondents typed in answers, all respondents and the moderators could view the answers, but no individual respondent could be identified. As respondents typed answers into the software application, electronic transcripts were automatically created, thus avoiding transcription costs and turnaround time. Later, data from the focus groups were loaded into the software application AtlasTI for content analysis.

FINDINGS AND IMPLICATIONS

Findings from the focus groups included lengthy, textual descriptions of hard-to-describe concerns.

In response to focus group question one ("Think about any search engines and Web sites that you currently use. What features do you like about them?"), many respondents reported a preference for "list of topic choices" and referred to Yahoo!'s directory as an example. The implication of this finding is that hierarchy-based searching should be implemented, and the hierarchy should be created by humans with topical expertise and who are conversant with user searching habits, as is Yahoo!'s Directory. This finding has implications for the interface design and functionality of digital libraries.

Findings from focus group question 3 ("What tools (electronic, hard-copy, etc.) are you using now as referral aids (name and describe them)?") showed that most respondents use many existing Organization-specific tools including the telephone directory, a domain-specific subject index, the Organization's Web site, the Organization's intranet, organizational charts, and consortia directories. The implication is that existing information tools may provide existing terms and hierarchies, to which employees are already acclimated, that can serve as a foundation for building a service.

Focus group question 5 ("How do you organize your referral records in any tools that you use?") was designed to discover how respondents organize their own resources, and how they would like resources organized in ORS. Most responses mentioned the need for retrieval of referral information according to a common set of categories, as well as some specific categories. The implication is that an I&R ontology must include, at a minimum, fields for "topic," "office," "contact name," "rank (title) of contact person," "date of receipt," and "medium."

The last finding discussed here, in response to focus group question 8 ("Where do we 'draw the line' around the boundaries of a referral system?"), was that employees often refer users to information sources that are located outside the boundaries of the Organization, including those at State and other Federal information systems, research centers, and independent experts. Some of these external entities are already designing metadata schema that will allow their systems to communicate with other systems. The implications are that the Organization must take measures to insure that its ontology does not become isolated. Specifically:

- data located or controlled from outside the Organization should be considered for inclusion in ORS, and
- the Organization should coordinate with external organizations to make information sharable across referring organizations.

This finding has implications for many digital reference services, as they must work with external entities for information provision.

The findings in Table 14–1, particularly 2, 4, and 5, have special importance to digital libraries and their personnel.

DISCUSSION

After having reviewed the referral activities of the Organization, the research team was able to create an ontology that captures the Organization's referral information, and that can serve as the basis for development of specifications for ORS. This section describes the ontology design, and describes three suggestions for the use of ontologies in referral activities and services organization-wide.

Designing an Ontology

There are three approaches to ontology creation: top-down, bottom-up, and combination (Noy and McGuinness, 2001). Top-down development is a deductive approach, starting with the highest-level concepts in a domain, under which sub-categories are iteratively determined, until irreducible categories are reached. Bottom-up development, on the other hand, is an inductive approach. It begins with objects in the real world, which are grouped into natural or logical categories with specific attributes, and ends

Table 14–1
Summary of Focus Group Findings

1. Hierarchy-based searching should be implemented in the ORS.
2. The hierarchy should be created by humans with topical expertise.
3. Terms and hierarchies should be reused from existing information tools.
4. Data in existing information tools located or controlled outside the Organization should be included in ORS.
5. Data in existing information tools created by the Organization should be shared with partner and referring organizations through the ORS.

with an articulation of the relationships between those categories. The combination approach employs both top-down and bottom-up methods. Combination development might work up from specifics to generalities, and then back down to more specifics that were not previously apparent. Or combination development might work from both high- and low-level categories toward some mid-range categories.

The Organizational taxonomy uses a combination approach, but one that employs primarily bottom-up, or inductive design. The terms and relationships in the Organizational taxonomy come from information sources created by users, including an organizational directory, a telephone directory, an official project index, an intranet, and several other sources. Some of these sources were organized hierarchically, reflecting the formal structure of the Organization and including both high- and low-level categories (e.g., the organizational directory and the intranet), and some were organized as "flat file" alphabetical lists including only low-level entities (e.g., the telephone directory and the subject index). In developing the ontology, it was therefore possible to utilize a combination development process, based upon these existing information sources.

The first task in designing an ontology is to determine its scope (Noy and McGuinness, 2001). The ontology's scope was first perceived—by the researchers as well as by the Organization itself—to be the Organization and the referrals that it was possible to make within it. The Organization's information sources, however, include programs that are only partially within the Organization's control (e.g., collaborative programs between the Organization

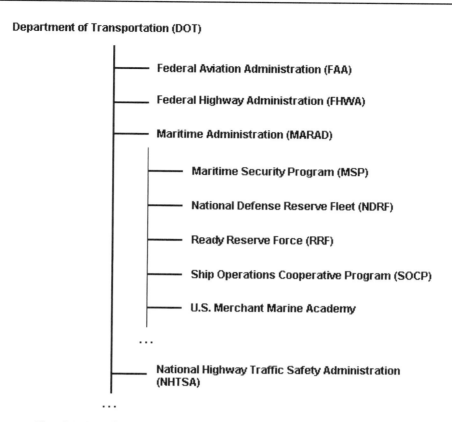

Fig. 14–1. A Small Sample of the Organization's Taxonomy

and other agencies), and employees not directly on the Organization's payroll (e.g., consultants, contractors, independent experts, and researchers). A challenge, therefore, was to determine where to "draw the line" around the ontology. Another challenge was to determine what information from these sources to include in the ontology. The Call Center staff provided consensus on both of these issues by agreeing that all information contained in the Organization's information sources, including external entities, should be contained in the ontology—but that external entities included only in informal sources should not be in the ontology.

In order for an ontology to be considered an ontology, rather than a classification scheme, it must be ensured that the model of the domain being employed "reflect[s] common understanding or consensus of the domain" (Studer et al., 1998: 186-7). This is because ontologies are intended to provide a basis for shared and reusable understanding of the domain in question. The ontology created for this project represents a "shared and common understanding" (Studer, 1998: 184) of I&R work within the Organization, as it is based on the hierarchies

and vocabulary used in existing information sources. Figure 14–1 shows a sample of the taxonomy on which the ontology was based, the generalities of which were drawn directly from existing information sources.

Due to contractual restrictions, the actual Organization and the offices and programs within it have been disguised as the Department of Transportation (DOT), an agency that was not part of this research project. The DOT was chosen as the surrogate for the Organization because its hierarchical structure is similar to the hierarchical structure of the Organization.

The ontology describes not only "is-a" but also other types of relationships between entities. These relationships are in the form of "inference rules"—that is, what sort of information can be inferred from any given entity. The ontology incorporates these inference rules by providing pointers from entities to additional information, thus dictating the content of information that will be provided to users of ORS. For example, one inference rule is as follows:

Term:	Maritime Administration
Scope Note:	The office that promotes the development and maintenance of the United States merchant marine. Also ensures that the United States enjoys adequate shipbuilding and repair service, efficient ports, effective intermodal water and land transportation systems, and reserve shipping capacity in time of national emergency.
Broader Terms:	Department of Transportation
Narrower Terms:	Maritime Security Program, National Defense Reserve Fleet, Ready Reserve Force, Ship Operations Cooperative Program, etc.
Related Terms:	Federal Aviation Administration, Federal Highway Administration, National Highway Traffic Safety Administration, etc.
Use For:	MARAD

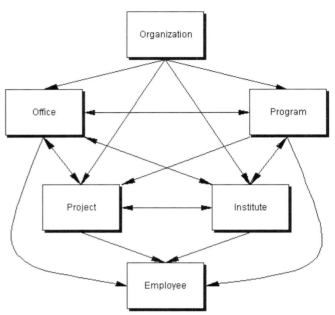

Fig. 14–3. Entities and Relationships

Term:	Ready Reserve Force
Scope Note:	Provides a ready source of "surge" shipping, available when needed by the Department of Defense's U.S. Transportation Command, to support rapid deployment of U.S. military forces.
Broader Terms:	Maritime Administration
Narrower Terms:	
Related Terms:	Maritime Security Program, National Defense Reserve Fleet, Ready Reserve Force, Ship Operations Cooperative Program, U.S. Merchant Marine Academy, etc.
Use For:	RRF

**Fig. 14–2. Two Entities and
Their Relationships**

1. Programs that are administered by an office are represented as narrower terms below the office.

The inverse inference rule is as follows:

2. For information about a program, contact the office that is the broader term above it.

Two entities and some of their relationships to other entities in the ontology are provided in Figure 14–2, above.

The combination of these relationships and inference rules allow for sophisticated behavior to be modeled. For example, a user of the ontology could determine that the Maritime Administration administers the following programs: the Maritime Security Program, the National Defense Reserve Fleet, the Ready Reserve Force, the Ship Operations Cooperative Program, etc. For another example, a user of the ontology could determine that the point of contact for information about the Ready Reserve Force is the Maritime Administration. The use of the ontology to model these relationships and inferences allows the creation of software to perform I&R functions based on these relationships and inferences. This is discussed in the section on software specifications, below.

Having described the scope, generalities, and structure of the ontology, and identified the information that needed to be reflected in the ontology, the researchers designed the ontology itself. The entities for this ontology are identified and their relationships illustrated in Figure 14–3, above. Arrows indicate the direction of inheritance; for example, Office is a subset of Organization, while a Program can be a subset of an Office and vice versa. Offices are hierarchical subdivisions of the Organization, and manage operations within a specific scope of service. Programs have a specific agenda and outcome measures, and manage specific activities. A Project is ongoing work under the jurisdiction of some working group within the Organization. Institutes sponsor research projects.

This section has described the design of an ontology for information and referral service functionality. During its design, the research team made several observations and present them here for other organizations to consider.

Suggestions for Use of Ontologies in Digital Libraries

Reference services take many forms, from library reference desks to I&R services to corporate help desks. There are two functions, however, that all of these different types of services perform:

1. Questions are received by the service, and assigned or routed to an individual who is qualified to answer the question, and
2. That individual makes use of the available information sources to answer the question.

In order to perform these functions there must be some mechanism in place in the reference service for determining to whom to assign questions, and some mechanism for determining what information sources to use. Pomerantz et al. (forthcoming), in a recent Delphi study of digital reference services, discovered 15 factors that influence the process of assigning and routing of questions, and also state that this process may be automated or may be performed by a human intermediary. Similarly, answering questions may be automated or performed by a human intermediary. The challenge for reference services and referral services alike is ensuring that both the assigning and routing and the answering of questions utilizes accurate and up-to-date information.

The research team concluded that referral activities—both manual and automated—can be streamlined, improved, and standardized by building ontologies based on existing information sources. Specifically:

- Existing information sources may provide terms and hierarchies—to which employees are already acclimated—that can serve as a foundation for building a sharable ontology for referral activities.
- Ontologies should be created only after

working with partner entities, thus ensuring interoperability among resulting systems. Cooperative ontologies must include terms and descriptions from external organizations to which users refer, and that can be used to create metadata schema.

- Ontology creation can provide specifications with which to create a software-based tool.

These conclusions are set out in greater detail in the remainder of this chapter.

Use Existing Information Sources

Existing information sources can provide a hierarchy of terms (a taxonomy) to which employees are already acclimated. The taxonomy can then serve as a foundation for building a sharable ontology for referral activities.

The taxonomy of terms in the case of the Organization, for example, comprises several hundreds of vocabulary terms, including "topic," "office," "contact name," "rank (title) of contact person," "date of receipt," and "medium" (these fields were suggested by respondents). This taxonomy is a fundamental component of ORS and imposes simple, hierarchical relationships among the terms.

On its own, however, the taxonomy provides only limited functionality. A taxonomy may provide definitions for each term and type of term, and it establishes relationships (such as "broader than" and "narrower than") between terms. These relationships are only part of the required functionality. A user could, for example, enter the term "FOIA" in a thesaurus and obtain a set of results that include "use for" synonyms, such as "Freedom of Information Act," but would not retrieve a list of FOIA resources and contacts. An ontology establishes more extensive rules than a taxonomy, thus allowing for broader functionality. An ontology-based referral service could respond to a user's query for "FOIA" with an office name, location, and phone number; the name and title of a contact person, URLs, and other referral information. Thus, while taxonomies may be equated with ontologies (Uschold, 1998), ontologies are not as limited as taxonomies (Gruber, 1993).

To the degree that digital reference services provide referral information, their vocabularies, the hierarchy of terms, the inference rules—all must reflect users' most commonly utilized information sources.

Ontologies Should Be Created After Working with Partners

Findings from focus group question 8 showed that some information sources important to the Organization are located outside of the Organization's boundaries. Respondents said they would be more productive if they could communicate across offices, both internal and external. This is certainly the case for many other organizations as well, and therefore external information sources should be considered for inclusion in any ontology for I&R systems.

Findings from focus group question 8 also showed that the Organization's external partners were creating their own taxonomies. Taxonomies from multiple organizations can be integrated to create an ontology that is sharable and reusable across organizations. The potential benefits of collaboration with external organizations are numerous and include:

- saving money by sharing resources,
- benefiting by others' experiences (adopting best practices, legal parameters, and procedures created by others),
- enhancing interoperability with other organizations, and
- providing faster and more consistent information access to users and the public.

These advantages would also accrue to digital reference services that use an ontology-based system, particularly if ontology creation is preceded by a review of the record structures, taxonomies, and ontologies of partner organizations. Resulting ontologies may then be used as foundations for cross-organizational referral services.

An increasingly useful way of ensuring inter-operability among organizations is the creation and use of metadata schema. Metadata is a topic too vast and involved to be addressed here in detail. Briefly, however, one use of metadata is to share information across distributed and heterogeneous sites and users.

Metadata schemas are currently being created by many organizations. Those schemas could offer insights into creating the optimal, shared referral service. Thus, in creating an ontology for a referral service, each organization should review schema from work partners, and investigate whether their own schemas may be shared. Organizations work together and must cooperate to avoid "splintering" their metadata schema. Ontologies created within an organization for a specific task may not have been built with reusability in mind. Nevertheless, reusability may be achieved through cooperation between organizations on arriving at sufficiently high-level categories that are generalizable across organizations. This function would be especially useful to digital reference services because they often draw on the resources of other organizations.

Organizations are finding new ways to work with each other, both to enhance their scopes, and to coordinate their information activities. Shared ontology design and metadata schema will be increasingly important as organizations realize they are facing similar challenges and opportunities in information provision.

Ontologies as Bases for Software

As Fikes and Farquhar state, ontologies "can be used as . . . class definitions for conventional software systems" (1999: 73). Certainly, the ontology resulting from the current research could be used to guide software specifications for automated referral applications.

The relationships in the ontology provide the backbone for the specifications for ORS's functionality. For example, a user who entered the term "RRF" would receive as a returned result the full name of that program (Ready Reserve Force), an explanation of what the RRF is (the Scope note), and contact information for the office that administers the RRF (the Maritime Administration). For another example, if a Call Center employee receives a call from a member of the public who is interested in the U.S. Merchant Marine Academy, that employee can search ORS for the phrase "merchant marine," "merchant marine academy," or some variation on those phrases, and retrieve information about and contact information for the Maritime Administration. The specifications for ORS's functionality include providing the following information:

1. The scope note for the term or phrase searched on, or for the appropriate "used for" term.
2. Contact information for the term or phrase searched on (if that term or phrase is an office), or for the administering office (if the term or phrase searched on is a program or project, the broader term above it).

The process of deciding to make or buy software is not addressed here, and will most likely be different for each organization. Each, however, is a lengthy process, and using an ontology to guide the process ensures that the system will do what is needed, rather than adapt organizational needs to available software functionality.

Commercial I&R software is used by thousands of community service organizations to assist employees in providing accurate information to customers of healthcare hotlines and local government services. What employees at those organizations have in common with workers at the Organization is the critical need for accurate referrals. An I&R application based on a shared ontology will allow employees providing I&R services to make such referrals faster and more efficiently. Similarly, the market is becoming populated with software packages that enable the functions crucial to digital reference services, and the caveats that exist for I&R organizations also apply to digital reference organizations.

Future Research

The limitations of this study provide suggestions for future research. First, the specific contents of the ontology are unique to the Organization. It would be useful to test the completed ontology in other organizations.

Second, the researchers found that ontologies streamline manual work and promote information sharing across an organization in an I&R service environment. Future research is necessary to determine if this statement would be true for other organizational environments, such as:

- consortial networks,
- digital and non-digital library reference services that seek to provide referral information, and
- other organizations that must perform high levels of internal coordination and thus must advise employees whom to call (such as hospitals and universities).

Future empirical studies are called for to test both the usefulness of shared ontologies in different environments, and the implications of such sharing on organizations and organizational processes.

Because reference services do make referrals, future work is necessary to create an ontology of re- ferral information built for the specific task of providing reference service, but designed to be reusable by the reference community at large.

CONCLUSION

This chapter has presented an approach to building ontologies to reflect existing information resources, using a combination of inductive and deductive methods. The chief implication of this research is that referral activities can be streamlined, improved, and standardized by utilizing I&R systems based on such an ontology. Further, this research indicates that ontologies are especially useful and effective when they are created in concert with partner organizations, so that they may be shared and used to create shared software tools. While this study was conducted within a large governmental organization, future research will determine the generalizability of these findings to other organizational settings. Organizational settings such as networked reference services and digital reference services may find the use of ontologies and ontology-based I&R applications particularly fruitful.

REFERENCES

AIRS. 2000. *Standards for Professional Information & Referral.* Seattle: Alliance of Information & Referral Systems.

Fikes, Richard, and Adam Farquhar. 1999. "Distributed Repositories of Highly Expressible Reusable Ontologies." *IEEE Intelligent Systems and Their Applications* 14, no. 2 (March/April): 73-79.

Gruber, Thomas R. 1993. "A Translation Approach to Portable Ontology Specifications." *Knowledge Acquisition* 5: 199-220.

Guarino, Nicola. 1997. "Understanding, Building, and Using Ontologies: A Commentary to 'Using Explicit Ontologies in KBS Development' by van Heijst, Schreiber, and Wielinga." *International Journal of Human and Computer Studies* 46: 293-310 [Online]. Available: www.ladseb.pd.cnr.it/infor/Ontology/Papers/vanHeijst.pdf [2002, May 24].

Hernon, P., and C. R. McClure. 1986. "Unobtrusive Reference Testing: The 55 Percent Rule." *Library Journal* III(7): 37-41.

Kwasnik, Barbara H. 1999. "The Role of Classification in Knowledge Representation and Discovery." *Library Trends* 48, no. 1 (Summer): 22-47.

Mahesh, K. 1996. *Ontology Development for Machine Translation: Ideology and Methodology.* New Mexico State University, Computing Research Laboratory, MCC-96-292.

Noy, Natalya Fridman, and Deborah L. McGuinness. 2001. "Ontology Development 101: A Guide to Creating Your First Ontology," Stanford Knowledge Systems Laboratory Technical Report KSL-01-05 [online]. Available: www.smi.stanford.edu/projects/protege/publications/ontology_development/ontology101.html [2002, May 24].

Pomerantz, J., Scott Nicholson, and R. David Lankes. (forthcoming). Digital Reference Triage: An Investigation using the Delphi Method into the Factors Influencing Question Routing and Assignment. *The Library Quarterly*

Studer, Rudi, V. Richard Benjamins, and Dieter Fensel. 1998. "Knowledge Engineering: Principles and Methods." *Data & Knowledge Engineering* 25: 161-197.

Uschold, Mike. 1998. "Knowledge Level Modelling: Concepts and Terminology." *The Knowledge Engineering Review* 13, no.1: 5-29.

Uschold, Mike, and Michael Grüninger. 1996. "Ontologies: Principles, Methods, and Applications." *The Knowledge Engineering Review* 11, no.2: 93-136.

Vickery, B. C. 1997. "Ontologies." *Journal of Information Science* 23, no.4: 277-286.

Chapter 15

Discovering a Defined Path: Information-Seeking Behavior of Users and Online Reference Services

Rui Wang

OVERVIEW

Users' social construction and innate characteristics define their information-seeking behavior. The path of information-seeking behavior of users impacts the developmental process of a service and technology. A survey was conducted in a community college with 84 students that aimed to explore the relationship between users and the use of online reference services. The survey was focused on users' social construction and cognitive styles in order to identify group differences in using online reference services. Multinomial logistic regression was used for data analyses. There were almost no group differences in using the new service. Even though no significant relationship between users' cognitive styles and using online reference services was found, the finding implied that users' social construction might play a more important role in using the services. The most demanding groups included students who hold full-time jobs, non-traditional students, and students who had prerequisite skills—e-mail users.

INTRODUCTION

As a new type of service, online reference service is emerging along with other innovative new online technologies. But questions about these services are still to be answered: how will these services, ultimately, be accepted? Who will be the users? How will users appropriate the services?

To investigate these questions is not only a mar-

keting strategy from service providers and vendors, but also it is a part of the developing process of services and technology products. In this sense, a user is not merely someone who is using the service at a specific time, but is more appropriately identified as the person who possesses his/her inner characteristic that are previously shaped in certain social contexts. These elements will largely define a path of users' behaviors in using the service. As the same kind of users become a group, the group will be closely related to the service and will give significant influences to the development of the technology and services. Thus, this study attempts to explore information-seeking behavior of users by examining users' social construction and cognitive styles, to identify relevant social groups, and to predict what types of users will be likely to use online reference services and how they expect the services will be functioning.

Fifty Years of Progress

In Tom Wilson's comprehensive review, "Information Needs and Uses: Fifty Years of Progress" (Wilson, 1994) he identified two dichotomous types of studies: systems studies and user studies. Systems studies were systems-centered and focused on how people used library systems and services, while user studies were person-centered and emphasized behaviors of information users. Wilson noted, "there has been some improvement in that situation over the last thirteen years, but, in the period covered by this review, it would be true to say that most 'user studies' have been about how people use systems, rather than about the users themselves and other aspects of their information-seeking behavior" (1994: 17).

Wilson used Oppenheim's 1962 study of student library use to describe some new elements in user studies. These new elements included gender differences, years of study, and the nature of students' courses. He thought that Oppenheim's study "was made to link information use to characteristics of discipline of the user" (1994: 30). As Wilson pointed out, "the movement away from system-centered studies to person-centered studies did not begin until the 1980s, and the various models for organizing the literature were, consequently, system-oriented" (Wilson, 1994: 30). With the development of information retrieval systems, more researchers were focused on a new element: individual cognitive style. Wilson followed the progress of user studies over 50 years. This progress was highlighted by "user studies" (1994: 17), which were person-centered information-seeking behavior. These user studies emphasized seeking users' innate characteristic rather than how users simply use library services.

Research on Cognitive Styles and Online Environment

Cognitive style has been an all-time favorite of social behavior researchers. The use of cognitive style as an instrumental tool of research can be found in a number of studies across psychology, education, communication, information science, business management, and marketing. Witkin (1978) and his group began the study of cognitive styles in the late 1940s. In Witkin's study, people's learning styles or cognitive styles were divided into two groups: Field-Independence (FI) and Field-Dependence (FD) by administering the Embedded Figures Tests (EFT). Witkin considered cognitive styles as a personal and cultural adaptation:

> Because internal references are not as available to them, field-dependent people are less able to structure situations on their own and so are likely to look to information from others as guides to structuring situations which lack it. In other words, field-dependent people tend to be information seekers under ambiguous conditions. Because field-independent people have recourse to internal referents in structuring situations, which lack it, they are able to function more autonomously of others. The tendencies

to be autonomous or to rely more upon others are expressions of the field-dependent and field-independent cognitive styles in the social domain and so are integral components of these styles (Witkin, 1978: 51).

As an online environment, a new information system challenges its users. The close relationship between cognitive style and information-seeking behavior naturally drew researchers' attention to how users' innate characteristics affect using new information systems. A number of researchers used the cognitive style approach to study users' behaviors in an online environment. One study used cognitive style and online database search experience as predictors of Web search performance (Palmquist and Kyung-Sun, 2000). This study found that cognitive style, field-dependence (FD) and field-independence (FI) significantly influenced the novice searchers, but not as much as for experienced searchers. Another study (Daniels and Moore, 2000) tested interaction of cognitive style and learner control in a hypermedia environment. The hypermedia contained text, graphics, still pictures, motion video, and sound. The effectiveness of the hypermedia was a primary factor in analyzing the relationship between hypermedia and individual characteristics. The study showed that there was no evidence that "learners who possess different cognitive styles benefit equally from educational hypermedia environments" (Daniels and Moore, 2000). A recent study explored users' metaphors for the Web (Palmquist, 2001). Palmquist intended to use metaphors as evidence of undergraduates' understanding of the Web. According to the author, "metaphors have become popular for describing new media environments like the World Wide Web. Metaphors like 'the Web is a highway' permit an individual to relate the complexity of Web to something previously experienced and concrete" (Palmquist, 2001). Thus, Palmquist believed that "if metaphors can function as possible mental structures or models for undergraduates' experience with the Web, they may provide an important tool with which to design instruction" (2001). The result of research showed that "cognitive style produced some interesting patterns in participants' verbal descriptions" of the Web (Palmquist, 2001). Field-dependents use metaphors to illustrate what the Web is, while field-independents use metaphors to describe what they could do with the Web.

Online Reference Services

Online reference services are a relatively new system in online environments. These services have been adopted and have become popular among libraries nationwide. Various terms are used to define these services. For instance, The Virtual Reference Desk ("Virtual Reference Desk," 2000) is a network digital reference (Internet question and answer) project. Other authors used the term electronic mail reference to define the service directly. Garnsey and Powell (2000) also used the term electronic mail reference services in their study. The two authors investigated pubic libraries in the U.S. known to be offering e-mail reference service and identified the characteristics of electronic mail reference services and variables affecting the use of the service. This study found that there were differences in how public libraries handled their e-mail reference services, such as time to get answers, frequency of received questions, types of patrons' questions, patrons' reactions to the service, and how to promote services. The responses to the services from users were positive. These positive reactions were mostly from users who had four years or more of college education with various occupations. The authors expected that people who were more exposed to new technologies would be more apt to use the services.

Digital library service seems a broader term. Prestamo (2000) presented what Oklahoma State University has done. As she explained, the digital library services help the university's students and faculty to access the library's catalog, online databases, e-mail and telephone reference services, interlibrary loan requests, electronic reserve, Web-based tutorials, and technical support for these services. The answer to the question, "if we build it, will they come?" was "yes."

Social Construction of Technology (SCOT)

SCOT is a descriptive model of studies for the sociology of technology. The model was depicted by these graphics (Figures 15–1, 15–2, and 15–3): developmental process of a technological artifact is a center surrounded by the "relevant social group" (Pinch and Bijker, 1987: 35), each social group is circled by problems, and a problem circled by its possible solutions.

According to Pinch and Bijker, "the social cultural and political situation of a social group shapes

Fig. 15–1
The Relationship Between an Artifact and the Relevant Social Groups (Pinch and Bijker, 1987: 35)

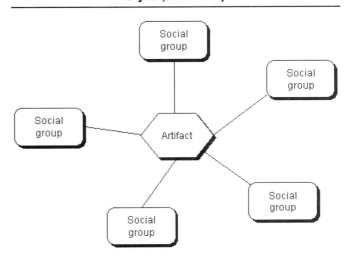

its norms and values, which in turn influence the meaning given to an artifact" (1987: 46). Pinch and Bijker indicated the importance of a social group in the process of development of an artifact or the technology.

Kilker and Gay reacted to the social construction of technology (SCOT) approach in a case study of online library services (1998). The authors applied the SCOT approach to investigate the development and evaluation of a digital library project at Cornell University and the University of Michigan. The project was to digitize selected nineteenth-century U.S. journals and monographs and provide access to the digital collection. As the authors stated, the necessity for "a social constructivist approach is ideal for examining digital library (DL) development because it can accommodate the multiple conceptions of DLs held by the various relevant groups" (Kilker and Gay, 1998: 60). The groups included the designer group, librarian group, faculty, and students. The SCOT approach in the study reinforced the notion of the utility of "the description of several social groups involved in the user-interface evaluation of a DL to argue that evaluations of this emerging technology should take into account the interactions among, and the differing needs of, such groups" (Kilker and Gay, 1998: 69).

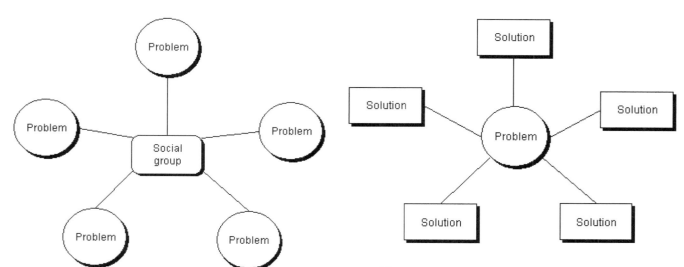

Fig. 15–2. The Relationship Between a Social Group and the Received Problems (Pinch and Bijker, 1987: 36)

Fig 15–3. The Relationship Between One Problem and Its Possible Solutions (Pinch and Bijker, 1987: 36)

HYPOTHESES

These studies mentioned above reflected current development of online library services, but more in-depth studies are needed. Especially, different users' characteristics and responses to the new system in academic settings need to be explored, as more library services have transformed from traditional services to non-traditional systems. Cognitive style may be one of the predictors in examining the new online system, online reference services. The SCOT approach has also shown a powerful influence in the developmental process of technology. Identifying relevant social groups is a crucial stage in the SCOT approach because of "interpretative flexibility" (Pinch and Bijker, 1987: 40):

> In SCOT, technological artifacts are culturally constructed and interpreted; in other words, the interpretative flexibility of a technological artifact must be shown. By this we mean not only that there is flexibility in how people think of or interpret artifacts but also that there is flexibility in how artifacts are *designed* (Pinch and Bijker, 1987: 40).

There is, however, no existing model to identify relevant social groups. As Pinch and Bijker admitted, "there is no cookbook recipe for how to iden-

tify a social group. Quantitative instruments using citation data may be of some help in certain cases. More research is needed to develop operationalizations of the notion of 'relevant social group' for a variety of historical and sociological research sites" (Pinch and Bijker, 1987: 50).

Thus, the objective of this study was to apply Wilson's "user studies" and the SCOT approaches to the investigation of relationships between users and online reference services. The operational definitions of concepts of users' social construction included users' gender, race, social construction (e.g., e-mail/non-e-mail users, traditional students/non-traditional students, and students who hold full-time jobs/part-time jobs/not working etc.). Different cognitive styles were identified by the Group Embedded Figures Tests (GEFT). The study tried to find whether or not users' social construction and cognitive style affect the use of online reference services and who was the "relevant social group"(Pinch and Bijker, 1987: 50). In other words, the study should provide some evidence of which social groups are closely related in using the services, how these groups react to and expect the services, and who will be most likely to use the services.

The independent variables included users' cognitive style (Field-Dependence/Field-Independence) and social construction (gender, race, traditional/non-traditional students, distance learning/non-distance learning students, full-time/part-time students, and AA/AS degrees). The dependent variable was the use of online reference services, including the awareness of online library services (knowing and not knowing), experience of using the service, evaluations of services (time of feedback and usefulness), and expectation (response time and preference of online reference service). In total, ten independent variables were modeled as predictors and 11 dependent variables were gathered from the survey and measured the use of online references. The hypotheses for the research are:

1. There are group differences in responses to the awareness of online reference service.
2. There are group differences in using online reference services.
3. There are different expectations of online reference services among different groups.

METHODOLOGY

The Group Embedded Figures Tests (GEFT) and a survey that included 21 questionnaires were used to collect data. The samples, 84 students from a homogenous population of a community college were administered the GEFT (Witkin et al., 1971). The GEFT was used to divide students into two cognitive styles, Field-Independence and Field-Dependence, and the cognitive styles served as one of the independent variables. The GEFT was administered by the procedure: two minutes for the first session (seven questions); five minutes for the second session (nine questions); and another five minutes for the third session (nine questions). Right after the GEFT, the survey containing 23 questionnaires was distributed and filled out by the same group of students. The survey was used to collect the students' demographic and social background information as well as their responses to online reference services. The data of demographic and social background information was collected for independent variables and the responses to the online reference services were gathered for the measurement of dependent variables.

DATA ANALYSIS

The 84 students were from three different classes of general education including biology and sociology.

Table 15–1.
GEFT Means and Standard Deviations by Gender

GENDER	Mean	N	Std. Deviation
MALE	11.67	21	4.397
FEMALE	7.27	63	5.093
Total	8.37	84	5.264

Sixty-three were females and 21 were males. They were administered the GEFT and participated in the survey by filling out the questionnaires. Fifty percent of them were identified as traditional students, and another half of them were non-traditional students. Among them, 69 percent were white, 17.9 percent were African Americans, 9.5 percent were Hispanics, and other minorities were 3.6 percent. Sixty-three percent were full-time students and 36.9 percent were part-time students. Most of them, 73.8 percent, were Associate in Arts degree (AA) seekers and 26.2 percent were in Associate in Science degree (AS programs). Fifty percent of them were full-time employees, 29.8 percent were part-time workers, and 20.2 percent were not working. Only 7.1 percent of them took Internet classes. Most of them, 78.6 percent, had Internet connections at home, while 20.2 percent could not go online at home. The survey showed 78.6 percent of the respondents had e-mail addresses compared to 21.4 percent who didn't have e-mail addresses.

Students' cognitive styles were identified by the GEFT. In total, 18 scores for 18 questions in the last two sections were accounted for as individuals' raw scores. The mean score for females was 7.27 with standard deviation of 5.093; while males' mean score was 11.67 with a standard deviation of 4.397. Scores above the means were relatively field independent (FI) and vice versa for relatively field dependent students (FD). Among the 84 students, 45 were FI and 39 were FD.

The data obtained from the survey questionnaires and the GEFT were recorded to SPSS 10.1. The multinomial logistic regression model was used in analyzing data because of the attributes of variables and the nature of prediction of the hypotheses in this study. Historically, multiple regressions are used when the researcher wishes to make a prediction. Variables, especially dependent variables, used in multiple regressions must be continuous or in intervals. Multiple regressions are restricted when

Table 15–2
Model Fitting Information (ASK WHOM DV)

Model	–2 Log Likelihood	Chi-Square	Df	Sig.
Intercept Only	130.280	35.242	22	0.037
Final	95.038			

Table 15–3
Likelihood Ratio (ASK WHOM DV)

Effect	-2 Log Likelihood	Chi-Square	df	Sig.
Intercept Only	95.03 [a]	0.000	0	0.000
GENDER	96.75 [b]	1.719	2	0.423
AGE	107.97 [b]	12.940	2	0.002
RACE	99.76 [b]	4.730	2	0.094
FORPSTUD	95.20 [b]	0.162	2	0.922
PROGRAM	99.64 [b]	4.602	2	0.100
INTCLASS	104.17 [b]	9.132	2	0.010
FORPWORK	96.64 [b]	1.604	4	0.808
EMAIL	98.07 [b]	3.037	2	0.219
INTERHOM	97.80 [b]	2.763	2	0.251
COGNITIV	95.13 [b]	0.092	2	0.955

The chi-square statistic is the difference in -2 log-likelihoods for the final model and a reduced model. The reduced model omits an effect from the final model. The null hypothesis is that parameters of that effect are zero.

variables are categorical or discrete. However, multinomial logistic regression can be used in analyzing data when both independent and dependent variables are categorical or continuous. Meanwhile, the strength of prediction is still kept in logistic regression: "Logistic regression is useful for situations in which you want to be able to predict the presence or absence of a characteristic or outcome based on values of a set of predictor variables" (Norušis, 1999: 3).

In this study, most of the variables were dichotomous and they were coded as 1 and 0. According to Norušis, "SPSS has two procedures that can be used to build logistic regression models: the Binary Logistic Regression procedure and the Multinomial Logistic Regression procedure. Both procedures can be used to build binary regression models" (1999: 65). Thus, even though some dependent variables were two categories, the multinomial logistics regression was still used.

FINDINGS

For answering the question, whom (online reference services, librarians in person, and teachers) are you going to ask, the outputs, –2 log-likelihood, Model Fitting Information (Table 15–2) showed that it was at a significant level, .037 < .05. The null hypothesis that there was no difference among groups could be rejected. This was the only significant number among all of the tests of dependent variables. In other words, there was a difference among groups pertaining to whom students would ask, if they had questions.

The Likelihood Ratio Test (Table 15–3) shows that AGE and INTCLASS are significantly related to the choice of whom to ask.

Some further explanation might be found in the output of Parameter Estimates. According to Exp(B) and B in the table, the group of students who were older than 20 years are more unlikely to ask online

reference services than the group who were under 20 years old. In other words, younger students more likely to choose online reference services than older students. Unfortunately, most of the numbers were not at a significant level due to the size of the sample, and there was no clear indication to see how the two groups (students who took Internet classes and students who never took Internet classes) reacted differently to this question.

There was no significant relationship between the dependent variable (KNOWING ONLINE REF SERVICE DV) and the set of independent variable predictors. In other words, there was not a significant difference among groups' awareness of online reference services. Apparently, 84 percent of students knew about online reference services. The null hypothesis was retained. Although the chi-square test of the model was not significant, FORPSTUD (full-time/part-time students) in the output of Parameter Estimates showed the lowest alpha level of .062 that closed to .05 (Table 15–4). The Exp(B) for FORPSTUD with an alpha level of .077 was the lowest significant level among all independent variables. It seemed to indicate that among these groups, full-time students were almost five times more likely to be aware of online reference services than were part-time students.

In testing the question, who used online reference services (USE ONLINE SERVICE DV) the chi-square

Table 15–4
Likelihood Ratio Test (KNOWING ONLINE REF SERVICE DV)

Effect	-2 Log Likelihood	Chi-Square	df	Sig.
Intercept Only	33.050[a]	0.000	0	**0.000**
GENDER	34.165	1.115	1	**0.423**
AGE	35.027	1.977	1	**0.002**
RACE	34.576	1.526	1	**0.094**
FORPSTUD	37.714	4.665	1	**0.922**
PROGRAM	33.477	0.427	1	**0.100**
INTCLASS	34.155	1.105	1	**0.010**
FORPWORK	35.322	2.272	2	**0.808**
EMAIL	37.886	4.836	1	**0.219**
INTERHOM	34.779	1.729	1	**0.251**
COGNITIV	33.059	0.009	1	**0.955**

The chi-square statistic is the difference in -2 log-likelihoods for the final model and a reduced model. The reduced model omits an effect from the final model. The null hypothesis is that parameters of that effect are zero.

a. This reduced model is equivalent to the final model because omitting the effect does not increase the degrees of freedom.

Table 15–5
Likelihood Ratio Test (AVAILABLE 24HOURS DV)

Effect	-2 Log Likelihood	Chi-Square	df	Sig.
Intercept Only	29.789[a]	0.000	0	**0.000**
GENDER	30.422[b]	0.632	1	**0.426**
AGE	29.896[b]	0.106	1	**0.744**
RACE	30.109[b]	0.319	1	**0.572**
FORPSTUD	30.809[b]	1.019	1	**0.313**
PROGRAM	35.448[b]	5.658	1	**0.017**
INTCLASS	31.465[b]	1.676	1	**0.195**
FORPWORK	32.000[b]	2.211	2	**0.331**
EMAIL	32.561[b]	2.772	1	**0.096**
INTERHOM	29.923[b]	0.133	1	**0.715**
COGNITIV	30.299[b]	0.509	1	**0.475**

The chi-square statistic is the difference in -2 log-likelihoods for the final model and a reduced model. The reduced model omits an effect from the final model. The null hypothesis is that parameters of that effect are zero.

a. This reduced model is equivalent to the final model because omitting the effect does not increase the degrees of freedom.
b. There is a possibility of a quasi-complete separation in the data. Either the maximum likelihood estimates do not exist or some parameter estimates are infinite.

test of the model was not significant, but FORPWORK (type of employment: full-time/part-time/not working) had a significant relationship with USE ONLINE SERVICE DV in the likelihood ratio tests, .033 < .05. In the output of Parameter Estimates, the variable FORPWORK 2's (students who have part-time jobs) significance level was .030 < .5. with B – 3.137 and Exp(B) 4.340E-02. This implies that students who had part-time jobs might be four times more unlikely to use online service than students who had full-time jobs might be.

For the question about using the services in the future, the null hypothesis was retained. It seems that the majority of students, 84 percent of respondents, were going to use online reference services.

Again, the test of the model for the relationship between the dependent variable AVAILABLE 24HOURS (should online reference services be available 24 hours?) and the set of independent variables were not significant with a 91 percent approval. An independent variable from the Likelihood Ratio Tests (Table 15–5) showed that PROGRAM (AA/AS) seemed to have a significant effect on the choice of "yes" with a significant level .017 < .05. To look at the negative B and Exp(B) in the table of parameter of estimates, it seemed that students in the AA program might be more interested in a 24–hour service

than AS students were. However, it is hard to draw this conclusion without seeing numbers at a significant level.

The dependent variable, HOW SOON DV (how soon do you expect to get responses?) was ranked as 1=immediately, 2=4 hours, 3=12 hours, 4=24 hours, 5=2 days, and 6=more than 2 days. Thirty-six percent of respondents preferred getting immediate responses and 26 percent of them could tolerate getting responses within four hours. The independent variables, AGE (traditional/non-traditional student) and FORTSTUD seemed to play some significant roles on the dependent variable from the output of parameter estimates .015 <.05 and .012 < .05, even though the alpha level of the Model Fitting Information was not significant. The table of Parameter Estimates showed FORPWORK 1's (students who have full-time jobs) significance level at .000. With a positive number of B and Exp(B)4.25+08, it might be a possibility that students who had full-time jobs might be four times more likely to want to get answers immediately from online reference services than students who had part-time jobs or were not working.

For the "four hours" choice, with PROGRAM 0 (AA) and INTCLASS, the significance alpha level was .000. This seems to indicate that the two groups of students had different preferences. Students in the AA program were 1.38 times more likely to choose the four hours option than AS students were. Interestingly, students who had never taken online classes were 8.7 times more unlikely to expect to get responses from online reference services within four hours. With a significance level at .000 again, for the choice of 12 hours, AA degree seekers and students who had full-time jobs seem to like it, but students who took online courses seem unlikely to have the choice.

The question to investigate the preference of the students in using local (the college) online reference services or remote (other Internet online reference services) was coded as 1=ircc (Indian River Community College) and 0=other. Eighty-four percent of respondents showed an interest in using local services and 16 percent wanted to use remote online reference services instead. The individual effect from E-MAIL (do you have an e-mail address or not?) was significant, .019 < .05, however, the Model Fitting Information was not significant.

For the last question, (do you think that the online reference services will benefit you in the future?), 92.2 percent of the respondents said "yes." The Chi-square of Model Fitting Information was not significant, but in the output of Likelihood Ratio Tests, the variable, FORPSTUD, was at the significant level, .031 < .05.

In the Parameter estimates table, part-time students (FORPSTUD 0) were 6.9 times more unlikely to believe in the benefits of online reference services than full-time students were. The students who had e-mails are almost 12 times more likely to believe the benefit of online reference desk than students who didn't have e-mails. However, neither one of the numbers was at a significant level in the table.

CONCLUSION

In general, almost all of the null hypotheses were retained. There seems to be no group differences in using online reference services, or in users' preferences and expectations. No matter what demographic backgrounds students were from and what kind of cognitive styles they had, online reference services seemed a general and popular choice to them. Nevertheless, there were still some subtle signs in which some groups seemed more demanding than other groups.

Table 15–6
Likelihood Ratio Test (WILL BENEFIT DV)

Effect	-2 Log Likelihood of Reduced Model	Chi-Square	df	Sig.
Intercept Only	33.050ᵃ	0.000	0	**0.000**
GENDER	34.165	1.115	1	**0.291**
AGE	35.027	1.977	1	**0.160**
RACE	34.576	1.526	1	**0.217**
FORPSTUD	37.714	4.665	1	**0.031**
PROGRAM	33.477	0.427	1	**0.513**
INTCLASS	34.155	1.105	1	**0.293**
FORPWORK	35.322	2.272	2	**0.321**
EMAIL	37.886	4.836	1	**0.028**
INTERHOM	34.779	1.729	1	**0.189**
COGNITIV	33.059	0.009	1	**0.923**

The chi-square statistic is the difference in -2 log-likelihoods for the final model and a reduced model. The reduced model omits an effect from the final model. The null hypothesis is that parameters of that effect are zero.

a.   This reduced model is equivalent to the final model because omitting the effect does not increase the degrees of freedom.

These more demanding groups included full-time students, students who hold full-time jobs, younger students (traditional students), students who had e-mails, and AA program students. The demands from these groups were specifically in these areas: students who hold full-time jobs are more likely to use online reference services and to want to get responses immediately. Full-time students seemed to be more aware of online reference services than other groups were and to be more likely to believe the service benefits. Younger students (traditional students and AA degree students) seemed to be more dependent on online reference services and to be more likely to want around the clock services. Rationally, e-mail users might have stronger faith to expect the benefits of online reference services than people who had never used e-mails would be.

As mentioned above, some social factors were behind these demands. The demanding groups include these types of people: people who are busy with their study and work, people who were not experienced enough to solve their problems, and people who were exposed to the technology and possessed such skills to be able to deal with the technology of the service. It seems undeniable that some groups were more related to some aspects of the services than other groups were because of their social construction. Ultimately, these groups will be the users who use the services more frequently, in turn to give influences and to shape the norms for the developmental process of the services and technology.

Interestingly, social construction seems a stronger predictor in this study. The needs for the services were straight from certain social contexts. There was not a sign of any effect of users' cognitive styles. Consequently, further studies need to be done in some areas. First, we need to find what other social factors can be accounted for by users' social construction for research of online reference services, and more operational concepts should add into the measurements of users' social construction. Secondly, besides cognitive style, what other users' innate characteristics should be studied in using online reference services? Thirdly, this study cannot draw the conclusion that there is absolutely no relationship between cognitive styles and using online services, because of an inherent weakness in this study: the size of the sample was not large enough. After 84 of the total respondents were categorized, the sample size became significantly reduced in each category. Some numbers in these categories were omitted and became zero or did not show any numbers at all. Interestingly, after the number of cases was doubled artificially, the attempt showed that five more dependent variables' chi-square's significant levels become less than .05 in the tables of Model Fitting Information.

Finally, there were not many students who actually were experienced in using online reference services. Only 13 students, about 16 percent of respondents, used such services. If most of the respondents were experienced users, the research evaluation could be led into another direction. Nevertheless, it is still worthwhile to take a look at the summary gathered from the responses of experienced users in this study.

There were only 13 respondents that used online reference services. Among the 13 students, eight students asked research questions rather than other types of questions. Eight students used the local college service and five used services outside of the college. Most of them, ten students, thought that the speed to get feedback was about right and that the services were useful. This seemed to show some optimistic signs: 1) students used the services for serious purposes; 2) there was a tendency of choosing local services for reasons; and 3) most of them were satisfied with the services they used. It would be more interesting to see further studies done based on thorough evaluations from experienced users. The key is that the evaluations cannot be merely satisfactory surveys but something that can reveal users' innate characteristic, connected to users' social construction, and lead us to solve the myth between information-seeking behavior of users and online reference services.

ACKNOWLEDGMENTS

I would like to thank Assistant Professor, Dr. Scott M. Lynch, Ph.D. in the Department of Sociology, Office of Population Research, and Princeton University for his important advice on using the Multinomial Regression.

REFERENCES

Daniels, Harold Lee, and David M. Moore. 2000. "Interaction of Cognitive Style and Learner Control in a Hypermedia Environment." *International Journal of Instructional Media* 27, no. 4: 369–374 [Online]. Available: http://search.epnet.com [2001, May 21].

Garnsey, Beth A., and Ronald R. Powell. 2000. "Electronic Mail Reference Services in the Public Library." *Reference & User Services Quarterly* 39, no. 3 (Spring): 245–254 [Online]. Available: http://search.epnet.com [2001, April 20].

Kilker, Julian, and Geri Gay. 1998. "The Social Construction of a Digital Library: A Case Study Examining Implications for Evaluation." *Information Technology and Libraries* 17, no. 2 (June): 60–70.

Norušis, Marija. J. 1999. *SPSS Regression Models 10.0.* Chicago, Ill.: SPSS Inc.

Oppenheim, A.N. 1962. "Reading Habits of Students: A Survey of Students at the London School of Economics." *The Journal of Documentation* 18, no. 2: 42–57.

Palmquist, Ruth A. 2001. "Cognitive Style and Users' Metaphors for the Web: An Exploratory Study." *The Journal of Academic Librarianship* 27, no. 1 (January): 24–32 [Online]. Available: http://search.epnet.com [2001, August 10].

Palmquist, Ruth A., and Kim Kyung-Sun. 2000. "Cognitive Style and On-Line Database Search Experience as Predictors of Web Search Performance." *Journal of the American Society for Information Science* 51, no. 6 (April): 558–566 [Online]. Available: http://search.epnet.com [2001, June 15].

Pinch, Trevor. J., and Wiebe E. Bijker. 1987. The Social Construction of Facts and Artifacts: Or How the Sociology of Science and the Sociology of

Technology Might Benefit Each Other. In *The Social Construction of Technological Systems, New Directions in the Sociology and History of Technology,* Wiebe E. Bijker and Thomas Parke Hughes. eds. Cambridge, Mass.: The MIT Press.

Prestamo, Anne. 2000. If We Build It, Will They Come? In *Proceedings of the 21ˢᵗ National Online Meeting,* M. E. Williams, ed. Medford, N.J.: Information Today, Inc.

"Virtual Reference Desk." 2000. *Ohio Media Spectrum* 52(2): 15 [Online]. Available: http://search. epnet.com [2001, May 21].

Wilson, Tom. 1994. Information Needs and Uses: Fifty Years of Progress. In *Fifty Years of Information Progress: A Journal of Documentation Review,* B. C. Vickery, ed. London: Aslib.

Witkin, Herman A. 1978. *Cognitive Styles in Personal and Cultural Adaptation.* Worcester, Mass.: Clark University Press.

Witkin, Herman A., Philip K. Oltman, Evelyn Raskin, and Stephen A. Karp. 1971. *Manual Embedded Figures Test.* Palo Alto, Calif.: Consulting Psychologists Press, Inc.

PART VI

Evaluating Digital Reference Service Quality

OVERVIEW

Evaluation has always been an issue for reference services. Indeed, when Samuel Swett Green outlined the basic tasks for a reference librarian in 1876, he also suggested how those tasks could be evaluated. The practices involved in providing reference service have been refined since then, but the central elements of the reference transaction have not changed. The advent of digital reference, however, has caused scholars and practitioners alike to question some of those elements that have been unquestioned in desk reference.

This section presents papers in which criteria and processes for this evaluation are presented. This section begins with a paper that reviews the literature on quality in digital reference, to provide a baseline for the discussion to come. The chapters that follow discuss measures and standards for evaluation, formative and summative evaluation, and evaluation in a variety of digital reference environments. Evaluation in reference has been a topic of discussion in the literature for decades. Only within the past two or three years have criteria and processes for evaluating digital reference services begun to emerge. Perhaps by beginning a conversation about evaluation for digital reference, we can begin a thoughtful and productive debate that will result in new and reliable assessment techniques and measures.

Chapter 16

Assessing Quality in Digital Reference Services: An Overview of the Key Literature on Digital Reference

Melissa Gross, Charles R. McClure, and R. David Lankes[1]

OVERVIEW

This review describes and discusses the key literature on digital reference service in libraries. Subtopics covered include the management, economics, staffing, training, users, and evaluation of digital reference. The objectives of this work are to determine the current status of digital reference in libraries, identify current issues in practice, identify the research needed to further advances in digital reference in libraries, and to inform the development of evaluation methods for digital reference services.

INTRODUCTION

This literature review utilizes the work of Bernie Sloan (2000) and Joanne Wasik (2001) who have both compiled major bibliographies in this area. These bibliographies were collapsed, duplicates removed, and the resulting list augmented with searches of the ERIC, Lib Lit, LISA, and INSPECT databases to ensure that all publications on this topic have been identified and retrieved.

The scope of this literature review includes articles and conference presentations in both print-based and electronic media and technical reports on the subject of digital reference service in libraries. For the purposes of this work, "digital reference is defined as human-intermediated assistance offered to users through the Internet" (McClure and Lankes, 2001). While the provision of digital reference service can certainly be informed by research on tradi-

tional reference services, electronic resources and search procedures, expert systems, and the literature on digital libraries—literature on these topics is included only to augment discussion. Further, not all of the literature identified is quoted here. Rather, many of the findings are summarized and key findings and issues are highlighted.

The main objectives of this chapter are:

- To determine the current status of digital reference in libraries.
- To identify current issues in the practice of digital reference.
- To identify areas in which research is needed to further advances in digital reference services in libraries.
- To inform the development of evaluation methods for digital reference services.

OVERVIEW OF DIGITAL REFERENCE SERVICE IN LIBRARIES

In assessing the state of the literature as a whole, it can be generally stated that the majority of what is available on the topic of digital reference service is anecdotal (of the "this is how we did it in our library" variety) or editorial in nature. Less of what has been written on this topic can be considered "research" in the formal sense. Discussion concerning the evaluation of digital reference services is also limited. While reference services are a well-established part of the traditional library environment, the provision of reference service in the digital realm is still very much in a formative stage.

Peters (2000) makes an analogy between the evolution of traditional library services and the development of digital library services by observing that in both cases initial interest centered on the provision of collections. Once these were somewhat in place, the provision of document surrogates became the center of attention. Only after these issues began to be addressed did interest in services begin to move center field. In this vein, it appears that discussion and experimentation with library services in the digital realm has begun, but there are still many issues, both practical and theoretical, that must be addressed to understand what the issues and needs are and to create true state-of-the-art services that meet user needs and can be professionally planned for, managed, and evaluated.

Digital Reference Service in Libraries

It appears that academic libraries were the first to provide digital reference services and that these services began in the early 1980s. Weise and Borgendale (1986), Howard and Jankowski (1986), and Bonham (1987) all report on the provision of e-mail reference services and make observations and predictions that remain valid today, including the understanding that the proliferation of digital reference was dependent on the adoption of computer technology by users, and that movement toward a computer on every desk would likely feed demand.

Since that time, the number of academic and public libraries offering e-mail reference continues to grow making e-mail the most common vehicle for providing digital reference services.[2] However, experience has shown that there are several limitations inherent in trying to provide service this way. For instance, the idea that users would provide better formulated questions if they wrote them out has not generally turned out to be true, and the process of question negotiation via e-mail is rather bulky and time consuming (Abels, 1996; Ryan, 1996; Schilling-Eccles and Harzbecker, 1998). This realization eventually led to a second standard of service in which a Web form interface is typically used to solicit specific information about questions from users and to limit digital reference requests to ready reference questions (Abels, 1996; Haines and Grodzinski, 1999; Sloan, 1998). Both of these measures appear to be effective in minimizing the e-mail traffic re-

quired to answer a query. However, librarians do report that it takes longer to answer a user's query when it must be text based, than it does to respond to a similar query orally in a traditional reference desk setting (Ryan, 1996).

A lot of what is known about the provision of digital reference services comes from the experiences of those involved in the development, ongoing refinement, study, and assessments of the Internet Public Library (IPL). The IPL began in 1995 as a class project at the University of Michigan. The interested reader can find several useful overviews of its development in Ryan (1996), Janes (1998), and Janes et al. (1999). Articles pertaining to specific aspects of the IPL are included in the discussion points below.

Current Trends in Digital Reference Service

Although e-mail remains the main vehicle for digital reference services in libraries, libraries are currently experimenting with various applications that provide synchronous interaction between the user and the librarian.

Several libraries, including the University of Michigan; University of California, Irvine; and a joint project with University of California, Berkeley and North Carolina State University, report undertaking synchronous digital reference using video conferencing, but these experiments have not been largely successful (Folger, 1997; Lessick, Kjaer, and Clancy, 1997; Morgan, 1996). Problems include low levels of utilization by users, the fact that most users and libraries do not own the equipment and software necessary to support this service and show little inclination to acquire it, problems with bandwidth when videoconferencing is available, and self-consciousness on the part of users to being visible on screen.

However, interest in other forms of synchronous services continues. For instance the IPL reports on reference provided in a Multi User Object Oriented environment (MOO), and the use of various types of chat programs and software adapted from the commercial sector, such as Customer Relations Management (CRM) systems, are increasingly being described in the literature (Coffman, 2001a, 2001b; Eichler and Halperin, 2000; Gray, 2000; Horn, 2001; McGlamery and Coffman, 2000; Shaw, 1996; Stormont, 2001). It appears that libraries in increasing numbers are adopting chat reference. Francoeur (2001) reports that as of April 2001, 272 libraries had a chat reference service in place. These chat services are not replacing e-mail or Web form reference, they are supplements to it that tend to be offered a limited number of hours a week.

Another recent trend in academic, public, and government libraries is interest in the idea of collaborative relationships with other libraries to provide various types of digital reference services. Francoeur (ibid.) reports that 77 percent of the 272 libraries he identified as having chat reference provide the service as part of a consortium agreement. Libraries are also participating in these agreements in order to develop 24/7 reference service. Representative projects in this vein include:

- The Virtual Reference Desk (VRD) project, which is a network of organizations that share expertise in providing human intermediated question and answer services on the Web (VRD, 2000).
- The 24/7 Reference project currently under way at the Metropolitan Cooperative Library System (MCLS) in California (McGlamery, 2000).
- The Collaborative Digital Reference Service (CDRS) project headed up by the Library of Congress (Kresh, 2000).
- The Ready for Reference Service under development by the Alliance Library System in Illinois (Sloan, 2001a, 2001b).

However, even as experiments in providing 24/7 reference are getting started, some are beginning to question the need for such extended service in every library environment. Sloan in his final report on the Ready for Reference project notes that, "the wee hours of the morning (1 AM to 6 AM) don't generate much activity at all" and he questions the need for both 24 hour and seven days-a-week service for these libraries (2001b).

General Management of Digital Reference Service

For the most part, libraries that provide digital reference services report they receive relatively few requests from users. This is in high contrast to the volume of questions received by non-library providers on the Web. For instance, Carter and Janes (2000) report that the IPL receives over 1,000 questions a month, but this number is quite minimal compared to reports that Ask Jeeves receives four million queries each 24 hours and that Webhelp received 1.2 million queries on the day it opened (Search Engine Watch, 2002; Tomaiuolo and Packer, 2000; Webhelp, 1999). Even the most successful digital reference services in libraries get nowhere near these numbers. Rather, academic libraries report numbers in the 26 to 56 *queries per month* range (Botts and Bauerschmidt, 1999; Bushallow-Wilbur, DeVinney, and Whitcomb, 1996; Folger, 1997; Hodges, unpublished manuscript). In public libraries the volume of digital reference questions is reported at "a mean of 5.6 e-mail reference questions per week; the modal or most frequent response was 3 questions per week" (Garnsey and Powell, 2000: 248).

Recent accounts of digital reference services indicate that libraries are becoming more in touch with the need to make services visible through continued promotion and publicity (Marsteller and Neuhaus, 2001; McLean, 1999; Wilson, 2000).

The volume of questions received by a library's digital reference desk is an issue that is worth keeping in mind in assessing the literature. For instance, a lot of what is written about digital reference service is editorial in nature or written with the goal of sharing anecdotal experience with other information providing organizations interested in starting a digital reference service. Most of these "case studies" fail to address issues like incorporating the development of digital reference services into the library's formal planning, user needs and/or community needs analysis, staffing and training issues, service efficiency, institutional benefits from providing this service, or how to properly measure or assess digital reference services. This may be the result of the minimal impact digital reference service has on these environments. The addition of an extra 50 questions a month is unlikely to tax any reference desk, even a desk in a small library. Perhaps the absence of strong demand on the systems within the organization that provide digital reference works against furthering study and consideration of many of the questions the profession has about how to best plan for, process, and evaluate digital reference services.

The Economics of Digital Reference

There is a major gap in the literature on digital reference services in the area of economic models and accounting. This may follow largely from the fact that the economic and costing models have not been fully developed in the traditional reference realm. This means that effective measures of cost need to be developed for all types of reference so that each can be assessed and compared in terms of efficiency and benefit.

In the literature of traditional reference services some approaches are offered toward the problem of determining what reference service costs. For instance, the Input/Output Model (Sayre and Thielen, 1989) focuses on measuring inputs and service utilization in small libraries. Functional Cost Analysis (Abels, Kantor, and Saracevic, 1996), a process explored in a variety of reference service environments, seeks to define the various costs of providing a service and then allocates these costs to that service. Hayes (1996) reports on the intricacies of assessing the costs related to the provision of electronic resources in support of reference within the framework of the Library Costing Model (LCM), but does not solve the problem for digital reference services.

Murfin and Bunge (1989: 17-35) offer four methods for assessing cost effectiveness in academic libraries. They are:

- Method One: Formula for Determining the Full Cost of the Reference Transaction.
- Method Two: A Reference Service Cost Effectiveness Index Based on Success, Helpfulness, Accessibility, and Time/Cost.
- Method Three: Cost (time taken) per Successful Question.
- Method Four: A Cost Benefit Formula.

These formulas were tested in academic libraries in a project funded by the Council on Library for Research Purposes and used in the Wisconsin-Ohio Reference Evaluation Program. There may be value in using this work as a starting point for addressing the current issue of how to evaluate digital reference services from a cost standpoint.

Cost issues also exist in the development and practical management of collaborative arrangements for providing digital reference services. As collaboration models form, the question of how to share the costs of providing 24/7 digital reference services, in what will inevitably be a global forum, has already come to light as an issue that will soon need resolution. In this regard the Library of Congress CDRS project will be interesting to watch as it learns how to share the cost of service among its members and finds its place in the information market.

Staffing the Digital Reference Service

Staffing for digital reference and the distribution of the digital reference workload are being handled in a variety of ways. At the IPL, reference questions are classified by subject and then staff members claim the questions they want to tackle (Ryan, 1996). At Rutgers University and the University of California, Irvine they use a team model in which designated staff handle digital reference queries (Borisovets, 1999; UCI Libraries, 1999). At both Rutgers and the IPL, staff members are encouraged to read the questions received by the service (and the answers), but to select only questions in their area of expertise to respond to. In these and other libraries there is a separate or select staff that provides digital reference services, but with the exception of the IPL, which is mainly staffed by volunteers, the digital reference staff is normally part of the general reference staff. They do not perform digital reference on a full-time basis. At other libraries staff performs both traditional and digital reference while at the reference desk (Botts and Bauerschmidt, 1999). In a study involving video conferencing the staff treated digital reference requests like telephone calls, giving preference to the face-to-face user at the desk (Folger, 1997).

The variety of approaches to staffing reflects the experimental nature of the digital reference services reported in the literature and also the minimal demand placed on these services in terms of the volume of questions received. However, the move from asynchronous to synchronous reference, with the spreading adoption of chat reference in libraries, is changing this. New staffing issues are erupting based on the special demands of this mode of service; even though chat reference tends to be offered only a few hours a day and does not necessarily attract a huge volume of users.

The literature appears to be moving toward a consensus that chat reference needs to be performed in a space away from the physical reference desk, even if this means hiring additional personnel (Boyer, 2001; Coffman, 2001b; Marsteller and Neuhaus, 2001; Stormont, 2001). Librarians are reaching this conclusion because they find chat reference service more demanding to provide. Not only does chat lack the physical clues of expression and body language, but because of its real-time nature, librarians worry about being able to respond quickly and concisely enough in type and about being away from a user too long as they research a question.

There are also many technology issues that librarians grapple with in using chat. They complain of users getting bumped off or leaving before the session is completed (Marsteller and Neuhaus, 2001). Librarians also complain about incompatibility between the software and proprietary databases, the high need for multi-tasking skills to handle multiple questions and resources at a time. Coffman (2001a, 2001b) and Francoeur (2001) provide excellent discussions of the various chat software products being used in libraries describing their functionality, strengths, and weaknesses.

Another development is the appearance of "outsourcing" in digital reference. One of the solutions to the problem of staffing for 24/7 reference is to pay someone else to do it. Sloan (2001b) provides an example of such an arrangement in which Library Systems and Services Inc. (LSSI) is used to provide reference services during time slots when regular library staff are not available. The potential outsourcing of services has also been discussed by others who predict the development of subscription services libraries might use to extend service hours or provide service during the graveyard shift (Francoeur, 2001). Another approach to this problem is to share the expertise of library staff through consortium and networking arrangements where librarians in different time zones can pick up off-hours requests for service or provide needed subject specialty expertise for an otherwise difficult to answer question. This can almost be viewed as a kind of "interlibrary loan" where instead of materials, it is the librarian's skill and expertise that is shared.

Staff Training for Digital Reference

It appears that librarians' reference skills are readily transferable to the needs of digital reference work, and some authors make the point that indeed, traditional reference must form the basis for the provision of reference in the electronic realm (Frank et al., 1999; Kasowitz, Bennett, and Lankes, 2000; Wasik, 2001). However, digital reference is also shown to require additional procedures, skills, and training. For instance, Abels (1996) offers a new model for reference service performed via e-mail, suggesting the use of a search request form and a minimum level of interaction between user and librarian to ensure the successful transaction of the e-mail reference

query. Further, the VRD network requires, as one of its quality standards, that information specialists receive training in how to respond to user queries and in the organization's policies and procedures for providing digital reference services (Kasowitz, Bennett, and Lankes, 2000). It is important to note that these reports on problems and successes in providing digital reference refer mainly to questions received via e-mail and Web form submissions.

The emergence of chat brings with it new demands and calls for an increased skill base that e-mail did not generate. Specific skills librarians need to perform chat reference as outlined in the literature include:

- Keyboarding skills. Chat requires librarians to be fast and accurate on the keyboard (Stormont, 2001).
- Ability to multi-task. In a chat session a librarian may have multiple windows open that he/she is actively using, may need to deal with more than one question/user at a time, and may be responsible for telephone and walk-in reference as well. Strategies are needed to prepare librarians to cope with this reference environment (Boyer, 2001; Francoeur, 2001; Horn, 2001).
- Better than average searching skills. Librarians tend to find chat reference stressful. The work is fast-paced and librarians need to be able to locate responses quickly (Boyer, 2001; Horn, 2001).
- Writing concise messages. The medium is not conducive to long messages, nor does it allow the librarian to take a lot of time to compose a response. The use of scripts or other pre-formulated text can help, but cannot do the job completely (Boyer, 2001; Stormont, 2001).
- Ability to deal with stress and demanding users. The synchronous quality of chat reference may have the effect of increasing expectations about service on the part of both librarians and users. The medium is instantaneous and at the same time somewhat bulky and slow leading to a reference interaction that is more intense than traditional reference typically is (Francoeur, 2001; Horn, 2001; Stormont, 2001).

The Digital Reference Model

While digital reference service has its roots in the traditional reference desk model, when reference is placed in the electronic realm one effect is that some aspects of reference service that previously received little attention become more visible. For instance, the fact that both the user's question and the librarian's response can now be recorded and stored allows for service enhancements that have the potential to make reference more efficient. One of the innovations of the CDRS project is the incorporation of question/answer sets resulting from digital reference transaction to develop a knowledge base that will be searchable and may shorten response time or allow for the automation of responses to redundant questions posed to the system (Kresh, 2000). The potential for automating responses (Lagace and McClennen, 1998), providing canned responses, developing frequently asked question (FAQs) pages, and using this data in the development of expert systems and intelligent agents has yet to be fully explored, but will likely impact how reference services are delivered in the future.

The Digital Reference Model developed by Lankes (unpublished manuscript) adds efficiency to the process by including a triage step in which questions are sorted and sent to the appropriate expert for handling as they are received, expediting the handling of questions and saving staff time that might otherwise be spent redirecting requests to the appropriate station. Concern about the efficient routing of questions in traditional reference service in staffing models is sometimes referred to as a tiered approach (Mardikian and Kesselman, 1995). Under this model non-professional staff is utilized to respond to directional questions and questions about the library's operation and may also answer simple or commonly asked questions. Lower-level staff is responsible for identifying which questions require the librarian's expertise and for directing users to the librarian when their expertise is needed. This allows for more efficient use of the librarian's time, which can then be focused on patrons who need more help defining their information needs, locating information that is difficult to find, providing instruction, and working on the development of systems and resources. A version of the triage idea is incorporated into the CRDS Request Manager software, which matches incoming questions with the appropriate member institution (Kresh, 2000).

Lankes' Digital Reference Model is also important because it emphasizes the usefulness of the intellectual products produced by librarians in the process of providing reference. Traditionally these products have included the development of bibliographies, pathfinders, instructional materials, and note cards indicating sources for particularly difficult or often asked questions. These products can now be captured and made more easily accessible to users and other information professionals. It may be that in the future reference librarians will spend more time developing these and other intellectual products that enhance access.

Digital Reference and the User

A major gap in this literature is the inclusion of the user in the design and development of digital reference services. While benefits to users, such as convenience (Garnsey and Powell, 2000) and the extension of service to users that are homebound or otherwise unable to visit the physical library, are discussed (Abels and Liebscher, 1994), there is little evidence that users have been consulted in the design and development of digital reference services. Rather, the understandings supplied about digital reference users come mainly from analysis of question logs and a few small surveys of current digital reference users asking about satisfaction with the digital reference services provided by the library.

This oversight is hard to reconcile. In a review of the user studies literature published in 1986, Dervin and Nilan heralded a change of paradigm in the field from a system orientation to a user orientation, documenting dissatisfaction with design, development, and evaluation techniques that are system based and that result in a reification of services the library provides that are uninformed by user needs and preferences. Likewise, the program and service development literature in the field has long promoted planning processes that include user needs and community analysis as an important step in determining the services a library will provide (Bolt and Stephan, 1998; Himmel and Wilson, 1998; McClure, 1980; McClure et al., 1987).

However, the developments reported in the digital reference literature largely ignore these views. Rather, the development of digital reference services appears to be largely system driven and based on the interests and vision of the service providers. Gray (2000) points out the need for libraries to re-evaluate who is included in their community, now that the Internet has made geographic service areas less relevant. This further emphasizes questions like, who is the user that digital reference services are being designed for and how are the needs of this user being determined?

Digital reference service does have the potential to expand the way libraries think about their service areas, but most academic and public libraries are funded locally and have missions that direct them to serve a defined community. Market place demand for digital reference services must be established first within these communities and user input solicited to help libraries establish what services are desired, what modes of delivery users prefer, and how to make the service visible to potential users.

Evaluating Digital Reference

The evaluation of digital reference is another underdeveloped area in the literature. While a variety of viewpoints are available in the literature concerning how evaluation should be approached from a conceptual point of view, there are few people actually undertaking this task. The points of view offered on how the evaluation of digital reference services might be conceived run the range of those who feel that evaluation techniques can be borrowed from traditional reference (Kasowitz, Bennett, and Lankes, 2000), to those who feel that digital reference requires a new approach to be properly evaluated (Saracevic and Covi, 2000), to the view that meta-assessment is needed now, before this service has totally evolved, to allow for the creation of a service that is not tied to traditional conceptions of what reference service is (Peters, 2000).

There are also pragmatists that have laid the groundwork for structured and well-thought out approaches to the question of assessment. White (1999), at the University of Maryland, has developed a scheme for analyzing question and answer services, including digital reference services, which is quite comprehensive in scope. The VRD has created a set of standards called "Facets of Quality" that clearly define what quality service means for participating organizations, and further, defines levels of participation that not only maintain a bottom line of quality service but also provide clear cut goals for service improvement (Kasowitz, Bennett, and Lankes, 2000). The CDRS has adopted the Facets of Quality for Digital Reference Services Standards as the criteria its members will use for their quality review (Kresh, 2001).

An important element of digital reference services

that is not yet explicitly recognized in the general literature on digital reference is that in moving to the digital realm reference service is losing much of its ephemeral quality. Lankes, in his general reference model, acknowledges that the intellectual products of reference (finding aids, resources notes, etc.) can be captured and more widely shared in the digital environment (1998). However many have noted, almost as an aside, that when the digital reference transaction is complete, a record of the e-mail question and response remains, or there is a chat transcript, or that log analysis can be used to retrace and analyze the steps taken during the electronic transaction, and some reference software packages produce reports on the reference service. Coffman notes in a discussion of knowledge base development that "up until now there has been no easy way to preserve our work" (2001b: 152). The presence of these records also points the way to evaluations of reference service and the librarian's reference skills that were not previously feasible.

Evaluations of Digital Reference

The majority of the evaluation attempts reported are anecdotal, suffer from weak methods, and provide only a limited analysis of the service. The main strategies used are the analysis of question logs (Borisovets, 1999; Bushallow-Wilbur et al., 1996; Carter and Janes, 2000; UCI, 1999) and user surveys (Bushallow-Wilbur et al., 1996; Garnsey and Powell, 2000; UCI, 1999). These reports depend on small sample sizes and in the case of survey efforts, often have low response rates. The data provided in these evaluations and in the "this is how we did it in our library" literature are highly redundant. Findings from these studies are summarized as follows:

- Turnaround time tends to be shorter than organizational policy dictates.
- Users of the service are mainly the target audience for the service. For instance, the users of the academic library's digital reference service are, for the most part, the faculty, students, and staff at that university.
- The majority of questions received are the type of queries sought by the service, i.e., ready reference questions.
- The volume of questions received is minimal.
- The users who respond to questions about satisfaction with the service say they like it, though

repeat use of these services appears to be minimal.

Sloan (2001b) recently reported a final analysis of the Ready for Reference collaborative 24/7 service provided by a group of academic libraries in Illinois. This work is descriptive in nature and focuses on understanding service utilization and workload issues and does not inform readers about the issues of quality of service, cost of service, or the impact of participating in this collaboration on other organizational activities.

There is much more that needs to be known about the provision of digital reference service in both stand-alone and collaborative efforts and how to properly evaluate it than the literature currently addresses. Issues of the accuracy of responses, appropriateness to user audience, the impacts of the digital reference process, the cost effectiveness of the service, and the overall efficiency and effectiveness of digital reference remain open questions. A common definition of what success and quality in digital reference is has not been achieved. Metrics and data are sorely needed that are practical in nature and designed specifically for libraries. In recent work on performance measures for networked services Bertot, McClure, and Ryan (2000) found evaluation in the digital environment to require the employment of multiple methods. The data such methods would yield are essential to support further service improvements and to substantiate resource allocation for digital reference services.

Fortunately, awareness of the need to develop strategies for formal evaluation and to collect this data is acute. This interest has found voice not only in the strategies shared above, but is also heard among the attendees at the VRD Annual Conference (McClure and Lankes, 2001), workshop attendees at the National Information Standards Organization (NISO, 2001), and in the efforts of the Assessing Quality in Digital Reference Services project.

KEY ISSUES IN THE CURRENT STATE OF DIGITAL REFERENCE

Overall, developments in digital reference work have sprung from practice environments and tend to replicate traditional reference models in the electronic realm. These services have provided the field with some insights, but mainly in an anecdotal way. This review of the literature indicates that while interest in digital reference is strong, progress is hampered by a lack of economic models, strong evaluative research, and a lack of user input.

New Models of Reference Needed

Clearly new service models are needed. No one is sure what "state of the art" reference service should look like or what quality in digital reference service means. It is most likely that reference service will need to be provided through a variety of media and modes that include both face-to-face and remote services that are available in both synchronous and asynchronous forms. To achieve this there are many questions research needs to address and ideas concerning what digital reference service is that need to be explored.

McGlamery and Coffman (2000) provide a rule of thumb from commercial sites that information on a company's Web site should be able to answer 80 percent of the user's questions. Can library Web sites achieve this? Certainly the use of FAQs on Web sites, providing access to the intellectual by-products of the reference process, and increased use of intelligent agents and expert systems may provide a tiered effect that saves the librarian's expertise for questions that truly require the training and expertise of a master's level professional. But what is the right mix of these approaches and how are they best organized to provide optimal service?

Clearly, research is needed to inform the profession about what kinds of questions are best suited to what media and what questions can be handled adequately without human intermediation. The literature indicates that e-mail reference works best for ready reference or simple factual questions that require few resources and can be stated in an unambiguous way. Instant messaging, video conferencing, chat programs, and applications from the commercial sector are all currently under investigation by libraries and will need to be fully evaluated for their utility in responding to the full range of user questions.

It is unlikely that these questions and many issues concerning system design can be fully resolved without input from the user. Opportunities have already been lost by not involving the user in the process at the front end, before the system and service are designed. User input concerning how they see reference, what they want from reference, how they want reference delivered, what an acceptable turnaround time is, how to best market these services, and many other questions will provide invaluable insight and save a lot of time and expense.

New Economic Models Needed

The economics of reference is an area that has long been neglected. Assigning costs to reference service is a complicated task but one that must be faced in order to realistically assess the true costs of doing business, to make assessments about the most efficient ways to provide services, and to determine how to share the costs of this service in setting up and participating in collaborative service models.

Understanding what it costs to provide reference, the various funding models (and cost recovery models) under which reference can be provided, what the effect of supporting digital reference is on other library expenditures, is important for planning, monitoring, and evaluating these services, as well as for performing cost benefit analysis and measuring the cost effectiveness of service.

Management Issues

Because of the ad hoc and experimental way digital reference has developed, there is little in the literature that informs practice on the management issues of planning, providing, and evaluating service. While there is evidence that some digital reference services are the product of committees or project teams, these efforts, as reported, do not appear to be part of the library's overall plan. Guidance is needed on how to incorporate the provision of digital reference into the library's planning process and to identify and include all the stakeholders needed to ensure its success. Data is needed to inform management on how digital reference fits into the array of reference services the library offers, as well as in the development of policy and procedures to support the service. Managers need to know how to budget for the cost of developing and maintaining digital service under multiple service models and how to develop models of future costs. The question of how to train staff to support the digital reference service and how to evaluate personnel providing the service has not been fully addressed. Managers also need to know how to determine the benefits of service to users and to the library and how to anticipate future needs.

Issues in Evaluation

As stated above, evaluations of digital reference suffer from a lack of adequate and innovative methods.

It is unknown to what extent methods used to assess traditional reference will be effective in the digital reference environment. New techniques need to be explored to evolve our approach to evaluating digital reference and to permit comparisons between various reference service modes. McClure and Lankes (2001) propose four main types of measurement needed to understand and set benchmarks for digital reference services. These are:

1. Outcome measures (quality of answers): Accuracy of responses, appropriateness to user audience, opportunities for interactivity, instructiveness, and impacts resulting from the digital reference process.
2. Process measures (effectiveness and efficiency of process): Service accessibility, timeliness of response, clarity of service procedures, service extensiveness (percentage of questions answered), staff training and review, service review and evaluation, privacy of user information, user awareness (publicity).
3. Economic measures (costing and cost effectiveness of digital reference): The cost to conduct a digital reference session, infrastructure needed to support quality digital reference services, and impact of these costs on other library expenditures.
4. User satisfaction (degree to which users engaged in digital reference services are satisfied with the process and the results): Satisfaction indicators can include accuracy, timeliness, behavior of the staff, technical considerations, physical facilities, and others.

With the exceptions of timeliness (in terms of actual question turnaround as compared to organizational policy), some technical considerations, and some interest in user satisfaction, little is known in a formal way about the other measures they propose. Evaluations of digital reference service that provide usable measures and benchmark data in these categories and for the various forms of service delivery are sorely needed.

Affective Considerations

Reference service is clearly in the midst of a transition fueled mainly by the proliferation of technology and communication formats. One feature of the literature that stands out is a sense of apprehension in the profession concerning the future and the perceived need to compete with commercial services. Falling statistics at traditional reference desks and fear of replacement through advances in technology also work as motivators for moving reference into the electronic realm.

But what can be interpreted as mixed feelings about service provision may also have roots in the economic models within which libraries exist. Kuhlman (1995) and Abels, Kantor, and Saracevic (1996) point out that libraries generally manage zero sum budgets where an increase in reference costs means a decrease in some other area of the budget. McGlamery and Coffman project that if the County of Los Angeles Public Library could provide a digital reference service that appealed to users and that was actively marketed, "it would more than double the reference load . . . and require double the staff, double the resources, and double the money" (2000: 384).

It appears that fear of the potential demand for digital reference and the new professional demands this technology brings are also professional issues that the field needs to deal with. The experience of a low volume of traffic in digital reference is coupled with descriptions of services that are not widely publicized, not very visible on the library's Web page, developed without user involvement, and only minimally evaluated. This review points out the strong need for libraries to be more proactive in planning, developing, marketing, managing, accounting for, and evaluating digital reference services if they truly wish to grow this service and compete with non-library providers on the Internet.

Directions for Research

This preliminary review of the digital reference service literature shows how great the challenges are that face libraries that wish to extend their presence to include the electronic realm. It reveals that there are many rich areas of research that need to be addressed and that will advance both the theoretical and the practice concerns of the field. In summary, research is needed that:

- Defines digital reference service. Is reference about providing answers, or giving advice on resources, or is it about teaching users to be independent in solving their information needs? Is it all of these things? Does it include every type of question? Do all questions posed to a service actually require human intermediation?
- Provides definitions of service quality. Quality criteria are needed for various library environments (academic, public, etc.), for various approaches (e-mail, instant messaging, chat, CRM, etc.), and for assessing reference service as a whole within organizations.
- Introduces the user's (and non-user's) voice into the design and provision of digital reference. What do people want from digital reference? What should digital reference services look like in terms of the technology required, services provided, and policies adopted if it is to meet real information needs? How can user satisfaction with digital reference services be meaningfully measured?
- Provides appropriate economic models for digital reference services. Answers questions like: What are the costs of doing business? What are the benefits and drawbacks? What reference models are most efficient economically? What is the level of demand for these services? How do libraries share the cost of services when engaged in collaborative agreements?
- Helps libraries incorporate digital reference service into their overall organizational plan. Provides data that facilitates library efforts to design, deliver, and budget for quality digital reference service. Informs management on staffing models as well as on how digital reference staff should be trained and evaluated. Provides insight on what policies need to be in place to support the provision of this service. Provides input on how to market, promote, and publicize electronic-based services.
- Demonstrates how digital reference services can be meaningfully evaluated. Provides multiple approaches, easily used methods, and related quality standards that address all aspects of service provision.

This future work is critical to supporting digital reference efforts, not only toward the design of better digital reference services and systems, but also to determine the means for their continuous improvement.

ENDNOTES

1. The authors would like to acknowledge the help of Ruth Hodges, Antoinette Graham, Mathew Saxton, Mike Pruzan, Katrina Meixner, and Tim Nelson for their work in compiling the bibliography.
2. The interested reader can find a list of libraries that provide e-mail reference at www.lis.uius.edu/~bsloan/e-mail.html

REFERENCES

Abels, Eileen G. 1996. "The E-Mail Reference Interview." *RQ* 35, no. 3: 345-358.

Abels, Eileen G., Paul B. Kantor, and Tefko Saracevic. 1996. "Studying the Cost and Value of Library and Information Services: Applying Functional Cost Analysis." *Journal of the American Society for Information Science* 47, no. 3: 217-227.

Abels, Eileen G., and Peter Liebscher. 1994. "New Challenge for Intermediary-Client Communication: The Electronic Network." *The Reference Librarian* 41/42: 185-196.

Bertot, John C., Charles R. McClure, and Joseph Ryan. 2000. *Statistics and Performance Measures for Public Library Networked Services*. Chicago: American Library Association.

Bolt, Nancy, and Sandy Stephan. 1998. *Strategic Planning for Multitype Library Cooperatives: A Planning Process*. Chicago: American Library Association.

Bonham, Miriam. 1987. "Library Services through Electronic Mail." *College & Research Libraries News* 48, no. 9: 537-538.

Borisovets, Natalie. 1999. *Ask a Librarian: Annual Report 1998/1999* [Online]. Available: http://newark.rutgers.edu/percent7Enatalieb/ask9899.htm [2001, May 15].

Botts, Carroll, and Rebecca Bauerschmidt. 1999. *Reference Issues Exploration: Electronic Mail Reference Service* [Online]. Available: www.unm.edu/~rebs/e-mailref/paper.htm [2001, May 15].

Boyer, Joshua. 2001. "Virtual Reference at North Carolina State: The First One Hundred Days." *Information Technology and Libraries* 20, no. 3: 122-129.

Bushallow-Wilbur, Lara, Gemma S. DeVinney, and Fritz Whitcomb. 1996. "Electronic Mail Reference Service: A Study." *RQ* 35, no. 3: 359-363, 366-371.

Carter, David, and Joseph Janes. 2000. "Unobtrusive Data Analysis of Digital Reference Questions and Service at the Internet Public Library: An Exploratory Study." *Library Trends* 49, no. 2: 251-265.

Coffman, Steve. 2001a. "So You Want to Do Virtual Reference?" *Public Libraries Supplement*: 14-20.

_____. 2001b. "We'll Take It from Here: Further Developments We'd Like to See in Virtual Reference Software." *Information Technology and Libraries* 20, no. 3: 149-153.

Dervin, Brenda, and Michael Nilan. 1986. "Information Needs and Uses." *Annual Review of Information Science and Technology* 21: 3-33.

Eichler, Linda, and Michael Halperin. 2000. *LivePerson: Keeping Reference Alive and Clicking, Econtent* [Online]. Available: www.ecmag.net/awards/award13.html [2001, May 15].

Folger, Kathleen M. 1997. *Virtual Librarian: Using Desktop Videoconferencing to Provide Interactive Reference Assistance, ACRL 1997 National Conference Papers* [Online]. Available: www.ala.org/acrl/paperhtm/a09.html [2002, May 24].

Francoeur, Stephen. 2001. "An Analytical Survey of Chat Reference Services." *Reference Services Review* 29, no. 3: 189-203.

Frank, Donald G., Katherine L. Calhoun, W. Bruce Henson, Leslie M. Madden, and Gregory K. Raschke. 1999. "The Changing Nature of Reference and Information Services: Predictions and Realities." *Reference & User Services Quarterly* 39, no. 2: 151-157.

Garnsey, Beth A., and Ronald R. Powell. 2000. "Electronic Mail Reference Services in the Public Library." *Reference & User Services Quarterly* 39, no. 3: 245-254.

Gray, Suzanne M. 2000. "Virtual Reference Services: Directions and Agendas." *Reference & User Services Quarterly* 39, no. 4: 365-375.

Haines, Annette, and Alison Grodzinski. 1999. "Web Forms: Improving, Expanding, and Promoting Remote Reference Services." *College & Research Libraries* 60, no. 4: 271-272.

Hayes, Robert M. 1996. "Cost of Electronic Reference Resources and LCM: The Library Costing Model." *Journal of the American Society for Information Science* 47, no. 3: 228-234.

Himmel, Ethel E., and William J. Wilson. 1998. *Planning for Results: A Public Library Transformation Process*. Chicago: American Library Association.

Hodges, Ruth. Unpublished manuscript. "Needs Assessment of Digital Reference Services at FSU."

Horn, Judy. 2001. "The Future Is Now: Reference Service for the Electronic Era." In *Crossing the Divide: Proceedings of the Tenth National Conference of the Association of College and Research Libraries*, March 15-18, 2001, Denver, Colorado.

Howard, Ellen H., and Terry A. Jankowski. 1986. "Reference Services via Electronic Mail." *Bulletin of the Medical Library Association* 74: 41-44.

Janes, Joseph. 1998. "The Internet Public Library: An Intellectual History." *Library Hi Tech* 16, no. 2: 55-68.

Janes, Joseph, David Carter, Nettie Lagace, Michael McClennen, and Schelle Simcox. 1999. *The Internet*

Public Library Handbook. New York: Neal-Schuman Publishers.

Kasowitz, Abby, Blythe A. Bennett, and R. David Lankes. 2000. "Quality Standards for Digital Reference Consortia." *Reference & User Services Quarterly* 39, no. 4: 355-363.

Kresh, Diane. 2001. E-mail correspondence with the author.

Kresh, Diane. 2000. *Offering High Quality Reference Service on the Web: The Collaborative Digital Reference Service (CDRS), D-Lib magazine* [Online]. Available: www.dlib.org/dlib/june00/kresh/06kresh.html [2002, May 24].

Kulhman, James R. 1995. "On the Economics of Reference Service: Toward a Heuristic Model for an Uncertain World." In *Library Users and Reference Services*, J. B. Whitlatch, ed. New York: The Haworth Press.

Lagace, Nettie, and Michael McClennen. 1998. "Managing An Internet-Based Distributed Reference Service." *Computers in Libraries* 18, no. 2: 24-27.

Lankes, R. David. Unpublished manuscript. "Integrating Expertise into the NSDL: Putting a Human Face on the Digital Library."

_____. 1998. *Building and Maintaining Internet Information Services: K-12 Digital Reference Services*. Syracuse, N.Y.: ERIC Clearinghouse on Information & Technology.

Lessick, Susan, Kathryn Kjaer, and Steve Clancy. 1997. "Interactive Reference Service (IRS) at UC Irvine: Expanding Reference Service Beyond the Reference Desk" [Online]. Available: www.ala.org/acrl/paperhtm/a10.html [2002, May 24].

Mardikian, Jackie, and Martin A. Kesselman. 1995. "Beyond the Desk: Enhanced Reference Staffing for the Electronic Library." *Reference Services Review* 23, no. 1: 21-28.

Marsteller, Matt, and Paul Neuhaus. 2001. *The Chat Reference Experience at Carnegie Mellon University* [Online]. Available: www.contrib.Andrew.cmu.edu/~matthewm/ALA_2001_chat.html [2002, May 24].

McClure, Charles. R. 1980. "A Planning Primer for Online Reference Service in a Public Library." *Online* 4, no. 2: 57-65.

McClure, Charles R., and R. David Lankes. 2001. *Assessing Quality in Digital Reference Services: A Research Prospectus* [Online]. Available: http://quartz.syr.edu/quality/Overview.htm [2002, May 24].

McClure, Charles R., Mary J. Lynch, Douglas L. Zweizig, Amy E. Owen, and Nancy A. Van House. 1987. *Planning and Role Setting for Public Libraries: A Manual of Options and Procedures*. Chicago: American Library Association.

McGlamery, Susan. 2000. "'Pushing' Reference." *Proceedings of the 15th Integrated Online Library Systems Meeting*, 111-117.

McGlamery, Susan, and Steve Coffman. 2000. "Moving Reference to the Web." *Reference & User Services Quarterly* 39, no. 4: 380-386.

McLean, Michelle. 1999. "Expanding Library Service Beyond the Walls." *Australasian Public Libraries and Information Services* 12, no. 3: 97-104.

Morgan, Eric L. "See You a See Librarian Final Report." 1996 [Online]. Available: http://sunsite.berkeley.edu/~emorgan/see-a-librarian [2002, May 24].

Murfin, Marjorie E., and Charles A. Bunge. 1989. "A Cost Effectiveness Formula for Reference Service in Academic Libraries." Grant No. CLR-4044. Washington, D.C.: Council on Library Resources.

National Information Standards Organization. 2001. *Report on the NISO Workshop on Networked Digital Reference Services* [Online]. Available: www.niso.org/news/events_workshops/netref.html [2002, May 24].

Peters, Thomas A. 2000. "Current Opportunities for the Effective Meta-Assessment of Online Reference Services." *Library Trends* 49, no. 2: 334-349.

Ryan, Sara. 1996. "Reference Service for the Internet Community: A Case Study of the Internet Public Library Reference Division." *Library and Information Science Research* 18, no. 3: 241-259.

Saracevic, Tefko, and Lisa Covi. 2000. "Challenges for Digital Library Evaluation." *Proceedings of the American Society for Information Science Annual Meeting* 37: 341-350.

Sayre, Ed, and Lee Thielen. 1989. "Cost Accounting: A Model for the Small Public Library." *The Bottom Line* 3, no. 4: 15-19.

Schilling-Eccles, Katherine, and Joseph J. Harzbecker. 1998. "The Use of Electronic Mail at the Reference Desk: Impact of a Computer-Mediated Communication Technology on Librarian-Client Interactions." *Medical Reference Services Quarterly* 17, no. 4: 17-27.

Search Engine Watch. 2002. *Searches Per Day* [Online]. Available: www.searchenginewatch.com/reports/perday.html [2002, May 24].

Shaw, Elizabeth. 1996. "Real Time Reference in a MOO: Promise and Problems" [Online]. Available: www.personal.si.umich.edu/~ejshaw/research2.html [2001, May 15].

Sloan, Bernie. 1998. "Service Perspectives for the Digital Library Remote Reference Services." *Library Trends* 47, no. 1: 117-143.

_____. 2000. "Digital Reference Services: A Bibliography" [Online]. Available: www.lis.uiuc.edu/~b-sloan/digiref.html [2002, May 24].

_____. 2001a. *Ready for Reference: Academic Librar-*

ies Offer Web-Based Reference [Online]. Available: www.lis.uiuc.edu/~b-sloan/ready4ref.htm [2002, May 24].

————. 2001b. *Ready for Reference: Academic Libraries Offer Web-Based Reference* [Online]. Available: www.lis.uiuc.edu/~b-sloan/r4r.final.htm [2002, May 24].

Stormont, Sam. 2001. "Going Where the Users Are: Live Digital Reference." *Information Technology and Libraries* 20, no. 3: 129-134.

Tomaiuolo, Nicholas G., and Joan G. Packer. 2000. "AskA Do's, Don'ts and How To's: Lessons Learned in a Library." *Searcher* 8, no. 3: 32-35.

UCI Libraries. 1999. "R & I Division. Electronic Reference Services Team Report and Recommendations."

Virtual Reference Desk. 2000. *Facets of Quality for Digital Reference Services* [Online]. Available: www.vrd.org/ facets-10-00.shtml [2002, May 24].

Wasik, Joan M. 2001. *Digital Reference Resources* [Online]. Available: www.vrd.org/pubinfo/proceedings99_ bib.shtml [2002, May 24].

Webhelp Inc. 1999. *Webhelp.com Ranks Among the Most Successful Launches in History with Over 1.2 Million Hits Per Day* [Online]. Available: www.webhelp.com/webhelp/newsroom/pr991203.jsp [2002, May 24].

Weise, Freida O., and Marilyn Borgendale. 1986. "EARS: Electronic Access to Reference Service." *Bulletin of the Medical Library Association* 74: 300-304.

White, Marilyn D. 1999. "Analyzing Electronic Question/Answer Services: Framework and Evaluations of Selected Services." *CLIS Technical Report no. 99-02.* College Park, Md.: College of Library and Information Services, University of Maryland.

Wilson, Marion. 2000. "Understanding the Needs of Tomorrow's Library User: Rethinking Library Services for the New Age." *Australasian Public Libraries and Information Services* 13, no. 2: 81-86.

Chapter 17

Assessing Quality in Digital Reference Services: Preliminary Findings

Melissa Gross, Charles R. McClure, and R. David Lankes[1,2]

OVERVIEW

This chapter reports the preliminary findings from the Assessing Quality in Digital Reference project. This study is designed to develop, test, and refine measures and quality standards to assess digital reference services provided by libraries and to produce a guidebook that describes how to collect, analyze, and report data for these measures and standards. Thus far, the study suggests that in addition to the need for developing statistics and measures, there is also a need to build organizational infrastructure and resources to support the assessment process.

INTRODUCTION

At the October 2000 Virtual Reference Desk (VRD) Conference in Seattle, the growing digital reference community identified assessment of quality as a top research priority. As patrons demand more services online, and as reference librarians seek to better meet patrons' information needs through the Internet, it has become essential to determine common definitions of success and quality. Library administrators need strong, grounded metrics and commonly understood data to support digital reference services, assess the success of these services, determine resource allocation to services, and determine a means for constant improvement of digital reference within their institutions.

For the purposes of this chapter, *digital reference* is defined as human-intermediated assistance offered to users through the Internet. Today, libraries are of-fering human-intermediated reference over the Internet at an increasing rate. Research by Janes and his colleagues (Janes, 2000) found that 45 percent of academic libraries and 12.8 percent of public libraries offer some type of digital reference service. Stephen Francoeur reports that as of April 2001 he was able to identify, "a total of 272 libraries [that] were being served by a chat reference service, 210 of which (77 percent) were served by one of eight chat reference consortia" (2001: 190). However, digital reference services are often ad hoc and experimental. Janes and McClure (1999) found that for quick factual questions, librarians using only the Web answered a sample of questions as well as did those using only print sources. Many libraries conduct digital reference service in addition to existing obligations with little sense of the scale of such work or its strategic importance to the library.

BACKGROUND

Digital reference, as an examination of the librarian's role in a digital environment, began with e-mail reference efforts. These efforts extended the traditional core reference function of the library past the reference desk to the desktop. Users were able to ask reference questions and consult with trained librarians through e-mail. Still and Campbell (1993) provide an excellent example of early e-mail reference studies. This thread of digital reference concerns issues such as the role of the librarian in cyberspace, the impact of distance service on the traditional reference interview, evaluation, and new skills needed by the information professional (Mardikian and Kesselman, 1995).

Previous work by McClure (Bertot, McClure, and Ryan, 2000; McClure and Bertot, 2001) suggests that assessing the quality of services in an electronic or networked environment is complex and requires multiple methods of assessment. Further, for the assessment techniques to be useful in a library setting, the procedures and methods need to be practical and easily implemented. Recent work in measuring and improving customer satisfaction suggests that there has only been limited attention to quality services and standards in libraries (Hernon and Whitman, 2000). Nonetheless, there is an evolving body of knowledge about designing and implementing "quality"-based services. Bertot, McClure, and Ryan (2000) and Hernon and Whitman (2000) provide a useful starting point for developing measures and standards for digital reference services.

ASSESSING QUALITY IN DIGITAL REFERENCE SERVICES

As discussed above, the Assessing Quality in Digital Reference project grew out of the practical interest of practitioners to be able to define quality and evaluate reference services. This study is examining the following areas:

- Quality criteria and benchmarks for digital reference services.
- Economic models and costing metrics for digital reference services.
- The use and importance of the human intermediary in digital reference services (LITA, 1999).
- Strategies for enabling librarians to assess electronic and networked resources for current and new services and describing digital reference work in economic and other terms.

Additional background and information about the study can be found on the project's Web site at: http://quartz.syr.edu/quality/.

CURRENT LARGE SCALE DIGITAL REFERENCE PROJECTS

It is important to note that digital reference issues are being considered in the context of ongoing digital reference service developments. There are a number of digital reference projects underway. Each of the following projects represents different aspects of the digital reference community (though the populations involved tend to overlap) and serves as starting points for this study.

- The Virtual Reference Desk—A project of the National Library of Education, this service has created a network of over 20 organizations, mostly from the AskA community. This project utilizes human intermediation in both answer formulation and triage of questions (VRD, 2000).
- The Collaborative Digital Reference Service—Spearheaded by the Library of Congress, this service is still in testing stages. However, it already involves over 60 libraries of different scales and missions. This service is asynchronous, and relies on the use of site profiles and service level agreements to automate routing of questions through the network (Kresh, 2000).
- The 24/7 Reference Project—A pilot network in the California Los Angeles and Orange County areas to provide real-time reference services directly to library patrons. This service utilizes commercial help-desk software and focuses on a limited geographic area (McGlamery, 2000).
- The Ready for Reference Service—A pilot project of the Alliance Library System in Illinois to provide 24/7 live digital reference service for students through the collaborative effort of eight participating academic libraries (Sloan, 2001a, 2001b).

These are just the major examples of digital reference systems. Others include AskERIC, the Internet Public Library, and the MAD Scientist Network.

STUDY GOALS AND OBJECTIVES

The overall goal of the Assessing Digital Reference Project is to better understand and describe the nature of quality digital reference services. Specific objectives include:

- Develop a model that helps to describe and explain the basic components that comprise digital reference services by reviewing existing

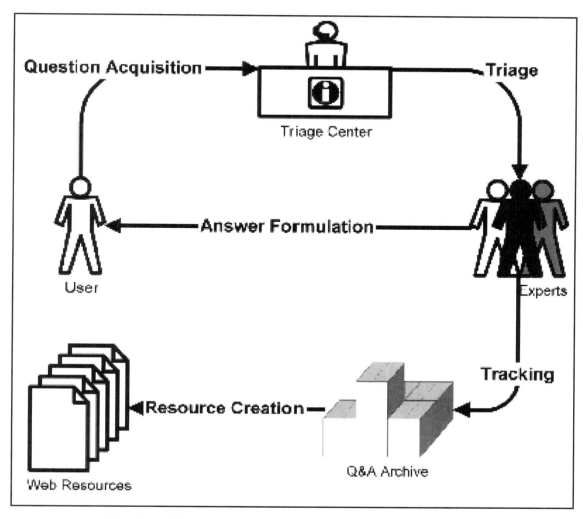

Fig. 17–1. The General Process Model of Digital Reference

sources of information (including best practices at participating organizations).

- Propose measures and quality standards based on this model.
- Develop and field-test proposed measures and quality standards at selected participating organizations.
- Produce a concise guidebook to assist libraries in assessing and describing digital reference services in terms of specific measures and quality standards.

Accomplishing these goals and objectives is essential if digital reference services are to evolve successfully and be fully integrated as part of library services.

THE GENERAL DIGITAL REFERENCE MODEL

The expansion of reference service to the electronic realm has had the effect of making the work of the reference librarian more visible in certain ways. For instance, the development of reference resources, which often include finding aids, bibliographies, pathfinders, and even note cards, are gaining new recognition as they can now be more easily shared not only among librarians, but with users too. The distribution of reference questions has also come under new consideration, as questions received electronically must be routed in some manner to librarians for handling.

Changes in how reference work is viewed and performed must be integrated into the question of what best practice is in reference services as well as the question of how to evaluate the provision of reference services in digital formats. To this end, this project is informed by the general process model of digital reference, pictured in Figure 17–1, developed through an empirical study of high-capacity digital reference services, primarily AskA services (Lankes, 1998).

The model consists of five key activities:

1. Question Acquisition is a means of taking a user's questions from e-mail, Web forms, chat, or embedded applications. This area of the model concerns best practice in "online reference interviews" and user interface issues.
2. Triage is the assignment of a question to a process or topic expert. This step may be automated or conducted via human decision support. Triage also includes the filtering of repeat questions or out of scope questions.
3. Experts Answer Formulation details factors for creating "good" answers such as age and cultural appropriateness. Answers are also sent to the user at this point.
4. Tracking is the quantitative and qualitative monitoring of repeat questions for trends. Tracking allows the creation "hot topics," and may indicate where gaps exist in the collection(s).
5. Resource Creation concerns the use of tracking data to build or expand collections and better meet users' information needs.

Every digital reference system studied thus far can fit into this simple model. The important question, however, is how efficiently and effectively can the digital reference model be implemented and optimized.

While this simple model is used as a starting point in this study, the model describes a single service or system. Increasingly libraries and other digital reference providers are seeking to build collaborative services. These collaborative services may be on a single campus, a city, a consortium, a region, a state, nationally, or internationally. As these services extend past the control and environment of a single library, it is assumed that different evaluative mechanisms will be needed. Certainly the economic model would change as shared resources are used. While this study will concentrate on the local setting, it is acknowledged that new metrics will be needed (or existing metrics modified) to accommodate consortia settings.

LIMITATIONS OF THIS STUDY

This project will provide much-needed criteria for determining the quality of digital reference services as well as baseline data about the success of and allocation of resources to digital reference services. However, it should be noted that there are some limitations on the kinds of data this study will provide. These are:

- Library type. This study will not address the needs of every type of library environment. Readers should be aware that library types not included in this study (such as school libraries and corporate libraries) might have policy issues, service objectives, and functional issues that are not addressed here.
- Based on services currently provided. Digital reference services currently take both synchronous and asynchronous forms. Criteria and measures will be developed based on current practices and organizational objectives.
- Data at the local level only. Definitions of the quality of digital reference will apply only at the local level of service provision. While this data will inform other levels of service, it is likely that there may be other issues for consortia and library networks organized according to regional or state, national, or international participation that affect the measures needed to respond to their needs. This study will not provide information on what the special needs or considerations of these other levels might be.
- Scaling issues. This research is dependent on the current experience of the participating libraries and cannot control the volume of questions processed or address issues of scaling within the measures it proposes.
- Economic analysis limited to information about costs. Issues of cost effectiveness and cost-benefit analysis are complex measures that are beyond the scope of this project. Economic analysis will be limited to determining the cost of providing digital reference in public and academic environments.

Despite these limitations preliminary findings suggest that useful and reliable statistics and measures can be developed.

PROJECT ORGANIZATION

The study began in May 2001 and is organized in a number of phases. Key tasks within these phases include:

- Phase I: Project Organization. Develop detailed project tasking; review existing work and resources related to evaluation of digital reference services and related topics; establish a project Web site; and organize an advisory committee for the project.
- Phase II: Review of Best Practices from Participating Libraries. Select the number and location of site visits with participating libraries that are actively involved in digital reference service evaluation or that have staff especially knowledgeable in this area. Solicit input from libraries that provide digital reference via a Web survey. Perform site visits; collect surveys. Analyze data.
- Phase III: Development and Field-Testing of Measures and Quality Standards. Based on the existing knowledge base, the site visits, surveys, and the study team's knowledge, develop a set of proposed measures and quality standards. Field-test proposed measures and quality standards in a sample of participating library organizations. Refine measures, quality standards, and the manual as needed based on input from the field test sites and comments from the advisory committee and others.
- Phase IV: Presentation of Findings and Final Report. Dissemination of findings began with the presentation of this report at the Third Annual VRD Digital Reference Conference in Orlando in November 2001. A final report that will be a practical guidebook of assessment techniques to produce measures and quality standards will be produced in May 2002.

As the study progressed, the study team realized that a number of additional issues and concerns would have to be addressed (see below) beyond the development of the statistics and measures.

PRELIMINARY KEY FINDINGS

This preliminary report discusses what the project team has learned on the basis of an extensive review of the literature on digital reference (Gross, McClure, and Lankes, this volume) and in-depth investigation into current practice that includes site visits at seven selected locations around the country at both academic and public libraries (Gross et al., 2001) and analysis of self-reports sent to the project by librarians around the country who volunteered to share their experiences in providing digital reference with the project team.

CURRENT TRENDS IN DIGITAL REFERENCE

This investigation reveals that what began as a small number of experiments in digital reference is giving way to a large number of experiments as more and more libraries choose to expand their services beyond their physical locations and explore various electronic formats that allow them to do so. Many of the early experiments in digital reference have become standard services and while there are still many libraries that do not offer digital reference service, the current standard for digital reference services appears to be asynchronous: generally e-mail service via a Web form on the library's Web page. There is movement toward providing synchronous service using a variety of modes—chat, video conferencing, and instant messaging. This is being achieved using a variety of software that ranges from applications that are internally developed at libraries to commercial applications developed especially for libraries or for customer relations management (CRM). Interestingly, the movement toward synchronous services does not appear to be displacing the provision of e-mail reference in libraries. Instead, libraries appear to be embracing the need to provide reference service in multiple formats.

Another recent trend in academic, public, and government libraries is interest in the idea of collaborative relationships toward the development of 24/7 reference service and chat. Libraries continue to show interest in exploring alternative modes of service delivery and for exploring collaborative relationships. Still, research is needed to inform program designers, managers, and practitioners about the strengths and weaknesses of all these and other potential modes of service as well as data on what they cost and how best to evaluate them.

GENERAL FINDINGS

The literature on digital reference, site visits, and survey data converge on several points:

- Turnaround time tends to be shorter for e-mail reference than organizational policy dictates. A typical turnaround policy informs users that it may take up to three days for them to receive an answer to their query. In practice, it appears that questions are often resolved within a day, if not within a few hours of receipt.
- Users of digital reference services tend to be mainly the target audience for existing services. This does not mean that people outside the legal service area of a public library or users other than the students, faculty, and staff of a given academic library do not send queries to these institutions, but rather that use by "outsiders" tends to be limited.
- The type of questions received is the type of query sought by the service. Users tend to submit ready reference or fact-based questions to digital reference services and it is not uncommon for libraries to formally state limitations such as, "only ready reference questions please." However, when more complex research questions are received electronically, they are often processed anyway, rather than being referred to the traditional reference desk or some other service.
- Volume is low. Digital reference services are not being heavily utilized, although some libraries report that volume does rise as the service matures. There is a lack of research available to sustain current efforts and support new developments in digital reference service. Objective, formal research is needed to improve design and development and to assist practice in getting support from governing boards and funding agencies by documenting service needs and issues, costs, benefits, and achievements.

PLANNING FOR DIGITAL REFERENCE

In terms of formal planning for digital reference the project team has found that:

- Digital reference services are often not integrated into the library's larger strategic plan. The development of digital reference service tends to be ad hoc and experimental or the result of a library's sense that the organization needs to make digital reference available to preserve a sense of providing state-of-the-art service.
- Digital services are developed without clear goals and objectives and without plans for evaluation. Oftentimes library staff simply "started-up" a digital reference service with little thought as to what the service would provide and how the service would be related to other library services.
- The low volume of questions results in few if any staffing issues. Chat services are changing this. Digital services provided via e-mail are much more readily integrated into the provision of traditional reference services than reference via chat is. Reference using chat applications is a more demanding service to provide, less easily integrated into the activities at a busy reference desk, and appears to require more training and a longer period of adjustment for the librarians providing reference service in this mode.
- Little formal research is being performed and reported on digital reference services. The main strategies used are the analysis of question logs and user surveys. Because the volume of questions tends to be low, small sample sizes are hard to avoid and in the case of survey research, efforts are hampered further by low response rates and the failure to consider evaluation plans as part of the design and development of digital reference services.

ECONOMICS OF DIGITAL REFERENCE

There is a major gap in our understanding of digital reference services in the areas of economic modeling and accounting. Unfortunately little has been written in this area as concerns traditional reference, so there is little established work to extrapolate from. It is not known what it costs to provide digital reference and it remains difficult to respond to this question as isolating and apportioning costs to the service is complicated and both budget lines and the accounting of costs are often expressed in very general terms. These factors make it difficult to determine the cost per digital reference question within a single library as well as to develop formulas that will allow for comparisons between libraries. This situation continues although libraries do report that they expect to be held more accountable for cost data in the future.

The development of economic models and reliable cost data must be emphasized in future research. Until we better understand the costs and benefits of digital reference, we will be unable to fully justify to funding sources why it is important to provide this service and to secure stable support for it.

"FEAR AND LOATHING" IN DIGITAL REFERENCE

There is a sense of apprehension in the profession concerning the future and the perceived need to compete with commercial services. Falling statistics at traditional reference desks and fear of replacement through advances in technology also work as motivators for moving reference into the electronic realm. Concerns include:

- Fear of competition with the commercial sector.
- Fear of loss of professional domain.
- Fear of replacement by intelligence agents or other advances in technology.
- Fear of falling reference statistics.
- Fear of potential volume of digital reference questions.
- Worry that per transaction digital reference questions take longer to respond to than traditional face-to-face questions do.
- Fear of using new technologies that support digital reference services and constantly having to update and be trained regarding new technology.
- Developing and providing digital reference services in order to be able to say the library provides it and then doing little to promote or grow the service after it is established.

It appears that fear of the potential demand for digital reference and the new professional demands this technology brings are professional issues that the field must address.

The experience of low-volume traffic in digital reference is coupled with descriptions of services that are not widely publicized, not very visible on the library's Web page, developed without user involvement, and only minimally evaluated. The profession needs to move beyond a fear response and self-soothing rhetoric about what librarians can provide that others cannot. Libraries must be more proactive in planning, developing, marketing, managing, accounting for, and evaluating digital reference services if they truly wish to grow this service and compete with non-library providers on the Internet.

WHAT ABOUT THE USER?

Reference service is clearly in the midst of a transition fueled mainly by the proliferation of technology and communication formats and the library's desire to expand into the electronic realm. In the midst of this the voices of users and non-users are largely missing.

- The development of digital reference services appears to be largely system driven. Services are developed based on the vision and interest of service providers rather than the interests and articulated needs of the intended audience.
- Users have not been consulted in the design and development of digital reference services. User needs assessment, community analysis, and usability testing have not been included in the development of digital reference services.
- Limited attention has been paid to the marketing and publicity dimensions of program development. Even after services are developed, the target user audience often remains largely unaware that the service exists.

Evaluations of reference tend to reify the existing system. Evaluation assumes the service is needed and that the mode of delivery is sound. User satisfaction surveys focus on input from a limited number of users and ignore non-users. Users are asked about satisfaction with the system, not what they want from digital reference services. It is unlikely that major innovations in service delivery, user awareness of service, or service excellence can be achieved without involving the intended audience in the process. This is especially true if libraries want to extend their reach to include non-traditional library users and to develop services that respond to actual human information-seeking behavior. Including the user is one powerful way to build commitment to and support for digital reference service within the library's defined service area.

EVALUATION OF DIGITAL REFERENCE

Evaluations of digital reference in the literature, reported during site visits, and documented by the project survey instrument focus on number of questions received, the day of the week and the time of day questions come in, question turnaround time, and general user satisfaction with the services offered. These evaluations tend to be based on content analysis of question logs and questionnaires directed at current digital reference service users. Evaluations of digital reference that provide usable measures and benchmark data in a variety of areas are sorely needed, as are innovative methods for assessing ways to evaluate service quality. The lack of data and measures makes it extremely difficult for libraries to justify the costs of providing and improving digital reference services to their communities, governing bodies, and funding sources.

KEY ISSUES

In addition to the findings presented above, several issues are raised by the data that may have implications for evaluation, but which may not be resolved during the course of this project.

- 24/7 reference. Is the continuous provision of reference service needed in every community or in every library environment? This question is especially pertinent when off-hours volume is demonstrated to be low.
- Librarians as technicians. What level of technical expertise should librarians have? How much technical assistance should they be prepared to provide in the context of reference services?
- Infrastructure needed to support ongoing evaluation and assessment. Libraries need to make investments in staff, staff training, assessment hardware and software, and other infrastructure if they expect to collect, analyze, and report evaluation data in a systematic manner. Without such infrastructure in place, meaningful service evaluation may not be possible.
- Need for digital reference skills. Technical train-

ing on the use of specific software is necessary for staff providing digital reference services. There may also be special reference skills needed for digital reference that differs from those required when reference is provided in person or over the phone. The specific skills needed may vary depending on the mode used to provide services (e.g., e-mail, chat, video conferencing, etc.).

- Need for continuing education. Librarians may need new skills that were not taught in graduate school, such as how to conduct online reference interviews, how to use online and print sources interactively, how to handle the input of multiple questions. How will they acquire these skills?
- Issues of cost. How much do digital and traditional reference services cost? Would cost-benefit data be of use to libraries? How will libraries that anticipate the need to provide cost data as a requirement for future funding calculate the cost of reference services?
- Choice of format. What preferences do library users have for reference formats (face-to-face, telephone, e-mail, chat, etc.)? Is this choice related to question type or other considerations?
- Collaboration. Should network agreements between libraries and consortia be clarified and structured so as to improve evaluation of digital reference services?
- User input. Would services developed with user input be significantly different from services that are uninformed by user needs assessment and community analysis? How can libraries best assess the usability of digital reference interfaces?
- Need for strategic planning. What advantages would preplanning and formal objectives provide libraries developing digital reference services? What is the best way to measure attainment of these objectives?
- Volume of transactions. How can libraries increase utilization of digital reference services and maintain quality service? Can growth be controlled to match the library's resources in terms of reference staff and resources?
- Need for evaluation. Useable measures and benchmark data are sorely needed in all areas. These include: effectiveness and efficiency measures, costing data, evaluation of staffing and

training, evaluation of technology/media used, user satisfaction, evaluation of marketing/publicity plans, and outcomes/impact measures.

These are only a preliminary listing of key issues that have resulted from the site visits and other data collection efforts thus far. Perhaps a most significant issue is the lack of a "culture of evaluation" (Lakos, 1999: 5) in libraries to support ongoing evaluation efforts.

NEXT STEPS

The initial phases of the Assessing Quality in Digital Reference project have revealed many shortcomings in the number and types of evaluation undertaken to increase understanding of what best practice is in digital reference. The lack of data and measures and the limited number of approaches documented make it extremely difficult for libraries to justify the costs of providing and improving digital reference services to their communities, governing bodies, and funding sources. Libraries want and need this data to help them describe and improve their services and to better understand their users. However, there are also practical limitations that libraries face in reaching this goal such as staff that are not trained in the collection, analysis, and reporting of evaluative data and the reality of limited fiscal resources. Therefore, the evaluation of digital reference must involve the use of methods and measures that are:

- Easy to collect, analyze, report. Evaluation is another responsibility to be integrated into the provision of reference services. The procedures used must maximize the quality and quantity of information they provide while minimizing the level of effort and special expertise required from staff.
- Accurate and reliable. Measures developed to assess digital reference must be capable of measuring what they are designed to measure and do so in a consistent manner.
- Address multiple dimensions. Many aspects of digital reference need to be measured to provide a holistic view of the service. Approaches to evaluation must address the complex nature of the service.
- Meaningful to decision makers. The results of digital reference evaluation must have utility for

decision making within the organization and for describing the service to the stakeholders and funding agencies that support it.
- Meaningful to staff. Evaluation efforts must have utility for staff in terms of providing feedback that addresses their concerns about services as well as information they can use to improve service provision.

In the next phase of the project, measures and quality standards will be developed that libraries of all types can use to assess digital reference services. These measures and standards will be based on understandings gained from the literature on digital reference and data provided to the project team during site visits and by librarians across the country who participated in the project's Web survey.

These measures will then be field tested in a sample of participating libraries and fine-tuned as necessary. The final product will be a concise guidebook to assist libraries in assessing and describing digital reference services in terms of specific measures and quality standards.

ENHANCING ASSESSMENT OF DIGITAL REFERENCE SERVICES

Increasingly, digital reference services are being developed and implemented at libraries across the country. Unfortunately, similar emphasis on developing assessment techniques, measures, and standards is not progressing at a comparable rate. This study is crucial in creating a series of standards and measures for developing quality digital reference services.

By developing common understandings of quality and the costs of quality, libraries can make informed decisions regarding digital reference service. By understanding the nature of quality assessment for digital reference, the library community can continue to provide high-quality information service on the Web and set the standards for providing expertise online. It is through this reference function that we can continue to demonstrate that librarians offer more than collections of links and data: they serve as essential human guides to information resources and services for all information users.

Finally, if digital reference services are to evolve successfully as bona fide library and information services, librarians need to engage in ongoing assessment and evaluation of those services. Such assessment is essential for the planning and development of these services, for cost and financial decision-making, and perhaps most importantly, to ensure that user information needs are met. This study is an important first step in better understanding how digital library services can be successfully integrated into existing library and information services.

ENDNOTES

1. The authors would like to acknowledge OCLC, the Digital Library Federation, and the individual academic and public libraries for their support and participation in the Assessing Digital Reference Project.
2. The authors would like to acknowledge Joanne Silverstein, Ruth Hodges, and Antoinette Graham for their participation on the Assessing Digital Reference project team.

REFERENCES

Bertot, John C., Charles R. McClure, and Joseph Ryan. 2000. *Statistics and Performance Measures for Public Library Networked Services.* Chicago: American Library Association.

Francoeur, Stephen. 2001. "An Analytical Survey of Chat Reference Services." *Reference Services Review* 29, no. 3: 189–203.

Gross, Melissa, Charles R. McClure, and R. David Lankes. 2002. Assessing Quality in Digital Reference Services: An Overview of the Key Literature on Digital Reference." In *Implementing Digital Reference Services: Setting Standards and Making It Real*, R.D. Lankes, C. McClure, M. Gross, J. Pomerantz, eds. New York: Neal-Schuman.

Gross, Melissa, Charles R. McClure, Ruth Hodges, Antoinette Graham, and R. David Lankes. 2001. *Phase II: Site Visit Summary Report* [Online]. Available: http://quartz.syr.edu/quality/Reports.htm [2002, May 24].

Hernon, Peter, and John R. Whitman. 2000. *Delivering Satisfaction and Service Quality: A Customer-Based Approach for Libraries.* Chicago: American Library Association.

Janes, Joseph. 2000. "Current Research in Digital Reference: Findings and Implications." Presentation at Facets of Digital Reference, the VRD 2000 Annual Digital Reference Conference, 17 October, Seattle, Wash.

Janes, Joseph, and Charles R. McClure. 1999. "The Web as a Reference Tool: Comparisons with Traditional Sources." *Public Libraries* 38, no. 1 (January): 30–39.

Kresh, Diane. 2000. "Offering High Quality Reference Service on the Web: The Collaborative Digital Reference Service (CDRS)." *D-Lib magazine* [Online]. Available: www.dlib.org/dlib/june00/kresh/06kresh. html [2002, May 24].

Lakos, Amos. 1999. "The Missing Ingredient—Culture of Assessment in Libraries." *Performance Measurement and Metrics: The International Journal for Library and Information Services* 1, no. 1: 3–7.

Lankes, R. D. 1998. *Building and Maintaining Internet Information Services: K-12 Digital Reference Services.* Syracuse, N.Y.: ERIC Clearinghouse on Information & Technology.

LITA. 1999. "Top Tech Trends" [Online]. Available: www.lita.org/committe/toptech/trendsmw99.htm [2002, May 24].

Mardikian, Jackie, and Martin A. Kesselman. 1995. "Beyond the Desk: Enhanced Reference Staffing for the Electronic Library." *Reference Services Review* 23, no. 1: 21–28.

McClure, Charles R., and John Carlo Bertot, eds. 2001. *Evaluating Networked Information Services: Techniques, Policy, and Issues.* Medford, N.J.: Information Today, Inc.

McGlamery, Susan. 2000. "'Pushing' Reference." *Proceedings of the 15th Integrated Online Library Systems Meeting*, 111–117.

Sloan, Bernie. 2001a. *Ready for Reference: Academic Libraries Offer Web-Based Reference* [Online]. Available: www.lis.uiuc.edu/~b-sloanready4ref.htm [2002, May 24].

————. 2001b. *Ready for Reference: Academic Libraries Offer Web-Based Reference* [Online] Available: www.lis. uiuc.edu/~b-sloan/r4r.final.htm [2002, May 24].

Still, Julie, and Frank Campbell. 1993. "Librarian in a Box: The Use of Electronic Mail for Reference." *Reference Services Review* 21, no. 1: 15–18.

Virtual Reference Desk. 2000. "Facets of Quality for Digital Reference Services" [Online]. Available: www.vrd.org/ facets-10–00.shtml [2002, May 24].

Chapter 18

Providing User-Centered Reference Services: Usability in Academic Library E-Reference Sites

Adrian Johnson

OVERVIEW

Providing e-mail reference to users is an important service offered by academic libraries. This chapter examines the user interface and accessibility of e-reference services in select research libraries to highlight possible reasons why e-reference has expanded at a slow rate and provide recommendations for improvement.

INTRODUCTION

In the last fifteen years, significant changes have been taking place at the reference desks of academic libraries. In many libraries, the number of patrons coming to the reference desk has steadily decreased as demands for traditional reference services have fallen (Coffman and McGlamery, 2000). Reference librarians have begun asking themselves why patrons are no longer coming to the reference desk, or even to the library, and what should be done to meet their needs. The advent of the Internet is at the center of these changes, and it is the online environment to which librarians are turning to remain a necessary and vibrant part of the academic community.

Students who are entering higher education right now have been using the Internet and the World Wide Web since their childhood, and are comfortable using these tools to fulfill their information needs, from reading the news and communicating with friends to doing research for their classes. As a result, many of them, instead of coming into the library, are performing the same functions from their

dorm rooms, computer labs, or anywhere they can plug in a laptop computer. Although students go to the library less, they have the same research needs that they have always had. The Internet has allowed an explosion in the availability of information, but due to a lack of organization the information is often more difficult to locate than in the past (Seiden, 2000). One can conclude from this that reference services are valuable today more than ever. For academic reference desks, the key to satisfying patrons' needs is providing them with reference services wherever they happen to be whenever they have a question. One of the obvious methods of doing this is by offering e-mail reference services. Although these services have been in existence in some form for almost two decades, they have not been accepted by library patrons as readily as the Internet or other online research tools. This chapter examines the user interface of e-mail reference services (hereafter called e-reference services) in an attempt to answer why this service has expanded at such a slow rate, and what can be done to improve it.

PROBLEM STATEMENT

Some people have discounted e-reference as a failure because the public has not embraced it as wholeheartedly as it has the Internet and other online services (Lipow, 1999). However, e-reference services do have a solid foundation of users. A 1999 ARL survey found that 75 percent of the academic libraries surveyed who provided e-reference reported a gradual increase in use since the services were implemented (Goetsch, Sowers, and Todd, 1999). This suggests that e-reference is becoming an integral part of academic library reference, and that every effort should be made to improve the service for patrons.

Slow acceptance of e-reference has been blamed on the disadvantages of the service, factors such as not having any live interaction with users and the extended time it takes to get an answer (Coffman, 2001). Other factors, however, seem to suggest that significant problems lie in the presentation of the service itself. Many different types of e-reference services have proliferated with the growing popularity of the Internet. Organizations, from government and private groups to hobbyists and commercial companies have created Web-based reference services (Richardson et al., 2000). Some of these services grow out of the need to serve specific clientele, while others are created simply because people feel they have something to contribute to whoever may be interested. Commercial services in particular, such as AskJeeves and Webhelp, have literally exploded. AskJeeves alone went from answering 500,000 questions a day in 1999 to answering 2,000,000 a day in 2000, and Kerry Adler, of Webhelp, has claimed that these services are "the librarians of cyberspace," (Coffman and McGlamery, 2000; 67). These statistics suggest that there is a great demand for e-reference services, and libraries are not doing a sufficient job of providing or advertising their own.

Why are library e-reference services not succeeding even moderately as fast as commercial help sites on the Web; especially given that most of the employees of these services have only several weeks of training? Many different reasons can be cited as to why commercial services are more successful. They have better funding, for instance, and their services are available around the clock. Their answers are not always correct, but they are obviously good enough for their users. Most academic libraries are not yet equipped to compete with around the clock service, but librarians can provide more consistent and better quality services than these companies. The first step in doing so is to improve academic e-reference services. The need for assistance in locating information obviously still exists. Academic libraries will probably never be answering questions for several million customers a day; but they can still provide a better quality service to patrons than commercial services.

Many types of improvements can be made to e-reference services, but this chapter will focus primarily on the accessibility of these services on the Web. Some libraries have done an exceptional job of making their services easy to find and understand, but generally there is a great amount of work to be done in this area. Many sites are difficult to find, and a few can only be located by wandering from page to page until one accidentally happens upon them. When they are located, some sites offer insufficient guidance as to what information to include, while others are extremely restrictive in what they allow. For this study, the usability of e-reference Web sites of 28 libraries in the midwestern and western United States were examined with a discussion included on how to make e-reference sites easier for library patrons to find and use.

REVIEW OF RELATED LITERATURE

Although there are limited articles specifically addressing the user-friendliness of library e-reference sites, the general topic of e-reference has been written about extensively. Bristow wrote some of the earliest analyses in 1992 from a survey of e-reference users in which she found that the respondents, mostly faculty and graduate students, liked using e-mail reference questions more than calling the reference desk on the phone. She also concluded that the questions asked were rarely too in-depth to be done by e-mail. Still and Campbell (1993), discussed the results of an Association of Research Libraries (ARL) survey showing that one in five ARL libraries were already using e-reference as early as 1988. For further general e-reference literature, a general bibliography entitled "Digital Reference Services: A Bibliography" has been compiled by Sloan. It can be found online at http://alexia.lis.uiuc.edu/~b-sloan/digiref.html.

In 1996, Abels proposed making e-reference more user-friendly when she, along with students in an Online reference course, examined the effectiveness and difficulties faced when they used e-mail to provide reference assistance to clients. The students decided after one semester that a "systematic" approach to e-reference, in which they replied to initial requests with a structured series of questions for the client to answer, was most efficient. In the final phase of the project, they used pre-made request forms that allowed students to answer reference questions without sending verification e-mails to obtain more information. Janes, Carter, and Memmott conducted a survey in 1999 of academic library Web sites, 45 percent of which offered e-reference services, to find out how the services were presented on the Web. Some had effective Web forms or e-mail instructions and policies that defined how the services should be used, but overall these were unclear. They concluded that "using the Internet as a medium for the reference process in academic libraries is still in its infancy" (1999: 150). Several similar studies were conducted in 2000, including one on AskA services by Richardson, Fletcher, Hunter, and Westerman (2000) and another by Stacy-Bates (2000). With the exception of these and a few other articles, the literature has focused more on the library side of e-reference services, discussing issues such as how to staff such services, deciding who can use them, and why they should or should not be promoted more heavily.

Web design principles constitute another important aspect in the accessibility of e-reference sites. The importance of these principles to library Web sites in general was addressed in 1996 by Hirshon (1996), who studied the importance of Web site design for organizing information in a technological environment. Sowards addressed design techniques several years later when he advocated creating typologies for library ready-reference sites to improve access for end-users (Sowards, 1998). These and other Web design studies are an important aspect to consider when addressing the accessibility and presentation of e-reference Web sites.

METHODOLOGY

To assess the user-friendliness of academic e-reference sites, the author collected and analyzed data from the Web sites of 28 different academic libraries between April 15th and 28th, 2001. The Greater Western Library Alliance (formerly known as the Big 12 Plus Libraries Consortium), made up of 29 libraries, was chosen as the subject group. They are a peer group of research libraries, and they have "common interests in programs related to scholarly communication, interlibrary loan, shared electronic resources, cooperative collection development, digital libraries, staff development and continuing education" (Big 12 Plus Libraries Consortium, 2001). Comparison of the libraries shows strong similarities in size, purpose, and their focus on research. Only one of the

libraries in the consortium is not a university library and did not have a reference presence online, so it was excluded from the survey. The other 28 libraries had some type of Web form or e-mail address that could be used to send reference requests. The libraries that made up the subject group, with the exception of two, were not contacted. The purpose of this survey was to analyze how the services are presented on the Web to the patrons of each university, without any input or data from the libraries surveyed. The two libraries contacted were both private universities, and access to their e-mail request forms was restricted to patrons with an identification number and password. A copy of each library's e-reference form was requested from reference librarians, and they promptly replied with copies of their forms. The data was gathered between April 15th and 28th, 2001. The author developed and answered questions for each aspect of the e-reference Web sites, navigating them as any undergraduate student might while doing online research or surfing the Web for information.

The questions were developed from literature covering the presentation and user-friendliness of e-reference and ready reference Web sites, and from examination of academic library e-reference sites outside of the Greater Western Library Alliance. The questions were pre-tested using five other academic library Web sites, and several questions were modified due to the results. A final survey of 24 questions, grouped in four general sets, was used to analyze each Web site. Each set deals with a key aspect of the ease with which a patron would be able to ask a question by e-mail or request form, first by locating it and then understanding what he or she is supposed to do. The first question set addresses the location of the service on the library's Web site, and whether patrons would be able to easily locate it at the time they have a question. The next set looks at what the service is called, and whether the name clarifies the purpose of the service. The third group looks at the information provided on the e-reference page, such as FAQs and how long the service will take. The final set of questions looks at the specific guidelines for what information should be included in the e-mail or form, whether there are so many instructions that patrons might be scared away, and if the form is thorough enough that librarians can answer the question with the information requested.

ANALYSIS OF DATA

All 28 of the library Web sites surveyed offered some form of e-reference. As expected, some of them were easy to locate and understand, others were extremely difficult to find and were not very clear, while some fell somewhere in between. For example, some were easy to find but confusingly worded, while others had clear, concise instructions and extra information, but were buried deep within the Web site. Overall, as the literature suggests, e-reference has a solid foundation in academic library services, but much improvement is necessary before use can substantially increase.

Location Within the Library Web Site

One of the keys to the success or failure of an e-reference service is whether a library's patrons are able to find it. Whether doing research, surfing the Web, or just sitting near a computer when they formulate a question, they must be able to go to the library's Web site and find the e-reference service with relative ease. If they cannot find it easily, they are more likely to give up and either ask a friend or go to AskJeeves than to continue clicking through page after page of search tips and services on how to locate information. If they are already on a page in the library's Web site, they must be able to find a link just as easily, either from that page, or by going to the homepage.

Having a link on the homepage that takes users directly to an e-reference service will assure maximum use, given that the name is self-explanatory. In a discussion about e-mail reference on the Dig_Ref (Digital Reference) listserv, a librarian from the University of Florida libraries described receiving "somewhere between 50–60 questions a month now that we have moved our link to the front page of the UF libraries' Website" (Patterson, March 17, 1999). Of the 28 libraries surveyed for this paper, exactly 50 percent had a direct link from their homepage, and the other half required looking deeper into the Web site to locate the service. Almost all of the Web sites that had the link directly on the homepage displayed it prominently, either at the top or on a sidebar. These results are identical to a survey done by Janes, Carter, and Memmott in 1999 of 67 academic library sites. Linking to a homepage obviously makes finding the service easier, but their conjecture was that "perhaps libraries that do not have direct links are

Table 18–1
Number of Pages with Links to E-Reference Services

Library Web pages with a link to e-reference service	Number of Libraries	Percent of Libraries
1 page	6	21 percent
2 pages	5	18 percent
3 pages	10	36 percent
4 or more pages	7	25 percent

trying out new services, concerned about volume, or just hoping to start out slowly" (1999: 153).

Another indicator of accessibility is how many hyperlinks one must click before reaching the actual e-mail address or query form. In this survey the number of clicks is counted from the homepage along the fastest route to the e-reference service page. This is not in itself an indicator of whether it is more or less difficult to find the e-reference page, but the more clicks that are required to locate a page, it will generally be more difficult to find. Of the libraries surveyed, 11 were only one click from the homepage, and 12 were two clicks away. Four e-reference pages were three clicks away from the homepage, while only one was five clicks away by the most direct path. When patrons are required to go through five levels to find an e-reference site, it is much less probable that they will locate it.

The most effective Web sites linked their e-reference services from more than one page (see Table 18–1). As a result a student who is in the middle of doing research and needs to ask a question can simply click a link from the page that is open at the time. Sixty-one percent of the sites surveyed had links to an e-reference service from three or more of their Web pages. Some of the sites had a navigation bar along the side or at the top of all of their main pages. These usually prominently featured the e-reference link, and no matter where a student was on the library site, reference assistance was only a click away. Even though the majority of the library sites had links from multiple places, 39 percent still only had one or two pages with a link. On some sites where a link was only available from one page, the page was deep within the site, such as the reference department's homepage, or a page dedicated to forms and queries. Some pages had a confusing array of forms, with links to blank forms for reserves, reference services, other questions, and some simply had one link that said "contact us." An experienced library user may understand the meaning of these different forms, but an incoming freshman who has yet to set foot in a campus library might have more trouble deciding how to obtain reference assistance.

Name of the E-Reference Service

A second important aspect of being able to find a library's e-reference service involves the name of the service. Most of the names effectively conveyed what the service was, but others were less clear. The most common name, used by 25 percent of the libraries, was "Ask A Librarian." "Ask A" services have become almost synonymous with online assistance, where commercial Internet services are called everything from Ask A Volcanologist to Ask A Mayflower expert. The second most common name was "E-mail Reference Service," and the third was "Ask A Reference Question." A majority of the other names had something to do with reference services, such as "Reference Assistance" and "Reference and Research Services," but a few had names that were less intuitive. One had a three-in-one service that was simply called "Comments, Suggestions and Questions." The order in which services are mentioned in this name demonstrate the importance e-reference service holds on the site. The most confusing name was "ISD Support: Research Consultants," where ISD stood for "Information Services Division." This name would perhaps be fitting for a business library, but as an academic library service the name would probably escape the majority of potential users.

Another consideration in finding an e-reference site is by the consistency of its name or description across multiple pages. Surprisingly, only nine of the Web sites, 32 percent of them, used the same name on each page that had a link to the service. Twenty-five percent of the libraries had more than three different names for the same links, depending on where a user is in their site. Some of the variations were fairly clear. For instance, one site had a link on its homepage that read "E-mail reference service," and the actual service was entitled "Ask A librarian." Other sites were less obvious. One, which was called "Reference and Research Services," could only be accessed by clicking on a link called "Not finding what you're looking for?" amidst dozens of other services on a "Reference Tools" page. Another service, which had the intuitive name "Ask A Question," could only be found if a user knew to click on the "contact us" link on one page, or a link on another page entitled "answer questions via the Internet." This sounds more like a user will be prompted to give answers than ask a question. Making clear links to an e-reference service is as vital as giving the site a good name. Even if every single person on campus knows that reference questions can be sent from the "Ask A Librarian" page, most will not be able to find it if none of the link names make sense.

The final question about the location of e-reference services combines previous questions into an overall assessment of how easy it was to find each library's e-reference site. To answer this, the library Web sites were re-entered from the beginning, and the overall experience, including combining the outcomes of all of the questions previously asked, was given a rating of "very easy," "easy," "not apparent," or "difficult" (see Table 18–2). While 61 percent of the libraries' e-reference services were either very easy or easy to locate, that still left 39 percent, or 11 of the 28 libraries, with services that were either not readily apparent or were difficult to find. It would be safe to say that information professionals such as librarians know how to make something easily accessible. This would suggest that either some academic libraries are still unconvinced that e-reference is an important part of the services they have to offer, or that they are unwilling to deal with a large amount of reference questions sent in electronically.

Information Provided on the E-Reference Web Page

The presentation of the e-reference page is another important aspect affecting use of the service. If little information is provided, patrons who are not sure about the details of the service may be less likely to use it. Extra information, such as how long the

Table 18–2
Overall Ease of Access to E-Reference Services

Very Easy	Easy	Not Apparent	Difficult
10 libraries – 36 percent	7 libraries – 25 percent	6 libraries – 21 percent	5 libraries – 18 percent

service will take, FAQ pages, and who answers questions, lets the patrons know what to expect from the service.

A majority (79 percent) of the e-reference services surveyed by the author had preset forms to be filled out by the patron. Six libraries (21 percent) provided only an e-mail address, although all but two of those had instructions on what information to provide in the e-mail. Three of the libraries provided both a form and an e-mail address, giving the user a choice of how to submit their question. Forms are usually more user-friendly than e-mail, because forms can display specific instructions for each section that needs to be filled out. Three of the libraries supplied more than one form. Two had various forms depending on the nature of the question, and the other had a restricted form for members of the university community and a publicly accessible one for visitors. One page had links to ten different forms, depending on what library or department (such as interlibrary loan, circulation, etc.) the user wanted to send a question to. Overall, with the possible exception of the two services that provide e-mail addresses without any instructions or guidance, the method of actually sending a question probably will not cause users to avoid using the service.

Different libraries provided extra non-essential information on their e-reference pages that is helpful in providing users with extra tips, options, and assistance in obtaining answers to their questions. FAQs can also be used to provide useful information for e-reference services. Of the libraries surveyed, only seven, or 25 percent of them, had FAQs linked to their e-reference page. These FAQs had information about specific library services, such as how to find a journal article, or how to renew a book.

Information about who answers the questions sent from e-reference services is also helpful to users. Of those surveyed, only 11 sites included information about who would answer requests. Eight of these said that "reference staff" would answer any questions, while another simply notes that questions would be answered by "a real, live person." Two of the services, however, provided names of subject specialists and general reference librarians that were available for assistance. Connecting a name to the service gives the patron a human connection, and makes it more personal than sending a request into cyberspace without any knowledge about who is receiving it. If someone needs an answer right away, a

Table 18–3
Answer Time for an E-Mail Reference Request
(not Including Weekends)

How long will a reply take?	Number of libraries	Percent of libraries
No length specified	8	29 percent
24 Hours	6	21 percent
2 Days	7	25 percent
3 Days	3	11 percent
As soon as possible	4	14 percent

direct phone number to the reference desk is helpful to have. Sixteen of the libraries (57 percent) in the survey provided their reference desk number, some even telling the patron to call if they need an answer right away. Five of these sixteen also provided the numbers or direct links to all of the subject specialists available for research assistance and consultation. Information such as this conveys a message that the librarians providing services are available to help in any way they can, and by whatever means are easiest for patrons.

For the most part, people using reference services need their questions answered as quickly as possible. Due to the nature of e-mail services, answers will not be instantaneous, but for patrons the sooner questions can be answered the better. Almost a third of the e-reference service pages (eight of them, or 29 percent) do not tell the patrons how long their service will take (see Table 18–3). The others vary from 24–hour service to three days. Still others did not specify a time, stating rather that questions would be answered "as soon as possible," or "in a timely manner." Many of them only check their mailboxes once a day, and all of the services examined stated that questions sent in on the weekend would not be answered until the following week.

Specific Directions/Guidelines for Asking the Question

The guidelines and instructions for filling out the form are an important aspect of how user-friendly a site is. If the instructions are long and unclear, or if there are no instructions at all, a user may not ask a question for lack of knowing what to say. On the other hand, they may not include enough information, necessitating verification e-mails that can infinitely prolong the process. Guidelines tell the users from whom librarians will accept questions, and what types of questions they will answer. These should be written with the overall mission of the university and the library in mind.

More than two-thirds of the libraries surveyed (68 percent) restrict who they will answer questions from. For the most part, these libraries will answer questions from students, faculty, and staff who are members of the university, and most say they will answer questions from others only if they pertain to special holdings in the libraries or are specifically about the university. One of the universities will answer questions from anyone residing in the same city, and another will answer questions from anyone in the state. Since 25 of the 28 universities are state universities, this was a mildly surprising statistic, because they are all supported to a certain extent by taxpayer dollars. Of the 28 libraries, nine of them (32 percent) placed no restrictions on who could use their service.

Seventeen of the e-reference services (61 percent) limited the types of questions they would answer by e-mail. Most say that they will only answer "brief, factual questions," and about half of those list examples of proper questions (e.g., fact finding, developing a search strategy, how to find a book). These guidelines make sense with many of the questions that patrons ask, but are confusing for many others, especially for someone who has never asked questions at a reference desk in the past. One library said they would answer "the same kind [of questions] you can call in by phone," but most people have never called a reference desk, and even those who have were probably not aware of guidelines. If a library wants to promote e-reference services, placing restrictions throughout the instructions conveys a negative attitude toward the service, and may turn users away. Attempting to limit the number of questions a service receives also risks turning patrons away by the tone of the site overall. On the other hand, several of the 11 services that placed no restrictions on what should be asked even said that questions that could not be effectively answered by e-mail would be referred to a subject specialist. These sites convey an attitude of helping patrons find the right answers, instead of the "don't bother us" tone of some pages that contain long lists about what should and should not be sent, or who can and cannot send questions.

Most of the Web pages had instructions that were relatively understandable, although some provided more specific guidelines on what to include in a question. A fine line exists between asking for too much information and not asking for enough. Too much can be a turn-off for users, while too little often forces the librarian to reply with an e-mail requesting background information instead of supplying the answer. Of the 28 libraries surveyed by the author, only eight (29 percent) asked for any extra information about the patron's question at all. The other 20 (71 percent) simply said something to the effect of "enter your question here." Those who request specific information usually ask what the subject of the question is, where the user has already looked, for any background information available on the question, and what the user needs it for, including, for example, a class assignment, personal use, or independent research. This information can be invaluable in answering a reference question that otherwise may be vague or confusing.

Various Web pages gave different options for actually sending the question. Most of the universities (71 percent) only provided one place to which the question could be sent, but almost a third of them (29 percent) gave a choice of places to send it to. Some of them allowed users to decide which campus library to send questions to, while others divided the choices up by specific subject specialist. Three of these eight gave a choice of whether to send the question to a general reference destination or to a specific library or specialist. The other five, however, required the user to choose a library or subject specialist. Some of the possible choices were clear. For instance, if someone has an engineering question, an engineering library or engineering bibliographer is an obvious choice. On the other hand, many questions do not readily fall into a category, and different subject specialists cover a diversity of topics, making it difficult for a user to decide where to send the question. In addition, some branch libraries are not clear as to what their specialties are, such as undergraduate libraries or those named after people (the John and Jane Doe Memorial Library, for instance). Offering a choice for users who know exactly where they need to send a question can be valuable, but forcing all users to do so will have negative results. The majority of users do not know or care where their questions go, as long as they get answered.

The final question compiles all of the previous questions for each library e-reference service's Web

Table 18–4
Instructions and Design on the Page: Ease of Use

Very Easy	Understandable	Difficult
17 libraries – 61 percent	6 libraries – 21 percent	5 libraries – 18 percent

page and rates it either "very easy to understand," "understandable," or "difficult to use" (see Table 18–4). Of the 28 library services, 17 (61 percent) were very easy to understand, six (21 percent) were understandable, and only five (18 percent) were difficult. Most pages had both good and bad points, although several of them were overly confusing. Just because a site was easy to understand did not necessarily mean it was the best site. Some requested very little information, which is easy for the patron, but makes it more difficult for the librarian to find what the patron really wants. Two of the sites rated difficult were not really e-reference sites, but had an e-mail at the bottom of a reference or research page with a description like "You can also mail basic reference questions to . . ." Overall, following the instructions at e-reference service sites was easier than trying to find the services on the libraries' Web sites.

CONCLUSION

Contrary to the claims of some librarians, e-reference services seem to be here to stay. While they surely cannot fill every need of library users, they are providing an important service for users who are not in the library and cannot or will not come into one for their information needs. This is especially true in universities, where students are doing research from their dorm rooms or homes, and sometimes live far from campus. E-reference services have not expanded rapidly, but they do have a solid foundation, and as long as they are addressing the needs of a substantial number of people, the service is fulfilling the library's mission of providing service to patrons.

Although one can see the improvement in e-reference services over the years, there is still much work to be done. From this survey of the Greater Western Library Alliance, some specific problems, which for the most part are easily improved upon, can be seen. The biggest problem that needs to be addressed is the accessibility of the site. This study

reveals that 50 percent of libraries surveyed do not have their e-reference service linked to their homepage, and some of them are three clicks or more away from the homepage. In a 1999 study of ARL e-reference sites, participating libraries reported that 99 percent of potential e-reference users find out about the service from the library's homepage (Goetsch, Sowers, and Todd, 1999). If a library wants to improve reference services to patrons, the best thing they can do is put an e-reference service link in a central location on the homepage. Another important improvement that libraries can implement is to ensure that they create a name that clearly describes their service and use that name on links to the page throughout the Web site.

The information provided on e-reference Web pages must be concise and clear, yet informative enough that users understand exactly what they need to include in their request, and what other options exist for assistance. FAQs can give users immediate assistance with simple problems they are having, like figuring out how to perform basic library functions. Providing phone numbers for reference desks or subject specialists also gives practical alternatives to potential users. Guidelines telling how long the request will take to answer are helpful, along with recommendations on what information a user should include in the reference request.

Recommendations for Improving E-Reference Services

Accessing the Web page:

- Service should be linked from the library homepage.
- Links should appear throughout the site.
- The name should describe the service.
- Links throughout the site should have the same name.

Improving appearance of the Web page:

- Include extra information—reference desk phone number, subject specialist names, FAQs, etc.
- Answer questions more quickly.
- Invite state/local residents to use the service.
- Tone of service economy—we want to help, not restrict!

The most difficult part of improving e-reference services is not necessarily making changes to an e-reference Web site. Rather it is convincing librarians that these services are a necessary step in continuing the vitality of the library in academic communities. E-mail reference is not a final solution to declining reference statistics. It does, however, cater to a market of users who will no longer enter the campus library to find answers to their questions, along with those who were never comfortable going to a reference desk in the first place. The tone of many of the e-reference services surveyed by the author imparted a vital lack of service economy. To bring more users to library services, librarians must market themselves and convince potential patrons that they can help them solve their information needs. Although some of the Web sites had a very helpful tone, many seemed to be more concerned with restricting questions than trying to assist patrons. Most of the Web sites are from state universities, and they are at least partially supported by taxes, yet only two specifically invited local citizens outside of the campus to use their services. This could be a great way to raise support for the university, and especially the university library. The amount of time patrons had to wait for a reply was another big limitation. Some of the sites stated that replies would be sent in three days, not including weekends, which means that answers might not be sent for up to five days. This is not very competitive when commercial companies like AskJeeves supply live assistance 24 hours a day, seven days a week, even if their answers are less than perfect.

Further research is needed on the usability of academic library e-reference sites. Because a library student conducted this research, there is a need for additional surveys where actual end-users test the usability of the sites. Further research should also be done integrating Web site design principles with e-reference usability. Finally, the development of specific e-reference Web site guidelines would make it easier for library users to find and use e-reference services from any library Web site. With continuing user interface and accessibility improvements, e-reference services can be a more attractive option for students, faculty, staff, and even the public, sitting at home, in dorms and in offices, debating whether to logon to their academic library's Web site or AskJeeves.com.

REFERENCES

Abels, Eileen. 1996. "The E-Mail Reference Interview." *RQ* 35, no. 3 (Spring): 345–358.

Big 12 Plus Libraries Consortium, 2001. *Big 12 Plus Libraries Consortium* [Online]. Available: www.big12plus.org [2002, May 24].

Bristow, Ann. 1992. "Academic Reference Service Over Electronic Mail." *College & Research Libraries News* 53, no. 10 (November): 631–633.

Coffman, Steve. 2001. "Distance Education and Virtual Reference: Where Are We Headed?" *Computers in Libraries* 21, no. 4 (April): 20–26.

Coffman, Steve, and Susan McGlamery. 2000. "The Librarian and Mr. Jeeves." *American Libraries* 31, no. 5 (May): 66–69.

Goetsch, Lori, Laura Sowers, and Cynthia Todd. 2000. *SPEC Kit 251: Electronic Reference Service.* Washington, D.C.: Association of Research Libraries, Office of Leadership and Management Services.

Hirshon, Arnold. 1996 "Running with the Red Queen: Breaking New Habits to Survive in the Virtual World." *Advances in Librarianship* 20: 1–26.

Janes, Joe, David Carter, and Patricia Memmott. 1999. "Digital Reference Services in Academic Libraries." *Reference & User Services Quarterly* 39, no. 2 (Winter): 145–150.

Lipow, Anne G. 1999. "Serving the Remote User: Reference Service in the Digital Environment." Keynote address given at the Ninth Australasian Information Online & On Disc Conference and Exhibition in Sydney, Australia, January 1999 [Online]. Available: www.csu.edu.au/special/online99//proceedings99/200.htm [2002, May 24].

Patterson, Mimi. 1999. "E-mail Reference Policies." From an e-mail to the *Dig_Ref listserv* (March 17). Available in the Dig_Ref listserv Archives at: http://vrd.syr.edu/Dig_Ref/drb.html.

Richardson, Joanna, Janet Fletcher, Alison Hunter, and Philippa Westerman. 2000. "'Ask a Librarian' electronic reference services: The importance of corporate culture, communication and service attitude." Presentation at AusWeb2K, the Sixth Australian World Wide Web Conference, Rihga Colonial Club Resort, Cairns, Australia, June 2000 [Online]. Available: www.bond.edu.au/library/jpr/ausweb2k/ [2002, May 24].

Seiden, Peggy A. 2000. "Where Have All the Patrons Gone?" *Reference & User Services Quarterly* 39, no. 3 (Spring): 221–222.

Sowards, Steven W. 1998. "A Typology for Ready Reference Web Sites in Libraries." *First Monday* 3 [Online]. Available: www.firstmonday.dk/issues/issue3_5/sowards/ [2002, May 24].

Stacy-Bates, Kristine. 2000. "Ready-Reference Resources

and E-Mail Reference on Academic ARL Web Sites." *Reference & User Services Quarterly* 40, no. 1 (Fall): 61–73.

Still, Julie, and Frank Campbell. 1993. "Librarian in a Box: The Use of Electronic Mail for Reference." *Reference Services Review* 21, no. 1 (Spring): 15–18.

Chapter 19

Comparing Online Library and "Ask an Expert" Sites

John Jaeger

OVERVIEW

This study examined six "ask an expert" and six online reference sites in terms of responses to a set of ten queries taken from various subject areas. The reference sites were found to be superior in response rates, accuracy of response, and comprehensiveness of response. Further research is needed, however.

INTRODUCTION

Two information finding services located on the Internet that have proven to be quite popular and regularly used are the "Ask an Expert" and online reference sites. "Ask an Expert" sites can be free (e.g., AskMe.com, ExpertCentral.com) or fee-based (e.g., Exp.com, Keen.com), or even require that the questioner "pay" by answering questions in turn (e.g., Frenzi.com). Also, "Ask an Expert" sites can be general in nature, where the user can choose from a listing of many experts in all major fields, or they can be specifically focused on one expert. The kind dealt with here are the free, general AskA sites. Reference sites can be of many kinds as well, representing academic, public, or other library organizations, but they are alike in allowing information seekers to offer questions of all types and then receive asynchronous answers to their questions. Of course, there now are synchronous digital reference services on the Internet as well, but for comparative purposes, these are not used in this study.

While the AskA sites and the online reference sites are not necessarily in competition with one another (one might even argue that they each offer Internet patrons a free service in research and in information gathering) they do stand alongside one another as patron options. A patron who chooses to use the AskA site may well not choose to use the reference site. With this in mind, it seemed a valuable idea to consider how one might do a comparative analysis of these two types of services. How might one compare the general "Ask an Expert" sites with the online reference sites and gain a reasonably accurate sense of the distinctions in their characteristics? This study intends to explore just this question.

To do so, it seemed necessary to reflect on digital reference theory, specifically related to determining quality standards for digital services. One needs to have some way of assessing quality standards before the key "characteristics" mentioned above can be established. David Lankes offered a framework for assessing digital reference based on his research into six highly successful digital reference services (Kasowitz, Bennett, and Lankes, 2000). His framework utilized Holland's systems analysis of how agents perform, with roles played by detectors, rules, and effectors. More specifically, though, Lankes worked with experts over a six-month period to establish "twelve quality characteristics of digital reference service" (Kasowitz, Bennett, and Lankes, 2000: 358). These were: authoritative, accessible, fast (turnaround of response), private (protects user information), consistent with good reference practice, clear in user expectations, reviewed regularly, provides access to related information, noncommercial, publicized, instructive, offers training to experts.

The comparative analysis in this study draws generally from Lankes's theory, in that the "Ask an Expert" and online reference sites are evaluated according to four qualitative categories. While the categories used here (promptness, accuracy, clarity, and comprehensiveness) do not all correspond exactly with those identified by Lankes, they do connect with the larger challenge of quality in digital reference service. These criteria allow for a general comparative framework between these types of services. More discussion will be given to the four criteria in the methodology section.

REVIEW OF RELATED LITERATURE

There have been a number of studies done that evaluate "Ask an Expert" sites in terms of their results in finding answers to queries efficiently and accurately. David Lankes provided a careful analysis of six specific AskA sites in his 1999 Syracuse University Ph.D. dissertation, *Building and Maintaining Internet Information Services* (Lankes, 1999). The sites he chose, however, were subject specific rather than general in focus. Thus, their relevance to this study is somewhat limited. Marilyn Domas White and others from the University of Maryland at College Park gave an excellent examination of eleven "Ask an Expert" sites in their *Analyzing Electronic Question/Answer Services: Framework and Evaluations of Selected Services*. This work was more helpful for this study because at least one of the sites examined, Dr. Universe, was of a general "Ask an Expert" nature. All eleven sites were evaluated according to the same criteria established to consider the sites in terms of their appearance, utility, and efficiency. The Dr. Universe site was evaluated favorably, both in terms of its framework and its functionality (White, 1999).

There are two articles that do provide evaluations specifically focused on general AskA sites. One of these is Zetter et al.'s (2000) *PC World* article, "How to Stop Searching and Start Finding," which carefully examined 20 search engines, directories, and AskA sites. Researchers examined the various sites by offering identical sets of queries and then evaluating the first ten responses from each electronic resource tested. Queries ranged from the very general to the very specific, while responses from the sites were evaluated in terms of their reliability, response time, relevance of answer, accuracy of answer,

and pleasantness of response. They rated AskMe.Com the highest, but also liked LookSmart Live and Exp.Com (Zetter, McCracken, and Garone, 2000)

A second article, by Nicholas Tomaiuolo, while not a research article so much as a discussion of the writer's own experiences using various general "Ask an Expert" sites, is also helpful. Tomaiuolo is a librarian who has experience responding to online patron queries, so he has bases for evaluating sites and offering comments concerning the different services. His method was to offer several queries to each site and then offer comments based on those encounters. His responses were related rather anecdotally: AllExperts provided several good experiences, with good and helpful experts. AskMe experts were flippant with him on a couple of occasions, actually ending correspondences abruptly, while those at Abuzz.com, he noted, do not actually claim to be experts but only a network of real people with knowledge. He indicated helpfully that Expert-Central has a knowledge base archive where one can search for questions that have been asked previously. Overall, though, Tomaiuolo believed that "while some 'expert' sites are promising, few have the necessary features to command the loyalty that they may desire. The quality of their output is simply too sporadic" (Tomaiuolo, 2000: 10).

Shifting the focus now from research available on AskA services to that present on online library reference services, there have been a number of studies on e-mail reference as performed in specific library settings. Ann Bristow provided one of the earliest of these with her article, "Academic Reference Service Over E-Mail" in 1992. In this study, based on the e-mail reference experiences at Indiana University at Bloomington, e-mail reference users were offered an opportunity to respond to a survey regarding their reference experience. Eighty percent responded, or a total of 51 different users. The users were comprised of faculty members, graduate students, staff members, and an undergraduate. Most considered themselves daily users of the computer. Most also reported that they used other forms of library reference, such as in-person service, though the telephone service was by far the least popular of all. Several suggested dropping phone reference altogether because of irritation with interruptions phones make with in-person reference (Bristow, 1992). In 1995, Bristow reported on another study done that updated the one mentioned above (Bristow and

Buechley, 1995). Here they added a brief survey to the reference staff at Indiana University concerning their preferences for receiving requests. Interestingly, they all chose in-person as their first choice, with e-mail or telephone coming in equally in second place. One complaint about e-mail was the time it took to write a long response.

Laura Bushallow-Wilber et al. (1996) studied three college libraries within the State University of New York at Buffalo system in terms of their use of e-mail reference service over an eighteen-month period, with quite interesting results. Surveys were distributed to 174 users, with 114 being completed, making for a 66 percent response rate. Users were comprised of faculty, staff, graduate students, undergraduates, alumni, and community patrons, in that ranking. Insights that came out of the study include: first, only one-third of the patrons asked a query by e-mail more than one time; second, users said they thought they could be more accurate in their questions by writing them down and thus the librarian would be more accurate in responding with an answer; third, immediacy was important to the e-mail users, in the sense of being able to write their questions down immediately.

Shifting from the academic to the public library, Beth Garnsey and Ronald Powell (2000) surveyed 22 libraries in terms of the services they provided. They also gave opportunity for e-mail patrons in each library to participate voluntarily in a Web survey. Beyond this, the researchers requested to view e-mail queries (with names/e-mail addresses removed) from the libraries for a three-month period in order to learn what kinds of questions were being received. In terms of results, libraries received a mean of 5.6 e-mail reference questions a week. Library response time for queries was one to five hours (14 percent) to 72 hours (10 percent), but the majority fell in the 24-hour (29 percent) or 24- to 48-hour range (43 percent). Over a third (36 percent) of the libraries had no restrictions on types of questions, while 55 percent stated that they could not handle in-depth ones. Patron responses indicated that they generally were satisfied with services provided and would be willing to use the e-mail services again.

A final study needing to be noted is David Carter and Joseph Janes' "Unobtrusive Data Analysis of Digital Reference Questions and the Internet Public" (2000). This analysis is based on data gathered from the IPL from January to March, 1999. The data

amounting to 3,022 queries received by IPL either via Web form or e-mail. Those received fell into specific categories, with the most being other, and the next ones, respectively, being education, science, humanities, government/law, business/economics, libraries/librarian, health/nutrition, entertainment, computers, Internet, social services/issues, environment, and news/current events. In responding to the questions, 56 percent received sources, 21 percent received factual answers, and 23 percent had their queries rejected.

The many studies mentioned above cover fairly well each of the two realms involved in the present study: that regarding the "Ask an Expert" sites and that regarding the online library reference sites. Where this writer found no research at present regards studies that give qualitative analysis of both areas together. There seems to be no research that provides qualitative comparative analysis of these two types of Internet informational services. It is this perceived gap in the research that the study seeks partly to fill.

METHODOLOGY

Six general, no fee or obligation, "Ask an Expert" sites and six online reference library sites were selected after a careful examination of potential sites on the Web. The expert sites generally function in similar ways, but certain distinctive elements need to be mentioned. While all the sites worked through categories of experts, two of them required the user to place the query to the category experts rather than select a particular expert from that category. Also, while five of the sites were independent, one was linked directly to a search engine; while this may not be significant, it is descriptive of the site and needed to be mentioned. The library sites represented something of the variety that is available online for reference searching. Three sites were from public libraries, one from an academic library, one from a state public library organization, and one from a library-related group focused on Internet users. All six library services, like their AskA counterparts, received queries through electronic mail. The sites used in the study will remain anonymous, but hereafter will be designated as E-1, E-2, E-3, E-4, E-5, E-6, and L-1, L-2, L-3, L-4, L-5, L-6.

Ten queries were chosen from different subject areas to present to each of the expert sites and each of the library sites. The subject areas were: literature, government, history, geometry, philosophy, gardening, biology, medical science, psychology, and religion (see Appendix I). The broad range of topics was selected with particular care and for two specific reasons. First, it was necessary to simulate the variety of topics covered on a general "Ask an Expert" Site. Also, it was important to provide a balance between questions that fell under the general classification of the humanities and those that fell under the categories of the sciences or social sciences for research purposes. With regard to specific questions, this writer patterned them after ones he himself had received at the reference desk. He also conferred with the other evaluators (reference librarians) for feedback. The difficulty here was in making questions challenging enough for experts to want to answer them, yet simple enough that they could be classified as ready reference and thus be dealt with in all e-mail reference service contexts.

Submitting the questions to the expert sites presented no particular difficulty, because different people would be receiving them—one e-mail account for query responses would be sufficient. Submitting the questions to the library sites, though, involved the same staff members receiving ten different queries. In order to address that problem, this writer developed ten different aliases with e-mail accounts from several large free Internet services, including Yahoo!, AltaVista, Hotmail, Excite, and Lycos. He then had to keep track of all those accounts as information was sent to them.

The responses from the expert sites and the online library sites were to be evaluated according to four basic criteria: (1) promptness of answer, (2) accuracy of answer, (3) clarity of answer, and (4) comprehensiveness of answer. The ranking scale for each of these for indicators was a range from one to five, with one being the lowest and five being the highest. This writer and three other reference librarians (Steve Baker, Marv Kaminsky, and Sammy Chapman) evaluated the gathered data, ranking each of the six expert sites and each of the six library sites on their responses to the ten questions, giving four numerical ratings for each question. After gathering all this evaluative information from the data, the librarians then returned their material to this writer for data calculation.

By "promptness of answer," it is meant the length of time from when the query is sent to the time when a librarian responds via e-mail with an answer to the query. A "five" ranking here would require that the response time be within the same day that the query was sent. The "accuracy of answer" phrase is intended to indicate that the information shared by the expert or the librarian is factually correct. This writer, as well as the other evaluators, scrutinized the sources given and information shared looking for accuracy. A "five" ranking in this category should not be so difficult—it might just involve using a high-quality, factual resource, such as a statistical abstract. By "clarity of answer" it is meant both that the answer given is free from unnecessary jargon or poor grammar, and that it is given appropriate to the age/background level of the patron requesting it. A "five" ranking in this area might be clearly stated but still quite in-depth if it is describing the elements of a nuclear chain reaction for a college student. The "comprehensiveness of answer" phrase intends to indicate the thoroughness with which the question has been addressed by the expert or the librarian. A "five" answer here is required to provide both a written (e-mail) answer as well as additional citations from books and/or Web sites/online articles. If only the Web sites or articles are provided, or only the e-mail communication, it does not count as a complete, "five" answer.

One other element of methodology needs further discussion. As evaluators, this writer chose himself and three other reference librarians. One could argue that ordinary library patrons or even people with no affiliation with libraries or background using AskA sites might make the best, most disinterested subjects for this study. My argument, however, would be that evaluators need a good understanding of queries and responses in order to evaluate *both* the AskA and the reference sites accurately; others without this background could do the evaluation, but not as accurately.

FINDINGS

One is cautious to do much generalizing on the basis of the findings of this study because of the small size of the samples; only six AskA and six online reference sites were being compared. Still, when compared in qualitative terms according to the four criteria of promptness in response time, accuracy, clarity, and comprehensiveness, they showed rather striking differences. While expert sites and library sites

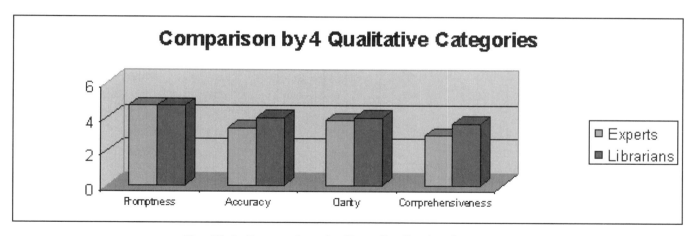

Fig. 19-1. Comparison by Four Qualitative Categories

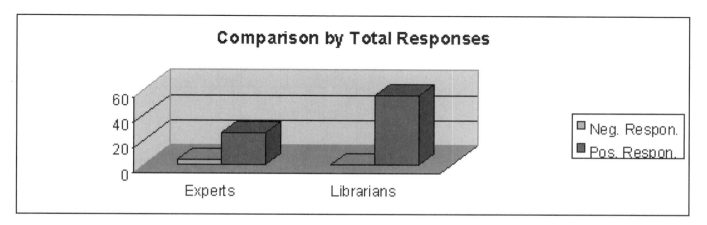

Fig. 19-2. Comparison by Total Responses

rated fairly closely in terms of promptness (4.68/ 4.64) and clarity (3.81/3.95), they diverged significantly in the accuracy (3.39/3.95) and comprehensiveness (2.93/3.63) categories. These are all mean rankings, as will be all that follow below. Librarians came out well ahead in accuracy and comprehensiveness, arguably the more significant categories in that they focus on the *content* of the reference answer.

Another interesting way of comparing the expert and library sites is by total response rates. As mentioned in the methodology section, each of the six expert sites and each of the six library sites received ten queries, thus making a total of 60 queries for each group. The expert sites responded to 30 of the 60 queries, and among the 30 responses were four negative responses (inability to answer the question). Thus, of the 60 queries received, only 26 were positively answered, making a 43.3 percent rate of positive response. The librarians responded to 55 of the

60 queries and there were no negative responses. This accounts for a 91.7 percent rate response.

A third way to analyze the data reveals more about the expert sites than it does about the two types of sites in comparison with one another. This analysis involves comparing how the sites did with arts and humanities questions as opposed to social science/sciences questions (see Appendix I). The arts and humanities questions were numbers 1, 3, 5, and 10, and they dealt with literature, history, philosophy, and religion. The social science/sciences questions were numbers 4, 7, 8, and 9, and they dealt with geometry, biology, medical science, and psychology. While this distinction between types of queries, as indicated on the graphs on the next page, showed a significant variance for the library sites only on the promptness category (4.48/4.83), this was not true for the expert sites; there, surprisingly, on all four categories of promptness (4.38/4.92), accuracy (3.27/

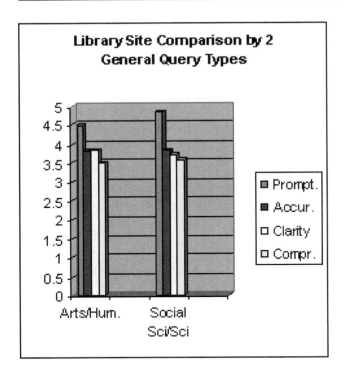
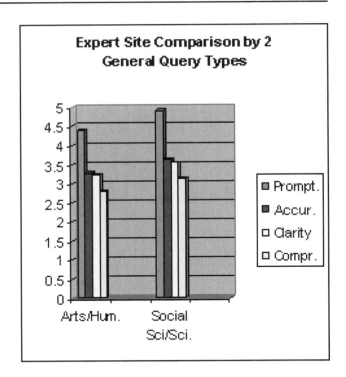

Fig. 19-3. Site Comparisons

3.65), clarity (3.23/3.54), and comprehensiveness (2.81/3.12) the social science/sciences responses came out superior to the arts and humanities ones.

CONCLUSION

This study was undertaken with an aim at providing some needed research in an area where little or none was available: studies providing comparative, qualitative analyses of online "Ask an Expert" and "Ask a Librarian" sites. In that endeavor, the study has been successful. Six expert and library sites were studied, results were tabulated, comparative information gleaned, and insights noted. However, this writer is aware that this effort is only a good beginning point in this area of research work.

First, other studies need to be done to confirm these findings. The relatively small sample sizes in this study make generalization difficult. Just six AskA and six online reference sites were examined. One of the expert sites, E-6, resulted in no responses out of ten, and another of the sites, E-5, resulted in only one response out of ten. Perhaps that was simply a bad sample, and a new study done with a different sample set would give an entirely different set of results. More research is needed to see if that is

indeed the case. There are dozens of other online library sites available, and there are several other expert sites.

Also, the present study sought to compare "free" expert sites with "free" library sites. The idea was that the experts were volunteers and the patrons received free information. Likewise, the librarians reached out beyond their normal boundaries of public, academic, county, or state librarianship and offered service to Internet patrons free of charge. In retrospect, I now think my expert/librarian comparison was problematic, for, while the experts truly were volunteers, offering their services for no payment, the librarians were professionals, offering their assistance while on the clock. They may well, with their larger library, have been reaching beyond their own community in service to others, but they nevertheless did so as professionals and not as volunteers.

With this in mind, it seems necessary to supplement this study in one of two ways. One is to search for online library sites that provide reference service on a completely voluntary basis, as is done at the Internet Public Library. If six such sites could be found, then they could be queried using the same set of ten questions as were given to the library sites, and the results then measured in comparison to the expert sites. A second, and perhaps more viable option is to select a sampling of six expert sites from those that accept fees for answering questions. By querying these sites and then comparing the results with those from the library sites, one would have something closer to a comparison between two sets of professionals. It is likely that the experts would have a much better response rate if paid than they did in this study as well.

Several other avenues of research come to focus at this point also. It would be interesting to compare experts from general AskA sites with those from specific ones. An example of this would be to compare a medical expert from a large site with an "Ask a Physician" site. It would be interesting to see where one found the better responses. A different study that also would be of interest is to compare "Ask an Expert" sites that charge fees with ones that require that you repay by answering queries. Which ones generally are better at answering patron questions? One might expect the answer would be the fee-based ones, but perhaps not. A third avenue of research might be to compare the online reference sites with one another on the basis of category; that is, it would be interesting to compare online public library, academic library, and state library sites of comparable sizes with one another to gain some sense of their effectiveness in online reference service.

"Ask an Expert" and online library reference sites each have found a successful role to play in the Internet world, and yet while so similar in services, they are also quite different as well. This study offered one glimpse into those differences by examining six expert and online library sites in terms of their query responses. By using a variety of questions and four qualitative criteria, the study was successful in bringing out some significant and interesting information concerning expert sites in comparison to library sites. The study only offers one glimpse, however, because in offering even that vision it points the way toward more needed research.

REFERENCES

Bristow, Ann. 1992. "Academic Reference Service Over E-Mail." *College & Research Libraries News* 53, no. 10 (November): 631-632, 637.

Bristow, Ann, and Mary Buechley. 1995. "Academic Reference Service Over E-Mail: An Update." *College & Research Libraries News* 56, No. 7 (July/August): 459-462.

Bushallow-Wilber, Laura, Gemma DeVinney, and Fritz Whitcomb, 1996. "Electronic Mail Reference Service: A Study." *RQ* 35, no. 3, (Spring): 359-370.

Carter, David S., and Joseph Janes. 2000. "Unobtrusive Data Analysis of Digital Reference Questions and Service at the Internet Public Library: An Exploratory Study." *Library Trends* 49, no. 2 (Fall): 251-265.

Garnsey, Beth A., and Ronald R. Powell. 2000. "Electronic Mail Reference Services in the Public Library." *Reference & User Services Quarterly* 39, no. 3 (Spring): 245-263.

Kasowitz, Abby, Blythe Bennett, and R. David Lankes. 2000. "Quality Standards for Digital Reference Consortia." *Reference & User Services Quarterly* 39, no. 4 (Summer): 355-363.

Lankes, David R. 1999. *Building and Maintaining Internet Information Services*, Ph.D. Dissertation, Syracuse University.

Stacy-Bates, Kristine K. 2000. "Ready-Reference Resources and E-Mail Reference on Academic ARL Web Sites." *Reference & User Services Quarterly* 40, no.1 (Fall): 61-73.

Tomaiuolo, Nicholas G. 2000. "AskA and You Shall Receive." *Searcher* 8, no. 5 (May): 56-67.

Vonder Haar, Steven. 2000. "Time to Ask the Experts Almost Anything." *Inter@ctive Week* 7, no. 8 (February 28): 54.

White, Marilyn Domas, ed. 1999. *Analyzing Electronic Question/Answer Services: Framework and Evaluations of Selected Services*, CLIS Technical Report No. 99-02 (July).

Zetter, Kim, Harry McCracken, and Liz Garone, 2000. "How to Stop Searching and Start Finding." *PC World* 18, no. 9 (September): 129-135.

Appendix I
Queries for "Ask an Expert" and Online Library Reference Sites

1. Many of Ernest Hemingway's novels and short stories deal with death. Didn't he die in a violent way? I'd appreciate any information you might have.
2. Who is the premier of Canada? Do you have any information on how I might contact him (or her)?
3. Did Dr. Mudd, the physician who (unwittingly) helped the assassin of Abraham Lincoln, John Wilkes Booth when he was injured, and who was imprisoned for this offense, ever gain a pardon or other official recognition of his innocence in his own lifetime?
4. I recently came across the term "non-Euclidean geometry" and had not heard of it before, having only known of Euclidean geometry. Could you please give me an explanation of non-Euclidean geometry?
5. Could you please provide me with a brief, but clear definition of what "postmodernism" means in terms of philosophy?
6. A neighbor just told me that I have bagworms on my shrubs. What are bagworms, and what kind of damage can they do to my shrubs?
7. I am a bit confused by the terminology used regarding the Human Genome Project. Could you please help me understand the distinctions between the terms "human DNA" and "human gene" and "human genome"?
8. A friend of mine recently went to the doctor with complaints of muscle pains, and the doctor gave him the diagnosis of fibromyalgia. Could you please give me a definition and any other information about fibromyalgia, so that I might pass this along to my friend?
9. What does the term "borderline personality disorder" mean as a diagnosis in the realm of psychology/psychiatry?
10. My question is related to the Druid religion—What areas of the world is this religion practiced in presently and in what approximate numbers?

Afterword

Jeffrey Pomerantz

A MATURE SERVICE

The continuing success and popularity of the VRD conference—and indeed, the very existence of this book—is evidence that digital reference is here to stay. Not merely a service or a technology, but a blending of both, digital reference has become a mature and indeed an omnipresent feature of the library landscape. Nearly all North American libraries offer some form of digital reference service; this is increasingly true internationally as well. Innovation in digital reference continues, as libraries build upon the success of existing mature services. As a result, the reference community's base of knowledge regarding digital reference—how to do it, how to improve it, how to evaluate it, what works and what doesn't—is increasing dramatically.

However, several issues remain unresolved in the provision of digital reference service.

SOME PERSISTENT ISSUES

Some issues that trouble digital reference services are similar, if not the same as issues that haunt more traditional reference services: users, policies, vendors, and training. The shift in the media used to deliver reference service has complicated existing issues and raised new ones as well.

Digital reference has motivated libraries to re-examine their marketing strategies. Libraries have traditionally not been overly concerned with advertising and marketing, relying on patrons to know about the library, to know their own information needs, and to come into the library when they need or want to. This is untenable for digital reference services: there are so many "places" online for users to go, why should they come to your site? How will users even know that your site exists? If you build it, they may come, but don't hold your breath. So the question is begged: how can digital reference services market themselves to "draw in" the appropriate user population? In Syracuse, New York, where two of the editors of this book live, the main branch of the public library is located in a shopping mall downtown. Libraries and digital reference services alike can no longer expect patrons to come to them; they must actively go to where the patrons are.

And once the connection with the user has been made, what is the best way to offer digital reference service? Question negotiation through the reference interview is frequently accepted as an absolute and unquestionable good. But what is the role of the reference interview in an asynchronous reference transaction? Or—to ask the really controversial question—does the reference interview have a role at all? Asynchronous communication media like e-mail have not been found to lend themselves well to the reference interview. However, synchronous communication media—like chat environments and instant messaging—might be a remedy for that deficiency. Advances in Internet technologies, such as voice over IP (VoIP) and video conferencing might bridge this gap and allow the reference interview to be re-invented in the world of digital reference.

As digital reference services grow, more libraries are discovering challenges in training. The issue of training has been referred to as "the Shazam problem." That is, many librarians trained and used to working in a physical desk reference environment have found themselves suddenly in the position of planning or working in a digital reference environment: "Shazam! You're a digital librarian!" Often this change occurs without adequate training, leaving librarians to invent—or indeed re-invent—practices in digital reference for their own institution, not benefiting from the progress made by others. Exacerbating this problem is the lack of available training materials to provide librarians with the skills required in digital reference. There is a great deal of experience in the community in providing digital reference; there is even a great deal of experience in creating training materials for individual services. What is sorely needed now is a more universal approach to the creation of training materials for digital reference services of all stripes.

And finally, there is the increasingly important issue of evaluation. To paraphrase Albert Einstein, development without evaluation is blind. Reference services have a long tradition of evaluation, and despite—or perhaps because of—some controversial issues (the "55 Percent Rule," for example) this evaluation is acknowledged to improve reference service. Existing evaluation criteria need to be further developed and integrated into digital reference services, just as evaluation—both obtrusive and unobtrusive—is integrated into the provision of desk reference service.

APPROACHES TO ATTACK THESE ISSUES

Dr. Charles McClure, in his closing remarks at the 2001 VRD conference, characterized the development of digital reference thus far as the "Plant A Thousand Flowers" approach: many different organizations start up their own unique digital reference service, based on the capabilities of their staff and institution and on the needs of their patron community, and over time we shall see what has taken root and grown. This approach was a sound one in the early days of the development of a new type of service. No one knew just what sort of a service would be required by the new environment, and therefore no one could foresee just what sort of services would thrive in that environment. Consequently, experimentation made good sense: through evolutionary trial and error some lived and others became extinct.

However, digital reference services have been in existence for over 15 years now, and the rate of growth has accelerated over the past five or so years. The time for evolutionary trial and error has passed, and the time for planned and coordinated development has arrived. It is time for the digital reference community to agree on an agenda for future research and practice. Every library, every AskA service has unique requirements and unique skills. However, the underlying mission of all of these services is very similar. The differences are differences primarily in degree, not in kind. It is the editors' hope not only that this book has contributed to that dialogue of agenda-setting, but that the reader will be inspired to contribute as well.

About the Editors

MELISSA GROSS

Melissa Gross, Assistant Professor, received her B.A., M.L.S., and Ph.D. from the University of California, Los Angeles. Her area of specialty is information seeking behavior and the major focus of her research is on imposed and shared information seeking. Her work isolates the fact that people are often put into situations where they are asked to find information for someone else. Dr. Gross is interested in understanding how information gets transferred between people, how this affects the structure, organization, and evaluation of information providing organizations, and what this means for the design of systems and services. She has a special interest in children as a user group. This interest has resulted in a second area of research concerning the provision of information to children, particularly information that is considered "sensitive" in nature. In this area she has published several articles and is co-author with Virginia Walter of the book, *HIV/AIDS Information for Children: A Guide to Issues and Resources*, published by H. W. Wilson Company.

Dr. Gross is a member of Beta Phi Mu, was one of twelve recipients of the Distinguished Scholar Award at UCLA in 1998, and was the 1999 Sara K. and Ted Srygley lecturer. She has taught at the University of California, Los Angeles and the California State University, San Jose. Her courses include research methods, the information needs of children and young adults, reference, and the development and evaluation of information programs and services.

R. DAVID LANKES

R. David Lankes, Ph.D., is Director of the Information Institute of Syracuse (IIS) and an Assistant Professor at Syracuse University's School of Information Studies. The IIS houses the ERIC Clearinghouse on Information & Technology, the Gateway to Educational Materials (GEM), AskERIC and the Virtual Reference Desk (VRD). Lankes received his BFA (Multimedia Design), MS in Telecommunications, and Ph.D. from Syracuse University.

Lankes co-founded the award winning AskERIC project in 1992. AskERIC is an Internet service for educators that offers resources and personal assistance for thousands of teachers a week. Lankes founded the Virtual Reference Desk project, which is building a national network of expertise for education. Lankes is also one of the architects of GEM. GEM is a standards-based system for describing and finding educational materials on the Internet.

Lankes's research is in education information and digital reference services. He has authored, co-authored, or edited four books, and written numerous book chapters and journal articles on the Internet and digital reference. He was a visiting scholar to Harvard's Graduate School of Education. He speaks and consults nationally on Internet issues in education, libraries, and business. He has worked closely with the National Library of Education, Library of Congress, Microsoft, the American Association of School Librarians, AT&T, OCLC, NEA, the White House Office of Science and Technology Policy, MCI WorldCom, and more.

Lankes serves on the boards of the Eisenhower National Clearinghouse for Mathematics and Science Education. He is the chair of the ERIC Executive Committee and is a founding member and member of the executive committee of the National Education Network. He is also a member of the board for the Onondaga County Public Library.

DR. CHARLES R. MCCLURE

Dr. Charles R. McClure is the Francis Eppes Professor of Information Studies at Florida State University. He is also the Director of the FSU Information Institute, a research center that studies the management and use of information. With R. David Lankes and Melissa Gross he is the co-principal investigator of the study, "Assessing Quality in Digital Reference." He is the co-author of Statistics and Performance Measures for Public Libraries (ALA, 2000) and Evaluating Networked Information Services (Information Today, 2001). Additional information about McClure can be found at his Web site at: http://slis-two.lis.fsu.edu/~cmcclure/.

JEFFREY POMERANTZ

Jeffrey Pomerantz is a Ph.D. candidate in the School of Information Studies at Syracuse University. His dissertation concerns classification of questions received by digital reference services. His previous research includes document genre on the Web and electronic scholarly publishing. He received a B.A. in Communication from the University of Massachusetts at Amherst, and an M.S.L.I.S. from Simmons College in Boston. Prior to his enrollment in the Ph.D. program, he was employed as a network administrator and a programmer. He is currently a Research Assistant at the Information Institute of Syracuse.

About the Contributors

BELINDA BARR

Belinda Barr is Head of Information Services, King Library, Miami University, Oxford, Ohio. She started her career at Miami as a Science Librarian and was one of the original Electronic Information Services Librarians who developed the Internet instruction program and was a member of the library Web development team. Miami has offered e-mail reference for years and offers chat ask-a-question service with a home-grown open source system. Belinda has presented at the Lilly Conference for Teaching in Higher Education, EDUCOM, and ALAO. She has been a member of the OhioLINK User Services Committee since 1994.

DAVID BRADBURY

David Bradbury is a Research Fellow on the OPAL (Online Personal Academic Librarian) project. Prior to this, David worked for various companies in the private sector in a variety of IT/software development-related roles in fields such as Web development, data mining, and computer games. David gained a Ph.D. in artificial neural networks from the Open University in 1996. He also has an MSc in cognitive science and a B.A. in psychology from Sheffield University.

BOB CARTERETTE

Bob Carterette has been the Head of Automation Services for the Cleveland Public Library since 1987. His duties include supporting all data, networking, and telephony for the library, as well as administering the CLEVNET Consortium. Prior to employment at Cleveland Public Library, Bob worked in a variety of capacities in public libraries in Illinois, including as a Head of Technical Services, Head of Adult Services, director, and board member. Bob's M.L.S. is from the School of Library & Information Science of George Peabody College for Teachers, Nashville, TN.

MIN CHOU

Min Chou is a reference librarian at the New Jersey City University. She coordinates the library's Web site, and is a member of the Task Force on Web and Communication of the University's Information Technology Steering Committee. Prior to her appointment at the New Jersey City University, she was a law librarian at White & Case in New York City. Ms. Chou has conducted research in copyright and ethics issues. She has published papers and presented at national and international conferences. She was a keynote speaker at the International Conference on "Academic Librarianship in the New Millennium: Roles, Trends and Global Collaboration." Ms. Chou received her M.L.S. from Pratt Institute in New York and her B.A. from Fudan University, Shanghai, China.

JULEIGH MUIRHEAD CLARK

Juleigh Muirhead Clark has been Public Services Librarian at the John D. Rockefeller, Jr. Library at the Colonial Williamsburg Foundation since 1998 and is the Webmaster for the library pages. She has worked as a private Web design contractor and published "Freelance Web Designer" in The Library Web (Julie Still, ed., Information Today, Inc., 1997). After receiving her M.S.L.S. from the University of North Carolina in 1978, she worked as a reference librarian in public and academic libraries, and as an instructor for Catholic University of America School of Information Science.

SARI FELDMAN

Sari Feldman has been the Deputy Director of the Cleveland Public Library since October 1999. In that capacity she actively works with the CLEVNET Consortium and worked on the development of the KnowItNow project. Prior to that appointment she was the Head of Community Services for the Cleveland Public Library and oversaw the 28 neighborhood libraries in the city of Cleveland, the Library for the Blind and Physically Handicapped, Children's Literature Department, and the development of family literacy services. She came to Cleveland from the Onondaga County (Syracuse, NY) Public Library in 1997. During her 14-year tenure in Syracuse, she was also an adjunct faculty member at Syracuse University School of Information Studies. Ms. Feldman serves on the boards of the Citizens' League of Greater Cleveland and the Shaker (Shaker Heights, OH) Family Center and the advisory boards for the ALA Office of Literacy and Outreach Services and the PLA Early Literacy Initiative. She is the co-author of several articles and books including *Serving Families and Children Through Partnerships* (Neal-Schuman, 1996) and *Learning Environments for Young Children* (ALA, 1998) and a frequent speaker at local, state, and national programs. Sari Feldman holds a master's degree in Library Science from the University of Wisconsin, Madison.

JOHN JAEGER

John Jaeger has been Reference Services Librarian at Union University in Jackson, Tennessee, for the past four years. He is also responsible for electronic collection development and online reference/instructional services for off-campus students. He received his Master of Science degree in Library and Information Science from the University of Illinois, Champaign-Urbana in 1997. He also has a Master of Divinity from Midwestern Theological Seminary, which he received in 1987. John has not published previously in the area of digital reference but is the author of "User Fees, Community Goods, and the Public Library," in *Public Library Quarterly* 17, no. 2 (Spring, 1999).

ADRIAN JOHNSON

Adrian Johnson is the Information Literacy Librarian at the University of Texas at Austin. He collaborates with campus librarians and faculty to implement information literacy skills into departmental curricula. Adrian teaches library instruction sessions and provides reference services, including e-mail reference, at the Undergraduate Library on campus. He has been teaching undergraduates to use the Internet and watching them surf it since 1995. He received his M.L.I.S. from the University of Texas at Austin's Graduate School of Library and Information Science in 2001. This paper grew out of research Adrian conducted for a course on academic libraries.

SCOTT D. JOHNSTON

Scott Johnston is a doctoral candidate at Rutgers University in the School of Communications, Information, and Library Science. He teaches courses in reference services and information policy at the School of Library Studies at Rutgers University and the School of Information and Library Studies at the Pratt Institute in New York City. Scott earned an M.A. in English and a Master's in Library and Information Science from the University of Western Ontario. He has worked as a reference librarian at the Columbia University Business Library and the Benjamin N. Cardozo School of Law and as a policy researcher for the Canadian Consulate General. His dissertation examines the feasibility of current privacy law addressing information privacy problems in the information age library.

ALICE KAWAKAMI

Alice Kawakami directs the digital reference program for the University of California, Los Angeles Library. As director she is responsible for the development and delivery of the library's digital reference service. This includes planning for system implementation and improvement; developing training and documentation, serving as liaison with software developers and service providers, and assessing and reporting on the service. Alice has an M.L.S. from the UCLA School of Library and Information Science.

KWAN-YAU LAM

Kwan-Yau Lam is an Assistant Professor / Librarian at Truman College, City Colleges of Chicago. Her research interest is library and educational technologies. She has an M.L.S. from Indiana University, where she also got her Ed.S. in Instructional Systems Technology.

MATTHEW R. MARSTELLER

Matthew R. Marsteller is the Physics and Math Librarian and a member of the Chat Reference Task Force at Carnegie Mellon University. Matt has also served as the Team Leader for Library Services at the Federal Energy Technology Center in Morgantown while employed by EG&G, Technical Services of West Virginia, Inc. and as an Assistant Science Librarian at the University of South Carolina. He received his M.S.L.S. in 1988 and a B.S. in Physics in 1987 from Clarion University of Pennsylvania. He also served from 1978-1984 in the United States Navy Nuclear Power Program.

LORRI MON

Lorri Mon has answered thousands of e-mail reference questions as a digital reference librarian for a variety of "Ask A" services including the Internet Public Library, Virtual Reference Desk, and Department of State Foreign Affairs Network (DOSFAN) at the University of Illinois at Chicago's federal depository library. Currently she is in the doctoral program at the University of Washington's Information School as a research assistant to Dr. Joseph Janes and is researching the digital reference interview.

PAUL NEUHAUS

Paul Neuhaus is the Social Sciences Librarian at Carnegie Mellon University. Previously he worked at the U.S. Bureau of the Census and Patent Office Libraries before coming to Carnegie Mellon in 1997. In addition to an M.L.S. from the University of Maryland, he holds master's degrees in Theology and Modern European History. His areas of focus are reference services and collection development issues.

LORRAINE NORMORE

Lorraine Normore moved to OCLC's Office of Research (OR) in 1997 from the Research Department at Chemical Abstracts Service. She does research designed to improve our understanding of the needs of libraries and their users and aims at using that understanding to design innovative interfaces that make library systems better able to meet user needs. She has acted as the OR's representative on OCLC's collaborative reference project since its inception. She received her M.L.S. from the University of Toronto and her Ph.D. in Experimental Psychology from the Ohio State University.

GEORGINA PAYNE

Georgina Payne is Learner Support Projects Officer for the Open University Library. Georgina currently works on a number of projects investigating the development of new library enquiry services, including OPAL (Online Personal Academic Librarian) and the library's WebChat project, a project to assess student and staff response to the use of real-time reference software. Prior to joining the Open University in November 2000, Georgina worked within Learning Resources at University College Northampton (UCN) where she was involved in the creation of Liberation, a suite of online information literacy tutorials. Georgina has a B.A. from Lancaster University and an MSc in Information Science from Loughborough University.

PAULA RUMBAUGH

Paula first came to OCLC, Inc., in 1985, as a writer in the User Documentation Department. In 1987 she joined the newly formed Reference Services Division and in 1990 became product manager for the development of a new, end-user online search service, FirstSearch. As manager of the FirstSearch Implementation & Database Creation Section, Paula devoted much of her time to exploring the needs of the library reference desk and the behavior of its end users.

In July of 2000, as part of the OCLC strategic planning process, Paula was named to a team of researchers, librarians, developers, and marketing individuals to study the environment and needs of reference librarians and users in the context of the World Wide Web. From this team has grown three projects: a collaboration with the Library of Congress in its ongoing study of a global reference network (CDRS); a pilot for a virtual reference desk cooperative toolset in a local or regional setting; and a prototype of a multi-purpose profile database of library/librarian expertise.

Before coming to OCLC, Paula was a reference librarian in the Lima/Allen County (Ohio) Public Library and prior to that an editor for Frederick Ungar Publishing Co., in New York City. She received her M.L.S. in 1983 from Ball State University.

JOHN A. SHULER

John A. Shuler is an Associate Professor and Department Head/Documents Librarian at the University of Illinois of Chicago. Since receiving his M.L.S. from the University of California, Los Angeles in 1983, Prof. Shuler has been a faculty member and documents librarian at universities in Oregon and New York. Writing, teaching, and lecturing extensively on information policy issues, political analyses of the U.S. Government Printing Office, and its system of depository libraries, he serves as reviews editor and editorial board member for *Government Information Quarterly*, editor for the American Library Association's Government Documents Roundtable quarterly publication *Documents to the People*, and writes a column for the *Journal of Academic Librarianship*.

JOANNE SILVERSTEIN

Joanne Silverstein is the Associate Director of the Information Institute of Syracuse (http://iis.syr.edu) and Assistant Research Professor at Syracuse University's School of Information Studies. She received her Ph.D. in 1998 and has a background in software design and management. Dr. Silverstein conducts research into the management of e-mail centers and customer communications in federal agencies, as well as human intermediation in digital reference environments. She has published articles and presented at international conferences about online business, digital reference, and information systems.

JUDITH SMITH

Judith Smith is a distance education librarian at Johns Hopkins University. Her main focus is to serve as the librarian for Excelsior College Virtual Library, a collaborative partnership between the Sheridan Libraries at Johns Hopkins, and Excelsior College. Judy provides research and reference assistance by phone, fax, and e-mail to the Excelsior community. Smith received her M.S. in Library and Information Science from the University of Illinois at Urbana-Champaign.

RUI WANG

Rui Wang is a reference librarian/social sciences bibliographer with assistant professor status at the Central Michigan University. Previously, she was a reference and government documents librarian at the Indian River Community College. In that position, Wang taught online courses for the Librarian Technician Assistant program, and taught sociology courses as an adjunct faculty member.

KATHLEEN WEBB

Kathleen Webb is Head of Client Services for Roesch Library, University of Dayton, Dayton, OH. Kathy began her career at UD as the Government Documents Librarian and then moved on to assume the role of Reference Team Leader. She led the library's first Web development team in 1995 and continues to serve on the committee. Kathy has been a member of the OhioLINK User Services Committee since 1998 and is serving as the Chair for 2001-2002. She received her M.L.S. from UCLA and her bachelor's degree from Penn State.

OLIVER ZHOU

Oliver Zhou is a practicing attorney in the states of New York and New Jersey, and member of the New York and New Jersey Bars. He has been admitted to practice at the U.S. Supreme Court, the U.S. Court of Appeals for the Second Circuit, and the U.S. Court of International Trade. His legal practice focuses on trademark and copyright registration and infringement litigation, international law, and immigration law. He has published extensively in these fields. He earned his J.D. from Rutgers University Law School-Newark, New Jersey, and his LL.M. and LL.B. from Fudan University, Shanghai, China.

Index

Note: Italicized page numbers refer to illustrations